Living in Heaven, Coping with Hell

Other Books by Clifford Sobin

The Pivotal Years: Israel and The Arab World 1966 – 1977

My Jackson Hole Favorites

Maryland Workers' Compensation

Living in Heaven, Coping with Hell

Israel's Northern Borders—Where Zionism Triumphed, the Kibbutz Evolves, and the Pioneering Spirit Prevails

Clifford Sobin

Copyright © 2019 by Clifford B. Sobin

Lean Forward Publishing 2020
Cover by JD&J Book Cover Design.
Cover image–Kibbutz Hanita perimeter fence facing Lebanon – from Alamy.

All Rights Reserved, including the right to reproduce this book or portions thereof in any form whatsoever, except for brief excerpts as part of critical reviews or other written materials without the express written permission of the author. For permission requests you may contact the author by accessing the author's website at www.CliffordSobin.com. December 31, 2020.

ISBN: 978-0-9986374-3-3 (paperback),
ISBN: 978-0-9986374-4-0 (eBook)
Library of Congress Control Number: 2019920426

Names: Sobin, Clifford, author.
Title: Living in heaven, coping with hell : Israel's northern borders -- where Zionism triumphed, the kibbutz evolves, and the pioneering spirit prevails / Clifford Sobin.
Description: First edition. | [Rockville, Maryland] : Clifford Sobin, [2020] | Includes bibliographical references.
Identifiers: ISBN 9780998637433 (paperback) | ISBN 9780998637440 (ebook)
Subjects: LCSH: Jews--Israel--History. | Zionism--Israel--History. | Arab-Israeli conflict--History. | Kibbutzim--History.
Classification: LCC DS123 .S63 2020 (print) | LCC DS123 (ebook) | DDC 956.94004924--dc23

*This book is dedicated to my wife, Julie,
My three children and their significant others,
My three grandchildren and those to come, and
The people living along Israel's Northern Borders*

Contents

Maps ix
Prologue 1

PART ONE

Ch. 1 **Gamla** 21
Ch. 2 **Rosh Pina, Pogroms, and the First Aliyah** 31
    Gai Oni 31
    Jews in Eastern Europe During the Nineteenth Century 32
    Palestine in the Late Nineteenth Century 36
    Rosh Pina 42

Ch. 3 **Degania and the Second Aliyah** 53
Ch. 4 **Hashomer, Tel Hai, Kfar Giladi, and the Third Aliyah** . 69
    Hashomer 69
    Tel Hai 79

Ch. 5 **Kibbutz Hanita** 89
Ch. 6 **Degania, May 1948** 105
Ch. 7 **Kibbutz Dan** 113
Ch. 8 **Merom Golan** 133
Ch. 9 **Kiryat Shmona** 165

PART TWO

Ch.10 **Fall of the Kibbutzim** 191
Ch.11 **Kibbutz Dan Now** 205
Ch.12 **Kibbutz Hanita Now** 217
Ch.13 **Kfar Giladi Now** 249
Ch.14 **Merom Golan Now** 259

PART THREE

Ch.15 People of the Land 271
    Sarit Zehavi 271
    Yael Barlev 291
    Shlomi Afrayat 303
    Stef Wertheimer 312

Ch.16 Three Communities on the Border 325
    Metula 325
    Majdal Shams 346
    Ghajar 355

Ch.17 Terror and Katyushas 365
    Terrorists 365
    Katyushas 371

Ch.18 Yesterday, Today, and Tomorrow 383
    The Lebanese Border 383
    The Syrian Border 392
    Medical Care 398
    Earthquakes 399
    Putting it all Together 401

Pictures 413
Acknowledgements 421
Sources and Background 423

Israel

Towns, Cities, and Kibbutzim Mentioned

Terror Attack Locations

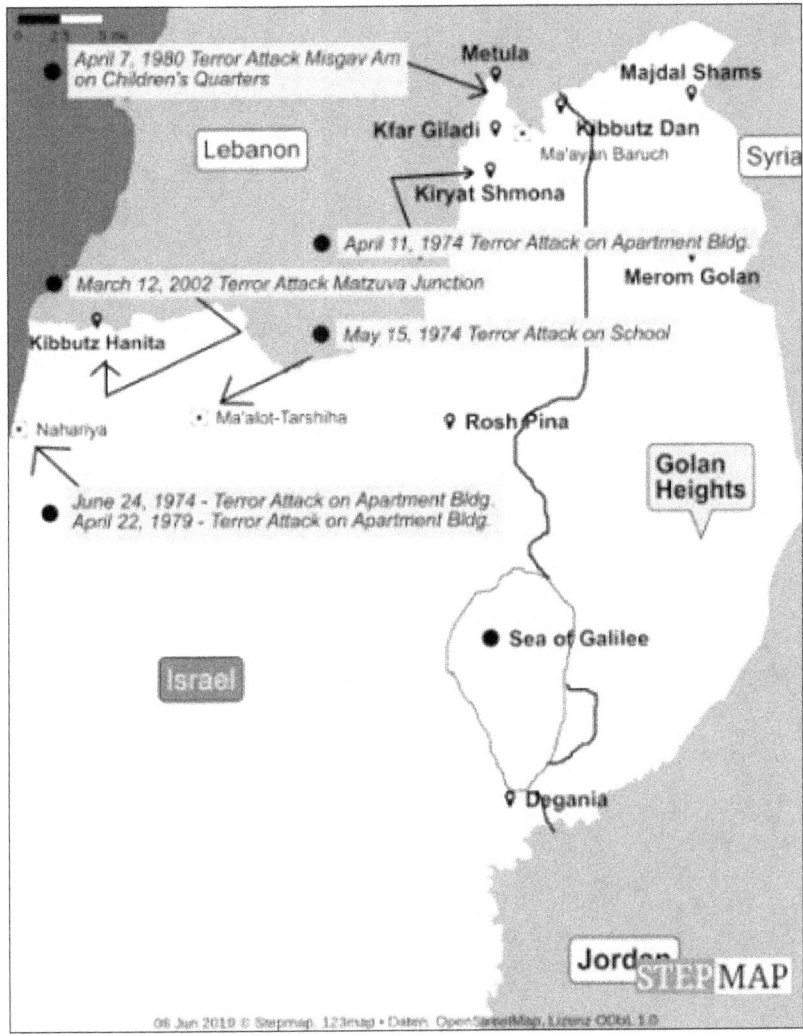

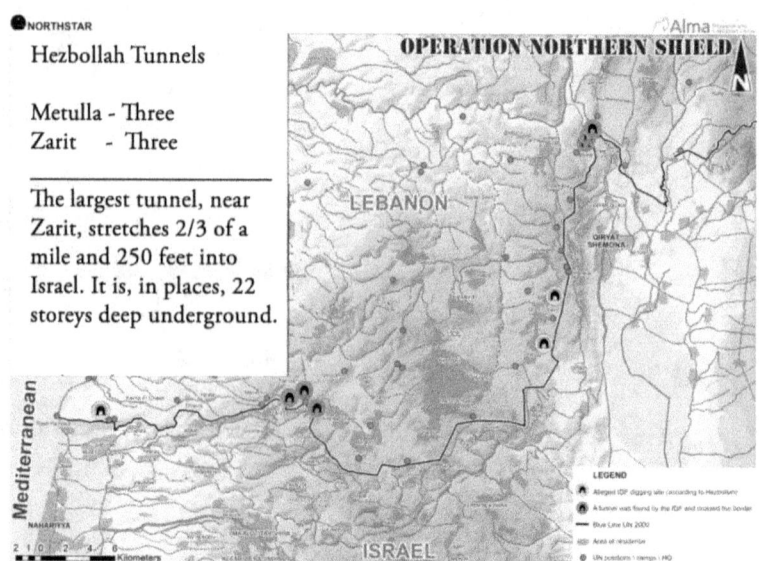

Map Courtesy of the Alma Research and Education Center

Text rectangle added by the author

Living in Heaven, Coping with Hell

Prologue

Israel's northern borders have always been breathtaking, haunting, and unpredictably violent. Here, amid widespread tranquility, a pervasive hint of danger lingers.

On May 15, 1974, 105 high school students from Safed bedded down at the Netiv Meir Elementary School, only a few miles from Lebanon after a terrorist alert had interrupted their scheduled three-day hiking trip. A few guards and teachers who would prove useless during the storm to come, accompanied them. The students had planned to sleep in the woods, but authorities ordered them to spend the night inside the school for their own safety. Why? A couple of days before, soldiers had found the tracks of three Palestinian terrorists crossing the border. The whereabouts of these terrorists were unknown.

One by one, the children fell asleep, girls on the third floor, boys on the second. By 3 a.m., all was quiet.

At 4 a.m., chaos erupted.

Having already killed three members of a family and wounded the fourth—a five year old—as well as another man, the three terrorists headed towards the Netiv Meir Elementary School where they planned to ambush students arriving the next morning. But when the Palestinians reached the school's parking lot in the dead of the night, to their surprise they spotted several empty busses that hinted of a group of students sleeping within the building.

Bent on mayhem, the three men burst into the school while firing their weapons in the air. Panic ensued. A few students escaped by diving out windows or running through unblocked doors. Some broke limbs in the process but their injuries were a small price to pay for reaching safety. Nearly eighty kids were not so fortunate. Within minutes the terrorists had herded them into a small room on the second floor. Then they ringed the room with explosives. As death lurked, hope departed.

Negotiations between the terrorists and Israeli authorities began in the morning. Many decades later, the details of those negotiations are no longer important. But the courage and fear felt by those innocent captives, intertwined with their alternating optimism and pessimism as the talks ebbed and flowed, remind us of the dangers faced then and now.

Ilana, one of the teenage captives, wrote:

> *Dear mom and dad, it is now 11:25 in the morning and I don't know how many more hours I have left to live so I am writing to you. I am sorry mom that I didn't listen to you and went on the trip. Yes, I know you didn't force me to stay but you were worried, and you preferred I didn't go. But I did go. Because I knew what I had to do.*
>
> *I [want] to say thank you for the education you gave me and the beautiful years I've had and it's all thanks to you.*
>
> *I am now fifteen and a half years old. And if I'm sentenced to die, I will die, quietly, with dignity and faith. Yes, faith is what you gave me. You always said to me that life without faith is pointless and much more painful. And now, in these hard hours, I am full of belief and I believe you are right. Life does not give much to a*

man. He does not have a choice in almost anything. Not when and where he will be born and to which parents. But for me it was great. I, a religious girl in Israel, with wonderful parents—you. Great hours I did not have. I didn't have that and very likely I won't ever achieve that.

Mom, don't cry a lot when I die. When Rivka will give birth, name the baby after me, Ilan or Ilana, and educate him like me to be strong and that he will know what his purpose is in life and the reason he was born. I know you have had a difficult life before and after I was born, and it will be even more difficult after I die. But always remember the pain and the suffering have always brought with them hours of happiness and satisfaction. I am not crying. My eyes are dry. My death is not painful to me, and I am not sorry, and when I will recite Shema Israel in my last hour, I will be thinking of you. I had to go on this trip. We must not stop our lives. The danger is in every place waiting for us. And if a decree was made in the heavens it will always be carried out. If we will hide in the shelters the danger will be greater. And it is better to live normal human lives and to be killed on Kiddush HaShem.

Give this letter, which is my last in this world, to all my family to read. And send them regards and lots of love from me. And to all of my friends and neighbors, send wishes of good luck. This is the last chance. In one small hour I will be gone. Yours always, see you sometime, with lots of love, Ilana.

Ilana miscalculated. An hour later she was still alive. Six hours later she wasn't. Ilana perished in a small room crisscrossed by a hail of flying lead, wracked by explosions, and filled with screams. She lay in a pool of blood among the jumbled, contorted bodies of nineteen other students who failed to escape those last frenetic seconds. She died in a town called Ma'alot.

Terrorists killed Ilana and those other students for no justifiable reason. But Ma'alot stands for more than its suffering. For those who live along Israel's northern borders, the threat of violence, of terror, has always been present. Unfortunately, however, that is not the only threat that persists here. Economic issues plague communities along the border where medical services are inferior to those available in the nation's center. And this is where the concept of the kibbutz, a community devoted to socialistic ideals, was born, almost died, and now struggles to reform.

So why live along Israel's northern borders? What was life like there? What's it like now? How did Jewish settlers meet the challenges? Why live there then? Why do people continue to live there now? What has the courage of the few who chose to brave hardship and desolation meant to the State of Israel?

I set out to Israel, where I have been a frequent visitor, to find answers to those complex questions.

My Personal Journey: Kibbutz Ma'ayan Baruch

Before writing this book, I had to determine which of the many border communities to focus on. Some were apparent; others became evident as my research progressed. Not on my list was Ma'ayan Baruch, a small kibbutz occupying a few thousand dunams (4 dunams constitute one acre) of land east of Metula, at the tip of Israel, bordering Lebanon.

Then I asked myself, how can I omit Ma'ayan Baruch? I had spent three weeks working the soil of that kibbutz, as a volunteer, when I was sixteen in 1971. It was Ma'ayan Baruch, coupled with James Michener's book *The Source,* which I had read while visiting Israel in 1969, that lit a Zionist fire within me that burns brighter today. Writing a book about northern border communities without visiting the source of my own relationship with Zionism seemed wrong. And so, in 2018, for the third time in three years, I found myself turning left off Route 99 and driving up a forgettable bumpy road that cut through farmland filled with crops.

Forgettable, that is, until I saw the kibbutz's tractor shed.

Then memories flooded. My pulse quickened. Images from nearly fifty years before danced through my mind!

Minutes later, I was talking with Phillip Pasmanick on a red-dirt knoll at the northern outer edge of Kibbutz Ma'ayan Baruch, a short stroll from Lebanon. We had ridden there in his electric cart. Along the way, we passed a memorial for a kibbutz boy, killed in his tank by Hezbollah soldiers who had violated the ceasefire from the 2006 Lebanon War. The boy's father, still a Ma'ayan Baruch member, has yet to reconcile why Israel did not respond to that egregious violation. What gets caught up in the politics of the outside world means little to a father mourning a lost son.

Before us rose stands of trees blocking our view of the border. Phillip told me farmers from nearby Metula had planted them. Previously, the land here had been barren, the view clear. I supposed it a small blessing that those I couldn't see were also unable to see me.

Phillip sported a small paunch and graying beard, both excusable for a man in his mid-sixties. His nondescript appearance and tone did not hint at the grave responsibility he once bore and his enduring passion for Israel, which still motivates him.

Phillip grew up in Atlanta, Georgia. At eighteen, he made aliyah (translated from Hebrew, the word means "ascend"; in practical use it is the term used for the act of immigrating to Israel). During the summer of 1973, Phillip enrolled in a Kibbutz Ulpan, an intensive, several-month study of Hebrew as part of the immigration process.

But things didn't go as planned.

On October 6, bombs dropped from Syrian warplanes flashing overhead altered Phillip's course in Israel. The Yom Kippur War had started. Phillip said:

> *All of a sudden everybody was being called up. Because on a kibbutz you are basically one, two, or three different units . . . we all go together. So, we are at the swimming pool, all of a sudden, the swimming pool starts to empty . . . and we don't speak Hebrew yet. We just got here a couple months earlier. Anyway, that was the end of our Ulpan. The Ulpan teacher got drafted.*

Several years later, a random event led to Phillip joining Ma'ayan Baruch, and he ended up overseeing security for the kibbutz for twenty-six years, from 1985 to 2011.

In the late 1970s, Phillip was part of an army unit stationed in Lebanon, tasked with a mission he would not tell me about. This was not a surprise. I found selective secrecy a common trait among Israelis who had engaged in security operations across the borders—even when decades had passed. But Phillip did provide many details about the random event. After a couple days, his unit ran out of water. Even though his unit was operating in Lebanon in close contact with the enemy, its operational base was also close to Ma'ayan Baruch. Sensing an opportunity, his commander ordered Phillip to drive to the kibbutz to fill up jerry cans with water, take a quick shower, and return. Phillip said:

> *So, we got here and there were a bunch of old folks who had set-up tables and they had kettles of tea and coffee, cakes, and cookies spread out. Back in those days when you heated up your hot water it was a kerosene heater. I was not part of the first group that came here. They finished all of the hot water. So, the old folks said 'listen, [while] we are waiting for the water to get hot . . . have*

something to drink, have something to eat, you can fill up the jerry cans in the meantime.' That very much impressed me.

He then clarified that the "old folks" he had just referred to are old today. When Phillip first encountered them, they were in their prime. Their kindness stuck with him. A few years later, after a short stint with a kibbutz on the Golan Heights, Phillip settled in Ma'ayan Baruch, where he still lives.

Phillip and I had missed each other at Ma'ayan Baruch by less than a decade. He was somewhere else in Israel while I was a volunteer picking apples, among my other duties, in Ma'ayan Baruch's fields in the summer of 1971. One of my tasks was less than enviable—a two-day slog shoveling wet cow dung at dawn into a tractor-pulled cart, sitting in it while the transport chugged over bumpy ground to another field, and then leaping out and distributing the stinking mounds evenly on a barren field. Those turds were great fertilizer. They were not so great for the unlucky ones, like me, who endured the inevitable oozing shit sauce that clung to our clothes and skin. Perhaps, though, it was even worse for our roommates when we entered the bunk at the end of the day!

Apple picking, however, was fun. To do so, I would lean a ladder against my target tree, reach out and cut the fruit from a branch with a clipper, and then place the apple into a canvas bag I wore around my neck. Once I filled the bag, I would dump its contents into a large bin placed between the endless rows of apple trees. Our prime directive was to ensure that the apple stem remained intact. Failure would render it unfit for sale. However, nobody taught me how to stay on the ladder while stretching for an apple out of easy reach. For that, I was on my own. Nor was I admonished to refrain from eating any of the apples. The best, I can attest, never made it past my mouth.

Those twenty-one days changed me forever. I loved working in the fields—excluding those two days in the cow shit. We would leave for work every day before dawn in a futile attempt to escape the oppressive heat. After walking under starlight to the dining hall for a quick bite, we would arrive at our work assignments by dawn. There, we sweltered as the sun rose higher in the clear blue sky. Then, at 8 a.m., we would have breakfast in the fields. Fresh bread was abundant, as were tomatoes and cucumbers and tubes looking like toothpaste that contained some unknown spread, which I would lavish on my starch of choice.

We ate as much as we wanted and washed it all down with copious amounts of juices and water. While working, I would cast glances at the Golan Heights to our east and the mountains marking the border with Lebanon to our west, which seemed filled with mystery and adventure. Frequently, we would hear roars in the sky followed by Israeli Air Force warplanes engaging in mock duels overhead. The planes would soar upwards in a straight line toward the stratosphere, disappear, and then, in a rush, swoop back down into sight.

It was bliss.

We spent our afternoons lounging, and on many evenings we played basketball with Israeli kids. Rules meant little during those games. When the hour drew late, we would gird ourselves for the next day's work. Sometimes, we would see flashes of light on the Golan from what likely were skirmishes between Israeli and Syrian soldiers.

My group slept in volunteer quarters; really just wooden shacks slapped together. They were quite a step down from our normal comfy suburban lifestyles. A toilet or two was attached to the outside structure, and somewhere there was a shower, although I can't remember where. On a pale-white exterior wall of my temporary home hung a brown sign with large black letters, "Volunteers Do Not Bomb."

Outside, there were trenches cut deep into the dirt that divided the volunteer bunkhouses. One volunteer fell into one and broke his leg. Our supervisor warned us not to cross the fence surrounding the kibbutz at night, saying, "We shoot what moves out there and come out in the morning to see what we got." I had thought it was mere hyperbole, a joke meant to scare us for the kibbutznik's merriment. In retrospect, I know the threat was real. I became especially aware of that reality after reading the diary of a 1965 kibbutz volunteer; his entries described in great detail Palestinian terrorists from Lebanon or Syria invading kibbutz land (both borders were very close then, now only the Lebanese border is).

In 1971, I had no idea where I was other than somewhere in northern Israel. All I knew was that I loved the life and the land—well, maybe not the cow shit part. Forty-seven years later, I was overwhelmed by the realization that I had come back to this place and its fields, a place that had been so integral in shaping my life.

Phillip and I continued our conversation. Around us, on three sides, agricultural fields hemmed us in. Fields I had surely worked in decades before. Meanwhile, the setting sun cast an ominous light over the pastoral scene, though perhaps it was not the light that spoiled the serenity but the presence of something else. There was a restored guard tower standing in front of us, and not too far away, security lights along the perimeter of an army base belonging to the Israeli Defense Forces (IDF) had just flashed on. Our proximity to the border, the gusting wind, and hints of music drifting toward us from the army base created a raw discord with the nostalgia I felt.

A young man lounged on top of the tower. The tower itself seemed out of place, more memorial than defense feature. I asked Phillip about it. His answer surprised me.

As is true throughout so much of Israel, that tower has a tragic past. In 1986, a PLO rocket struck it, killing two IDF soldiers inside. Afterward, Phillip obtained permission from the IDF to restore the guard tower for kibbutz security purposes. His concerns were not trivial. Not too long before, terrorists coming from Lebanon had twice tried to sneak into the kibbutz.

After the second incident, Phillip spoke up at a meeting attended by IDF area commanders to assess and improve security in the area. He said, "Here I am on the border, there is no army base in front of me. I'm front line. You guys are depending on me to stop [the terrorists] or contain them until you get here, and yet the radio I have is with the police and everybody behind me, I don't have any radios with anybody in front of me on the border, so I can't call a patrol on the border."

Incredulous, I asked whether he had been able to communicate with the army back then. Phillip answered, "I was tied into the military . . . the military behind me not in front of me. And I want it in front of me. We are only 300 yards from the border. And they were on the border. I want these people on the border. I want people to get here as fast as possible."

Recognizing the danger Phillip had expressed, the IDF, rather than station troops at the kibbutz, gave him an extra searchlight to affix to one of the kibbutz's guard towers. At least then kibbutz security would have a chance of spotting infiltrators before they reached the fence. Little did anyone know then the role that searchlight would soon play.

On November 25, 1987, two Palestinian terrorists took off from Southern Lebanon in separate hang gliders. Both gliders were equipped with small, jury-rigged propellers powered by lawn-mower-sized engines. Each took with them an assault rifle, a pistol equipped with a silencer, and a few hand grenades. Several IDF soldiers heard one of the hang gliders and sounded an alarm. IDF forces shot flares into the night sky while helicopters searched for the terrorists without success. The terrorists avoided discovery by flying level with the treetops. One landed at approximately 10:30 p.m. very close to an army camp near Kiryat Shmona. He killed one soldier and wounded another, then commandeered a truck and drove into the base. Inside, he killed five more soldiers and wounded seven before the battalion cook shot him. An investigation revealed that the alert sounded thirty minutes before the attack had been ignored throughout the north, except at Ma'ayan Baruch.

That night, Phillip said:

> *I got into my jeep to go check my soldiers at the gate. Whenever I turn on my jeep I always turn on all the communications . . . . So, I am listening to four different radio stations chatter at the same time. [All] of a sudden I hear somebody saying, 'send an ambulance quick.' So, the first thing I did, I went down to the gate and said turn off the lights, everybody outside. [Then] I picked up some chairs . . . and I said, 'Ok, you watch this way, you watch this way, and you watch this way.'*

Phillip then listened closely to the radio tuned into the regiment's medical radio frequency. He explained, "[The] people who have to get information right away are the medical people. So, I listen to intelligence, the medical, and the actual guys patrolling. I don't listen to the command; I'm not interested in the command. That's protocol. I'm not interested in protocol. I want to hear what is actually happening in the field."

Continuing further, he said, "Now I hear somebody saying it's not the Moshav, it's the army base. Send ambulances. Apparently, a hang glider landed. So, the first thing I did was get on my radio to my commanders on that side." Phillip told them, "We're going on alert because of something in the air." And then he further explained to me, "The code that you use for crossing the border coming in the air wasn't really being used very much. Almost never heard it. After that incident you heard it every night. But before that almost never heard it. But I used it, and they said 'wait, wait let command protocol decide and then you decide what to do'."

Phillip ignored the IDF's advice and pushed the alarm button. The siren went off, and everybody came out. He stationed some people in a different guard tower than the one now in front of us. "We turned on the [searchlight]," he said, "and all of the sudden the second glider that was coming at us [appeared in the light beam]. [The hang glider pilot] was blinded [by the light] and he crashed."

Was it luck that you spotted the hang glider, I asked?

Phillip answered modestly. He said the kibbutz had a second guard tower and he had "told those guys from here to here you keep searching back and forth. I told this guy from here to here. I told this guy from here to here. So, there was a little crossover, but not much." Was it luck, his tactics, or both?

The hang glider incident was the third time terrorists had tried and failed to attack Ma'ayan Baruch in the 1980s. For Phillip, change was needed! He met with the IDF Northern Commander and said:

> *Three times they tried to come in, three times we stopped them. Two things: 1) It is not our job to stop them it is your job. 2) Three times [they tried], there is not going to be a fourth. No other settlement in the country can say that they have been able to stop them . . . . Misgav Am failed, Manara failed, Kfar Yuval failed, I am the only one who didn't fail.*

He then added:

> *You got to put somebody up there. We are going to have people killed. Then I am going to feel responsible and I am going to leave. I can't stay here if anybody dies. I've got kids. My kids cannot be going to school with the children of people who died because terrorists came in on my watch. I told him I am a Zionist. Don't make me leave this country!*

As he spoke, I looked at the base in the distance, its security lights shining and from which music wafted. Clearly, it was there, at least in part, because of Phillip's persistence after the night the hang gliders attacked. And because of his persistence, the people of his kibbutz were safer. When the base became operational, Phillip loaded his jeep with tables and chairs and drove to it to make breakfast for the soldiers stationed there: eggs, sliced vegetables, and all the accouterments. Phillip had learned from the kibbutz's members when they had pampered him a decade before.

Near the end of our circuit around the kibbutz we passed chicken houses that were now enclosed by a fence because of the dangers of bird flu. Below them, I spotted the dairy farm. They were probably the very fields where I had shoveled cow shit almost fifty years before.

As we headed back to my car, I asked Phillip the question that been hanging in my mind over our entire interview, "Do you worry?"

> *I'm not concerned. I'm not worried at all. But I'm not the average person on the kibbutz. There might be only two or three other people that understand. How come we don't use a projector anymore? Because we see better in the dark than we do during the day. Now a projector is not for us to find somebody like in the night of the hang gliders. A projector is [for] anybody trying to sneak in will see it and maybe he will turn around and leave. But the army is not like that. The army is saying come on a little closer, a little closer, we are waiting for you.*

"So, you don't have a concern?"

"There are enough electronics around, and we also have satellite," Phillip said. "So, the border is now protected. You don't hear about people coming to the border in the north anymore. Because anything suspicious is dealt with immediately."

But how is the kibbutz kept secure on a typical night? I asked.

Phillip answered, "Times change based on the political situation." Decades ago, when the PLO were on the border, he had commanded several regular IDF soldiers living at the kibbutz. They, along with kibbutz civilian residents, would patrol the community. Phillip required that two men, one soldier and one civilian, drive the kibbutz perimeter throughout every night. He told me, "I would take the keys to the jeep off [the rubber hose it was attached too] . . . hit myself on the knee [with the hose] and say I want you to do 60 kilometers . . . . It is three kilometers around the kibbutz. I want twenty times in nine hours."

Phillip then said, "For decades I knew every millimeter of this kibbutz. I [would] dig up Katyushas when they fell. I have a hell of a Katyusha collection!" But, I asked, do you fear that more Katyushas might hit the kibbutz? "I don't think about it," Phillip answered. And, "I developed an ear for booms. So, I could tell if it was artillery going out or a Katyusha rocket coming in."

While Phillip spoke, his connection to the land, his land, was obvious. Intrigued, I asked him why he loved it here. Phillip told me:

> *If I had taken you to my house, we would have sat on [my] porch. You would have seen the entire Hula Valley in front of you. You would have seen about six different fruit trees that I planted. The oranges and tangerines that I planted are growing now . . . kumquats are also growing now; the other fruits are not in season. You would have seen the mango tree, you would have seen the little lemon tree, there are wild parrots that fly overhead. They fly in little groups of five or six. They squawk a lot. The storks are not flying around so much. If we had been here about four o'clock, 5 o'clock you would have seen them. I live in paradise. Nothing short of paradise.*

Then his lyrical discourse on the wonders of his home abruptly stopped. Distracted, he revealed that security concerns were never far from his mind. Twenty-six years of safeguarding the kibbutz had left its impact. "The helicopter you just heard. Did you hear the helicopter? See nothing gets by me, not military, the helicopter you just heard is the United Nations flying across the border."

Phillip stopped our cart at the dining hall, filled with young people. It was the same dining hall where I had worked in, ate in, and met friends in when I was sixteen. What used to be the kitchen was now the kibbutz grocery store. Decades ago, the now dilapidated rooms of the dining hall reverberated with the sounds of kibbutzniks and volunteers eating and socializing. Now the patrons were neither kibbutznik nor volunteer. They were part of an alternative educational program. Most Israelis go into the army after high school. However, before fulfilling their army commitment they can delay their service by entering an educational program that trains them for certain jobs. One of those preparatory programs is called an army "Mechina." Ten teenagers in that nation-wide program drowned in the Negev during a flash flood in 2018. Ma'ayan Baruch hosts one of those Mechina programs. Now, the dining room is dedicated to those young adults where they meet, attend classes, and put on plays and skits.

It was time to go but I found myself lingering in the cool night air because I wanted to keep talking to Phillip. He then asked without expecting me to answer, "Why is it that we have a border road on our entire border and Lebanon does not have one at all?"

Before I could respond, Phillip answered his own question:

> *When UNIFIL [the United Nations Interim Force in Lebanon] patrols, why do they [use a] helicopter [rather than a vehicle]? Because we have to protect our border, we are afraid of infiltrations, so we built a border fence with sensors and we patrol there all the time for footprints, checking out why the sensors went off. And the reason they don't . . . is because they don't have to. There is no threat of us sneaking [in] we're not going in. So when you hear the helicopters, usually around this time of night, it is dark enough where they can start using infrared and seeing stuff,*

> *it's also where they are not really sure with enough light with binoculars [that] they can see some things . . . . It is standing operating procedure.*

And then, with more frustration than venom about UNIFIL, he said:

> *I don't think they've done a single goddamn thing to protect us. Hezbollah are professionals. It is an army, nothing less. Not just because they spent [several] years in Syria, even before that these guys are not intimidated by the United Nations. As a matter of fact, I once hosted a Norwegian group here that [said] six months earlier Hezbollah walked into their base, held them at gunpoint, I'm talking about the whole base, held them at gunpoint, made them fill their rucksacks with radios and wallets. You see, UNIFIL does not intimidate!"*

Phillip made it very clear that he respects Hezbollah, takes them seriously, and does not "underestimate them even a little bit."

My visit to Ma'ayan Baruch overwhelmed me. The kibbutz of my memory had grown and prospered. Yet, in so many ways, it still reminded me of the kibbutz of my youth. Located in the far north, steps from ever-present danger, Ma'ayan Baruch had seemingly thrived despite its close proximity to danger.

But I was disturbed to learn from Phillip that the kibbutz had problems of its own making. The average age of its 180 members was sixty. When Phillip had moved to the kibbutz in the 1980s, it was thirty. However, it's not for lack of trying that the kibbutz is growing older. One solution to address the problem was to entice members' children to move back by partially subsidizing them. If eligible adult children would agree to pay approximately $5,000, the children would receive kibbutz land and membership contingent on their pledge to build a home on that land and live there for five years. In addition, Ma'ayan Baruch recruited sixty unrelated families to live at the kibbutz and tried to include them in kibbutz cultural events.

But the quest for new, younger members did not go smoothly. Litigation erupted when the new residents sued Ma'ayan Baruch over funds they had paid to the kibbutz, in addition to the contractors, when the non-members' homes were built. They argued that the amount they paid Ma'ayan Baruch was greater than the value they received. The battle ended with a victory for the kibbutz. Lingering animosity from that dispute still divides some members and non-members.

Now the kibbutz is implementing a more radical solution in hopes of enticing younger members. It is trying to change its format from kibbutz to moshav. This will be a significant change. A kibbutz is a socialist enterprise where even today, despite kibbutz reformation over the last few decades, the community, as a whole, generally owns the means of producing income. Even though there is far more individual responsibility and differentiation now than in the pre-reformation days, the present-day kibbutz model still bears a semblance to those early days. Whereas moshavs generally allow more room for individual ownership and profit, though resources are pooled for many endeavors.

Phillip seemed excited about the proposed change. That surprised me because the kibbutz concept was a foundational part of the Zionist enterprise. But Phillip's main objective was to create opportunity for members to own more land and build homes there to support succeeding generations. Thus, he was willing to jettison the kibbutz concept in hopes of solving the community's problem.

However, changing the community's structure from kibbutz to Moshav is not easy. Land is owned and controlled by Israel's land authority. One Haifa professor concluded, after studying relevant law in Israel, that only two other nations share its archaic land system:

Cuba and North Korea—hardly beacons of modernity. Israel's government grants land to kibbutzim and oversees how it is used. Changes require much paperwork, legal effort and, in the case of Ma'ayan Baruch, a seven-year wait.

Phillip was a joy to spend time with: passionate and knowledgeable about his country, proud of his achievements, and dedicated to his community. Sadly, I did not have time to join him at his home for coffee and cake.

Driving south, on the only road that led to the main highway, I again spied the tractor sheds where I had mustered as a teenager in the pre-dawn hours before heading to the fields. But competing with my nostalgia was the realization that I had much to learn if I hoped to understand life in the north. To my left and right, forlorn, twinkling lights marked communities on top of the Golan Heights and the mountains bordering Lebanon. A few minutes earlier, while the sun still cast a dimming glow, I had seen the development town of Kiryat Shmona to my west. A town that had suffered so much from rockets, terrorists, and economic malaise. Northwest of me sat Metula, a town of perhaps 1,500 souls. To the northeast, but not far away, was Ghajar, an anomaly to say the least. An Alawite town that wants to be part of Israel, Ghajar is coveted by Hezbollah, which claims it is part of Lebanon even though Syria controlled and administered Ghajar before the Six-Day War of 1967.

As I neared the highway, I thought of my home near Washington, D.C. There are no implacable foes there living behind a fence just yards from my door. There, amid shopping malls and high rises, nobody is actively trying to kill me. Nor am I required to help secure the perimeter of my community. While distractions, annoyances, and some dangers abound, existential threats do not. And I certainly don't feel, as one northern Israeli resident expressed when I asked what it is like to live in the north, that I am living "under a volcano."

But Israelis living along their country's northern borders have a different perspective than me—even though they usually refrain from discussing the dangers unless prompted. Even though they are less than three hours car ride to Tel Aviv, and most are less than two hours' drive from Haifa, every man or woman who calls a northern border community home say the same thing: They live on the periphery. They say it with pride tinged with the annoyances they experience as a result.

Why do they call it the periphery? What is the history of these communities? What social, economic, and security challenges do residents face, and how do those challenges impact their lives? Who are some of the personalities making a difference? That and more were on my mind as I traveled from one community to another.

Answering these questions required me to dig into the past. Two thousand years ago, the northern Galilee and the Golan Heights contained many thriving Jewish communities. In the late 1880s, the northern Galilee was a wilderness with only small Jewish enclaves at Safed, near the Lebanese mountains and at Tiberias, adjacent to the Sea of Galilee. What happened to those thriving communities that populated the region during the Roman era? How and why did Jews return in the modern era? How did they survive and thrive? All of that is an integral part of today.

I have tried in this book to capture the reality of life on Israel's northern borders by focusing on a few places, people, and events. I am not trying to provide a comprehensive history of the region. I will happily leave that task to academics. Instead, my hope for this book is that it sparks your desire to learn more about Israel's north, inspires you to travel the region yourself, and provides you with some context for what you might encounter there. Then I will be satisfied, for I will have done my small part in thanking the people of northern Israel for standing strong.

Clifford Sobin, January 2020

Chapter One

Gamla

I knew better.

Over the last two decades I have hiked hundreds of trails, some a mile or less, and many ten miles or more. I have hiked under blazing suns and through air thick with humidity. One safeguard was a constant. I always brought plenty of water.

Sometimes, I would marvel at hikers who carried, at best, one small bottle of water, mostly empty, their faces red and sweaty. "Idiots, they are going to die out here!" I would think.

Now, I was the idiot.

I arrived at the parking lot at the Gamla Nature Reserve, located on the Golan Heights plateau, in mid-morning. The sun was already hot and high in a blue sky absent of clouds. A liter of water sat on the seat next to me, but I was in a hurry. I had an appointment in Metula, an hour drive away, at 1 p.m., and since I had forgotten to take my backpack, I thought carrying the water bottle by hand would slow my descent on the craggy rocks. The hike down to the ruins of Gamla was less than a mile. I reasoned it should not take me more than twenty minutes down and perhaps thirty minutes to scramble back up. Having my hands free would facilitate traveling along the boulder strewn path. So, I opted for speed over caution.

Why did I want to go to Gamla? Simple. Two thousand years ago Gamla was a thriving Jewish border community. The tale of its fall, the last fortified Jewish city in the region, rivals the better-known story of Masada.

* * *

Gamla is located on a hill, in the southern Golan, six miles east and slightly north of the Sea of Galilee. Its shape is often described as reminiscent of a camel's hump—although frankly I didn't see it until I saw a drawing depicting the view from the northeast. To me, it is better described as a pyramid with two sides, divided by a spiny ridge, having a slightly gentler slope than its third, which sheers starkly down to its base. Nevertheless, the city of Gamla's name is derivative of the Hebrew word *gamal,* meaning camel.

Deep gorges separate Gamla from the mountain plateaus that surround it. Its ruins occupy the rocky southern saddle, part way up the hill. They include an ancient synagogue featuring intact stone benches along the walls and the remains of a *Mikvah* (ritual bath) at its entrance. Today, the synagogue is used for Bar Mitzvahs. The hill steepens rapidly above the town before narrowing to a point. The only plausible approach for an advancing army was on the eastern side of the hill. There, Gamla's Jewish defenders constructed robust fortifications, including a stone wall six meters thick with a circular tower at its highest point, plus other towers spaced intermittently along the wall.

Jews first came to Gamla in large numbers during the 200 years that preceded Christ's birth. Some theorize that Jews returning from exile in Babylon were its first settlers. Eventually, they came under the rule of King Herod, the Roman-appointed ruler of Judea. Herod used tax incentives to promote Jewish settlement in Gamla—not unlike tax gimmicks used worldwide today to promote government objectives.

Then, in 66 C.E., Jews revolted for the first time against Roman rule. It would not be the last time. Nero, Rome's emperor, directed

Vespasian to squash the revolt. A year later, Vespasian arrived in the Galilee, at the head of three Roman legions that, along with allies, totaled 60,000 soldiers.

Vespasian first directed his attention to settled regions in the Galilee. After a short siege, he took Yodfat, a Jewish town on a hill about thirteen miles southeast of modern-day Acre. There he captured Josephus, commander of Jewish forces in the Galilee. Rather than kill him, as he did the 40,000 inhabitants of Yodfat, Vespasian made Josephus his slave and interpreter.

Evidently, Vespasian became quite taken with Josephus. Within two years, Vespasian granted Josephus his freedom and gave him his family name, Flavius. Later, Josephus fully defected, became a Roman citizen, and chronicled the Roman-Jewish wars. Whatever one might think of Josephus's loyalty to his fellow Jews, he, along with modern archaeological efforts, is responsible for most of the information we have about Gamla.

Jerusalem was Vespasian's ultimate objective. But after taking Yodfat, Vespasian turned his attention to Gamla. He had no choice; 9,000 Jewish zealots inhabited the fortress. Leaving them astride his supply lines would have caused havoc and threatened his conquest of the Galilee. And so, in September 67 C.E., Vespasian turned 30,000 of his soldiers towards Gamla.

Vespasian must have found the defenses of Gamla rather imposing. Barren, hot terrain, steep ravines, a thick wall, and imposing towers stood in the way of a walkover. However, the Romans held some cards too. In addition to outnumbering Gamla's defenders more than three to one, the Romans had battering rams and catapults, more properly called ballistae, capable of hurling heavy stones. The trick was to get them close enough to the wall to inflict damage. Therefore, upon arrival, Vespasian ordered his men to fill in the ravine on the northeast side so that his soldiers could drag their ballistae to where they were needed. Within weeks, all was ready.

The ballistae hurled rocks into Gamla's stone fortification, rupturing the wall in three places. The main breech was five yards wide and "V" shaped. With trumpets blaring, the Roman army poured through. The Jews fled uphill to the town and the ridges. Roman soldiers shoved through the narrow alleyways and swarmed over the roofs of the terraced structures. Vespasian and his guards triumphantly joined his men. The end was near. The defenders of Gamla, in their death, would join the departed souls of Yodfat.

Except Gamla's defenders refused to flee. Panic was not welling within them. Rather than retreat up the rise, they turned to fight. The Romans, jammed into alleyways and atop uneven rooftops, could not organize themselves to bring their superior training and numbers to bear. Jewish arrows drew Roman blood. By the hundreds and then thousands, Romans fell and then retreated. Vespasian barely escaped. To protect him against the furious onslaught of arrows and slashing swords, Vespasian's guard created a *testudo*, a wall and ceiling composed of their personal shields. They held this barrier in place to shelter Vespasian and themselves while inching away from the fight. Imagine the resolute discipline required to accomplish that maneuver successfully amid such carnage. One slip, one false step, and a hole would open, which would cause the loss of one man, then another, then all. But training won out. Vespasian survived.

The defeat did not deter Vespasian. It made him craftier.

A few days later, Vespasian ordered several Roman soldiers to sneak close to the base of the large circular tower anchoring the defensive wall under the cover of night. Quietly, one by one, they removed many of the heavy stones supporting the structure's base. The soft chalk ground that encapsulated the stones made their job easier. As their mission neared completion, their excitement must have grown.

Suddenly, it happened. With a loud boom, the tower collapsed. According to Josephus, the inhabitants of the fortress panicked for they knew what the crashing sound meant. Their key battlement had fallen, and a large hole had been torn in the defenses. Soon hordes of Romans thirsting for revenge would pour through that hole.

Vespasian's son, Titus, led the onslaught. Once again, Romans filled the alleyways of the doomed city. But this time, there was no ambush, only failure and fear. The Jewish defenders fought valiantly, but the attacking Romans steadily pushed them up the narrowing hill, closer and closer to the point at its crest.

However, a stand-off developed that for a while staved off defeat. The Jews shot their arrows and threw stones downhill with great effect while the Romans struggled to fight while clamoring up the steep hillside. Having walked the terrain without water, I suspect thirst and fatigue, mitigated by adrenalin, must have assailed both Roman and Jew.

But then fate intervened.

Josephus wrote that a heavy wind blew up the hill with such strength that it turned aside Jewish projectiles aimed downhill at the Romans. Conversely, the wind helped the Romans, enhancing the strength and range of Roman arrows shot uphill. Modern meteorological observation is consistent with Josephus's story. During early fall, occasional eastern winds, some near gale force, sweep the area. The narrow gorge surrounding Gamla increases the velocity of those winds. Some gusts are so strong they interfere with breathing and create thick clouds of dust. Arrows shot down into that maelstrom would not have a chance of hitting their mark. Arrows aimed uphill in such wind would be far more lethal.

The Jews who survived Titus's charge into the city and whom the legionnaires were now pressing hard, no longer had a chance. Facing death, they had only one remaining choice—decide by whose hand they would leave this earth. Josephus wrote that 4,000 died by Roman sword, while 5,000 flung themselves into the ravine, not unlike the desperate souls that jumped from the Twin Towers on September 11,

2001, preferring death by impact to fire. At the end, Josephus says only two women survived to tell the story.

How much stock can be put into this story? Josephus's mention of two female survivors is suspect since he also said there were two women survivors at Masada (along with five children). Coincidence or artifice? And the telling of the mass suicide is questionable. Josephus says that men first flung their wives and children and then themselves into oblivion. While very steep, the sides of the hill in many places do not lend themselves to mass suicide by falling into the ravine. At least one scholar has posited an alternative: that probably thousands of Jewish non-combatants scrambled to escape down the sides of the hill. Having been there, I can attest that anybody trying to rush down that hill would stumble and fall. One can only imagine what it would be like if thousands were trying to pick their way down the sides of the hill in a jumbled mass of panicked humanity. Those that did not tumble into the abyss would be easy pickings, laying broken on the steep slopes, for Roman soldiers bent on revenge. But in the end, the manner of their demise does not matter. All 9,000 inhabitants of Gamla, with the possible exception of those two women, died horrible deaths. By the end of the day, Gamla was no more.

No more, that is, until 1967.

Sometime after the Six-Day War ended, Shmarya Guttman conducted an archaeological survey of the Golan Heights. While taking a break to eat a sandwich, he by chance looked down on an oddly shaped hill covered with foliage. My guess is that his view offered the same perspective depicted in the drawing I had seen of Gamla resembling a camel. Astonished, Guttman realized that the oddly shaped hill below him conformed exactly to Josephus's description of ancient Gamla. It took Guttman six years to raise funds for initiating excavations. It was to those excavations and that hill that

I now tread, six days short of 1,951 years after the massacre.

* * *

After I left my car and walked a short way on a flat path, Gamla came into view on my left. I spent a moment at the overlook, and then I began my descent. Steep, barren, and rocky would be understated adjectives. Along the way, brief signs informed me about the history of where I would soon tread. The wind rattled around me without respite. Each step, I soon realized, was a step into my ancestral past.

At the bottom of the gorge a small parking lot, accessible by a road on which hikers are not permitted, brings a hint of modernity to the somber scene, even though replicas of Rome's catapults were also present. Their proximity to Gamla's walls visibly demonstrated that ancient warfare required an immediacy unnecessary in modern times when Hezbollah can shoot rockets from miles away.

Then I began my trek up to Gamla.

From a distance, Gamla looked imposing. From close, Gamla felt forbidding. The breach in the wall was self-evident. The ruins clear. As I struggled up the spine of the "Camel's back" I thought about how the Jewish defenders must have felt as the Romans chased them higher and higher up the hill, until they had nowhere else to go.

Gamla's ruins are majestic and forlorn, a monument to Jewish presence on the Golan and a testament to how fragile that existence was—and still is. It is also visual proof that Jews have lived on this land for millennium and that their presence here only ceased because they were driven from it.

While retracing my steps down Gamla to the gorge below, my thoughts drifted to other evidence of Jewish presence on the Golan in ancient times. I remembered a few months before when I had visited the Synagogue at Ein Keshatot ("Spring of the Arches"). Jews built that synagogue in the fifth century and improved it in the sixth. Also located in the Golan Heights, this impressive structure presently undergoing renovation was fifty-nine feet long, forty-three feet wide and thirty-nine feet high! It is one of twenty-five Jewish Synagogues whose remains have been found on the Golan Heights and that existed between the period of the Jewish revolt against the Romans and Muslim conquest of the area in 636 A.D.

Until I had visited Ein Keshatot, I did not know that Jews had inhabited the Golan long ago. When I did more research, I learned that the Kingdom of Northern Israel held the Golan Heights for some 200 years until 720 B.C.E. For the following 1,350 years, a Jewish presence remained and then was forcibly made absent until after the Six-Day War in 1967.

Such thoughts of the ancient past trickled away after I crossed the flat area beyond Gamla and began my ascent along the same path I had descended less than an hour before. By then it was mid-day, the sun blazing. The twenty-minute trek down the hill, during which I practically leapt from rock to rock, had turned into an interminable slog back up rather than the relatively easy jaunt I thought it would be. The ceaseless wind, a cooling breeze on the way down, left me parched and impeded my progress. Lack of water was no longer a thought; it was an increasingly persistent issue. My rest stops increased, often under whatever sparse cover I could find. Still, I was confident that I would reach the top.

Suddenly, my confidence faded. As my tongue clove to my parched throat, my physical condition began to concern me. I was still sure I would reach the top, but now I understood that I had to be careful, rest strategically, and watchful of my effort. Wisps of alarm began to sap my faith that I would overcome the challenge I faced.

Just as I began focusing on remaining calm to avoid any energy-sapping panic, relief came via a young Israeli man. Earlier, I had spied his group of three beginning their descent. About two-thirds of their way down, our paths crossed. I must have looked poorly because he immediately offered water. His act reminded me of an incident twenty-five years earlier when I descended into the Grand Canyon and had done the same for someone in dire straits struggling uphill. I guzzled down several gulps without regard to the risks of sharing the same bottle. I'd like to think that his water did not make the difference, that I would have made it to the top without his assistance. But I can't say that. What I can say is that when I reached my vehicle, the liter of warm, sunbaked water lying in my car felt more refreshing than the coldest beer.

And so I left the Golan voluntarily; I was not forcefully ejected, as the Jews had been long ago. The fall of Gamla presaged the end of Jewish presence on the Golan and the end of Jewish rule in northern Israel. A void on the Golan that did not begin to refill until after the Six-Day War in 1967. But eight decades before that war, idealistic Jewish settlers set the stage for the return of the Jews. Those settlers left lands where they were not welcome for a dream. It was a dream to re-establish the Jewish State lost two thousand years before. Undaunted, they faced a dangerous journey followed by an uncertain future in what was then called Palestine and later became part of Israel. A few especially hardy ones came to lands in the northern Galilee, west of the Golan. It was the 1880s, the place was Rosh Pina, and they were part of the First Aliyah.

Chapter Two

Rosh Pina, Pogroms, and the First Aliyah

Gai Oni

Rosh Pina sits above Route 90, a busy highway less than ten miles from Safed. Today, Rosh Pina is a bustling tourist town and vibrant art center snuggled into the mountains. In 1878, it was where the roots of modern Zionism first took hold. Then, seventeen religious Jews set out from Safed with the dream of creating, with their own manual labor, a new Jewish agricultural settlement. They were among the 2,000 Jews living in Safed at the time and perhaps 10,000 Jews in all of Palestine. They had little money and no agricultural experience.

The parsimonious financial support they received from fellow Safed Jews was enough to buy land in an Arab village called Ja'una, several miles walk from Safed. The land was available because the Arab inhabitants of Ja'una had a strategic plan. They knew their land was too poor for them to thrive, and they had identified more fertile ground in another area of the Galilee. Yet they had no money to purchase it. Their solution was to raise money by selling half their property, about 2,500 dunams, to the foolish Jews from Safed. After the sale, many of the villagers left to establish their new village. The remainder planned to follow.

Meanwhile, the seventeen idealistic Jews from Safed settled on their newly purchased land and called it Gai Oni (Valley of my Strength). Except strength was not a characteristic associated with the settlers. Abject poverty was. A wonderful fictional account of the difficulties those settlers faced is the subject of Shulamit Lapid's *Valley of Strength* which recounts the turbulent years of Gai Oni's struggle to survive, and its ultimate demise.

They failed because the land was difficult to cultivate, and the Jewish settlers had far too little knowledge of soil cultivation. For example, after planting potatoes the settlers were dismayed to find that the potatoes did not appear on the plants. Determined, they tore up the fields and tried again. That was how they first learned that potatoes grow under the earth! Adding to the settlers' problems, they were not alone. Turkish authorities prevented Arabs who had remained at Ja'una from leaving because local Effendis told them that Ja'una's residents were trying to avoid military service.

At first, the Arabs stuck at Ja'una had accepted the Jews, and the Jews were happy too. With Bedouin raiders in their midst, living together was the safest option for all. But drought and crop failure accentuated the poverty that plagued both groups. Their mutual suffering was the perfect petri dish for conflict. The Jews felt hardship, not redemption. After three years, only three remained. But then came the First Aliyah.

Jews in Eastern Europe During the Nineteenth Century

For many today, their only knowledge of Jewish life in Eastern Europe comes from productions of *Fiddler on the Roof* or *Yentl*. But those romanticized versions of Jewish life hardly convey the hardships Jews in Eastern Europe endured. For the most part, they lived in the "Pale of Settlement," a large swath of western Czarist Russia that incorporated parts of Poland. Others lived in Romania, where they suffered similar privations. In total, five million Jews lived in Eastern Europe at that time—nearly half of the world's Jewish population.

They lived in *shtetls* (a Yiddish word for "town"). Stuffed with wooden homes that lined twisting streets with confusing means of ingress and egress, shtetls were jumbled slums. The homes stank from reeking stoves and other rank smells that heralded the poverty of those dwelling inside. Their rooms were dark, their floors creaked with every step, and their stairways wobbled. Their inhabitants spoke Yiddish, a hybrid combination of German, Hebrew, and a smattering of other languages.

Invariably, each town center had a bustling market. Christian peasants would come from miles away to trade livestock, vegetables, fish, and hides in exchange for Jewish dry goods, clothing, lamps and boots, among other imported and manufactured goods. The reverse was never true. By law, Jews could not own land, work as farmers, or engage in other professions such as law and medicine. Instead, many became blacksmiths, tailors, butchers, shoemakers, and the like. These men with side curls and beards could be found in the town's commercial corridor—weaving, hammering, stitching, and haggling. Others, less fortunate, called "l*uftmenschen*" (Yiddish for "Flying Men"), moved from *shtetl* to *shtetl* in their eternal search for work where, without much hope, they would accept the most menial of jobs.

Yet their plight did not interfere with their piety. Most *shtetl* residents embraced the 613 commandments derived from the Torah, Judaism's most holy document. Those commandments dictated every facet of their lives. So, while they could not control their external life, they used religious teachings to exert absolute control of their internal lives. Boys began religious school at an early age, obligated to sit in squalid conditions. Their pale faces evidenced the *shtetl* Jews' obsession with religious learning. Perhaps because laws prevented them from turning outward, Jews living in shtetls turned doggedly inward. Restricted and hopeless, that was Jewish life in Czarist Russia.

Then, life for them got worse.

The difficulties Jews endured in the late 18th century and early 19th century, increased after Nicholas I became czar in 1825. He called Jews "regular leeches" and wanted to rid them from the land. In an ironic parallel to the 613 Torah commandments, Nicholas I issued more than 600 edicts during his thirty-eight-year reign that were specifically aimed at disrupting Jewish life. One was to "bring about their gradual merging with Christian nationalities and to uproot those superstitious and harmful prejudices which are instilled by the teachings of the Talmud." Other edicts censored Yiddish and Hebrew books, interfered with Jewish educational practices, mandated mass expulsions, and even conscripted young Jewish boys into the army for up to twenty-five years. Furthermore, Nicholas I made it even harder than before for Jews to own land, live outside the "Pale of Settlement," and practice professions such as medicine or law.

After Nicholas I died, there followed a period of optimism when his son, Alexander II, became czar in 1855. For twenty-six years, life improved. The State still conscripted Jews into the army but only for five years instead of twenty-five. Alexander II also permitted some Jews to enter universities and allowed a few Jewish businessman to travel to areas of Russia, previously out of bounds for Jews, to ply their trades. Slowly, reforms became reality. Life for Jews was better.

The enlightenment ended on March 13, 1881.

As he did every Sunday, Alexander II traveled in a closed carriage to a military roll call. He was accompanied by six Cossack guards and two trailing sleighs filled with additional security personnel. An assassin lurked on a narrow, paved area parallel to the road. He carried a small package wrapped in a handkerchief. As the czar's carriage drew near, the erstwhile assassin threw the camouflaged bomb he held "under the horses'" hooves in the supposition that it would blow up under the carriage," killing the czar. He failed. Although one guard died in the blast, the czar exited the carriage shaken but not wounded.

However, the assassin was not alone. As the remaining Cossacks urged Alexander to swiftly exit the area, a second man approached. He too had a bomb to throw. It landed at the czar's feet. The explosion shattered the czar's legs, tore open his stomach, and mutilated his face. Royal blood poured into the street where it mingled with the blood of wounded commoners caught in the fray. The czar's guard took him to the winter palace, where he died minutes later.

The killers were members of a movement called the "People's Will," a Russian revolutionary organization that embraced terror to overthrow the czar and force political reform by sparking a peasant uprising. Ethnic Russians dominated the group. It was by no means led or instigated by Jews. At best, less than fifteen percent of its members were Jewish.

And yet, rumors quickly spread: the Jews were responsible for Alexander II's death. Drunken peasant mobs attacked Jewish communities. At least forty Jews were killed, more than 200 Jewish women were raped, and thousands of properties destroyed by the hordes of rioters. Those who survived without injury were traumatized.

The Russian word for such wanton behavior is "*pogrom*," meaning the attack, looting, raping, and destruction of one part of a minority group that is condoned or approved by the authorities. Although others might appropriate the word for their own purposes, its clear purpose is to reference state agitation, or at least acquiescence, for wanton attacks on Jews. These attacks, spurred by rumors surrounding the death of Alexander II, continued sporadically into 1882. Years later, these kinds of baseless attacks would be repeated.

During the rioting, many Jews shamefully cowered in hiding or remained inert, helpless with fear. A man in Vilna lamented that he knew it would be better to kill those he loved so that "some drunken riffraff [could not] come along, ravish [his] wife and daughter and throw [his] infant Sonia from the third-floor window." He continued, "What a miserable creature is the Jew! Even when the advantage is clear to him, he cannot summon the courage to do a good thing. Death awaits us in any case, so why should we wait?"

Meanwhile, Alexander III, the son of the assassinated czar, became the Russian empire' new leader. He brought his father's reforms to a screeching halt. A year after his father's death, the czar issued the "May" law that imposed new restrictions on where Jews could live and what work they were permitted to do. One of his leading advisers said, "One-third will die out, one-third will leave the country, and one-third will be completely dissolved in the surrounding population."

The new restrictions, combined with the pogroms, forever changed the mindset of the Jews living in the region. Rather than relying on religious fervor for escapism, many considered leaving. Despite stops and starts to the process and fears expressed by some that they should avoid antagonizing the Russian government and the Russian peasants, eventually organizations were formed, and choices were made. Over the next thirty-three years, an estimated 2.5 million Jews left. Most found their way to the United States; others went to Canada, Argentina, and Britain.

However, a small number made their way to Palestine. And within that group were a few hardy settlers who traveled to northern Israel where they founded the first Jewish settlements, the first of many kibbutzim, and paved the way for the creation of the State of Israel.

So, it is to Palestine that our story now turns.

Palestine in the Late Nineteenth Century

The Ottoman Empire, ruled by Turks in Constantinople, took control of Palestine in 1516. Four years later, Suleiman the Magnificent began his rule as Sultan. Until his death in 1566, life for

Jews in Palestine improved to the point that some immigrated from without to Safed, less than ten miles from what is now Israel's border with Lebanon. Many of those immigrants were Sephardic Jews, including leading rabbis who came from Spain after their expulsion in 1492, the same year Columbus left to discover the Americas. By the time Suleiman passed away, the number of Jewish families in Safed had more than tripled to over 700.

Now a fascinating collection of cobbled streets, ancient synagogues, and small covered shops off alleyways, with the arrival of the Sephardic Jews, Safed became a home for the study of Kabballah. Often called the "soul" of the Torah or the "Wisdom of Truth," Kabbalah provides believers mystical insights into the "essence of G-d, his interaction with the world, and the purpose of Creation."

Unfortunately, Safed did not continue to attract Jewish immigrants for long. Nor did any of the surrounding lands, the sole exception being Tiberias along the Sea of Galilee. Those lands were harsh, and not ideal for Jewish settlement. By and large this was thanks to the Ottoman Empire. Two hundred years after Suleiman had died, absentee landlords owned most of the land, which they leased to poor Arab and Druze farmers. Since no resources were devoted to protecting or developing the land, the huge forests present in the Galilee during ancient times disappeared; in turn swamps, which shrunk the amount of land available for agriculture, replaced them. Further burdening the poor farmers, the Ottomans imposed upon them oppressive taxes and a corrupt administration open to bribery. In essence, Palestine was a backwater of no consequence that contained a few people scratching away their existence, mostly from the soil.

Things began changing in 1879 when Napoleon's invasion brought Palestine to the forefront of some European minds. Soon after, more and more Europeans traveled to the region, and European nations aimed to influence events in the Levant. Their struggle for dominance brought scraps of modernization to the region as power began to slowly shift from the Ottomans to the Europeans.

During the 19th century the "Capitulation Agreement," first reached in the 16th century, was more rigorously followed. That agreement exempted European resident citizens and traders from Ottoman law and placed them under the protection of their European consuls. By the mid-1800s, slightly more than 10,000 Jews lived in Palestine under this context, amid 400,000 Muslims. More than half of those Jews lived in Jerusalem, while 2,000 lived in Safed and another 1,500 in Tiberias. Few Jews resided outside those three cities.

In 1858, the Ottomans created confusion locally and spurred the avarice of greedy absentee landowners—all while sparking conflict between Arabs and Jews—when they passed a law that required farmers to register their holdings. The new law provided for five different types of ownership. Only one, called "mulk," allowed individuals to have outright control. Another—the type of ownership called "miri"—designated land leased by the State for agricultural purposes. The remaining three ownership classes were designed to reflect different forms of government control or uses. The Turks did this to organize and identify landowners to facilitate taxation and land transfers, both of which were major sources of revenue for the Ottoman Empire.

A land's designation could not be changed without approval from the government. Similarly, owners could not build on land or plant orchards without the government's permission. Permits were required for land sales and if there were no heirs, the land would revert to the government. All this created revenue sources for the government and, through bribery, for many local officials that administered the process.

There also was another catch. Ownership of *miri* land that lay uncultivated for three years would revert to the government. In practice, this rule was not uniformly enforced if a farmer left his land fallow for several years. However, when it came to the Bedouin, because of their propensity to raid others, scrupulous enforcement of the three-year requirement was the rule rather than the exception.

By 1912, most of the restrictions the 1858 law placed on land sales were lifted. And by World War I, the Ottomans had established thirteen offices in Palestine to handle land sales. Yet problems still abounded. Tax assessments were based on the size of a registered property—measured in dunams, a unit equal to roughly a quarter acre or about 900 square meters. Therefore, landowners would lie about the number of dunams they owned while simultaneously marking the exact boundaries of their land. The differences between stated dunams and boundary markers that could shift with time and reflect different dunam totals, caused much litigation when land ownership changed hands, especially between Arabs and Jews.

The ostensible purpose of the 1858 law was to grant those working *miri* land ownership rights. The corollary objective was to raise government revenue by taxing *miri* landowners. The reality was that few farmers could afford to pay those taxes, and when they did pay them, the tax collectors kept much of the money. This left the poorer owners at the mercy of government officials who had no mercy. Thus, much of the land passed from the poor to wealthier individuals who could afford to pay taxes and stand up to the petty avarice of local officials. Soon half of the arable land in Palestine belonged to owners of large estates, many of whom who lived elsewhere.

The process whereby local Arabs lost their land to the wealthy often involved some, or all, of the following:

1. *Miri* land was taxed at ten percent of the gross value of the crop yield, not the profit. Tax collectors would descend on a village, assess taxes for each owner, all the while eating and staying at the village for free. Police officers and military officials accompanying the collectors would squelch any objections. When landowner had the temerity to take legal action, resolution would take a long

time. The ten percent tax was equivalent to thirty to forty percent of profits from the crop yields. After paying the taxes, peasants would be unable to both take care of their family's needs and shell out the cost of planting the next season's crops. As a result, they were forced to seek help from moneylenders who charged usurious rates. Year after year this process would repeat, until the peasant had nothing left. The lenders then evicted the peasants and kept the land or sold it to a wealthy buyer. Meanwhile, the same peasant would continue to work the land as a tenant farmer while paying fees for the privilege to the new owner.

2. Many ruling families in Beirut and Damascus seized much of the land in Northern Palestine. Some by taking *mawat* land (land not owned by anybody) and cultivating it, thereby permitting them under Turkish law to gain ownership of the land after paying to the government its value (after the British took control in the 1920s, such land did not even need to be cultivated once seized). The wealthy obtained other tracts of land voluntarily from poor peasants who feared the taxes they would be assessed, dealing with government officials, and even conscription of their sons into the Ottoman army. To avoid that problem, peasants would ask someone wealthy, and thereby powerful, to record ownership of the peasant's land in their name for a fee. The peasant, depending on the good graces of the person he was doing business with, figured the wealthy would be better able to handle the taxation and corruption problems, leaving the peasant to work his land. Of course, this meant they no longer officially owned their fields and had no future right to challenge their sale or usage.

3. The semi-nomadic nature of the Bedouin in the Jordan valley worked to the government's benefit. When three years would pass without the Bedouin cultivating a plot, the government would

seize their land and sell it to the highest bidder.

4. The Ottoman regime would sell land for token amounts and grant ownership of large tracts to influential and supportive families. The government granted the Sursuk family in Lebanon hundreds of thousands of dunams in this manner. The Sursuk family sold some of that land to Jews.

Whenever they could, Jews bought land when it became available in the north. Sometimes individual Jews bought it, sometimes Jewish organizations. Sometimes they obtained the land at the public auctions that followed foreclosures. Other times, they bought directly from the Ottoman government, sometimes from individual local Arabs or villages, and often from wealthy landowners sitting in Beirut, Damascus, or elsewhere.

But with almost every purchase came problems.

All Jewish purchases were of *miri* land, which required a permit. And obtaining permits meant having to bribe local officials and, occasionally, high-level officials to overcome "technicalities."

And then, after the purchase, Jews often experienced friction with local Arabs who refused to accept Jewish ownership where it conflicted with their tenant farmer and grazing practices. Complicating the issue, land records and local Arab understanding of who owned what did not always match. After the Ottomans enacted the 1858 law, many Arabs avoided or reduced their registration taxes by lying about the amount of land they owned. In the land records they understated the size of their property while accurately recording their property landmarks. Taking advantage of that practice, sometimes sellers would destroy the physical landmarks and then argue that the sale was only for the lesser number of dunams recorded. Feuds—legal and otherwise—would then ensue.

Rosh Pina

In 1881 and 1882, the first wave of Russian pogroms jump-started two nascent movements that promoted settlement in Palestine. Later, they would become part of the Zionist movement.

BILU, founded in 1882, stood for a Hebrew phrase that meant "O House of Jacob, come and let us go!" Members of BILU were socialist and secular. The second line of their manifesto said it all, "If I do not help myself, who will help me?" The second-to-last line made clear their belief that creation of a homeland in Palestine would be the only salvation for Jewish suffering. BILU's first Jewish pioneers arrived in Palestine in July of 1882.

The second movement, also founded in 1882, was called "Lovers of Zion". The Lovers of Zion movement urged Jews to gradually return to the soil by creating agricultural communities in Palestine. Since czars had barred Jews from being farmers for centuries, this represented a fundamental change in the way Jews saw their future. The Lovers of Zion also embraced national unity of the Jewish people on a secular as well as religious basis, but that required territory and a common language to replace weakening religious homogeneity. Perhaps most importantly, the Lovers of Zion believed that a national revival required actual Jewish labor working the land, not the labor of others. Lastly, this was an activist movement that decried passivity. After enduring the pogroms, Lovers of Zion believed Jews could no longer afford to rely on others for security.

During this time, a Polish Jew named Leon Pinsker, published a powerful tract entitled *Auto-Emancipation*, in which he observed: "Judaism and anti-Semitism passed for centuries through history as inseparable companions. Like the Jewish people, the real wandering Jew, anti-Semitism, too, seems as if it would never die." Pinsker argued for the establishment of a Jewish homeland, although he did not say that it had to be in Palestine. Without a homeland, he warned,

Rosh Pina, Pogroms, and the First Aliyah

Jews would continue to experience the hardships and injustices imposed on them since the loss of their country 2,000 years ago. Given Hitler's subsequent rise and his slaughter of six million European Jews, his warning was prescient.

Of the 25,000 Jews who lived in Palestine by 1881, 15,000 lived in Jerusalem. Few lived outside the cities. Only three remained at Gai Oni. That changed in 1882, when the first major wave of Jewish settlers arrived in Palestine. Approximately 7,000, many passionate to create a better future for Jews, came from Czarist Russia and Romania. They called Jews who had lived in Palestine for hundreds of years the "Old Yishuv" and themselves the "New Yishuv." The Old Yishuv were the repository of past values and traditions; the New Yishuv saw themselves as the embodiment of a new spirit and hungered to innovate.

Like many immigrants, these new arrivals did not find the land they had idealized. Rather than a land flowing with milk and honey, they encountered hardship.

At the Arab port of Jaffa, now just south of modern Tel Aviv, many even encountered problems reaching shore. Since Jaffa did not have a deep-water port, Arab oarsmen would take immigrants in rowboats from their ships to shore. When the waves were high, they had to time jumping onto the rowboats for when they were on the crests of the swells.

Once on land, immigrants burned under a blazing sun and endured soaking rains while they waited for Turkish officials to decide whether to permit their entry into Palestine. By August, so many Jews arrived that the Turks stopped granting Jews from Russia, Romania, and Bulgaria entry into Palestine if they intended to settle there. New arrivals circumvented this restriction though a combination of bribery and deceit, saying they were only visiting. If permitted entry, immigrants would ride on donkeys to their new homes—often just mud huts or crowded rooms replete with insects, rodents, scorpions, and snakes. Few had any furniture, and nobody had access to running water. In many cases, daily nourishment consisted of a single meal limited to pita, canned fish, and olives.

When the lucky few reached their new homes— whatever piece of rocky or marshy land that had been acquired for them—they often found it teeming with flies and malaria-laden mosquitoes. Developing this land required backbreaking labor to which they were not accustomed. If the work was not enough to fill their hearts with despair, they also had to contend with various diseases—including dysentery, malaria, and typhus—and roving bands of Bedouin, who delighted in stealing the little they possessed. It's no wonder that many Jews returned to Eastern Europe.

But not everyone failed to adapt to these discouraging circumstances. One success story took root in the north.

This group of settlers came from the Romanian city of Moinesti, located near the Russian border. The city's 2,000 Jews composed about half of the city's population. Life for them in Romania, where sanctioned anti-Semitism and outbursts of peasant cruelty made Jewish life difficult, was not much better for Jews than in Russia. In 1866, the Romanian Constitution was amended by adding Article Seven. It stated, "Only such aliens of the Christian faith may obtain citizenship." With no hope of becoming full citizens in the future, some Jews in Moinesti prepared to leave. They included one group that was an offshoot of the Lovers of Zion, which focused on re-settlement in Palestine.

* * *

On December 11, 1881, David Shorb and two other individuals left Moinesti for Palestine, hoping to purchase land there for establishment of a village composed of Moinesti Jews. Shorb's two-year old son and pregnant wife stayed behind. Four days later, Shorb's wife gave birth to their daughter. He traveled from Istanbul to Beirut on a Russian boat. From Beirut he rode a donkey to Safed, assisted by two Arab guides.

Months later, by the start of summer in 1882, Shorb had identified land suitable for settlement. He telegraphed Jews in Moinesti, "I found it." The land was like his hometown: it was 1,000 feet above sea level, had access to freshwater springs, and featured a mix of hilly and flat terrain. The land stayed dry because of its elevation, much different than in the valley below where swamps predominated in many places. And the air was crisp, clean, and cool thanks to winds drafting off the slopes of Mount Hermon to the Northeast. On July 24, 1882, he closed the deal.

The property, close to the seemingly friendly Arab village of Ju'ana, was the same site where Jews had previously tried and failed to make a new community—ill-fated Gai Oni.

The Jewish community in Moinesti was thrilled by Shorb's news. Thirty families quickly packed everything they thought they needed to establish a new village. They brought tools for farming, materials for building, and two guns. On August 18, 1882, they set sail on the SS Thetis.

Their route first led them to the Port of Galati on the Danube River. From there they traveled east by boat to the Black Sea, and then south through the Bosporus to the Dardanelles before spilling out onto the Mediterranean Sea. They then headed to Haifa on Palestine's coast.

But then they encountered a problem—the Turks administering the port refused entry.

The problem was twofold. First, the Turkish government was no longer inclined to permit Jews to settle in Palestine. Secondly, Romanian Jews faced more obstacles than most because of Romania's alliance five years before with Russia to fight the Ottoman Empire. Rather than trying to sort out the matter in Haifa, the boat carrying the Moinesti Jews shuttled between Beirut, Jaffa, and Egypt. But they were denied entry at each. At last, they successfully disembarked near Haifa. One story contends they masqueraded as Christian Pilgrims.

As Shorb had done, the new arrivals journeyed several days to Safed by donkey. Along the way, one gave birth to a baby girl. They arrived in Safed in September 1882, where Jews living there sheltered them and where, together, they celebrated Shabbat.

Soon after the Moinesti Jews arrived, Shorb realized that money was going to be an issue.

Sometime between the ten days that divide Rosh Hashanah and Yom Kippur, Shorb scheduled a meeting for the Romanians. As a condition of making the trip, each settler family was supposed to have brought with them at least 2,000 francs (equal to tens of thousands of dollars in 2019). But few had done so. Most had brought far less. Only a few had brought more. To resolve the problem, Shorb proposed that they would farm as partners during the first year—sharing labor, resources, and crop yield. He also suggested pooling all their money, electing a treasurer, and forming a committee to run the village's business ventures and to determine who would work where and when. After a year, equal plots of land would be distributed among the settlers. It was a proposal eerily like the future makeup of the kibbutzim. Most agreed, some didn't and left. Twenty-five families remained.

To buttress their finances, the remaining families sold off some of their land to a few Jewish settlers from Russia who joined them.

Building homes was the next step. The settlers constructed fourteen structures close to the two that already existed near Ja'una. Most stayed in Safed during the construction phase, traveling several miles each day to the construction site. Arab laborers, who also lived in Safed, joined them (insistence on using only Jews to farm their land did not then extend to building their homes). Much of that path still exists. I have walked it. It is steep, open, and lonely, and certainly not something I would enjoy traversing down each day, with only arduous construction to look forward to as a break before returning up the formidable incline to Safed.

Unfortunately, soon the settlers encountered a new problem. Construction of their new homes at Gai Oni ground to a halt after Turkish authorities issued an edict banning Jews from settling in Palestine, which prompted local officials to intervene at Gai Oni.

Once again, Shorb stepped into the breach. He traveled through Lake Hula's adjacent swamps, filled with mosquitoes, past the village of Banias, and up the Golan Heights, all the way to Damascus where he appealed their cause. Upon arrival, he met with the designated Ottoman governor for the region, known as the "wali." Shorb offered a concession: the Jews would become Turkish citizens if they could establish their new village. The *wali* agreed to consult with his bosses in Istanbul. Shorb thought a response would come in a few days. After six weeks, he still hadn't received one. His patience gone, Shorb returned to Safed only to learn that permission to continue building their new homes had been granted weeks before. Not mentioned in the histories I reviewed, but almost certainly, money must have exchanged hands locally to broker the deal. Money the Jews were already short of.

After the arrival of necessary rain, the settlers began planting crops in December 1882. In commemoration, they also named their community Rosh Pina, Hebrew for "cornerstone." It was an apt name. The settlers were inspired by a phrase found in Psalm 117:22, "The stone the builders rejected has become the cornerstone." It was the same for those settlers. Rejected by their mother countries, they had set out to a new world to build a new life.

Rosh Pina, built on the foundation of Gai Oni, was the first of those communities to emerge in the north. Two other communities, near Lake Hula, soon followed.

Life was not easy for Rosh Pina's settlers. They lacked money and agricultural knowledge, lived with the constant threat of marauding Bedouin, and suffered violent interactions with local Arabs. Several incidents—some due to inevitable cultural clashes—illustrate how difficult and precarious life was for the setters in those early years.

One happened during the construction phase, when workers encountered ancient Arab burial remains. This, of course, caused some conflict with Arabs in the area. Although the settlers resolved the dispute by paying restitution and reburying the remains, the event further crippled the community's finances.

A more dangerous encounter arose out of a misunderstanding—this one occurring at the wedding of a Jewish couple at Rosh Pina. In attendance were several Arab laborers from Safed who had helped build Rosh Pina's new homes. Then, an Arab custom was to shoot rifle bullets into the air during a wedding celebration. At this wedding, an Arab laborer tried to grab a gun held by another guest, a Jew, to fire it into the air. The Jew did not know the Arab's intent. A fracas ensued, the gun was fired, one Arab was dead.

For the Arabs in Safed, it did not matter whether it was an accident or not. Livid, a crowd made its way toward Rosh Pina, bent on revenge, but the Mukhtar (leader) of Ja'una, interceded. He brought all the Jews into his house. Then he told the Arabs outside, if they wanted to murder the Jews, they would have to start with him.

The crowd calmed down.

Eventually, the impasse was resolved yet again with the Rosh Pina Jews paying a sum they could scarcely afford.

And, as it is in so many agricultural regions, water was also an issue for the settlers. Rosh Pina's land contained three springs. The Jews further developed their water sources by digging an open canal for irrigation and created a pond where they could water their livestock. But they weren't the only ones who wanted to use the pond.

In normal years, the Bedouin tribe of el-Zangariya, which lived east of Rosh Pina, could access all the water it needed from the Jordan river. In dry years, though, the tribe wandered toward Rosh Pina's lands to water its flocks. And because the Jews and Bedouin—unlike the Jews and Ja'una Arabs who generally got along—were not on the best of terms, the seeds for conflict were ever present. Inevitably, whenever the Bedouin trespassed into the settlement to water their animals, fights would break out. Some of the conflict was caused by their differing cultures. The Bedouin believed that water belonged to everyone. The Jews believed that because the water was on their land, land they had worked on to develop the water resources, that the water was theirs.

Nobody had died because of the water dispute, yet both sides knew it was a very real possibility. Since neither side would back down and each side had something the other needed—the Jews had water, the Bedouin had excellent land for grazing—a deal was struck beneficial to both. Jewish livestock would graze on Bedouin land, and Bedouin livestock would drink on Jewish land. If only all conflicts in the Middle East could be resolved so simply.

Still, in less than a year, Rosh Pina was already failing. The settlers, all hailing from different socio-economic backgrounds, struggled to adapt to their new lifestyle. Like the Gai Oni settlers before them, they had little knowledge of agriculture. Nor did Shorb's proposal for communal efforts attract many of them. All that, coupled with their dwindling financial resources—an issue that Romanians back home refused to address and that international Jewish organizations ignored despite Rosh Pina's appeals for help—signaled the imminent demise of their community.

But just as the settlers' optimism began to wane, salvation arrived—Baron Edmond James de Rothschild.

Baron Rothschild belonged to the French branch of the mega-wealthy Rothschild family whose money stemmed from their banking empire. Different from the typical philanthropist, Baron Rothschild was not so concerned with the individual people he helped. Instead, he wanted to create model solutions to help millions of Eastern European Jews settle in Palestine—in essence, making the dream of reestablishing a Jewish homeland in the historic land of Israel a reality. In 1883, Rothschild provided Rosh Pina residents with agricultural training and initiated changes in its management. He built an administrative building at Rosh Pina now known as the PICA house, staffing it with agronomists and other specialists. Because of Rothschild, the settlement survived.

While Rosh Pina grew over the years—it established a school in 1899 that was the first to teach all manner of subjects in Hebrew—it was slow to prosper. It wasn't until Rosh Pina's residents began to produce tobacco and silk products to complement its agricultural base that the community began to flourish. World War I halted that progress, though, and Rosh Pina did not grow into a more vibrant community until modern years. Now tourists flock to Rosh Pina, where they visit its restored buildings, the museum at the PICA house, and its active artist colony.

* * *

So why was Rosh Pina important? After all, it was not the first Jewish settlement in northern Israel. Outside of cities, that distinction belongs to Gai Oni. Yet Gai Oni's attempt to realize the dream of reestablishing a Jewish homeland by creating facts on the ground ultimately failed. Or did it?

Building upon the ruined grounds of Gai Oni, the Rosh Pina Jews overcame countless obstacles in their way, and hung on. By surviving they showed that life here was possible. In short, they were trailblazers.

Other Jewish settlements soon emerged in the northern Galilee. They hung on too. Mishmar-Hayarden—begun by Americans in

1884, destroyed by the Syrians in the 1948 Arab-Israeli war, and reborn over the last fifty years—became a going concern. So did Yesud Hama'aleh, where malaria claimed many. Yet, neither of those settlements, or any others, were the cornerstone, the place where several families, oppressed where they had lived for centuries, overcame hardship to plant the first Jewish roots in a region that had not seen Jews for 2,000 years.

In 2019, when I walked the two slick, stony main streets of the old Rosh Pina while enduring a soaking rain, I couldn't help but gaze down at modern Rosh Pina spreading over the hillside below me. I felt proud of those people who had created something out of nothing in a harsh land. The beautiful homes, the art galleries, the restaurants, the entire town—none would now exist without them. Nor, perhaps, would Israel have its present border with Lebanon—or perhaps even exist at all—but for their determination. Thirty families, a baron, and a large supply of perseverance set the stage for a story that would take decades to unfold.

But Rosh Pina is just part of the story. Another ingredient that needed to be thrown in the mix was the invention of the kibbutz. Rosh Pina was not a kibbutz. The distinction of being the mother of the Kibbutz Movement belongs to a settlement called Degania, to which my story of the north now turns.

Chapter Three

Degania and the Second Aliyah

On November 22, 1913, Moshe Barsky set off towards evening on a mule for a nearby Jewish village to obtain medicine for a fellow community member, Shmuel Dayan. Barsky's return home would require him to cross the Jordan River at a narrow point that remains desolate and hauntingly beautiful to this day. It was no trivial mission. With bands of marauders everywhere, traveling alone at sunset was dangerous.

Barsky was just another eighteen-year-old boy, energetic and beloved by the twenty to thirty idealistic Jews then living at Degania, when he left on his mission of mercy. He did not know then, and never would know, that he would become a symbol of Jewish determination and would be forever connected to another Israeli hero.

Eight months earlier, Barsky had traveled from the Ukraine to Palestine and then Degania, leaving his family behind. He was one of thousands who constituted the Second Aliyah, which took place between 1903 and 1918. For the most part, they were Jews fleeing more pogroms in Russia and Romania—instigated, in part, by false rumors that Jews had killed Christians to obtain blood for Passover rituals. These rumors had sparked the nightmarish pogrom in the city of Kishinev, where Russian mobs killed eighty-five Jews, raped many

Jewish women, and damaged 1,500 Jewish homes on Easter Sunday 1903.

In October 2018, I went to Degania again. My previous visit to the kibbutz had been confined to standing outside its fence where a rusted Syrian tank sits. I was aware of the role Degania had played in Israel's War of Independence in 1948, yet I knew little about its creation. There is now a sign at the entrance to Degania that says in both Hebrew and English, "Degania, the First Kibbutz." Perhaps the sign says what it does because the complex truth would exhaust the short attention spans of tourists. Technically, however, the sign is wrong.

Degania today features lush, grass lawns, well-kept gardens, tall trees, and numerous flowers. Driving into the kibbutz, you'll find a small parking lot on the right and a large factory to the left. Across the street from the parking lot is the kibbutz grocery store. To the northwest is a courtyard with a fine restaurant and stately looking buildings that suggest but don't shout importance. If you drive on the road leading south of the parking lot you will pass fences, the factory, and agricultural fields. After turning right at the road's end, you will pass impressive stands of banana and date trees. And beyond that there is a fence with a gate, a rather desultory parking area, some old looking structures, some dilapidated farming equipment, and a decidedly unimpressive languid stretch of water that looks more like a massive ditch than what it is—the Jordan River.

There, near the Jordan River, even in October it was hot. It was also barren and forlorn. And it is precisely where Degania's story begins.

Degania began as a test—for a dream and for an ideal. But before it was established, close by there was an Arab village called Umm Juni sitting on land owned by a Persian family living in Beirut. The village's fields were located alongside the western bank of the Jordan River, just south of the Sea of Galilee. By the end of the first decade of the nineteenth century, twenty Arab families, living in the village in mud huts, worked those lands for their absentee landlord.

In 1907, the Jewish National Fund purchased Umm Juni's land as well as adjacent terrain east of the Jordan river. During the fall of 1908, Dr. Arthur Ruppin—the head of the Palestine Office of the Zionist Organization and regarded by many as the father of Zionist settlement—sent pioneers to work Umm Juni's land. He didn't have a choice. As we know, if left untouched, under Turkish law the land would otherwise have reverted to the Ottomans. Ruppin had jumped at the chance to purchase the land because it was sparsely populated, which presented the opportunity for Jews to become the majority in the area.

In 1909, when those pioneers evidenced failure due to conflicts within the group, Ruppin replaced them with several men and one woman, selected for their talent and motivation. It was a yearlong test to see if Jews working independently could turn a profit farming the land. Unlike Rothschild's model of producing products to sell, Ruppin's goal was to develop self-sustaining Jewish settlements. "We want not dividends, but men," said Ruppin.

The test worked, but with their one-year commitment about to end, Ruppin needed to find a new group to live and work at the site.

On October 28, 1910, ten men and two women, handpicked by Ruppin, arrived at Umm Juni. This group had already lived together, at a different location, for a full year. There, living with each other in a commune, they had learned farming techniques and had pooled their wages. Motivated by their socialist principles, they wanted "to establish an independent settlement of Hebrew laborers, on national land, a collective settlement with neither exploiters or exploited . . . ." Ruppin agreed to pay each member fifty francs per month (which they pooled into a common fund) and supply whatever they needed, such as mules, horses, and plows. He would also advance them money to purchase seeds and other essentials. In return, the twelve pioneers would pay Ruppin fifty percent of their profits.

They called their new home Degania, Hebrew for "cornflower," to commemorate the five types of grain they planned to grow: wheat, barley, oats, corn, and sorghum. But there was no sign of those crops when they arrived. Unlike the lush view that greets visitors at the entrance of the community today, the land was empty and difficult to irrigate. For irrigation, the new settlers resorted to filling cans from the mere trickle that often was all that flowed in the Jordan, which they transported on mules to whatever location needed water.

At first, they lived in the temporary huts the previous group had used. But those huts were in terrible condition, and the settlers, with their lack of carpentry skills, had trouble repairing them. Rain destroyed much of the fodder for the animals before they could cover it. Even obtaining building supplies proved problematic. Armed Arabs had attacked two members of the group who were on the way to buy wood in Tiberias. They escaped unharmed but one of their mules was wounded. That said, the group's relationship with the few remaining Arabs at Umm Juni was good. Those Arabs taught the settlers their farming techniques in exchange for medicine. Despite the challenges, the twelve young settlers were ecstatic to be there.

Yosef Bussel was the intellectual leader of the group. Only nineteen and taller than most, he sported long curly hair and eyes that beamed self-confidence and determination. Bussel wanted to build "a system that will truly give the worker individual freedom, without his having to exploit the work of others."

Another member, Joseph Baratz, of stockier build than Bussel, said, "What we wanted was to work ourselves … and to do it not for wages but for the satisfaction of helping one another and of tending the soil."

Collectively, they were determined to build a new Jewish society. Now there was a chance. For the first time they were working for themselves rather than for others. They directed their strength to the soil. And soon, others joined them.

That first year was backbreaking. The oppressive summer heat pressed against them "like a hot plate." Vegetation would burn brown, and during the dry season the Jordan was a mere trickle. When the rains came, the parched land flooded. And when the water receded, it left behind swampy havens for disease-carrying mosquitoes and muck so thick it sucked boots off workers' feet. Most settlers contracted malaria and other diseases. On most days, one of five were too sick to work. Some days only half were well enough to labor in the fields. Speaking of the conditions, one pioneer said, "The body is crushed, the legs fail, the head hurts, the sun burns and weakens." Still they persevered.

After such a challenging first year, some of the pioneers suggested they move to a more favorable environment in the mountains across the Jordan River. But Tanhum Tanpilov, one of the original settlers and the hardest worker among them, reminded them that Jews have always been capable of creating change but not always capable of preserving their achievements. He insisted that they stay where they are and "make the desert bloom."

They stayed. They renewed their contract with Ruppin and did so every succeeding year until they assumed complete responsibility for the land. Shmuel Dayan wrote of that time, "[E]veryone relates how he felt during the day. You feel the partnership. You are not alone! The new family, the family of the *kvutza*, is very strong and powerful." But rather ominously, well before the kibbutz movement encountered significant issues, he added, "Not everyone was equally conscientious, skilled, and energetic. Some were careless and even lost their tools. There were crises and arguments."

While work predominated during their waking hours, common social activities contributed to their cohesiveness. Despite their Orthodox Jewish backgrounds, the *kvutza* did not place religious practice high on their priorities. Yet, Shabbat remained special. On Friday nights they would make their best meals and then sing and dance, melding their past cultural background with their hopes for the future. Many of the songs were folk songs that came from Russia and elsewhere in Eastern Europe. But new songs, which the pioneers sang in Hebrew, were added to the mix. Inevitably, these cheerful evenings would end in exhaustion—not from the drudgery of work but from dancing the Hora arm-in-arm.

Each evening, the *kvutza* would determine work responsibilities for the next day while sitting around the rough dining room table. In the early days, no votes were taken. Instead, the settlers would talk until they reached a consensus. Sometime these conversations went through the night.

However, as the size of the group increased, the settlers struggled to manage themselves. While all members still shared most things, such as animals, tools, equipment, and even clothing, newcomers began to demand control of the community's funds and, at first, were not fully committed to the commune concept. Even though new members gave everything they had to the community when they would join it, and were required, like the founding members, to share gifts from the outside with the community, accommodations were made in the form of separate accounts for each new member in which financial credit was given for work performed and debits were recorded for food and supplies consumed. Meanwhile, the founders remained true to their organizing principle and shared everything. Thus, for many years, the founders' commune community remained embedded within Degania's socialist society.

And then there was the problem of the women. Although all were focused on revolutionizing Jewish life through strict equality, that equality did not extend to the sexes. Changing the traditional role of women did not occur to them—at least right away. For example, Baratz later wrote that there was a reason for the size and gender of the original group. Each day, six men would leave before dawn to perform brutal plowing work in the fields, they would not return until after dark. Two men would stand guard during the day and all would take their turn at the night watch to protect the community against Arab marauders. Occasionally bullets would whistle by. Another man would devote himself to administrative duties and the tenth would be in reserve or off-duty. The two women were needed for housekeeping duties. Despite their exhaustion, this arrangement made the men happy. But not the women.

The original group had only two women because it was assumed that women could not physically and emotionally bear the burden of arduous labor—or protect themselves when left alone—in this dangerous and unforgiving land. But those concerns did not shield the two women from jealousy and displeasure. They had no stoves, kerosene, or electricity. Every day they performed the same tasks—whether during the summer heat or in the midst of winter's soaking rains, the women would cook over open wood fires while smoke blew into their eyes. Then there was sewing, cleaning, and washing. Their pioneering spirit ebbed in the face of unending drudgery and disparity of roles that robbed them of opportunity.

And so, the women rebelled.

They insisted Degania needed cows, chickens, and vegetables that they could take care of. After argument, the women convinced the men, and the community purchased livestock. But that alone did not end the problem. When one of the women, Miriam, returned to Degania from a short trip, the men barred her from taking care of the two newly purchased cows. One man told her that she was not allowed to go near the "large and dangerous beasts." Miriam would have none of that. She promptly went to some local Arab women for lessons in how to milk cows. Upon her return, she rose from bed well before the man assigned to the cows, went to the cowshed, and milked them. Her activism changed the dynamic at Degania. Going forward, the role of women changed. They milked the cows, plowed the fields, and even stood guard.

Children also posed an issue for the new community. Even though children bring great joy they also require resources for their care—financial and laborious attention—resources the *kvutza* had in short supply. Shmuel Dayan, who had joined the *kvutsa* soon after the original twelve had arrived at Degania, declared that no one in the group should marry for five years because "living as we do in this climate and in danger from the nomads, how can we have children?" But hormones are a powerful counterbalance to ideology. Baratz refused to listen. He married Miriam. Dayan didn't follow his own suggestion, either. He married an immigrant from Russia named Dvora, the third woman to join the *kvutza*.

* * *

Josef Baratz, one of the original settlers, was born in a Ukrainian village along the Dniester River in Russia. In his autobiography, he gives a suspiciously idyllic description of growing up in a community of whitewashed cottages among cherry and apple orchards. His father was an innkeeper. But as life became increasingly harder for Jews, his family moved to Kishinev in 1888, when Baratz was eight. Five years later came the Kishinev pogrom.

After witnessing the violence, Baratz was inspired to join a local Zionist youth movement. But simply talking about Zionism wore on him. He became determined to move to Palestine to work the land. Baratz wrote, "[to] construct our country we had to first reconstruct ourselves. We had been intellectuals [and] middlemen for too long. We had to work with our hands and above all we needed peasantry—that had to be the foundation of it all." His view was the same as many other young Zionists who had taken up the slogan "To build and rebuild" and who felt the only way to accomplish that would be by the "conquest of labor," which meant only Jews should work the land and defend it.

In 1905, after the failed Russian revolution, the Russian government banned Zionist movements, but Baratz's group continued to meet secretly. Two years later, when Baratz was sixteen, after his parents relented and gave him the money he needed, Baratz traveled to Palestine.

* * *

In 1912, with the help of Ruppin's financing, the *kvutza* had finished building new barns, stables, and storerooms from black basalt stone quarried in the area, along with a large hut for a kitchen, a new dining hall, and a two-story wooden building for living quarters. Still in existence today, everything was built around a courtyard some distance from the Jordan River.

That distance between their structures and the river would soon create an Israeli legend.

On the evening of November 22, 1913, after Moshe Barsky had set out to get medicine for Shmuel Dayan, Josef Baratz returned to Degania from Damascus, where he was buying more mules for the community. His several-day journey took him up and down the Golan. Baratz had expected a warm welcome, but instead found commotion. The men had rifles in their hands.

Just after sunset, Moshe Barsky's frightened mule had returned. Barsky had not.

Although song and dance helped the Degania settlers to cope with their isolation, joyous celebration could not abate the fear they lived with on a daily basis—the persistent threat of an Arab attack. Most of the Arabs living in the area were helpful and friendly. Some, however, were murderers and thieves. And the Jordan River ford was known for its common usage by Arab robbers frequenting the area.

With lit torches in hand, the settlers broke into small groups. They searched for hours. Winds blowing off the Sea of Galilee made it difficult for the groups to coordinate their efforts by calling to each other. Then a few settlers came to the ford.

Barsky's body lay on the riverbank, with a stick and a pair of shoes by his head. Those symbols had meaning. They meant there would be vengeance. Barsky had fought back, but he also had kept in mind how important his mule was to the community. After jumping off the animal, he had sent it back to Degania before facing his attackers.

It's likely his actions surprised the six Arabs who had accosted him. The Bedouin disdainfully called the Jews "Children of Death," because they were usually easy to rob and would not defend themselves. In older colonies, Jews often hired Arab Bedouin as security for their communities, to protect them from other Bedouin. In reality, it was more of a protection racket. If the Jews didn't hire Arab guards, those same "guards" would attack them. But the *kvutza* at Degania refused to play that protection game. They wanted to work the land themselves and protect themselves. So, Barsky fought back. That fight cost him his life. But he also took the life of one of his assailants while defending himself.

In his death, Barsky accomplished more than perhaps he would have by living. For decades, his death became a symbol for Jews: of their connection to Eretz Israel, of their determination to free themselves from anti-Semitism, and through their own labor and self-defense to create a base for the Zionist mission. What happened to him that night highlighted the lonely quest by a few Jews to settle the land, the dangers inherent with that quest, and their insistence on doing so by virtue of their own sweat and blood. Those traits continue to this day; embodied in Israel's insistence to rely on its own strength of arms, not promises of others, to defend itself against foes seeking to destroy it.

Chaim Weizmann, Israel's first president and at that time a globally respected leader of the Zionist movement, immortalized both Barksy and Barsky's father when he wrote:

> *We Jews have not as yet made many sacrifices: that is why we own only two percent of the Palestinian soil. What value there is in real sacrifice, the example of a Jew from Kiev will show you: his name is Barsky. One of his sons, a worker, was killed on Palestinian soil, at Degania. The bereaved father writes a letter of comfort to the workers of Palestine and sends his second son into this most dangerous life to take the place of the fallen one. This is the continuation, writes the bereaved father. And it is this Jew who is the greatest Zionist after Herzl.*

Over time, Barsky's courage and death also contributed much to Degania's fame and survival.

Barsky was the first community member to die, and his body was the first to be buried in Degania's new cemetery. Soon, another member joined him after succumbing to illness. Within a few years, two more settlers would die, this time by suicide. Both suicides occurred during a time of great difficulty when the Turkish army, during World War I, occupied Degania and forced its Jewish inhabitants out of their homes and into tents. One settler left a suicide note addressed to Baratz, leaving it next to his body that was found sprawled across Barsky's grave. It said in part, "You have faith, I have lost mine." More deaths followed. Yosef Bussel, the community's intellectual leader, drowned in the Sea of Galilee in 1919.

Despite the suicides, the climate, and Bussel's accidental drowning—Degania took root. Barsky's death unified the community and inspired them to persevere. When times were tough, they would gather at Barsky's grave to make confessions and reaffirm their dedication to Degania. Through sheer willpower and memory of personal sacrifice the community overcame its many mistakes and survived its many challenges. Then came joy. Miriam and Baratz welcomed their son, Gideon, to the world in Tiberias, where Miriam gave birth. The couple soon had a second child.

And this is where Degania's story takes a coincidental turn—which helped keep the community in the public eye.

* * *

Although he never explicitly said so, Shmuel Dayan never lost a sense of guilt, or appreciation, for Barksy's selfless travel alone into a lawless land to fetch him medicine. After Barsky died, Shmuel corresponded with Barsky's father in Russia. On the tenth anniversary of Barsky's death, Shmuel gave a eulogy. So it's no surprise to learn that in 1915 he and his wife named their son Moshe, after Moshe Barsky.

Moshe Dayan, the first child actually born on the grounds of Degania and the second child born to Degania's settlers after Gideon, became a revered leader of Israel's Defense Forces during the Sinai War of 1956 and defense minister during the 1967 War. Although his leadership failures during the first few days of the Yom Kippur War tarnished his reputation, Moshe Dayan is still widely revered. He also played a role in saving Degania in 1948, a story that we will come to later. Sixty-one years after his birth, Moshe Dayan wrote his autobiography. It starts, "My name Moshe was born in sorrow. It had been inscribed a year before on a solitary tombstone in an olive grove in Degania . . . ."

* * *

After World War I, Degania became independent. Ruppin had stopped providing assistance. And, even though Degania did not own its land—the community leased the land from the Jewish National Fund—Degania was on its own. And its population grew.

Word of Degania's new lifestyle spread. Famous personages visited and worked there for a time. One of the most unique and remarkable was Aaron David Gordon. Gordon was a frail man who sported a long, white beard. And, he was a mystic. Although he never became a Degania member, his frequent presence had a significant impact on the group.

Despite being an intellectual and a writer, Gordon passionately believed in the virtues of hard labor. Along with the other members of the *kvutza*, he thought that Jewish revival in Palestine required working hard to revive the soil. Gordon wrote, "An alienated people with no roots in the soil, deprived of the power of creativity, we must return to the soil, to independence, to nature, to a regenerated life of work." And, recognizing the possibility of a future confrontation between Arabs and Jews, Gordon warned that those who worked the land the most would inherit it.

Upon arriving at Degania, Gordon insisted on performing a full day's work, even though he spent his nights bent over a crate recording his thoughts. He also had a gentle soul. Believing there was a "covenant between man and nature," that included a love for animals, he would pick grass to feed the mules during his rest periods.

Gordon died in 1921 but he lives on at Degania where a museum is named after him.

But despite Degania's growing notoriety, its population growth brought problems. The first was children. Before Bussel died, he told the group that they must all share responsibility for the children of the community so that their way of life does not end. He said, "There must be no privacy. All privacy interferes with our communal life. All of us are obligated to participate in the expense of raising the children—not just the parent." To facilitate that, the community built a special house where a member of the group cared for the children during the day, but unlike what later became common at kibbutzim around the country, at night the children slept at home.

The second problem that population growth brought was governance. While decisions were originally made by consensus of the entire group, by 1919 that was becoming increasingly difficult as the number of voices grew. To alleviate the problem, the *kvutza* tried electing a committee of four to oversee daily routines. Some opposed that solution as a perversion of their goal to operate as a commune. Instead, they suggested that their group should be limited to ten families. But given the workload required to farm the land, the community needed more than that. In 1920, the group decided to split into two separate communities, the new one to be called Degania B. To this day Degania B sits adjacent to Degania A. Two years later a third group emerged, but since there was not enough land to support all three, the third group moved twenty-five miles away.

Even so, Degania A continued to feel the impact of the internal ideological divide. In 1921, Shmuel Dayan and others left to form a new moshav called Nahalal. The term moshav means a workers' cooperative village. Within it, the inhabitants would cooperate by sharing the work and many of the assets of production but the moshav would permit each family to keep its own profits and would not require the families to maintain a communal lifestyle.

Although the departures shook Degania, the community still prospered. In 1923, Degania rid itself of the newcomer individual accounts and reverted to becoming a pure commune. Over time, it developed numerous agricultural products and eventually built a factory. Meanwhile, others sought to emulate its communal life while trying to grow larger than Degania's consensus governance system would permit. They also wanted to experiment more broadly with the family model that Degania pioneered. Out of that, the kibbutz movement came into being. And eventually, Degania joined their ranks. Out of the *kvutsa* came the kibbutz.

But no matter how large Barsky's legend grew, and as important as Degania was to the future of Israel, across the valley another legend was growing, and men rode, alone, steeled by their courage to secure the Zionist ideal. There, another important foundational element of today's Israel emerged.

Chapter Four

Hashomer, Tel Hai, Kfar Giladi, and the Third Aliyah

Kfar Giladi sits nestled into the Naftali mountains in the far north of Israel, little more than a mile from the Lebanese border. There, tucked away from much bustle, the kibbutz offers a breathtaking view of the Hula Valley below. Scattered within and just outside its fence are hints of its gloried past. But they are hidden from those who drive by uninformed. My first four visits didn't reveal much. On my fifth, I struck gold. I met Gideon Giladi.

But first a bit of history.

Hashomer

At the start of the twentieth century, the farming community of Sejera (now called Ilaniya) was established on land purchased by Baron de Rothschild. Located in the lower Galilee, close to the Sea of Galilee and Degania, Sejera played an integral role in the development of Israel's north. Here young, idealistic Jewish pioneers learned farming techniques and became accustomed to the physical work required to establish new agricultural communities. Sejera also became known for Arab violence—specifically, Arabs harassing Jewish settlers.

In 1909, during one particularly violent cycle, four Arabs robbed a Jewish traveler on his way to Sejera. The victim wounded one of his assailants who died days later. The following week, local Arabs wounded two Sejera residents and killed the watchman on duty before stealing some cattle and destroying crops at the settlement. When some of Sejera's settlers chased after them, they stumbled into an ambush, and one was shot.

One of the settlers chasing the Arabs was twenty-three-year-old David Ben Gurion, who forty years later became Israel's first prime minister. That wasn't Ben Gurion's only brush with death. While walking back to Sejera from a nearby village, an Arab attacked him with a knife. Ben Gurion suffered light wounds and the loss of his pack. Those incidents remained with him for a long time after it was over. He later wrote that they highlighted "the severity and dangers of the Arab problem" and that "our Arab neighbors hate us."

Sejera was not the only location in Palestine experiencing security issues, and it was not only travelers who were being accosted. Isolated farming communities felt the need to secure their livestock and possessions from theft. Fear and anxiety were constant companions for those determined to pursue their idealistic dreams.

At first, some Jewish communities hired Arabs in the service of local Sheiks. Ineffective at times, this strategy also violated the self-help philosophy held by the Second Aliyah pioneers. Simply put, they hated employing people to defend them who otherwise would be among the first to attack them. But those that stopped hiring Arab security faced retribution. Those same Arab guards would revert to robbery and mayhem to demonstrate the folly of villages trying to defend themselves. And so, the violence and pilferage increased.

Into the brewing crisis rode the Hashomer. Established in 1909, it had twelve founders; its membership never exceeded forty at any one time; and the organization accepted fewer than 100 members in its twelve-year existence. Eleven members died in service of its cause.

Yet, despite its small size and brief tenure—it disbanded in 1920 and was incorporated into the Haganah (a nationwide underground paramilitary force organized by the Jewish leadership in Palestine)—the Hashomer played a critical role in defending Jewish outposts in the North, as well as other parts of Palestine, and was an inspiration to pioneering Zionists.

Hashomer's philosophy influenced the Haganah, and then continued after the establishment of the State of Israel in 1948 when its courageous and honorable ethic played a large role in the IDF's development. Winston Churchill's famous line, "Never in the field of human conflict was so much owed by so many to so few" could be applied to the Hashomer as well.

Hashomer was born in the attic of a residence in Jerusalem. Its founders sat on upended crates placed on a rug spread out for the occasion. All the participants were young, and all were members of the Po'alei Zion party, which believed strongly in the necessity of the "conquest of labor" in order to establish a Jewish State. At heart, they embraced socialistic principles. To further their goals, they had first established a secret order in 1907 called *Bar Giora*, named for a leader of the Jewish revolt against Rome, 2,000 years before. The new organization's motto was "In fire and blood did Judea fall; in blood and fire Judea shall rise." There, in that room, dim due to a setting sun, "The seed was planted, the seed from which shortly after a large tree grew—Hashomer."

Bar Giora took on the responsibility for protecting some existing Jewish communities, establishing new ones, and defend land purchased by the Jewish National Fund. Its members had some experience in defensive measures, many after having fought to survive the pogroms in Russia and Eastern Europe. But to enhance their agricultural skills, they established a base of operations at Sejera.

In 1909, as conditions in the Galilee worsened for Jews, an increasing number of communities asked the organization for help.

Helping them required growing *Bar Giora's* membership. As part of the process, *Bar Giora* decided to re-brand itself as *Hashomer*, meaning "The Watchmen."

Hashomer members had quite the dashing image. Dressed in Arab clothes with Keffiyas affixed to their heads by woolen bands and wearing long riding boots, they usually sported mustaches and bandoleers filled with ammunition. On top of their horses, brandishing rifles, pistols, and sometimes swords—they were imposing figures. All possessed a flair for horsemanship, dollops of courage, and exceptional fighting skills. They needed those attributes because they often traveled alone and thought little of challenging groups of Arab intruders.

Joining *Hashomer* was no trivial thing. After all, it was a secret organization, Ottoman authorities didn't take kindly to armed civilians banding together. Prospective members had to endure many nights of guard duty to prove their worth. They also had to pass tests involving navigation at night, overcoming fear of suspicious sounds in the dark, and had to react appropriately when gunfire rang out. *Hashomer* members would bring worthy prospects to an isolated cave or hiding place. These prospects were sworn in by torchlight. The ceremony included an oath of allegiance to *Hashomer*, made while their hand rested on a Bible and a gun. New members swore to abide by many rules, including:

1. "First of all—be human"
2. "Be courageous"
3. "Do not be intimidated by danger."
4. "When in trouble, be quick witted."

Israel Shochat, Hashomer's leader, infused the organization with his belief that Jews must rapidly transition from exiles to living in a nation of their own. The key for that to happen, Shochat believed, was rooted in Jews cultivating their own land. From their efforts and their acceptance of self-responsibility, Shochat thought that a moral society would emerge that would shape the character of the forthcoming Jewish nation.

Shochat extolled heroism and defense of Jewish property and expected each Hashomer member to further the organization's goals while honoring its collective spirit. To new members, he warned that anyone who betrayed Hashomer would receive a death sentence. Shochat was a serious man with a serious mission.

Soon Hashomer members were wandering from place to place, passing through lonely landscapes, to protect Jewish communities. While they had many clashes with hostile Arabs, they also made conscious efforts to befriend Arab villagers in their areas of responsibility, to understand their issues and cultural differences, and to learn Arabic. In 1910, the Palestine Office in Jaffa hired Hashomer to guard, and begin cultivating, newly purchased land until permanent settlers could take over. Within a few years, Hashomer had won contracts to guard several Jewish communities in the Galilee.

In 1916, Hashomer founded Kibbutz Giladi on land owned by the Jewish Colonization Association. They named it after Israel Giladi, one of the founders of the organization. The man I met in 2019, Gideon Giladi, was Israel Giladi's grandson.

* * *

To meet Gideon, I drove through the kibbutz gates and then turned right into a parking area for a nondescript building housing the offices of the kibbutz's main industry—Kfar Giladi Quarries. Gideon had twice served as general manager of Kfar Giladi Quarries and once, general secretary of the kibbutz. His office was filled with books and notebooks teeming with information pertaining to past, present, and future projects. Now in his mid-70s, Gideon is a man of average height with gray hair surrounding a receding hairline. Dressed in blue jeans, a blue shirt, and white under-shirt, he hardly resembled the dynamo, still filled with energy and enthusiasm, that he very much is.

We exchanged pleasantries, and then Gideon dove in. Hashomer, he said, was the "father and mother of Israeli defense forces to come." And then Gideon told me about his grandfather.

Israel Giladi grew up near Kishinev. Like so many who came to Palestine as part of the Second Aliyah, he had endured the pogrom in Kishinev. Giladi had been living with other students in the Yeshiva while the nightmare unfolded.

The 1903 Kishinev pogrom, Gideon told me, seared the consciousness of Jews who had been living there, impacted the development of Zionism, and still resonates within the psyche of Jews today. C.N. Bialik wrote a 400-plus-line poem entitled "The City of Slaughter" that details in a macabre and meticulous manner the horror the Jewish community in Kishinev suffered during the pogrom, and the unfathomable passivity of its men. Even now, Israeli students are taught the poem and tested on its contents. Later, I found an English translation—and after reading it I understood. The following lines are a sampling:

> *Of murdered men who from the beams were hung,*
> *And of a babe beside its mother flung,*
> *Its mother speared, the poor chick finding rest*
> *Upon its mother's cold and milk-less breast*

And:

> *This is the place the wild ones of the wood, the beasts of the field,*
> *With bloody axes in their paws compelled thy daughters yield:*
> *Beasted and Swiped!*

Hashomer, Tel Hai, Kfar Giladi, and the Third Aliyah

Note also do not fail to note,
In that dark corner, and behind the cask
Crouched husbands, bridegrooms, brothers, peering from the cracks

Bialik's poem, written in 1904 and first published in English in 1906, with its description of rape, bloodshed, and Jewish men cowering in fear rather than defending their loved ones, was a wakeup call. It shone a light on the need for Jews to fight for themselves and remake their society. It still does.

Hashomer sprung from that need. It would prevent such barbaric deeds from happening again. It would fight, not sit idly by while Jews suffered at the hand of others.

Israel Giladi's group was one of the very few that had organized for defense prior to the Kishinev pogrom. Their preparation included obtaining a few rifles, which they put to good use in killing several rioters bent on mayhem. However, the local police did not appreciate those acts of Jewish self-defense. When they began investigating in earnest, Giladi's group had to leave.

Israel Giladi was seventeen when he arrived in Vienna as a fugitive. There, with the help of a Jewish organization, his group found lodging in a hostel and worked as dishwashers in restaurants. At night, they gathered with others to discuss the future of the Jewish people.

One night, after learning that a local Jewish agency was purchasing tickets for Jews to travel to the United States, a group of twenty-five young Jews, which included Giladi, met at the grave of Theodore Herzl. Together, they made an oath that they would instead immigrate to Palestine.

In 1905, Israel Giladi arrived in Palestine.

Giladi first worked in agricultural fields near a town called Zichron Yaakov, where many new arrivals congregated. Then he learned that the manager of a nearby orphanage was looking for "strong and serious people [for] something he had in mind." Giladi answered the call. There, he met the man responsible for the message, Israel Shochat. Shochat told Giladi that he planned "to create the basis of the Israeli state to come."

At that point in the story, Gideon asked me in a steady voice betrayed by the emotion evident in his eyes "Who were the orphans?" After pausing, Gideon said that every time he talks about this he tears up. "They were the orphans from the pogrom Kishinev," he said. "Look how the circles closed—the orphans and the defenders [of Kishinev] meet at the orphanage [with Shochat] from the Galilee."

Gideon was quiet for a moment, and then said, "Never again. Never will the Jews stand again in front of such an attack from the pogroms."

In Gideon's voice, his determined expression and especially his eyes, I heard and saw the trauma of the pogroms; of the endless persecution Jews have endured and of the Holocaust. That moment made me acutely aware of how those traumas mix with modern events for the Israeli people, especially for those living along Israel's northern borders. For them, the threat of violence is a daily reality, it can come from anywhere and anytime, but there will be no more Kishinevs. Israel will stand, fight, and never cower.

Gideon went on to tell me that when his grandfather and the others founded Bar Giora they made a flag out of a Talit, writing on it, "In blood and fire Judah fell, and in blood and fire Judah will rise." Gideon then repeated with pride what I had already known, that their first founding principle was "Be a human being." But then Gideon added a twist when he highlighted there was nothing in that first principle limiting Hashomer to fighting or stopping criminals. Instead, it was about the rise and defense of a Jewish State. This concept he said, to be a human being, became part of the "DNA for all Israeli defense forces in the future."

After Bar Giora ended its secrecy and morphed into Hashomer in 1909, thereby exposing its existence, but not its clandestine activities, to the occupying Ottoman authorities, Israel Giladi's role became more public. In part because he could read Arabic, a large part of Giladi's Hashomer duties transformed into mediating disputes between Arabs and Jews. This role garnered him respect and success. Much of his success was due to his studying the various cultures in the area. To emphasize the point, Gideon clarified that Hashomer did not primarily rely on force of arms. Instead, Hashomer made it a priority to understand the interrelationships of all who lived in the region. If a Hashomer member shot first, he would be kicked out of the organization. Having strength, Gideon said, doesn't necessarily mean you should use it, for strength is "not the best solution for all problems."

Gideon then gave me an example of how his grandfather resolved a dispute between Jewish farmers in Metula and the Muslim communities surrounding them. Three cows had been stolen. Metula's residents suspected that a particular Muslim village was harboring the thieves. Rather than charging into the village and causing a confrontation, Giladi's grandfather sought to create a better future by not poisoning the present. Instead of demanding that the cows be returned and that the villagers identify the thieves, he obtained a written promise that nobody from the village would attack Metula again. That, said Gideon, was the power of Hashomer: "Be strong, but also to think, be practical, and be a human being."

Gideon explained that Hashomer had three functions: Jewish defense and security; Jewish labor for Jewish pursuits; and creation of new Jewish settlements.

Defense and security did not always require fighting. It just required a willingness to fight and a show of strength. Hashomer members would go into Arab villages astride their horses, armed to the teeth. Speaking Arabic and wearing Arabic clothing, except for a

Russian shirt, they commanded respect. While Gideon told me about them, I thought back to when I had interviewed a Maryland State Police Officer, perhaps twenty years ago, during my former life as an attorney. He told me that in Western Maryland, when he made a traffic stop at 3:00 a.m. on an isolated road there, he would be the only police officer within tens of miles. Therefore, perhaps in a manner not considered politically correct in these times, for his own safety, when he walked up to the driver, he made very sure the driver knew who was boss. The same was true for the isolated Hashomer Jew, who rode alone into Arab villages armed more with bravado than the rifle slung over his back.

Its second function—to increase the prevalence of Jewish laborers—impacted Hashomer's ability to prosper. Because it emphasized the need for Jewish labor to redeem the land, Hashomer would only contract to provide security for communities that proved that at least half of their workers were Jewish.

Hashomer's third goal went hand-in-hand with its first two. New settlements would only flourish if they were secure. In part, the purpose of new communities was to provide opportunities for Jews to connect to Eretz Israel and remake their society. Kfar Giladi fulfilled that purpose. It was built on land purchased by Jewish philanthropy; it provided a base for Hashomer; and it held an important part of the frontier near the Lebanese border that linked Metula, farther north, and Tel Hai, just below and to the southeast, to the lower Galilee and the rest of Palestine.

But by 1920 the Jewish community's need for a larger, stronger defense force was apparent. A village had been overrun in the north and Arab strength and organization were increasing. In keeping with that need, Hashomer formally disbanded in May 1920 and its membership was folded into the Haganah. The Haganah then assumed the task of defending Jewish towns from increasingly strong and virulent Arab attacks. When Israel became a state in 1948, the

Haganah provided the structure and the majority of the manpower for the IDF.

However, as David Ben Gurion said, "There are many fathers to the IDF, but only one grandfather, which is Hashomer."

Tel Hai

Hundreds of Bedouin surrounded Tel Hai on March 1, 1920. Thirty-five determined Jews defended the outpost, led by Joseph Trumpledor. They anticipated the possibility of having to confront an Arab force. Still, its arrival that day was a surprise.

The Tel Hai stockade today is tucked into a revered corner of the Tel Hai University campus. I found it difficult, when I visited the grounds on a hot, sunny day in the fall of 2017, to envision what had happened there in 1920. The area is immaculately kept, and its rooms are sterile with rather bland markers and a boring visual presentation that tell much of the Tel Hai story. They don't do justice to what happened that March day. Or at least they don't if you arrive as I had, with only a vague understanding of the events that unfolded. It was only later that I realized Tel Hai's hallowed place in Israel's history.

* * *

The Tel Hai story traces back to 1896, when a few dozen families moved to Metula, several miles north of Kfar Giladi, on a mountain plateau only reachable by a road that snaked up a steep hill. Baron Rothschild had purchased the land from its Lebanese owner living in Beirut. Metula then was the latest manifestation of Rothschild's mission "to see whether it is possible to establish Jews on Palestinian soil." Despite his purchasing agent's belief that Metula was the "Shangri La of Mount Hermon" and that it had a sufficiently temperate climate to grow apples, pears, and other crops, that wasn't the case. Temperate it was not. Winters could be bitterly cold. I experienced that during my visit on a rainy day in early March 2019. Also, one third of the land was so rocky it could not be terraced for agriculture; and the remaining soil was limited, given the agricultural methods of those times, to growing cereal crops and some tobacco.

But there was another problem: the Druze who once lived there.

For years, Druze (a non-Muslim sect that broke away from Shia Islam) tenant farmers worked the land owned by their landlords in Beirut. In 1895, many Druze men living in the area left to fight in the ultimately unsuccessful Druze rebellion of 1895. While gone, the land no longer produced, and therefore the landlord no longer received their rents. This prompted the owner to sell the land to Baron Rothschild. That's when Jewish families moved to Metula, encouraged by the opportunity they thought was there. Instead, they encountered Druze families, whose men were now returning after the fighting ended, who insisted they still had the right to farm—and live on—the land now owned by the Jews. Naturally, this did not sit well with the new Jewish residents who refused to relinquish their legally purchased rights. Conflict ensued. The offended Druze frequently shot at the Jewish settlers, killed one, and repeatedly stole farm animals and destroyed crops.

The Jews of Metula complained to Joshua Ossovetski, Rothschild's land purchasing agent. Ossovetski complained to the Ottoman authorities that were only too happy to arrest and imprison the recently rebellious Druze. Ossovetski seized the opportunity that arose from what he had set in motion. He offered the displaced Druze a financial settlement to end the dispute. They accepted and used the money to buy land near the source of the River Dan in the Hula Valley. However, they had trouble adjusting to living in the valley, where malaria took a toll on them. Some returned to reassert their claim on the Metula land. After years of clashes, Ossovetski negotiated a new deal in 1904 in which the Druze received another 60,000 francs (the equivalent of about $300,000 in 2019). The Druze used the settlement to purchase land on the slopes of Mount Hermon, and that ended the dispute.

Three years later, six agricultural workers from Metula traveled four miles south, back down the steep, windy road to intermittently live and work newly purchased agricultural land not far, and slightly downhill, from Kfar Giladi. Eleven years later, Hashomer established a permanent settlement there, named Tel Hai, after the former name for the region, Talha.

Thus, by late 1919, three Jewish villages had gained a tenuous hold along the northernmost part of what became Israel three decades later. They constituted the only Jewish communities in the far north. Tel Hai and Kfar Giladi were very close. Metula, farther north and connected to the other villages by a primitive, uphill path, takes only a few minutes to reach today by car, but then must have required several hard hours of travel. Developed with the hopes of establishing individual self-sufficiency, the three communities were also built with the idea of providing mutual security support and establishing part of the boundary for a future Israel.

But this was the north, so it was only natural there would be a problem.

Because to victors often go the spoils, after World War I, the British gained control of Palestine and part of Lebanon. However, France was unhappy with that state of affairs. In deference to the French, British forces withdrew to a point south of all three Jewish settlements. The French, greatly weakened by the war, did not immediately fill the void. This created a virtual no man's land, which roving bands of armed Bedouin, equipped with ammunition left by the defeated Ottoman empire, quickly filled.

The Bedouin, loosely linked with Arab nationalists, virulently opposed France's presence in the region because they wanted to assert their own control. Their hopes for control included ejecting Jewish settlers from the region and aggressively pursuing their hunger for plunder. The Bedouin, some coming from as far as the Golan Heights, harassed French forces that occasionally made an appearance to assert France's claim. They also attacked local Christian Arab villages that had expressed allegiance to France. And, of course, despite occasional assertions from rebel Arabs that they meant no harm to the Jews, Jews were often fair game as well. It did not help matters when Jewish settlers opted for neutrality in the Bedouin's dispute with the French. Adding further to the already volatile mix, relations with the Bedouin worsened after they observed French forces occasionally camping at Kfar Giladi and Tel Hai.

The increasing danger of the situation weighed heavily on the isolated Jewish community in Metula. Because they knew they could not alone repel a concerted attack—and because the surrounding landscape would prevent assistance from reaching them quickly—the Jews abandoned Metula.

But the young Jewish inhabitants of Kfar Giladi and Tel Hai stayed put. They wanted to preserve the panhandle region of northern Palestine as a home for the Jews. As one Zionist leader put it, "Retreat would be decisive proof of our weakness.... The only proof of our [linkage] to the land lies in a stiff-necked and desperate stand with no looking back." Ben Gurion echoed that view, "If we flee from robbers, then we will have to leave not just Upper Galilee but the whole Land of Israel."

On December 12, 1919, Bedouin murdered a Jew outside of the Tel Hai stockade. One who saw the danger, Israel Shochat, head of Hashomer, acted. That same December, he asked Joseph Trumpledor to go to Tel Hai and Kfar Giladi to investigate the extent of the danger. And so, the saga of Joseph Trumpledor began.

Trumpledor grew up in Russia. The Russian government allowed his father, called a "useful Jew" because of his accomplishments during the Caucasian War, to live outside the Pale of Settlement. Though proud of his Jewish heritage, Trumpledor volunteered for the Russian army in 1902, later losing his left arm to shrapnel during the Russo-Japanese War. After convalescing for 100 days in a hospital, he returned to the fight. When some discouraged him from heading back to the front lines because of his injury, Trumpledor responded, "I still have another arm to give to the motherland." He was subsequently captured by the Japanese. While in captivity, Trumpledor printed a newspaper that covered Jewish affairs and initiated educational classes. After his release and return to Russia, Trumpledor received four decorations for bravery, making him the most decorated Russian-Jewish soldier. In 1906, he became the first Jew to receive an officer's commission in the Russian army.

In 1911, Trumpledor organized and led a group of young Zionists in immigrating to Palestine. During his first years in Palestine he labored at a farm along the shore of the Sea of Galilee, and then, worked at Degania for a brief period.

When World I started, because he was a Russian citizen, Trumpledor needed to leave Ottoman controlled Palestine because the Turks were on the opposite side of Russia in the war. Soon after he arrived in Egypt, Trumpledor, and others, pushed the British to create a Jewish Legion to fight with the British army. These efforts led to the British forming the Zion Mule Corps, the first completely Jewish military unit in nearly 2,000 years. After the war, during which he suffered a shoulder wound at Gallipoli, Trumpledor returned to Russia for a spell. There, he taught Jews to defend themselves and established a youth organization that prepared members to make aliyah to Palestine. Shortly thereafter, Trumpledor returned to Palestine where he had already made quite a name for himself.

When Trumpledor arrived at Tel Hai, he immediately assumed command. His January 4, 1920, diary entry says:

> *The question was raised, if a battalion of French troops equipped with [cannons] and machine guns was unable to withstand an Arab assault, how could we, a small handful of people armed only with rifles, do so? . . . at a hastily arranged meeting it was decided that we would remain in place, come what may . . . and that when the decisive moment comes, we shall hold firm and shall raise the cost of our lives to the utmost.*

Aaron Sher, a settler at Tel Hai, was not as confident as Trumpledor. He wrote a plea for help in early 1920. Although Sher's plea was not so memorable, his reasoning was, "A place once settled is not to be abandoned." That phrase became a slogan for the Zionist movement. It still resonates today.

The Provisional Council for Jews in Palestine was divided as to whether it should send assistance. Some thought resistance futile and that Jews at Kar Giladi and Tel Hai should withdraw. Others feared that a relief column could not get through. Some favored providing help but did not act with urgency. While they dithered, on February 6, 1920, Aaron Sher was shot and killed by Arab thieves while working in Tel Hai's fields.

Then, on March 1, Trumpledor's fateful moment came to pass.

* * *

Five armed Arabs stepped forward from the hundreds of Arabs surrounding the Tel Hai stockade. One, a local resident whom the defenders knew, addressed them. He asked for permission to enter the walls of the outpost to make sure no French soldiers were sheltering there. Since none were present, and it was not the first time such a request had been made and honored, the request did not alarm the Jews. They agreed.

A rectangular, fortified stockade surrounded Tel Hai. One side featured living quarters with outward-facing windows reinforced by sandbags. The entire structure was one story tall—save an attic room in the center that could be accessed from the interior courtyard by an external stairway. Entry into the main building could only be accomplished from the same interior yard. The defenders allowed the Arabs to enter the stockade through a gate opposite the entrance to the living quarters.

Trumpledor accompanied the five Arabs. They asked to look in the attic room. Meanwhile, a sixth Arab had slipped inside, unseen, amid the commotion. He set up a machine gun somewhere inside the living quarters. Within the attic were two women accompanied by three men.

As Trumpledor moved to join the Arabs climbing the steps to the attic, one of Tel Hai's defenders, who spoke Arabic, told Trumpledor that this time something was awry. He had overheard the Arabs saying they planned to confiscate all their guns. Although the defender did not yet know of the Arab machine gunner in hiding, his instincts were on the mark. Why else would the Arab have sneaked in during what was supposed to be a routine inspection?

Trumpledor responded decisively. He ran back down the steps, into the open yard, fired his pistol as a signal, and ordered his men to open fire. The Jews immediately discovered the Arab with the machine gun and killed him. But Trumpledor was shot as well, in the hand and stomach. Meanwhile, the five Arabs heading up the stairs threw hand grenades into the attic room, killing both women and two of the three men.

The settlers, outnumbered more than ten to one, were not prepared to fight the Arabs both inside and outside of Tel Hai. But the Arab leaders were trapped inside, and the Arabs outside showed little initiative without them. The settlers firing at them from the inside forced the Arabs outside to move further back.

Two settlers placed Trumpledor, his entrails hanging out of a gushing hole in his body, on the floor of the living quarters. There, he advised the only person present with any medical knowledge how to return his intestines to his abdomen, verbally guiding him as he performed the task. Because all the first aid equipment had been destroyed in the attic, no bandages were available to dress Trumpledor's wound. A towel was used instead. In that time of extreme duress, Trumpledor ordered, "These are my last moments, tell everyone that they must stand firm till the very end for the sake of the people of Israel's honor."

The two sides fought for three hours without respite, during which the Arabs pinned down on the attic landing had managed to escape out the gate. Then came a brief ceasefire that allowed the Arabs to remove their fourteen dead and the many more who had been wounded. When the fighting flared up again, Tel Hai's defenders continued to hold off the Arabs, thanks in part to the machine gun they had confiscated.

That night, three Jews covertly exited the compound to fetch medical help for Trumpledor and the others who were injured. They returned with a doctor who asked Trumpledor how he was feeling. Trumpledor famously responded, "It is no matter, it is good to die for our country."

The doctor ordered that the injured be taken to Kfar Giladi. They had no stretchers to carry the wounded, only blankets. Trumpledor died en route.

With the Arabs massing for another attack, ammunition dwindling, and food supplies low, the settlers abandoned both Tel Hai and Kfar Giladi. Seven months later Jews returned to both locations, never to leave again.

Because of that battle, and the continued violence throughout the region, attendees of an international conference agreed to the British re-assuming control of the Upper Galilee. Also, in part because of the battle of Tel Hai, Jews in Palestine realized they needed a strong, organized defense force. That is why Hashomer formally disbanded in May 1920, to make way for the Haganah.

Trumpledor's valor and deathbed statement—"It is good to die for our country"—is legend in Israel (some question whether he really said that). Both left and right-leaning movements in Israel consider him a hero. The same is true of Hashomer, the determined settlers of Kfar Giladi and Tel Hai, and the courageous defense of Tel Hai. All are heroic reminders deeply embedded in Israeli culture and passed down from generation to generation. Their simple tenets were: land must be defended with courage and determination, borders must be held against all odds without wavering, and that all have a duty to secure Israel's future.

If you want to understand the character of the people who to this day stubbornly maintain their hold along Israel's northern border regions, visit Tel Hai. Step toward the stockade, walk into the pristine courtyard, mount the steps to the attic, and all the way don't say a word. See the inside of the living quarters where Trumpledor bled out on a dirty floor. Close your eyes and imagine the chaos. Then think what it must have been like within the compound: surrounded by angry Arabs; a grenade exploding leaving carnage in its wake while defenders manned the walls cutoff from help, far from civilization; and all the while, a Jewish hero, knowing he was going to die, thinking of his nation before himself.

Trumpledor now lies buried in front of a large monument, in a cemetery just outside the gates of Kfar Giladi. Near his remains are the silent graves of many valiant members of Hashomer. At the entrance to the cemetery there is a memorial to another tragedy in 2006 that also will never be forgotten, but we have not yet reached that part of the tale. Instead, the next step of the story of the north centers on Kibbutz Hanita, where heroes again staked another claim that would one day help establish Israel's future northern boundaries.

Chapter Five

Kibbutz Hanita

There is only one way to reach Hanita—by a steep road that winds up the face of the mountain separating Israel from Lebanon. That road begins at well-developed communities at the base of the mountain and takes you up through Hanita forest until finally you reach the kibbutz, set behind an imposing yellow metal fence. It is a journey from the present to the scene of a hallowed past.

After passing through the entrance gate, resist the temptation to make an immediate left and instead drive straight, where you'll encounter a circle and a little sign with a tower and stockade emblem on it. It's the first inkling a visitor gets that there is something special here. To the right and below are the kibbutz's major industries. To the left and above is the kibbutz. Everywhere is the sense of quiet and solitude. Nowhere is a sense of what was accomplished here.

I first visited Hanita in the fall of 2017. I came as part of my search for a community with a storied past, uncluttered by Palestinian issues, that could serve as a sister city to the Jewish community in Jackson Hole, Wyoming. Soon I found myself at a long table outside with a friend, my brother-in-law, Lieutenant Colonel Sarit Zehavi, and the kibbutz's financial director, Orly Gavishi-Sotto. Zehavi and Orly, a young mother of three, briefed me about the kibbutz while we ate omelets outdoors, cooled by a light breeze and shade from a tree.

Stretching before us, a couple thousand feet down and several miles away, was a remarkable view of the Mediterranean, the beach town of Nahariya, and a hint of the outskirts of Haifa far in the distance. A short while later we visited the kibbutz museum. There, we watched an old film and studied a few exhibits that seek to bring Hanita's history to light.

My interest was piqued, especially after learning of the challenges Hanita faces today. Before leaving, I had decided that Hanita was the community I had been searching for. But more so, I realized that I had much to learn if I wished to understand why people choose to live in such a dangerous place. And I could only do that by digging into Hanita's past.

By 1938, the Fifth Aliya was in its seventh year. The Fourth Aliya, which began in 1924, had petered out around 1928. The Fourth Aliyah saw another 80,000 Jews immigrate to Palestine—mainly from Eastern Europe, Russia, and a few from Yemen and Iraq. Most settled in the cities, especially Tel Aviv.

Then, in the early 1930s, a new and even more virulent force emerged to drive Jewish immigration—Nazi fascism's brand of anti-Semitism. Approximately 160,000 more Jews arrived in Palestine within the first five years of the Fifth Aliya. That pace quickened over the next three years.

As more and more Jews came to Palestine, Arabs began attacking Jews more frequently. Although these attacks had been commonplace since the First Aliyah, their frequency and lethality reached new heights in 1929 throughout Palestine and especially in Hebron. Half-hearted efforts by British occupying forces did little to stop the violence. In 1936, there was yet another round of Arabs targeting Jews. Isolated Jewish farmers were killed, and Arabs bent on interrupting Jewish commerce randomly shot at Jewish buses and trucks on main transportation routes.

The violence inspired the British to conduct multiple studies. Each was different and each incorporated information gleaned from so-called fact-finding missions. Yet they all had a common theme. The basic idea was twofold. First, partition Palestine in some manner into separate enclaves—one controlled by the Jews, another by the Arabs, and a third by an international regime of some form. And second, limit Jewish immigration to Palestine in order to appease the Arabs.

However, the British couldn't find a solution to the problem that their policy enunciated in the Balfour Declaration in 1917, based on belief in the righteousness of the Zionist cause and British self-interest, had helped create. That's when they promised a homeland to the Jews, while in other pronouncements and conversations the British promised Arabs a homeland in Palestine in return for their support in World War I against the Ottoman Empire. Jewish immigrants desperate to escape their circumstances and determined to re-establish their own state in Palestine where they could be safe, created pressure on the British to fulfill the Balfour Declaration's promise. But pressure also came from a growing Arab population composed of some who had long lived in Palestine and others attracted by the increasing economic activity spurred in large part by the influx of Jews.

The British tried to reconcile what couldn't be reconciled. On one hand there were the Jews, who had a need, right, and desire to re-establish a Jewish nation on land where, long ago, invaders had destroyed the then existing Jewish state; on the other hand there was an Arab population that had never had a state of its own in Palestine but now wanted one despite the existence of many other Arab states. And to complicate matters, Palestine in its entirety, and in particular locations such as Jerusalem and Hebron, contained the only land that has deep religious significance to Jews, but which also contains within Jerusalem the third holiest site for Islam.

But Jews were certain of one thing. It was crucial to establish a presence on the boundaries of land deemed critical to the future of a

Jewish state. Establishing and securing borders were top priorities. All the studies focused on fixing borders based, in part, on who lived where. If there were no Jews in a location, the study would designate it for future Arab control. That's why PICA, the Rothschild development fund, changed its focus in 1936. Previously, it aimed to purchase land in the lower Galilee where agricultural pursuits would be more promising, and geography and proximity made the new communities easier to defend. Similarly, the Zionist Jewish Fund had followed the same purchasing priorities for the same reasons in the Hula Valley. But priorities changed. Borders needed to be established.

Terrorist groups frequently crossed into Palestine from Southwestern Lebanon, descending from the mountains that stretched east from the Mediterranean until making a northern turn after twenty some miles. The Haganah needed a base from which to stop them. And a future Israel needed borders it could defend effectively. Ben Gurion, by then an acknowledged leader of the Jews in Palestine, said, "First of all we have to purchase [land] in the Upper Galilee, close to the Lebanese border, and to put settlers immediately on the land. We have to do everything in order to make it difficult to exclude the Galilee from our possession." As a result, Jewish organizations once focused on purchasing land that had high chances of becoming productive changed to purchasing as much land as possible, especially in strategic locations, without regard to soil fertility or climate.

But the question remained: Where to put the sorely needed settlement? Clearly, for defensive purposes, its location had to contribute to the Haganah's control of the mountain ridges overlooking the western Galilee. And control of those ridges would also be crucial for arguing that any partition plan must leave Jews in charge of much of the Galilee when securing a new state. Still, establishing a community on those mountains would be dangerous. Could it survive in a remote location while surrounded by Arab villages and faced with an increasingly virulent Arab population in Lebanon? Or would it become the new Tel Hai—lost under pressure and leaving nothing other than a new symbol of courage and martyrdom?

Fortunately, the Jews had come upon a promising strategy. Traditionally, under Ottoman law, buildings once constructed could not be lawfully torn down. British mandate law grafted onto and/or added onto many Ottoman legal precepts. Whether possession of a newly built building conferred absolute title is beyond the scope of this book. But the tradition surely had force, at least in the minds of Zionists determined to build a nation. Thus, the Jewish leadership believed it important to erect buildings wherever they wanted to hold land. But how would they defend those buildings? Their answer was to build tower and stockade settlements.

The tower and stockade concept was simple in theory but sometimes difficult to execute. The base of operations would be a Jewish community located as close as possible to the site of the new settlement. For transport, laborers would construct an outer stockade wall, with walls and roofs for living quarters, and a watchtower, all made of wood. Other materials such as barbed wire and gravel would be collected. On the eve of the appointed day, all would be condensed into loads appropriate for lorries and wagons. Then a convoy would travel to the new site at dawn with all materials, armed guards, and workers.

Upon arrival, each worker would feverishly work to complete their pre-planned tasks in hopes of finishing a Spartan, defensible outpost by nightfall. Perimeter defenses would be a top priority. To make the sheltering structure bullet proof, two outer walls would be placed around the encampment. They would consist of wooden panels set into the ground parallel to each other and spaced thirty centimeters apart. Workers would fill the space between the panels with gravel. Equally important was raising a watch tower within the stockade for surveillance purposes. The tower would feature a powerful searchlight run by an electric generator. They would not build the living quarters and dining hall until the stockade and watchtower were finished. The workers would then leave after installing a barbed wire fence around the perimeter of the stockade. Remaining behind were those designated to garrison the new settlement. By nightfall, if things went well, all would be in place—usually before Arabs in the surrounding areas would learn of their existence.

At dawn on March 21, 1938, 400 workers set out from their assembly point. Accompanying them were ninety-one pioneers and forty Jewish police officers. Their ambitious goal was to build the first Jewish settlement in the western portions of the upper Galilee—high on the hills adjacent to the Lebanese border and five miles from the Mediterranean coast. The land had been purchased from Arab owners in Haifa. There were no Jewish outposts nearby, only Arab villages. Driving north, the vehicles went as far as they could until they reached the rocky slopes of the mountains that prevented further motorized travel. The group then left their vehicles. Some cut a new path upward that would provide means for transport. Others didn't wait for the path. They climbed the mountains by foot, bearing packs heavy with materials.

Construction did not go as planned. High winds bedeviled them. The steep slopes impeded them. Trucks could not carry workers and materials to the site like at other tower and stockade projects. At Hanita, everything depended on sturdy backs and willing legs. Sunset found the project incomplete. The access road and the living quarters were not finished but at least the wall, tower, and barbed wire were in place.

The workers and police headed home. The ninety-one pioneers remained. Among them were Yitzhak Sadeh, accompanied by his two deputies, Yigal Allon and Moshe Dayan. All three would become famous leaders of the future Jewish state. Years later Sadeh would lead

Haganah's strike force, the Palmach. Yigal Allon would become a leading IDF military commander, a deputy prime minister, and a temporary acting prime minister of Israel. And, Moshe Dayan, eventually became a renowned chief of staff of the IDF, then defense minister, and later, foreign minister. Thus, gathered on that lonely hilltop outpost, at a young age, were three of the most impactful personages of the first thirty years of Israel's existence.

There is a photo of Sadeh standing between Allon and Dayan taken during the construction of Hanita. Keen observers will see that Dayan had placed himself on higher ground, making it appear he was Allon's senior. Many saw in that picture demonstration of Dayan's political instincts, looking for every opportunity to gain a step on Allon, his competitor. Allon, who was no different, later said to put Dayan in his place, "I taught Moshe Dayan how to throw a hand grenade."

When the stars came out, all was quiet. Until midnight.

Shots rang out from two nearby hills. Sadeh radioed for permission to lead a force "beyond the fence" to clean out the attackers. The regional Haganah commander denied his request. Sadeh ignored the order and did so anyway. Cowering behind a wall was not in his playbook. In later years, Dayan valued the aggressive commander who sometimes made mistakes over a more timid one. What Dayan saw that evening helped shape his views.

The confrontation continued for over an hour. It ended with the Arabs returning to Lebanon. But they had exacted a price—two dead Jewish defenders and several others wounded.

The Jews continued to work on the Hanita outpost for the next three days while the Arabs regrouped. On the fourth day, Arabs opened fire on some of the Hanita defenders working on the access road. To expedite the construction, Dayan took a car, customized with steel plate to ward off bullets, to Nahariya, several miles away along the Mediterranean, to gather more manpower to help build the road. Meanwhile the pioneer-soldiers in Hanita persevered.

Of the fifty-two tower and stockade settlements—all built in remote areas that lacked a Jewish presence—only Hanita was attacked during its construction phase, proving the viability of its concept. To this day, Hanita plays an important role in holding the border due to its physical presence. Similarly, the other fifty-one tower and stockade settlements proved their worth, claiming and maintaining their hold on strategic land.

* * *

Sadeh, Allon, and Dayan were not the only interesting people who walked Hanita's ground. Perhaps the most fascinating, and certainly the most unique, was Orde Wingate.

The British army assigned Captain Wingate to Palestine in 1936. Wingate had a deep love and understanding of the Bible and almost immediately upon arrival felt great sympathy for the Zionist cause. He saw the fledgling communities as evidence of the Bible's prophecy of Zion's redemption and the idealistic kibbutz members as great soldiers in the making. He felt it was his duty to help create a Jewish State in Palestine.

Soon after stepping foot in Palestine, Wingate asked his commander for permission to create joint squads of British-led Jewish commandos that would engage the Arabs in unconventional ways, primarily at night. His request drew sympathy because the Arab revolt that began in 1936 had been targeting British mandate officials as well as Jews. Wingate's superiors approved the proposal and he initiated training.

The Jewish combatants under his wing revered him. He taught them that there was always a way to accomplish a mission, and the most unorthodox way was often the best. Although he was sloppy looking and often rude, Wingate was also fearless. After undertaking his frequent nighttime missions, Wingate would often be seen sitting in the dining hall, naked, eating an onion and reading the Bible. Crazy as a fox is an understatement. But the Jews he led called him "Hayedid" (the friend) and quickly embraced his philosophy that the best defense was to attack. Wingate, perhaps more than anyone else, influenced the future doctrine of the IDF.

Wingate arrived at Hanita in 1938 carrying only a backpack. Its contents included maps, a couple of pistols, and a bible. Wingate made two requests: To be taken to the base leader, a man named Ben Ya'akov, and for someone to clean his guns. When he met with Ben Ya'akov, Wingate demanded that he describe his defensive plan for Hanita. Ben Ya'akov was in the process of patiently explaining his placement of the guards, timing of shifts, and other details when Wingate stopped him, asking:

"Why are you defending this place from the inside and not from the picket-line outside?"

Ben Ya'akov answered that it was difficult to keep the outposts supplied with munitions.

Wingate was incredulous, "Why?"

Wingate's response confused Ben Ya'akov. He thought Wingate understood the restraints the Jews operated under. Ben Ya'akov explained that the British had made it illegal for the Jews to have weapons, and so they hid them underground until needed. That necessity made it impossible to man positions outside Hanita's perimeter.

But Wingate refused to be mollified. He insisted that they needed to aggressively patrol outside the stockade. And, Wingate followed his convictions. He would leave the settlement for hours at a time, ignoring standing orders that nobody could leave without the commander's permission. Because Wingate always returned without a scratch some started to suspect that he worked with the Arab gangs in the region.

One time, Wingate asked Zvi Brenner to go out with him. When Ben Ya'akov got wind of the plan he ordered thirty of his best soldiers to arm themselves and accompany Wingate and Brenner. Wingate would not permit it. Finally, after haggling, he agreed that one extra man could accompany them.

The three hiked so far from Hanita that Brenner felt certain that if they went any farther, they would have little chance of returning alive. But Wingate would not stop, and he held to a pace that kept him 100 yards ahead of the other two. Finally, when they reached a set of hills, Wingate stopped them to rest. It was then he revealed his plan. Wingate wanted to reconnoiter a house from which Arab bandits had previously launched an attack. Brenner, both frightened and ashamed of his fear, responded that they should first return to Hanita for reinforcements. Wingate would have none of that. He told his two companions to stay put and he would go alone. If he was not back within a short time, Wingate told them to return to Hanita.

Sure enough, Wingate did not return by the expected hour. His two companions waited and waited and eventually thought Wingate dead and headed back to Hanita. On the way they discussed how they would explain to Ben Ya'akov what had happened, including their violation of Ben Ya'akov's orders to stay with Wingate. Fortunately for them, Wingate returned to interrupt their explanation. He said he had searched the house for arms but there were none.

Wingate then told Ben Ya'akov it was time to change tactics. Rather than wait for an attack, the defenders of Hanita should go out at night, he said, and ambush their attackers near their own villages. Ben Ya'acov accepted his advice and offered a platoon for Wingate to lead. Wingate refused. Instead, he handpicked just seven men.

The small group made its way to the Lebanese border after leaving Hanita. When they reached the border, Wingate stopped and turned to the men. He told them their mission was to uncover the infiltration routes Arab gangs had been using. There are two ways to accomplish that, he said. They could sit, observe, and write a report. Or they could "go to the spot and obtain results." Of course, Wingate preferred the latter. They proceeded into Lebanon.

Wingate's nighttime navigation skills were extraordinary, far better than those that better knew the countryside. And his endurance was legendary. Those skills were crucial when traversing such forbidding terrain where the hills curved back and forth and sometimes run perpendicular to each other, creating narrow valleys. Along the way, one of the men fainted and needed to be carried to a water source. Two others went back to get a donkey to carry him home. Meanwhile, Wingate stayed with the stricken soldier. Instead of returning by 10 p.m. as planned, the small group returned to Hanita at 7 a.m.

Later that year, while Wingate was in Hanita, a collection of ragtag Arab raiders, thought of as an army by its leader, Fawzi el-Kaoukji, attacked Hanita. Although they killed two of its defenders, Hanita held.

In early June, Wingate's squads went into action on a nightly basis, embarking from Hanita and two other settlements. Wingate hoped that his well-trained Jews would eventually form the nucleus of a Jewish army. The total number under Wingate's command was never more than a 100 Jews accompanied by sixty British soldiers. Each squad's schedule was based on a six-week cycle: three weeks for training, two weeks on duty carrying out missions, and then one week off to relax. While on duty, they would patrol at least nine out of fourteen nights. If one of the men misread a map, Wingate would give him hell. If they coughed or made other noise while on patrol, he would hit them with the butt of his rifle. Wingate told them, "The Arabs think that the night is theirs . . . the British troops and police shut themselves up in their camps during the night, but we, the Jews

[sic], will show that we can destroy their plans. We will not rest until a fear of the night, as of the day, assails them."

In the first month of their operation, Wingate's squads ambushed and killed sixty Arab gang members and retaliated against villages that harbored the marauders. To accomplish his aims, Wingate was constantly on the move, training his men and planning and leading operations. Many of those men came from Hanita.

On June 17, Wingate arrived at Hanita to find his soldiers formulating a plan for an attack based on information from an Arab informant. Suspecting treachery, Wingate pretended to believe the informant but put together a contingency plan to implement if the Arab was lying.

Hoping to surprise and confuse the Arabs, the special night squad divided into three groups as they headed for the Arab village of Jurdeih, three miles away. But their maps were bad. Rather than reaching Jurdeih without being noticed, they stumbled into a small hamlet where they ran into a Bedouin man in the dark. He told them fifteen Arab gang members were sheltering nearby. Wingate's men didn't take the man into captivity because several women were watching from their tents. Wingate feared that the women would scream if they tied up the man. Instead, he moved his unit to positions surrounding the gang.

But the Bedouin man spoiled Wingate's plan. Running, the Bedouin crossed the border into Lebanon and screamed, "My brothers! My brothers! The children of the Jews are upon us!" The women then added to the commotion with their warning cries.

The gangsters ran out of the tents, saw that the Jews had surrounded them, and then fired their guns with little effect. Wingate's men returned fire and attempted to block their escape. Some of the Arabs got away, but others died during the battle. Despite its victory, the patrol force did not risk spending time searching the shelters for weapons and information, for the fight had most certainly been heard in Lebanon. The group feared that Arab reinforcements would arrive soon. Wingate depended on stealth and surprise. The Arabs had superior numbers and would have the upper hand if a pitched battle would have been fought on ground not of Wingate's choosing. Rather than risk a fight that they might not win, Wingate's force retreated, returning to Hanita at 6 a.m.

Their attack had accomplished more than they first thought. The mukhtar of Jurdeih sent an emissary to Hanita with a peace proposal. The mukhtar's capitulation was not surprising given the reputation that the night squads were gaining among local Arabs. He knew his village had literally dodged a bullet. As a result, the next few weeks saw quiet and the local gang that had been the target of the attack did not return.

The Wingate era did not last long. The British became increasingly skittish over his overt favoritism of the Jews. Too successful for his commanders' liking, Wingate was ordered to leave Palestine. By 1939, the British authorities had abolished the special Jewish-British night squads. Later, Wingate proved he was not a one trick pony. In Burma he achieved notoriety fighting the Japanese during World War II, where he was promoted to major general before dying in a plane crash in 1944. But his short stint in Palestine had a profound impact.

Thanks to Wingate, the once-more-passive Jews defending the settlements transformed into proactive defenders willing to be aggressive and take risks. Though brief, his presence played a large role in the establishment of Israel's northern border with Lebanon. The IDF will never forget him.

* * *

Hanita continued to prove valuable for military pursuits after the end of the Arab revolt in 1939 and the threat of Arab attacks diminished.

In June 1941, future two-time prime minister Yitzhak Rabin traveled to Hanita. He had heard rumors that Germans were in Lebanon with the consent and knowledge of its Vichy government. In Hanita's reading room, Rabin met with Dayan and other Haganah leaders. A British officer briefed them. He advised that the British would soon invade Lebanon to prevent the Germans from using it as a staging area for an attack towards Egypt from the north. The German army already threatened Egypt from Libya. An attack from Libya alone could spell Egypt's fall. But of more immediate concern to the Jewish leadership in Palestine, Jews living in Palestine would be doomed if Germany were to wrestle control of the region. Given the stakes, the Haganah had agreed to cooperate with the British army. Rabin, Dayan, and the other Haganah soldiers at Hanita were there to help.

After their meeting, small Haganah units patrolled in Lebanon. One night, Rabin joined a mission that required a fifty-kilometer march deep into Lebanon to cut phone lines to prevent the Vichy army from summoning reinforcements after the British army attacked. Since Rabin was the youngest member of the unit, the job fell to him to climb the designated telephone pole. But he had a problem. Rabin didn't know how to use the pole irons that attached to his boots for climbing. Nonplussed, Rabin took off his boots and shinnied up the pole. When he reached the first wire, Rabin promptly cut it. That's when he realized that he had another problem. The cut wire was not a telephone wire. It was a wire that stabilized the telephone pole. The pole swayed and Rabin fell back to the ground. But Rabin completed the mission. He shinnied back up the pole and cut the appropriate wire.

Meanwhile, another future star of Israel also faced adversity that same night, the outcome of which would disfigure him for life. Dayan was leading one of two Jewish companies that the Haganah had provided the British army to aid its attack into Lebanon. Yigal Allon commanded the other company. Leaving from Hanita, their objective was to take control of a bridge six miles north of the frontier. Dayan joined an advance party that would lead the attack. While observing the terrain, a stray bullet hit his binoculars, driving it into his left eye. From then on, he would always wear in public an eye patch, which became his trademark, to cover his empty left eye socket from which his eye had been removed.

* * *

My first trip to Hanita has already led to five more. Hanita today sits on top of the ridge, within easy rifle shot of Hezbollah. For the first few months of 1938, Hanita was located a few hundred feet lower, nestled into the hills. Any higher would have asked too much of the men who feverishly pushed themselves to lug heavy materials up the hill in order build the stockade and tower before nightfall. But later in 1938, intrepid souls moved Hanita to its present location on the ridgeline separating Lebanon from Israel.

Every time I head up that steep, twisting road that always takes far longer to navigate than anticipated, I look to my right two-thirds of the way up. There, a rough track leads through the trees to the first site of Hanita. My mind drifts, imagining what it must have felt like, surrounded by people who wanted to kill you, going out on missions designed to cause contact that would lead to combat, and led by the cream of Israel's future leadership. There, history was made amid the now silent trees now gently swaying in the breeze.

But history is always being made everywhere, not just at Hanita. It's just that some history is more important than others.

Shortly after World War II, new and important history was made at a location already famous for its contributions to Israel. The time was May 1948. Several months earlier the United Nations had voted to approve a partition plan that would separate Palestine into two independent states, one for the Jews and one for the Palestinians. The Jews accepted the plan. Surrounding Arab nations and indigenous Palestinians rejected it. When the Jews declared their independent state on May 14, 1948, the Arabs responded by attacking. Overnight, the Jewish War for Independence, already simmering after the UN Resolution in November 1947 signaled international approval for Israel's creation, had begun—fed by the surrounding Arab nations and indigenous Palestinians out for blood. Among them was the Syrian army. It went on the march. Its purpose was to cut through northern Israel and end the Jewish dream. A few intrepid souls at Degania stood in the way.

Chapter Six

Degania, May 1948

There is a ruined Syrian tank that sits on a grassy field outside of Degania A's fence. Children were climbing on it the first time I saw it. Most people in vehicles whizzing by on the adjacent highway don't pay it any mind. This is true of so many hallowed grounds in Israel. Descriptive plaques, written in Hebrew and sometimes also in English, can be found in many of these locations. Occasionally, there are recordings one can listen to, again in Hebrew and sometimes in English as well, that provide basic details. But unless you learn about these places before visiting them, unless you stop and walk the grounds, unless you close your mind to the distractions, it's hard to appreciate their significance. That small gray tank doesn't look like much at first sight. And yet it stands as a reminder of the courageous Jews who defended the Jewish communities in the Galilee there, near Israel's 1948 border, and the strategic impact they had that far outweighed the number of their casualties or the violence of the battle.

On May 13, the Syrian invading force was in southern Lebanon, prepared to attack towards Safed, fifteen miles east of Hanita. In a sudden change of plan, the Syrian Command ordered its forces to move back to Syrian territory, traverse the Golan Heights and descend to a point at the southern tip of the Sea of Galilee. Their new plan entailed crossing the Jordan River at the narrow bridge located there and then by moving west, cut off the Galilee from the rest of Israel. The changed plan reduced the power of what the Syrians could initially bring to bear since not all their invasion force could make the journey in one day. But it also circumvented Israel's strongest defenses. The Israelis had gathered forces to block Syria's anticipated attack from Southern Lebanon as well as an expected Syrian move north of the Sea of Galilee, a lake that ran several miles along the border. Israel had few forces south of the lake. All that stood in the way was an ad hoc group of defenders buttressed by the buildings, fences, and inhabitants of Degania.

On May 15, 1948, the commander of Syria's invading force stood on a grassy hill that overlooked the Arab village of Samakh, an Israeli-held strategic point along the southern shore of the Sea of Galilee. The day before, Egyptian, Syrian, Lebanese, and Iraqi forces had attacked Israel's fledgling state. Palestinian irregular forces joined them, as did Jordanian forces. The Arab nations had been preparing their offensive for weeks, knowing that pursuant to United Nations vote, Jews in Palestine would declare their sovereignty on May 14 over land designated in the U.N. Resolution.

The Syrians thrust into Israel on May 16. Their first objective was the police station at Samakh. After succeeding there, the Syrians planned to punch through Degania A adjacent to the Sea of Galilee and Degania B immediately to its south. The Syrians had many infantrymen, a tank unit, and artillery. The vastly outnumbered Israelis had a couple hundred men armed mainly with rifles.

Before the Syrian forces arrived, Jewish forces, some of which were from Degania, occupied the strategically important police station. They also tried to trick the Syrians by sending many vehicles west with their lights off so the Syrians wouldn't see them. Then they turned the trucks around with their lights on, hoping to convince the Syrians that Jewish reinforcements were coming. But this didn't work. And so, early on May 16, the Syrians unleashed their artillery. After hours of shells dropping where the Syrians thought to be critical points, they began their ground attack at 7 a.m.

From a hastily dug trench, three platoons of Golani infantry along with residents of Degania A and B faced the Syrians. Degania A stood only a few hundred yards behind them. The Syrian infantry descended from the nearby hills. The Jewish forces began firing when the Syrians were 150 yards away. Their defensive fire forced the Syrians to break off their attack and call for reinforcements. Over the next two days, more Syrian soldiers and armored vehicles arrived. On May 18, they launched another concerted attack.

It took approximately an hour for the Syrians to drive the Jews from the police station. Sixty-one Jews died in the fight. The Jewish defenders then made a quixotic attempt to retake the ground they had lost, which failed miserably. Five more died in their charge through a field already littered with corpses. However, it did help delay the Syrian advance on Degania another day.

But the writing was on the wall. Degania would be next. As shells crashed and Syrian planes dropped bombs, Degania's children and their mothers evacuated from the community. Desperate, Degania's leadership sent a delegation to Tel Aviv to meet with David Ben Gurion, Israel's newly minted leader, to secure assistance. The delegation consisted of three men. One was Joseph Baratz, part of the group that founded Degania thirty years before.

The delegation arrived in Tel Aviv at dusk and went straight to Ben Gurion with its message of impending doom. "The Syrians have tanks, guns, and planes" they said, "and we have nothing but rifles and a few machine guns with too little ammunition. You must give us arms; we can't hold out like this!"

Ben Gurion responded: "We have nothing. We have a front in Jerusalem, a front in Galilee, a front in the Negev. There are not enough arms anywhere."

Ignoring his tears, Baratz fired back, "Ben Gurion, don't say this. Do you realize what this means? If Degania is taken, the way is open to the whole of Galilee, to Tiberias, to Haifa."

"What can I do?" said Ben Gurion. "There are not enough guns, not enough planes; men are lacking on all fronts. The situation is very severe in the Negev, is difficult in Jerusalem, in Upper Galilee. The whole country is a front line. We cannot send reinforcements."

But then the prime minister thought better of his message of despair. "Wait until midnight," he said, "and we'll see what we can possibly do."

Ben Gurion then left the room, leaving the delegation to wait. Waiting with them was Yigael Yadin, a staff officer destined to become Israel's second chief of staff. The wait was interminable. Finally, Yadin broke the silence. "This is my advice to you. Go back to Degania. Let the Syrians come, let them come right in; then you'll beat them."

"Are you crazy?" Baratz answered. "We have seen what happens in other places: once they get in, within an hour they've destroyed everything and . . . once they're in, how can we drive them out with our rifles?"

Yadin tried placating Baratz. "I know," he said. "But I know you Deganians. If you meet them face to face, you'll drive them out. If we could give you tanks it would be better, but if we can't this is the only way." Yadin later wrote:

> *I was suddenly shocked at that moment, when I realized that the fall of Degania would mean that the whole north of the country might be lost. In the south, the Egyptian army was advancing on Tel Aviv. Jerusalem was cut off, and the Iraqis were putting pressure on the middle of the country. This was a moment that I suddenly felt that the dream of generations was about to disintegrate.*

Yadin's words fell flat. His exhortation did nothing to lift the delegation's gloom.

But then a message from Ben Gurion offered a small measure of hope. He said that he would try to send help but could not promise. Meanwhile, Moshe Dayan had made his way north. Earlier, Ben Gurion, had ordered him to "hold the Jordan Valley." Ben Gurion knew full well what was at stake at Degania, but there were emergencies everywhere and not enough resources to deal with all of them.

The delegation headed home empty handed. Dawn was approaching, and with it, the Syrians. As the delegation neared Degania, soldiers guarding the road hesitated to let them pass because of the danger ahead. Syrian Shells began hitting Degania A & B at 4:30 a.m.

The Syrians advanced at sunrise in three columns. The northernmost column headed towards Degania A. The southernmost set its sights on Degania B. The column in the middle aimed for the garden that lay between the two communities. Several tanks accompanied each column. Artillery swept the ground in front of their advance. Overhead, Syrian planes swooped over Degania's roofs, dropping ordinance and firing their guns.

Degania A's defenders were in trenches. Dayan, who had arrived in the middle of the night, had ordered Degania B to stop working on improving the trenches and instead to focus on building individual firing positions. He also took a calculated risk by sending some of the men to an archaeological mound outside their perimeter, which flanked the anticipated path of the Syrians. This weakened Degania B's main defenses but improved their ability to stop the attack by firing from an unanticipated direction. Their rifles and machine guns could do little against Syria's armored vehicles. Instead, they hoped that their home-brewed Molotov cocktails would stop the tanks. The cocktails were simple, yet effective, incendiary weapons; airtight glass containers filled with a liquid flammable substance that you could light. Once lit, these poor man's bombs would explode on contact, bursting into flames and hopefully igniting the target.

The seventy Jewish defenders at Degania A worked hard to improve their positions but suffered in the heat from their exertions. When they complained, Dayan tried to cheer them with the thought that when the Syrians attacked, they would have no shade.

The Syrian infantry, led by armored cars and several tanks, closed in on Degania A. Their tanks smashed through the hastily constructed defensive positions and breached the outer fence. The Jews used their three handheld-bazooka-like Piats to stop two of the tanks. But the other armored vehicles pressed forward followed by foot soldiers. Within moments, the tanks crossed the adjacent road and knocked down any trees in their path as they headed for the trench line.

That's when one brave soul became a legend. He jumped from the trench holding several Molotov cocktails and then threw them at one of the tanks. At least one shattered on the tank's steel wall and burst into flames. The two officers inside the tank had been directing the attack in that sector. They died in the conflagration, which also engulfed surrounding trees. Others followed suit with their Molotov cocktails.

The destroyed tank that now sits on the grassy area outside Degania is a monument to the courage of those defenders. While some have suggested that that tank was the one destroyed by the hand-thrown Molotov cocktails, modern investigation has uncovered that an explosive shell from one of the handheld Piats actually destroyed it. But there is little doubt that Molotov cocktails, thrown by courageous young farmers exposed to fire when they stood up close to the Syrian vehicles to hurl the glass containers, played an important role in the overall defense of Degania.

The Syrian infantry, now separated from its supporting vehicles, of which many had been destroyed, pressed forward. The embattled defenders of Degania A struggled to hold them off, finally succeeding in causing them to break off their attack. At Degania B, the battle was still in doubt. The Syrians got to within thirty yards of the trench lines when artillery shells began to fall on them. It wasn't friendly fire from poorly aimed Syrian artillery. They were Jewish shells. But from where?

It turns out that Baratz's desperate mission to Tel Aviv had not failed. While the dejected delegation was on its way back to Degania, Yadin went to Ben Gurion. Four artillery pieces (one account says two) that lacked aiming sights had just arrived at Tel Aviv. Ben Gurion had wanted to employ them to help open the road to Jerusalem. But Yadin argued, "The situation is critical [in the north]." Ben Gurion stood his ground. For hours they debated the pros and cons. Finally, Yadin wrote, "I pounded Ben-Gurion's glass-topped desk with my fist and the glass shattered." His emotional physical outburst turned the tide. Ben Gurion agreed to send the artillery pieces north.

A little after noon, a truck approached the area. Inside were the artillery pieces. Dayan ordered them placed on a hill overlooking the battle a couple miles away. I had an opportunity to visit the location, a rocky field now strewn with trash. It lies adjacent to a restaurant where I had one of my best lunches in Israel. Below, the Sea of Galilee shimmered to the left and straight ahead, the Golan Heights lay beyond. Slightly to the right, I could see where the battle in 1948 had been fought. Given the tranquility of the moment, it was hard to imagine the artillery pieces, the many shells, and an inexperienced crew operating those guns. But it was easy to understand why Dayan had picked that spot. It was safe from Syrian interference and offered a perfect view of the battlefield.

Made before World War I, the guns were so old that the Jews nicknamed them "Napoleonchicks," because they had no aiming sights. Before firing for effect, the crew had to adjust them for proper aim by firing shells into the lake. Still unable to aim precisely, at least one shell reportedly hit a Syrian ammunition dump causing massive explosions. Other shells caused fires in the dry fields.

The Syrian commander, Colonel Wahab, was observing the Syrian attack from atop the police station taken previously. With dismay, he saw his troops retreating as artillery shells exploded within their ranks. Initially, he thought it friendly fire. But then one of his officers came to him and said, "Sir, those are Jewish shells. They've got artillery!"

The Syrian's bravado quickly faded. Not knowing how many artillery pieces the Jews had, Wahab ordered, "Head the troops into the hills!"

The attack on Degania was over. The Jordan valley and the Galilee had been saved.

The defenders were too exhausted to take advantage of the Syrian soldiers' confusion. When they retreated the Jews did not pursue them. The next morning the Syrians retreated further, to the slopes of the Golan.

Over the next few days a hot wind called a "hamsin" blew over the battlefield. The stench of corpses strewn everywhere was overpowering and there was a growing risk of pestilence. The Arabs never collected their dead nor asked to. So the residents of Degania collected Syrian bodies as well as their own. Since Syria continued to conduct air raids, it was too dangerous to dig individual graves for the Syrians. They were buried together in a communal grave.

Degania A and B would never face another attack. Thanks to the courageous defenders, Northern Israel had dodged the Syrian bullet.

Chapter Seven

Kibbutz Dan

Fifty feet above the countryside sits Tel Dan, an ancient site that features verdant vegetation, bubbling brooks, and archaeological digs that have uncovered ruins dating back thousands of years. This was where the Jewish tribe of Dan established its home under King David's rule as part of the Kingdom of Israel and continued to dwell there in the turbulent wake following King Solomon's death. But I wasn't interested in the area's beautiful walking paths or its wading pool fed by snowmelt from nearby Mount Hermon. Instead, I was interested in Kibbutz Dan, which is located less than a mile away from its namesake. When mainly Romanian immigrants established the kibbutz in 1939, they, along with Jews in Metula, had staked Israel's northernmost claim on the future state's border.

In the mid-1960s Kibbutz Dan sat directly across from territory that Syria controlled. It was there that Syria's war over water with Israel had devastating consequences for the kibbutz. Then, in 1967, Kibbutz Dan was the only kibbutz attacked during that war by Syrian ground troops. It was not enough for me to just read about those events. I wanted to see the ground for myself and meet the people who lived there.

* * *

After driving through the entrance gate, I made a hard-right turn and motored past part of the kibbutz's industrial plant. Although I read the company names on each building I passed, my mind was elsewhere. I was thinking about my upcoming interview with Samuel Gardi, a longtime resident of the kibbutz.

Gardi was the first of over forty people I eventually interviewed in hopes of learning about life along Israel's dangerous northern borders. Frankly, I was nervous. How would Israelis react to my questions? Since I only speak a few words of Hebrew, would the language barrier cause confusion or negatively impact the interviews? I wondered if Samuel would allow me to record our conversation, and I fretted over how I might broach the subject. On a more mundane level, I worried that the new tape recorder I had purchased for the trip would prove too cumbersome to operate.

My fears reached a crescendo when I turned left and saw a lean, athletic-looking man waving me towards a gravel parking lot. Smiling, Samuel approached me with his hand out. He was vibrant and appeared younger than his sixty-eight years. We shook hands and walked past a few residences to his home. Thanks to Samuel's demeanor, I was already at ease.

Perhaps because it was the first kibbutz residence I had been in; I was surprised to find his home very nice and modern. The kitchen was on the right, a living room on the left, and a dining room and multiple bedrooms lay beyond. Hours later, we would stand on his covered porch and watch as an unusually strong thunderstorm dropped hailstones.

We made small talk as Samuel prepared coffee and brought out a bottle of sparkling water. Then I asked him if I could record our conversation, and he casually waived his hand and said something akin to "of course." I soon learned why he was so fit. Samuel is a long-distance biker. Now retired, he once worked as the marketing director for NanDanJain, one of the industries I had passed on my way to his home. Months later, I learned that he also had held leadership positions with the kibbutz.

But we couldn't sit for long. Samuel had lined up two other residents for me to interview.

A few minutes later we drove in my car through an older section of the kibbutz to pick up Yossi Lev Ari. When we arrived, a somewhat frail eighty-three-year-old man wearing oversized dark sunglasses and a floppy hat walked into my view with help of a cane. Despite his obvious age, Yossi's step looked surprisingly spry as he approached my vehicle and then settled himself in the back seat. Samuel had told me how important it was for me to meet him: Yossi has been living at Kibbutz Dan since the mid-1950s. Samuel knew most of the stories, he said, but Yossi had lived them.

Our destination? Tel Dan. But we weren't going to the archaeological dig and tourist sites. We were going to where Yossi, when called up for reserve duty, had served during the war over water with Syria. There, with his fellow soldiers, he had stood guard opposite a Syrian village defending his home, Kibbutz Dan.

Despite Yossi's appearance, I soon realized that he still had a young man's spirit. My first indication was the friendly argument that Samuel and Yossi had in the car. They couldn't agree which of the many dirt roads I should take to reach the shortcut Yossi wanted us to use. They were speaking in Hebrew, but I could tell that Yossi was dishing it out as well as Samuel.

We soon came to the shortcut: a steep, rough, road leading to Tel Dan's border with Syria, which had been the scene of bitter fighting with Syrian forces that had occupied the area beyond the border fence. Not only did the Israeli positions guard the border there, they also overlooked the Golan's hills, where the Syrians had embarked on their water diversion project. There, IDF soldiers had had a bird's eye view of the unfolding crisis that eventually brought Israel and Syria to blows.

But there was a problem. The gate to get in was locked. While waiting for a guard to come open it, Yossi told me about a defining moment in his life and the history of the kibbutz.

It was November 13, 1964. His voice turned serious, "No warning—shells started coming. [The Syrians] knew all the children were in the kindergarten.... We had shelters for each kindergarten. My kids for example go down to the shelter."

When the shelling began, Yossi and his wife had been driving back to the kibbutz after an excursion to Kiryat Shmona, several miles to the west.

He continued, "So they stopped us because of the bombardment. I make a circle around and [made my way to the kibbutz]."

Immediately, Yossi and his wife went to where his oldest child lived in the children's home. Their child was not there. Instead Yossi found "a shell in the bed—a part of [a] bomb had hit the bed, but he was not in it." It "took some terrifying minutes," Yossi said, "to find he was not hurt . . . My father [had] taken him to the shelter." Yossi then explained what had happened, "Three thousand shells destroyed the kibbutz completely."

The kibbutz was flattened, "electricity, every house, everything." Rebuilding it required government assistance and help from many other kibbutzim.

The November 13 conflagration was largely caused by the terms of the armistice agreement reached between Israel and Syria in 1949, after the end of the Arab-Israeli War of 1948. First, Israel and Egypt signed an armistice agreement after almost two months of talks. A month later, Israel and Lebanon agreed to one; ten days later a deal with Jordan followed. The agreement with Syria took another three months. But the signed documents were not a peace agreement. The Arab nations had no interest in that. In fact, they refused to sit in the same room as the Israelis. All that was accomplished was a supposed end to the fighting. To no one's surprise, it proved to be very temporary.

Israel's agreement with Syria was unique compared to the agreements it had with other nations. Syria had captured a small amount of territory in three locations that the 1947 United Nations Resolution, favoring Israel's statehood, had granted to the forthcoming Jewish state. Syria did not want to return the land—not without strings attached.

Thus, Israel's agreement with Syria established three demilitarized zones where Syria had taken Israeli territory that would remain demilitarized until a final agreement could be reached. In exchange, Syria agreed to withdraw its military from those enclaves. Unfortunately, Israel and Syria had different interpretations of the agreement and what their obligations were in those designated zones. Syria believed that, although free of the Syrian army, the zones would remain under Syrian sovereignty. Israel believed that there could be no military presence in the zones and that since the three enclaves were officially Israeli land, it was free to farm what was Israel's land. Based on that interpretation, Israeli farmers plowed the land and raised crops, not just for agricultural reasons but also to assert Israel's sovereignty. Not surprisingly, these differences resulted in armed conflict.

The smallest of the demilitarized zones lay east of Tel Dan. Within that zone was Tel Azaziat, a hilltop Syrian fortification equipped with Syrian artillery. This was a direct violation of the armistice agreement. Nevertheless, from that hill, Syrians would shell Israeli tractors in the fields.

On November 3, ten days before the devastating shelling on Kibbutz Dan, two Syrian tanks from bunkers just north of Kibbutz Dan fired on Israeli tractors performing agricultural work in the demilitarized zone. Ten Israeli tanks, prepositioned to respond to the expected Syrian military response, returned fire for several hours without success. Neither side's accuracy—a deficiency the IDF quickly corrected— was enough to harm the other's tanks.

The November 13 attack that Yossi had spoken of, which put his child in danger, began when Israeli troop carriers drove along the border road Israel had built that encircled Tel Dan—a road that some argue lay beyond recognized Israeli territory (in this region borders are squishy—credible arguments are many). Syrian guns fired on them, killing three Israeli soldiers. The IDF responded by firing its artillery against Syrian positions, and then Syria shelled the kibbutz. Some commentators point to several IDF tanks, not involved in the fighting, that had been sitting in Kibbutz Dan's open yard as the cause. But that doesn't explain the devastating fire directed at the kibbutz's civilian buildings. Prime Minister Levi Eshkol responded to the shelling by authorizing Israel's air force to attack the Syrian emplacements. After a little more than thirty minutes of air strikes, the battle was over.

The guard arrived and unlocked the gate just as Yossi's story concluded, and we drove to a spot near the top of the Tel. An expansive view of Lebanon and the Golan Heights greeted me after exiting my vehicle and walking the few remaining feet to the top of the Tel. In front of us was an old Israeli trench, lined overhead with rusted iron ribs that once supported some form of metal roof. I was in the sun. Yossi lingered in the shade of a tree, an Israeli habit that I came to know well—why stand or park your car in the sun when shade is so much more comfortable? Close by were remnants of one of the tractors the Israelis had used to farm the demilitarized zone.

A few yards down were the dirt remains of the Israeli patrol road. Then barbed wire. Then a white road just a little lower, which prior to 1967 was Syrian controlled. To the northeast lay Ghajar, a town half controlled by Israel, half in Lebanon under an ambiguous control scheme. Before the Six-Day War, its Alawite residents had given their allegiance to Syria, but after Israel took the region from Syria, Ghajar's residents preferred Israeli control to the alternatives. Theirs is a complicated story, which I will address in Chapter Sixteen. To our northeast (to the right) were the slopes of the Golan Heights and the mountains and extinct volcanoes that litter the Golan plateau. And straight ahead, I could see a destroyed Syrian tank sitting on a hill the Israelis called "Nohala,"

Yossi had stood guard in the military position we were standing on. At times, he said, up to ten Syrian tanks would aim their guns at the Israelis from Nohala. It was from there that Syrian guns had fired on Israeli vehicles on November 13, 1964, kicking off the ensuing violence. All this was within a few minutes stroll from where I stood. Beyond that, Hezbollah controls. And all the while there was a man standing next to me, old now but young then, who had witnessed the terror of those times.

According to Yossi, the IDF did not base his unit on the position where we stood until 1964. Only when it became clear that Syria would try to change the course of the Hatzbani and Banias Rivers did the IDF garrison the location. The headwaters of those two rivers lay in Lebanon and Syria before draining into the Jordan River and eventually the Sea of Galilee. That water was crucial for Israeli irrigation.

Yossi then showed me what the Syrians tried to do. Perhaps two miles off to the right, along the downward slope of what he called the Syrian Heights rather than the Golan Heights, was a path that looked like a road. It gently descended downward. Yossi explained that the Syrians hoped to build a canal where the path was that would connect to the water sources. They were going to rely on gravity to divert the water away from Israel and into Arab land. Parts of the planned route were only within a few hundred yards of the border.

Israel had just completed a national water carrier that would take water from the Sea of Galilee to the Negev in the south of the country.

Had the Syrians succeeded, half of that water—water that flowed past Tel Dan, water the Israelis counted on—would no longer be there. Since water is life, the Syrian scheme was a potential death knell. Israel had to prevent it.

Soon, Syrian bulldozers working on the canal came less than a mile from Israel's border. Israel was determined to stop the construction work. Then Chief of Staff Yitzhak Rabin hoped to find a way without crossing the border, but the previous tank exchanges at Tel Dan had demonstrated that the accuracy of the tank gunners was insufficient for fulfilling his goal.

But the head of the armored corps, Yisrael Tal, was determined to do something about that. Rabin later wrote, "Tal instituted up-to-date training, [found] shells most suitable for targets of this nature; worked out new firing techniques for tank guns; and improved the marksmanship of the gunners."

The best officers and gunners were then assigned to tanks in the region. Soon, the Syrian bulldozers were destroyed. When the Syrians tried again by moving the water diversion route farther back, the IDF found ways to increase their range. Again, the Syrian bulldozers were wiped out. Eventually, the Syrians stopped trying after the Israelis destroyed equipment as far as two-and-a-half miles away. The techniques learned made a significant difference in the Six-Day War and may well have saved the Golan and the northern Galilee from Syrian capture in the 1973 Yom Kippur War.

Yossi found his wife at Kibbutz Dan. He now has four children, fourteen grandchildren, and eight great grandchildren. To his joy, two of his children live on the kibbutz along with several of the grandchildren. Listening to him and watching his body language, it was clear—he will never leave Kibbutz Dan even though the kibbutz has changed since its establishment under the auspices of the Hashomer Hatsair, "The Young Guard," movement.

Hashomer Hatsair grew out of a merger between the Hashomer and a youth group called *Zeire Zion* (Youth of Zion) that studied Zionism, socialism, and Jewish history. It believed that Jewish youths could be liberated from the chains of oppression in Eastern Europe by immigrating to Palestine and living in a kibbutz. Members of the group who were unable to leave Europe before the Germans invaded their countries became leaders of many resistance movements that sprung up to fight the Germans, including in the Warsaw Ghetto.

As we drove to Yossi's home to drop him off, I asked him whether he missed the old days. Yossi quipped, "I was younger." Turning more serious, he added: "It was more of a community."

I could have happily peppered Yossi with questions for hours but clearly fatigue had caught up with him. And we had another appointment— with another man in his eighties.

After Yossi left us, Samuel directed me down several roads until we reached another dirt road, this time heading south to the main highway outside of the kibbutz. On our left was a modest wood with a small hill running parallel to the road amid the trees. On our right was a large field. Straight ahead and across from the highway a large hill was within sight and along the road perpendicular to us, within the field, were some ruins of an old building. As I took in the scenery, Samuel told me to stop and pull off the road. Within a minute or two, another car pulled up. Out of it strode Amiram Efrati, another eighty some year-old man, but with far more pep in his step than Yossi, and an energetic, engaged look in his eyes.

After introducing us, Samuel drew quiet as Amiram spoke.

His part of the story, Amiram said, is Syria's attack on Kibbutz Dan on the first day of the Six-Day War. To orient me, he pointed to the hill I had spotted in front of me. It was Tel Azaziat. From there he said, "They could look down to see if the kibbutz workers shaved their cheeks in the morning."

The Six-Day War began on June 5, 1967 and ended six days later with an overwhelming victory for Israel. But in the run up to the war, although the military was confident, Israeli citizens were anything but. As Amiram put it, "People were very worried."

Amiram spent his days leading up to the war working as the dairy manager at the kibbutz. At night, he and others would dig holes in which they would place mines. The Syrians were only a few minutes march away. Kibbutz Dan had experienced Syrian attacks in the 1948 War for Independence, devastation that was a byproduct of the War over Water, and various Palestinian terrorist infiltrations. So, its residents were used to danger. But this was different. The tension had been building for weeks. Arab propaganda had been vitriolic, and their apparent capabilities and proximity was frightening.

Two weeks before the war, with tension ramping up, Moshe Dayan came to the kibbutz dining room—a central meeting place for the kibbutz, where members would eat all their meals together, socialize, and engage in other communal activity. Thus, it was natural that Dayan would come to the dining hall to speak to them.

Amiram heard Dayan say, "You have nothing to worry about. Maybe on the Egyptian border, maybe." Dayan's hope was to calm their nerves. So, he emphasized, "On the Syrian border, nothing [will] happen."

But, Amiram told me, "During the night [we] could hear the chains of the tanks gathering on the Golan Heights." As he spoke, I thought what it must be like to live in a small village along a border with a hated enemy who was broadcasting their intent to kill you and your family—an enemy all the while staring at your wife, your children, your home from up high—and wondering what the next day will bring? What, I thought, is it like to have no control of events but be controlled by them? What must have it been like then? What is it like now?

And then things got worse.

The IDF withdrew the regular soldiers stationed at the kibbutz, so confident that the Syrians would do nothing, and placed the soldiers elsewhere. Most of the younger men from the kibbutz were long gone, having been called up to do their reserve duty or already serving in the active army. This left thirteen members in total—including six elders over the age of fifty and Amiram, who then was thirty—to defend the kibbutz. They were armed, Amiram told me, with three machine guns and simple Czech rifles that could fire no more than five bullets, with each shot causing a massive recoil that would bang the stock of the rifle into your shoulder. Then, with your shoulder smarting from the pounding and your arms aching from the weight of the rifle, Amiram said, you would have to ask the enemy to kindly stop charging forward while you reloaded.

Amiram then gestured to their post. It was the ruined building I had seen when we drove up. When I focused on it, I could make out one of the three bunkers still there that they had used for defensive positions. That ruined building had an ancient past. During the Ottoman era it was the local custom post. Similarly, during the British Mandate, farmers and merchants coming from the Damascus region to British controlled territories, would have to stop there to pay taxes on the items.

"Twenty-four hours exactly after the beginning of the war," Amiram said, "on Tuesday at ten minutes to six" the Syrians started to heavily shell the kibbutz and their post. The reason, they learned from documents the IDF later uncovered, was that the Syrians thought there was some secret military activity going on at the kibbutz. "We were here. Thirteen warriors, half of them elder people."

"Mortar shells, artillery. Two hours exactly," explosives rained down on their positions. It was incredibly loud. "After that silence." The silence presaged what they already knew: the Syrians were only a few hundred yards away. They would come soon.

Amiram took a moment to diverge from his story. As I eagerly waited to hear what happened next, he instead pointed to the trees behind us—the ones to the left of the road as we were driving up. He pinpointed an old anti-tank ditch built by the British to stop any potential attack by Vichy France during World War II. I then didn't understand why he had interrupted his narrative to point that out to me. I soon learned why.

The pregnant pause that followed the end of the shelling ended with something worse, Amiram recounted. They heard sounds of infantry coming. Rejecting stealth, the Syrian soldiers shouted as they moved forward that they were going to overrun the kibbutz. All they could do, Amiram said, was check their rifles and prepare to fire. A company sized unit of Syrian soldiers, perhaps a hundred, soon appeared. Like a wave, they relentlessly moved toward the thirteen defenders.

Then Amiram surprised me. He said, "Our commander was Yossi, he has nerves of a fish." The same Yossi whom I had just spent an hour with at Tel Dan. With admiration, Amiram recounted Yossi's order, "Wait until you see the white of [their] eyes before firing."

The Syrians were running toward them. Amiram, Yossi, and the others could see they were carrying Bangalore torpedoes to blow a hole through the kibbutz fence. They knew, Amiram said in a quiet voice, that if the Syrians passed them, "the women and children were in the bomb shelters." He didn't need to explain what would happen to them if the Syrians got past their thin line.

"When close, Yossi gave the order to fire," said Amiram. Their bullets killed several and wounded others. But their ammunition ran low. They desperately called from their field phone to the kibbutz headquarters for more. Only children from the High School were available to carry supplies to them. Running through trenches, risking their lives, they delivered the needed munitions to the thirteen. The

Syrian charge faltered and then stopped. Their morale devastated; they retreated.

But the battle was not over. Just as the Syrian infantrymen were pulling back, a new threat appeared. Six tanks crashed through the trees, rolling over the filled-in British anti-tank ditches, which were no longer effective after almost thirty years of erosion. At first the Syrian tanks had stopped near the road we were standing on and fired shells at Amiram and the others. The small group of desperate defenders had nothing to fire back with that would stop the tanks if they came forward. Bullets from their rifles wouldn't pierce a tank's armor and machine guns wouldn't do much to tanks but make a racket.

Desperate, they radioed IDF regional headquarters for help. But the IDF's resources were stretched thin, and a distance away. Other than one mortar firing shells from Kibbutz Dan, and a couple other mortars from surrounding villages, they were on their own.

Then the Syrian tanks began moving toward the thirteen. Crossing the road, they entered the field. Amiram and the others crouched low in their positions, which were in clear sight of the tanks because the surrounding wheat field had been cut down a few days earlier. The defenders could hear the tank treads crushing the dry stalks littering the ground as they moved forward. Now the tanks were just a couple hundred yards short of overrunning the bunkers. In seconds it would be over.

And then, a modern miracle happened. Like when Moses had led the Jews through a parted Red Sea before it closed up on the Egyptians in pursuit, heat generated by all the shooting and explosions ignited the straw-like residue littering the wheat field. Fire bloomed within the tanks' treads. The Syrians panicked. Three of the tanks were destroyed, engulfed in flames. One stopped functioning as it retreated along the same road we now stood on. Another got as far as the Banias, a few miles away. It's still there today. The last tank, also disabled by the fire, has found a new home and a new purpose. It now resides outside of the museum at Kibbutz Dan on soft grass where children play. And, in case you are wondering, all thirteen defenders survived.

Amiram's story taught me a lesson. There is no substitute for walking the ground and seeing history through the eyes of those who shaped it. I have studied the Six-Day War for decades and have probably read almost everything that has been written about it in English. In addition, I wrote a two-volume study about an eleven-year period in Israel that includes the Six-Day War. What Amiram and Yossi experienced is described at best in two sentences in all of the histories. It usually goes something like this, "The Syrians made a desultory probing attack in the direction of Kibbutz Dan that the IDF beat back." Nowhere is there mention of the desperation the few defenders of Kibbutz Dan felt to save their homes and families and how isolated, devoid of any assistance, they were.

Standing on that road with the former Syrian-fortified hill in front of me, the wheat field and the bunker to my right, the woods to my left that the six tanks had burst through—it was an experience I will never forget. On numerous occasions, I have driven on the highway past the field, past the old Ottoman Custom House, past the intersection of roads that is now called "Tank Junction," and past the ghosts of a desperate history I will now never forget.

* * *

Naturally, I was curious about Amiram after listening to his story

Amiram came to the kibbutz in 1954 but he had grown up as a child in the new city of Jerusalem. Food and water were scarce after the 1948 War of Independence broke out. Jewish leadership arranged for the city's children to leave during a ceasefire. Amiram was on the first bus out. It left via a bumpy, poor excuse for a road, which had been carved through rough hills out of desperation during the fighting to avoid an Arab-held chokepoint along the main road. He was ten years old and had three Liras in his pocket, a relatively paltry sum.

His parents' plan, when the bus deposited Amiram in Tel Aviv, was for him to hail a taxi that would take him to the home of family members nearby. Next, they told Amiram, he was to make his way to Tiberias where other family members lived. It was dark when Amiram exited the bus, he was in an unfamiliar place, and there were no familiar faces. When a taxi drove up, Amiram announced where he wanted to go. The driver asked how much money he had. When Amiram showed him the driver said, "It's not enough." But then said in a kinder tone, "You are from the children from Jerusalem." That knowledge tugged at the driver's heart. He said give me what you have and then took Amiram where he wanted to go.

Like Yossi, Amiram fascinated me. I would have been happy to converse with him for hours. Unfortunately, he had another appointment.

But just before leaving, Amiram spoke of the pre-1967 days when Kibbutz Dan was little more than an outpost, its children always under the eye of malevolent Syrian soldiers planted in the hills above. He compared that experience to his daughter's. She now lives with her children in a nearby kibbutz, built on territory held by the Syrians before 1967. When he visits his daughter, Amiram says to her: "You think you are in Israel? You're not in Israel. [When we are here] we are traveling abroad."

Now there is no marker on the road to delineate when you leave the boundary of old Israel. To the uninformed observer, one blade of grass is no different from the next, one rock undifferentiated from the others. But Yossi emphasized to me that the difference between those blades of grass and rocks was once real. Sixty years ago, death lurked from across a marked divide, which today is a seamless transition. Yossi's memories will never leave him. But memories alone do not inform the present. I was sure the people in the cars whizzing by had no idea of the stoic courage of those thirteen young and old men, pressed into the walls of those three bunkers, with their loved ones sheltered behind them, outnumbered and desperate—and heroic.

* * *

Fortunately, Samuel had more time for me. After Amiram left, we eased into my car and headed to a parking lot outside Beit Ussishkin, Kibbutz Dan's museum highlighting Tel Dan and the natural environment in the area. As we walked through the parking lot a several foot-high, tan-colored half-circle anchored in the ground caught my attention. This marks the beginning of the Israel Trail. More than 600 miles long, it extends from Kibbutz Dan to the southernmost point of Israel at Eilat. Similar in concept to the Appalachian Trail, it traverses mountains, cities, seascapes, and desert.

Leaving the parking lot, we walked through the open raised walkway that divides the museum in two and then exited into a shaded grass yard. There, sitting near the vegetation that lines the Dan River, sat the sixth tank that had been stopped by flames in the wheat field.

By then, the nervousness I had felt upon entering the kibbutz had been replaced by awe for the two men Samuel had introduced me to. But I was sure Samuel had a story too, perhaps less captivating than Yossi's or Amiram's, but I was certain that it would be interesting and, like almost every Israeli I met in the north, indicative of his deep and abiding love for the land. So, with confidence and eagerness to learn more, I walked with Samuel back to my car, got in, and turned the key in the ignition.

The car made a sound like it was starting, but never quite got there. With a sinking feeling, once again I realized that I had messed up the sequence required of anyone driving an Israeli rental car. With patience and a smile, Samuel reminded me that before turning the ignition, I had to punch in, to the left of the steering wheel, the secret code provided by the rental company. Given his background as an engineer who kept logistics convoys moving on the Golan during the Yom Kippur War and his specialty for clearing mines in the military, for Samuel to explain to me how to operate my car was not a heavy lift! I followed his instructions, and the engine roared to life. My feeling of stupidity lessened greatly when he invited me back to his living room for more conversation.

Of course, upon entering his house, we both had the same need, which he expressed eloquently, "At our age you don't go to the bathroom when you need it, you go to the bathroom when you can." While I am half a decade younger than Samuel, and innately rejected being grouped together by age, I agreed with his logic.

Samuel and his wife, Haviva, came to Kibbutz Dan just days after the Six-Day War had ended. They were just eighteen. Upon arrival, Samuel saw the destruction that Syrian artillery shells had brought to the kibbutz and its fields. He then went up to the Golan Heights to see what was going on there. Samuel was very curious, "For many years this place was on the other side of the border, suddenly it was not on the other side of the border." On the Golan, he made his way through the litter of war; Syrian bodies were strewn about.

Haviva, still attractive and engaging after more than forty years of kibbutz life, dominated our discussion soon after I sat down. Hours earlier, when I first came to her home, Haviva had told me that she had immigrated to Israel with her parents from Communist Romania at the age of ten. So sudden was her departure that she didn't know she was leaving until she got onto the plane. They left because life was hard for Jews in Romania in the wake of World War II.

Haviva first met Samuel when she was about fifteen. They had both joined the same Zionist youth movement. Rather sheepishly, Haviva said that Samuel had fallen in love with her immediately. Samuel remembered it the other way around.

According to Samuel, the Zionist youth movements of the mid-sixties "[were] very, very significant." He said, "Almost everybody had a part of [their] history . . . in the youth movement. In those days, city kids too. There were four or five youth movements and [that is] a very significant part of [Israel's] history." And then, perhaps, Haviva made me think Samuel's side of the love story was the more accurate one. She showed me an old picture of her husband and said softly, "It was impossible not to fall in love."

In their youth movement, it was typical that members would consider where they would live after finishing school. Both knew by the eleventh grade that Kibbutz Dan wanted them to live there, and when they neared eighteen, the movement had given both a pin to signify their worth. Nevertheless, going to Kibbutz Dan was not a done deal. Many graduates of the youth programs were determined to further the Zionist dream. Haviva remembered having a discussion with Samuel as to whether Kibbutz Dan was located far enough on the edge, despite being on the border with Syria and Lebanon (the exact location of those borders then and now is contested to this day), to fulfill their sense of mission. Then further complicating their decision, the border with Syria went away after the Six-Day War. Nevertheless, they decided to move to Kibbutz Dan together.

"We came with nothing," said Samuel, yet the kibbutz accepted them, not as newcomers, but as if they had been born there. What they had "was ours." Samuel told me a story that demonstrated the communal norm of those days. The kibbutz had issued him clothing when he arrived. When dirty, the routine was to go to the kibbutz laundry and exchange the clothing for clean attire. A few days after arriving, he found a nice jacket on his shelf. Thinking there had been a mistake, Samuel said to the laundry attendant, "This is not mine." The attendant responded that he had earned it.

"How could I [have earned] it?" Samuel had asked.

Samuel answered his own question: "Everyone got a coat after three days."

Haviva then interjected with a comment that even further illustrated kibbutz life, though she admitted it was "a little embarrassing" for her. The norm in those days was for couples to live together. They were no different. Samuel and Haviva lived in a very small home with one room, a bathroom, and a kitchen—together without any commitments other than their feelings for each other. In love, they had no thought of marriage. At least none until the kibbutz intervened.

One day, while walking around the kibbutz, the kibbutz secretary stopped Haviva and said, "Haviva, during this summer three couples are going to get married . . . . Do you and Samuel want to get married too?"

Haviva responded, "[I] will think about it." Later, she told Samuel of her conversation with the director and asked, "What do you think?"

They both had forgotten this story for some time, only remembering it after their kids asked which one of them had proposed. They could not recall at first. Samuel's explanation for that lapse of memory was "there was no ceremony, no fireworks, no one knee." When they finally did remember the origin of their nuptials, the story became a family legend of which Samuel shortcuts, "The proposal came from the kibbutz secretary."

Neither Samuel nor Haviva thought the circumstances of their engagement odd. Tradition on the kibbutz in those days was that a couple would not marry by themselves. Instead, they would have to wait for a few other couples to make the same decision. Then the kibbutz would put on a group wedding. Collective celebrations saved the kibbutz money. Later during my visit, Haviva rummaged through a storage area in another room before bringing me a picture of the four brides. Haviva was the black-haired radiant one on the far right. A shy happiness marking her facial expressions.

I left the Gardi's just after a thunderstorm had dropped hailstones on the area. While walking together on my way out, Samuel and I spoke of family. As my wife and I do, the Gardis also have children. One son lives 200 yards away in another part of the kibbutz. A second son lives in the center of the country where he holds a regular job and writes. Their son's family was coming for dinner later, as they do every week. A few months later, when I returned for a second visit, Samuel took me to meet one of his grandchildren at her school, also within the kibbutz. His life is a simple one now, riding his bicycle many miles on a frequent basis, dabbling in kibbutz business and politics, and being with family. Especially his grandchildren. If twenty-four hours goes by without seeing them, he "has problems." Not so different from me. We bonded, one grandfather to another.

Chapter Eight

Merom Golan

Driving up the Golan Heights in late February is a totally different experience than in summer or fall when it's dry and haunting. But in February I was shocked and pleased to see green, not brown, and towering above everything was the pure white of beautiful, snow-bound Mount Hermon, which contrasted well with the plateau below.

For me, the Golan Heights has always been a source of awe. I well remember reading as a teenager about soldiers who performed the impossible, breaking through minefields and withstanding withering fire as they scaled the heights to take Syrian positions in 1967. As an adult, I have walked those battlefields and rode in a jeep that seemed on the verge of falling backwards as we climbed the same impossibly steep route that those young soldiers had taken. Also, with book and maps in hand, accompanied by a former IDF commander on the Golan, I walked step by step over hallowed ground as I sought to understand what Israel's young defenders faced in October 1973 when attacked by a much larger Syrian force. And, of course, I remember working while a teenager in the early morning light, picking fruit, viewing the Golan a short distance away, then at night seeing on the crests of those same heights, flashes of light emanating from likely Syrian and IDF artillery fire. But perhaps most meaningful to me is the relief I felt every time I gazed from one of the multiple vantage points offered by the Golan's ridges upon the many Jewish communities in the Hula Valley. Every building of every community along what was once the border is in plain view. So are their streets and schools and playgrounds. All within easy range of the Syrian artillery that used to routinely fire on them. All now safely shielded by the rocky slopes, plateaus, and volcanic cones of the Golan—now controlled by Israel.

* * *

My destination in February 2019 was Kibbutz Merom Golan—my sixth trip there in five years. I had visited the kibbutz four months earlier with the goal of meeting Yehuda Harel. I didn't expect then that I would also be enthralled by the simple wisdom of Omer Weiner, the Golan's first cowboy. This time, while I very much wanted to speak with Yehuda again, I was equally looking forward to again bask in Omer's humor and zest for life.

Yehuda appeared old and frail at our first meeting in October 2018; nothing like the image I had conjured of him. We had chatted in the reception area of Merom Golan's hotel. This time, we met in the sitting room of Omer Weiner's home. On both occasions, despite his physical appearance, Yehuda's words were measured and meaningful. His every sentence captured my attention.

Yehuda's story is the story of Kibbutz Merom Golan, now located in the shadow of Mount Bental, within a couple miles of the current Syrian border on the Golan. But it's also more than that. It is the story of a resurgence of pioneering spirit in 1967 that brings to mind the settlers of Rosh Pina, Degania, and Tel Hai. Simply put, it was the Zionist enterprise reborn. They transformed the Golan from captured territory to settled land. Without Yehuda, Omer, and a few intrepid others—all of whom seemed to live by the immortal words in a children's book, "If you think you can, you can"—it is doubtful that Israel would still control the Golan. Because of them, the Hula Valley was not at risk in 2011 when civil war broke out in Syria, during which Al Qaeda and ISIS affiliated forces held Syrian territory along Israel's present border on the Golan. Because of them, when Hezbollah with Iran's help tries to turn the Israeli-Syrian border into a confrontation zone similar to Israel's border with Lebanon, the Hula Valley does not face the perils that Kibbutz Hanita, Kfar Giladi, Kibbutz Dan, Kiryat Shmona, Metula, and so many other communities now face on a daily basis.

But the Merom Golan of today is not the Merom Golan of 1967. That Merom Golan had been located just steps from the Syrian border. It stretched into Kuneitra, taken by Israel in the Six-Day War and returned to the Syrians after the Yom Kippur War. Now only ruins remain to mark Merom Golan's first location. But those ruins have a hallowed place in the story of Israel and its settlement of the Golan Heights. Then, there was just a rocky plateau in the western shadow of Mount Bental, a couple miles from the fence line. Now within that shadow, sits the new Merom Golan, a well-developed kibbutz with industry, agriculture, a restaurant, and a hotel.

Merom Golan owes its existence to Israel's victory in the Six-Day War in 1967. Rather than being overrun by the Arab armies surrounding it, Israel emerged from the war in possession of new lands, which for the first time would leave the tiny nation with defensible borders or, as many in government thought, bargaining chips for peace. In the south, the vast, desolate Sinai was now occupied by the IDF. In the center, the Old City of Jerusalem and the West Bank—sites of religious, historical, and military significance—were Israel's. And in the north, the victorious Israeli army now held the Golan Heights.

The fighting stopped on June 10, and with success came a decision. What would Israel do now? Would it trade land for peace?

Would the world force Israel to withdraw its forces in return for empty promises? In 1956, after Israel destroyed the Egyptian army and occupied the Sinai, the United States pressured Israel to pull back in return for supposed United Nations peacekeepers. That did not work out so well. When Egypt's president ordered them to leave in May 1967 and then sent his army to replace them in the desert sands adjacent to Israel, war broke out as a result just three weeks later.

These questions lingered four days after the war ended as two middle-aged men and an enterprising younger man—all members of kibbutzim in the Hula valley along Israel's northern borders—took the first steps toward placing a settlement on the Golan Heights. They were determined to prevent the Israeli government from returning the Golan to Syria. Yehuda Harel, who would win the Israel Prize fifty years later, would soon join them.

"I have a problem with a German doctor. Do you know him? Dr. Alzheimer!" said Yehuda Harel. But his self-deprecating humor could not have been further from the truth. Concisely, and with precision, Yehuda's deep voice demanded attention as he told me his story.

Yehuda's parents arrived in Palestine from Europe in 1931. But it was only for a short time. Soon, as dutiful members of the growing Jewish youth movements coalescing in Europe and Palestine, they were back in Europe, this time in Germany. Their mission? To help get Jews out of Germany. While I am sure they were at least somewhat successful, they did experience one temporary setback. Instead of decreasing the number of Jews in Germany they increased the amount by one. Yehuda, their son, was born in Berlin in 1934. Two years later, Yehuda's family returned to Palestine.

When Yehuda was twenty-one, the youth movement he belonged to sent him to live at Kibbutz Manara, along the Lebanese border. By 1967, Harel had married, had the first three of his five children that would eventually give him sixteen grandchildren, and lived full time at Manara, where he worked in the kibbutz's fish pools. Three months earlier, he had been the secretary (leader) of the kibbutz. His life was integrated with Manara. But his intellectual outlook, heavily influenced by Yitzhak Tobenkin, ranged far beyond.

Tobenkin was a philosopher, who though somewhat of an outlier, wielded much influence on his devotees. From age sixteen in 1906, Tobenkin advocated for the establishment of more Jewish settlements. He thought Zionism had no chance without an official state, but first Jews needed to create settlements that hewed close to socialistic philosophies. Those settlements would mark the borders, and then there could be a state. Tobenkin despised what he viewed as western imperialism unilaterally marking the borders. To counteract that, he strongly supported the concept of Jewish national liberation, mainly with Jews living in "communes, as part of a worldwide alliance of communist peoples." But his primary priority was clear: worry about statehood later and instead, build from the bottom up, one settlement at a time. Although Tobenkin never became a political leader his philosophy—settle first—proved prescient when Israel became a state in 1948. Where there were outlying Jewish communities—Hanita, Dan, Kfar Giladi, Metula, and others—Israel's borders encompassed them.

Already an old man by April 1967, Tobenkin was friendly with his doctor, who happened to be Yehuda's father. Perhaps that is why Yehuda describes himself as Tobenkin's student. In April, two months before the Six-Day War, Syrian guns situated on the Golan Heights brutally shelled Kibbutz Gadot. Yehuda said, "Within twenty minutes, the Syrians fired 400 shells in a highly precise operation. The kibbutz was destroyed almost down to its foundations." At a subsequent meeting with members of the kibbutz movement, Tobenkin said of the Golan, "This is a fascist Height.... We have to have settlements on this Height." Yehuda told me, "Everybody thought he was crazy."

But he wasn't so crazy. Two months later, the Six-Day War created an opportunity to fulfill Tobenkin's pronouncement. Eytan Sat took up the challenge.

Eyton Sat was seven years old when his father died. His mother then sent him to a children's home in a kibbutz in the Jezreel Valley, south of the Galilee. He later moved to Kibbutz Gadot. When the Six-Day War broke out in June 1967, Sat was thirty-one. But he had already proved his worth. The members of Gadot had elected him executive director of the kibbutz.

With the Golan Heights now in Israel's hands, the IDF released Sat from active duty days after the fighting ended so he could help restore Kibbutz Gadot. As leader of the kibbutz, his services were needed more at home than in the army. Especially, because significant damage remained from the April shelling. In addition, more shells had struck the kibbutz during the war, but with less effect. But Sat's focus was twofold. He wanted to restore Kibbutz Gadot, and he also wanted to ensure that the Syrians would never again be able to destroy it.

Yehuda explained, "Everyone figured that Israel would give [the Golan Heights] back within a couple of months, people called it the 'Syrian Heights'. Not Sat, he telephoned to all communities in the Upper Galilee and asked them to send members to a meeting in Gadot." About a week later—two weeks after the war had ended—twenty-five people came. They sat in the former clubhouse of the kibbutz, its walls still showing damage from Syrian artillery shells, its electricity out. The destruction was a vivid reminder of what residents along the former border with Syria had endured. Yehuda was there too. Sat didn't ask for their help to fix the kibbutz. Instead, he spoke to his vision of creating a new settlement on the Golan to ensure the Syrians would not return. If there was a civilian presence on the Golan, "no one could just order a withdrawal. There would have to be a debate in the Knesset," Sat thought. "This [was] the beginning," said Yehuda. "The man who started this was Eitan Sat."

But convincing those in attendance was difficult. Most opposed Sat's idea. "It seemed crazy," said Yehuda, or even "delusional." Yehuda explained that many Israelis thought Hebron and Jerusalem "historically part of Israel . . . . But nobody [said] the Golan [is] part of Israel. I was in Manara, from the window I saw the Golan Heights. I never thought it is part of Israel."

But Yehuda had no qualms. "Count me in," he said at the meeting's conclusion. As a disciple of Tobenkin, he could say no less.

Before Yehuda finished his story, I asked Omer Weiner what he had originally thought of the idea. Omer had been patiently listening to Yehuda and I wanted to include him in the conversation. I knew that Omer had not been at that original meeting, coming to the region later, but he was a founder of Merom Golan. And he was a cowboy, which made him a bit of a philosopher in his own way. Omer answered in his characteristic straightforward manner: "I knew that all the time we have fights with the Syrians here. And, it can't be the Syrians sitting on our neck all the time."

Yehuda then continued describing that initial meeting.

"Most people didn't think it was a serious thought. [But] Sat was clever, not asking for agreement, but just looking to explore the idea." However, Yehuda was very much enthused with Sat's plan for two reasons. "First of all, I was a pupil of Tobenkin. And Tobenkin was for settlements in all the areas . . . . Second, I was a very good friend of Eitan Sat, because I was with him in the youth movement in Tel Aviv . . . . After a week, I wrote him a letter, how come that we have the idea to make a settlement and why there is not already a settlement up there?"

Harel smiled. A year ago, when he got together with Sat, Sat had showed him that letter.

Meanwhile, Harel said that two others were involved. One was Raphael Ben-Yehuda, a member of Ne'ot Mordechai, near the northern tip of the Galilee valley. A few days after the initial meeting,

Sat held another meeting at Ne'ot Mordechai. This time, 200 attended, and Sat had the chance to meet Ben-Yehuda, who already had been considering the same idea.

At forty-six-year, Ben-Yehuda was an interesting character. Born in Austria, he left Vienna in 1938, while a teenager, a month after the Anschluss when German stormtroopers marched into Austria without opposition and took it over. Ben-Yehuda arrived in Palestine by boat but not at a dock. He had to swim ashore with other immigrants. During the war years he worked in communes of workers that had no land of their own, became a disciple of Tobenkin, and subsequently helped found Ne'ot Mordechai along the Jordan River.

Ben-Yehuda said to Sat, "I will help you."

Ben-Yehuda had another sympathetic friend. An important one. He was General Dan Laner, the second highest-ranking officer of the IDF's northern command, charged by the IDF with conquering and then occupying the Golan. Not surprisingly, Laner was also a Tobenkin disciple. Laner promised his active support.

Sat, Ben-Yehuda, and Laner were right to worry. Already, Israel's Cabinet had secretly adopted a policy regarding Egypt and Syria. In return for a full peace treaty, Israel would withdraw to the international border consistent with changes required by Israel's security needs and with Syria's agreement that the "Syrian Heights" be demilitarized. A withdrawal to the international border meant that the Golan (Syrian) Heights would revert to Syrian control. It was too soon to then know, but Syria had no intention of agreeing to a peace treaty with Israel.

Laner spoke with his boss, General Elazar, who was the highest-ranking officer in the IDF's northern command, about building a settlement on the Golan. Elazar would later become the chief of staff of the IDF. Harel recruited Yigal Allon, then Minister of Labor, whose roots were with Kibbutz Ginosar in the north. All knew they couldn't be complacent or wait for Israel's political leadership to decide—not without dooming the project to failure before it would start. Yet moving quickly would require a degree of subterfuge. So they focused on finding a legitimate reason for Jews to work on the Heights. Cows offered the perfect opportunity!

Omer interjected, "Many of the Arabs who ran away [after the war] left thousands of cows in the Golan. The Minister of Agriculture had [tasked] Bedouin from Tuba to collect all the cows and sell them. So, they had to be [quarantined] for a couple of months first to make sure [they were] not ill."

Yehuda then clarified like old friends do: "There was a contract between the army and the Minister of Agriculture to put them in a quarantine to see if they are healthy, and then to sell them to the Ministry of Agriculture and the money [would go] to the army."

Omer added that despite the agreement there was an ongoing argument whether to sell the cows or leave them for people who might move to the Golan. "In the end they left about 1,500 cows." The cows provided the perfect excuse. Jews would be permitted to manage the cows on the Golan while they were in quarantine.

While Laner, Ben-Yehuda, and Sat pursued their parts of the dream, Yehuda remained in contact with Sat. He also worked the political angle. Soon, Yehuda's activities bore fruit. Yigal Allon prevailed on the Cabinet to permit the Settlement Department (an independent organization that contracted with the government to assist settlements but was for all practical purposes part of the government) to establish a couple of temporary work camps on the Golan to house laborers. Those laborers would primarily herd the abandoned cattle and perform some additional agricultural work, including harvesting ripening crops in the fields and planting seeds for new crops. Allon also agreed to provide some funding through the Labor Department by characterizing the effort as "work projects for the unemployed." Though not a permanent community, a temporary work camp would be a beginning.

But where would the temporary camp be and who would live and work there?

Sat and Ben-Yehuda went looking for a good location. They left Kibbutz Gadot; crossed the nearby bridge over the Jordan, which had previously been the border with Syria; and then they drove east up the series of steep switchbacks leading them to the plateau on top of the Heights. Along the way, Sat observed that the buildings of Gadot "could be seen as clearly [as] if they were in the palm of your hand." They were also within easy range of the Syrian gunners that had peered down at Gadot before the war. During their drive they saw cattle, left by Arab villagers that had fled, grazing amid the minefields the Syrians had dug. Close to the former Arab village of Nafekh was a deserted Syrian army base, but the land there was poor for farming. Further east, near another deserted Syrian army base, the land was better, but the buildings dilapidated. With no better choice available, they agreed that they could make do with the base near Naffekh. They named their encampment Aleika, same as what the Syrians had named the spot.

Ben-Yehuda then went about gathering the material and manpower to fulfill his dream. He needed food, mattresses, guns, and tools, among other items. He also needed permits from the army, money to buy the items required, and the people to use them. All required cooperation from the governing entity in the region, the Upper Galilee Council. The Council promised a small sum and the use of a jeep. Needing more, Ben-Yehuda and Sat met with Yehiel Admoni, second in command of the Settlement Department. While sitting in a restaurant in Rosh Pina in the middle of July, they pressed their case. Admoni realized that "they weren't talking about gathering cattle . . . but settling in the Golan." Given his sympathy for their cause, he didn't mind. The Settlement Department quietly gave them more supplies and a van.

To solve the manpower issue, Sat went from kibbutz to kibbutz in the north looking for volunteers. Everywhere he went, Sat met with the general secretary of each kibbutz first. Sat knew that he would need the general secretary's permission before recruiting that kibbutz's members. At first, Sat felt he had failed. Only eighteen responded positively. He did not know then that many throughout Israel would answer his call. One of them was Omer Weiner.

Frustrating for Sat, he was unable to move to the new community. As the elected leader of Kibbutz Gadot, Sat had responsibilities. In addition, his wife had refused to move to the new settlement. Who could blame her? Her childhood had been rootless. Yehuda told me she had no memory of her parents, nor knowledge of when she was born. Somewhere, along the route to Auschwitz, her parents threw her out of the cattle car taking them to their deaths. She was just a baby, about one year old. Peasants found the child and brought her up as their own. Three years later, somehow—and somehow is how to describe many Holocaust survival stories—soldiers of the British created Jewish Brigade had learned of her Jewish background. Those soldiers were part of a special unit created to look for orphaned Jewish children. Not surprisingly, her foster parents did not want to give her up. But perhaps their attachment was not so strong. They let her go in return for a payment from the Jewish Agency. The Jewish Agency brought her to Israel.

I would have tried to interview Sat's wife, but she passed away three weeks before my meeting with Yehuda. I did not have the heart to ask Yehuda to arrange a meeting for me with Sat.

Yehuda also wanted to move to the new "temporary" settlement on the Golan, but he too had a problem. To do so, "I had to have the permission of my kibbutz, Manara. And they were absolutely against it because Manara was in bad shape . . . and I had already three children. They were absolutely against it! I put it to a meeting. In those times every Saturday there was a meeting of the kibbutz."

He asked the kibbutz to let him have one year on the Golan. "It took me about two or three months arguing with Manara, three or four meetings, and every time they were against it. And I have to tell you in those times I could not [go] against Manara because I was a member and I had to obey the General Meeting."

But then, Yehuda conveyed to me with a seriousness that hinted at his determination, he lost his patience. "I told the Secretary of Manara, the sister of Yitzhak Rabin—she was a very strong woman—if you decide not to give me permission . . . I will go without permission."

At this point, Omer groaned. He understood full well how unusual and significant, especially in those days, was Yehuda's defiance.

Yehuda continued, "It was very difficult for me. And then in the [subsequent General Meeting] she said she was for letting me go." But Yehuda knew she had only changed her public view because of their private conversation. Rabin's sister did not want a public break with such an important member of the kibbutz. It was October of 1967. Rabin's sister thought Yehuda would only be gone for a year. He never returned. Soon, his family joined him.

Meanwhile, I sat riveted and stunned.

Over and over as I traveled the north, I listened to stories like Yehuda's that reminded me what a small world Israel is. The coincidence of Rabin's sister playing a role in this story struck me. At that time, Rabin was the top officer in the IDF. Several years later he would be involved with negotiations with the Syrians after the Yom Kippur War. Two decades later, before he was assassinated, he would decide to return the Golan to the Syrians if they fulfilled certain conditions, which they never did. The irony of his sister unwillingly opening the floodgate to settling the Golan by blessing Yehuda's departure astonished me. I'm sure her brother Yitzhak knew the story, but one wonders.

* * *

The first settler arrived at Aleika on July 16, five weeks after the war ended. Soon others floated in. They slept in a eucalyptus grove adjacent to a stream because the buildings, despite their good condition, were bleak cement blocks that needed to be cleaned and prepared for permanent use. A persistent bedbug problem bedeviled them. Food was scarce, so the IDF allowed them to eat canned Chinese meat found in the storerooms. A generator did not arrive until a week had passed, and a radio link to Kibbutz Gadot took another week to establish. Meanwhile, the army provided guards for security.

The settlers also needed official permission from the army to remain there. That meant a permit. Sat drove to Kuneitra, the abandoned Syrian capital of the Golan and location of the Syrian military headquarters for the entire Golan before the war. The IDF had established its Military Governor for the region there. Sat remembered the air filled with flies, attracted by an enticing food source—Syrian corpses that still littered the area. Sat carried a note from the deputy minister of agriculture to the military governor of Kuneitra. A heavy-set fellow named Akiva Feinstein was the military governor.

Feinstein had a storied past. During World War II, he spied for Britain in Syria and Lebanon while simultaneously smuggling weapons into Israel for the underground Jewish army, the Palmach. Later, Feinstein helped bring illegal Jewish immigrants into Palestine. In 1946, the Lebanese captured him and then transferred him to the Syrians. The Syrians tortured Feinstein but failed to break him. He never gave up the names of others involved in the operation. Four years later, the Syrians released Feinstein. Nevertheless, Sat had little respect for his appearance and apparent disinterest. Seemingly bored, while swatting flies from his face, Feinstein signed a document approving the new settlers' presence at Aleika.

Immediately, the settlers got to work gathering and inoculating cattle they had rounded up and building corrals for them. Some tended sheep found in the fields and harvested the few acres of barley and chickpeas they found. Their governmental salaries, paid for their efforts, went into a shared pool. Despite the temporary nature of the approvals that allowed the settlers to be there, it was evident that a permanent kibbutz was forming on the newly occupied lands of the Golan. Even Prime Minister Eshkol, with tongue in cheek, was in on the game. When the Cabinet discussed the Aleika site, he said, "It's clear that you neither destroy orchards nor start permanent settlements. But if orchards exist, you have to maintain them. Certainly, we can permit workers to use buildings there, and then we'll see."

When Yehuda arrived at Aleika in early September, after receiving Manara's blessing, he saw a notice on the bulletin board from the work director asking everyone to inform him when they were taking vacation. This upset Yehuda. He believed in socialism to his core. In fact, in those days, he admitted further: "You could say I was a communist." But he also had organizational capability and experience as a prior general secretary at Manara. Since he was older, Ben-Yehuda, had been in charge but was not living there on a permanent basis. He recognized Yehuda's worth and immediately made him secretary of the budding community. His responsibility was to create order out of the chaos.

And chaos there was. Men would shoot wild dogs straying too close to the dining hall with AK-47s. Others thought nothing of slaughtering a sheep to supplement the canned food. Women performed the cooking duties. Men herded cattle from horseback with no real idea of what they were doing. It was a wild and disorganized bunch, yet joyful. The nouveau cowboys—clad in khaki shorts, their hair bleached by the sun—were having a grand time herding the cattle. Black and white photos from those days depict images reminiscent of the pioneering kibbutzniks decades before. After working hours, the spring-fed swimming pool once used by the Syrian officers became a meeting place where the young men and women would gather and sing. The night sky provided enough lighting. Yehuda was infused with passion for what they were trying to accomplish. He later said:

> *We thought we'd missed the War of Independence . . . . The kibbutz movement was no longer what we'd thought it was . . . . We dreamed . . . that a new era was beginning, that we would be the first settlement of hundreds, that thousands of young [Jews] would immigrate from abroad, that everything we'd read in books about the kibbutz movement and the War of Independence, we were doing."*

When I read that quote in Gershom Goren's fascinating book, *The Accidental Empire*, I immediately understood. How many of us have longed to perform something important? How many of us have thought the opportunity to do so was no more and that we would have been happier living in a bygone age where great things could be accomplished? At that moment, Yehuda felt that he now had that opportunity. It was there for the taking and he took it.

Omer Weiner arrived at Aleika before Yehuda did. Omer is a gregarious man. It takes only a few seconds for you to like him. After a few more moments in his company, you can't help but like him a lot. He laughs from the gut, speaks from the gut, and gives you his unvarnished gut feelings. There is nothing calculated about Omer. He is what he is—a cowboy in the absolute best sense of the word. When we drove through the fields of Merom Golan in 2018, Omer gave me a book of pictures that he had taken with the camera that he always seems to be carrying. The pictures in the book are accompanied by poems Omer wrote while wandering the fields on horseback, by foot, and in his 4-wheel drive vehicle that he is proud of. The book is entitled appropriately enough, "The Songs of a Getting Old Cowboy." Omer told me, "They are short poems, [but] I don't like to call it poems." He doesn't see himself as a poet but as a "cowboy that likes to write songs." A year later, Sarit Zehavi, who you will meet in a later chapter, said of those poems, "They are amazing!"

Omer is sensitive, knowledgeable, and capable. When I learned that I would meet with a cowboy, I never imagined I would meet a man I would never forget. He was the perfect counterpoint to Yehuda, whose every word had a precise purpose. Omer's words exploded from him in joyful bursts. "When you have something on your heart or your mind," Omer said, "you can take it out with little songs."

Omer had fought in Jordan during the Six-Day War. He grew up opposite the West Bank Arab town of Tulkarem. Omer was able to see his home from the Jordanian side, when his unit had moved into Jordan. He told me, to see where he lived from that vantage point was like "to go to the moon. You knew it was a place you couldn't ever cross [to]." But there he was. Those words resonated and reminded me of Sat looking down from the Golan Height's ridges on his home at Kibbutz Gadot. What a feeling of jubilation, shock, or some other adjective that poorly describes the sober euphoria of the moment when you see your home from the eyes of your tormentors on ground that you now hold. That emotion always come to mind when I look down on the Hula Valley from the Golan.

After the war ended, Omer tried going to what he called field school in Sde Boker in the Negev, where he said you learn about nature and stuff. Omer thought it was what he wanted and planned to stay there a year. But then he changed his mind: "After two weeks [I] learned [it] was not for me. I became a cowboy instead."

Omer then heard of the encampment at Aleika and decided to give it a try. For a nature lover, living there seemed like an opportunity to love your job. Also, Omer is a socialist. So the lifestyle appealed to him. Although I never asked him, I wouldn't be surprised to learn that Omer was also attracted to the craziness of the enterprise. And even if he weren't, I would bet a considerable sum that Omer was one of the guys creating havoc.

On Omer's first working day at Aleika, the work director assigned him to the cows. He knew nothing about cattle. That said, those that got there before him were equally clueless. Omer explained that before Aleika, the biggest herd in Israel was 100, perhaps 150 cows. They had to deal with up to 2,000. "So, we had to learn it by ourselves. There was nobody to teach us."

But Omer learned a valuable lesson that day. A lesson that wasn't really about cows.

The work director had ordered Omer to make sure that none of the cattle wandered off and that the herd did not move too far away. Omer said that when some get too far in front, the trick is to get ahead of them, make them turn, and then when they start to go, get to the other side to push them back where you want them. That sounded reasonably easy to me. But then I remembered that the Syrians had littered the Golan with mines. I asked whether they caused a problem.

Omer responded that he had had the same concern and asked about the mines before starting to herd the cattle. Herders with a little more experience told him it wasn't a problem there. Omer thought, "Ok. If there [are] no mines there are no mines." And along with a dog that trotted alongside him, he began herding the cows.

As expected, eventually some of the cows got too far ahead of him. Omer moved to cut them off when "I come to a wire," Omer emphatically emphasized, "that looks to me that is smelling bad. It looks to me like a wire for the mines. There is one wire or two, then about 50 meters or 60 meters there is another. It's not looking good.

But the cows were on the other side about fifteen or twenty [meters further away]."

Omer continued:

> *I saw this area that looks like minefield, but the cows were in the other side in total safety. If I [do] nothing, what will I tell them, that I lost part of the herd because I was afraid? They told me there were no mines. So I crossed the fence and I went to the other side and saw it's alright So I pushed the cows back and they start to go like they told me and I let them cross it again and then I knew that it is nothing and it's alright.*

Omer, feeling more comfortable with the situation, headed toward what looked like an archaeological prize that he had spotted—a stone knife. To get closer to the object that had piqued his interest, Omer had to move to the other side of the herd. Then:

> *When I was about 100 meters [away from the cattle] I heard BOOM and in the back one of the cows [became steaks]. And after this one, another one, and another one, about eleven cows flying in the air. And the herd [scattering]. You know, in two minutes I was by myself in the fields. No cows in the area. I thought about the cows but the people who heard the booms thought about me and they came just to see if I was still alive.*

Omer acknowledges his good fortune. Twelve cows died that day, 300 were temporarily lost when they ran off, and a cowboy was born.

The mines were for tanks, not people. A person's weight would not set them off; a cow's would. Since Omer was new, the work director had not assigned him one of their horses. If he had, Omer might have tromped all over that field and ended up like those twelve other cows. He then understood "that my luck was that I didn't have a horse and I did . . . what they told me. Exactly to work like they told me. Every guy that came to work with the cows that started to make problems, I told them it was dangerous work, for me it saved my life just to do what they told me." Those mines made holes three or four meters long and more than a meter deep. "A half a ton rocks flying in the air. It was very lucky to get out from it."

The cowboys of Aleika had other problems. They struggled to move the cows from pasture to corrals. And even when they succeeded, sometimes they would return to find them gone. Tracks in the dirt would invariably uncover the culprits. As Omer once said to a reporter with the New York Times, Syrians would come across the border that was not nearly as well defended as it is now to "steal the cows back."

About a year after the Six-Day War ended, and after many months of preparation, the supposedly temporary settlers moved from Aleika to Kuneitra, where they declared themselves Kibbutz Golan. Approximately 100 people made the move, after which, the community grew. Like at Aleika, "friends brought friends." More and more people from all over Israel, not just the Galilee, came to join. Prior to the war, Russian officers advising the Syrians had used the buildings in the area. Now, Jews filled the dreary structures. The pioneering spirit was alive and well on the Golan.

In this new community, Omer had found love. A widower of two years when we first spoke, he seemingly had come to peace with his loss. I found him eager to tell me of the life he and his wife had, and I was honored to listen. "It is a nice story," he said.

Omer was seventeen when he met Atalya, at a party. Atalya was fifteen. "She was so pretty that I was afraid to speak with her," Omer said. With that opportunity lost, he thought little more of her while serving in the army and during his time at Aleika.

One day, while sitting in the new Kibbutz Golan's dining hall he heard, "Erev Tov Omer, how are you?"

And there she was again, seated at a table.

"What are you doing here?" Omer asked.

"I came to see if it is good for me to come here."

"I left her," Omer related, with a twinkle in his eye, "[then] ran to my house, wrote a letter to my girlfriend, 'I'm sorry that I have to finish our relationship. Somebody came to the kibbutz I have been waiting long to see.' I put it into the mailbox. From this day for fifty years we were together." Throughout his story, as the wind swirled around us while we stood amid the ruins of Kibbutz Golan, just steps from Syria, he seemed warmed by those thoughts, his mind caressed by the thought of his lost love.

I couldn't help myself. "Who loved who first?" I asked.

Omer laughed with that earthy gut laugh of his, and then admitted that he had to chase her a bit before she fell in love with him. Recalling the day his chase ended, "It was cold," he said, "and you can't go outside so after one day we changed places, so I went to live with her and the girl that was with her went to another house." Laughing again, he said, "We were young," Soon Atalya became pregnant: "Our daughter, [in 1968], was the first child [born] in Kibbutz Golan." They named her Noah.

The winters were brutal because they had difficulty heating their homes. Kibbutz members attempted to use old Syrian heaters fueled by gasoline flowing through a pipe, which they'd place on the porch. But in winter the pipes would freeze. While Noah was just a baby, Omer and Atalya would put her between them at night in their one room home to keep her warm. When Noah was a toddler, the thin walls dividing them from another couple led to an uncomfortable question. The settlement was filled with young people. When not working there wasn't much to do. One afternoon, Noah came to Omer and asked, "Why is Gila crying." But it was passion, not pain that caused Gila to cry out. How to explain sex to a toddler? Noah was their first child, but Omer and Atalya eventually had four more, and now Atalya's memory and Omer's life is blessed with twelve grandchildren.

But Omer had kept a dark secret from his new wife for some time. Atalya's brother was a pilot. The Syrians had shot down his plane during the Six-Day War. He landed by parachute on a hill near present day Route 99, just south of the turn close to the Syrian Headquarters, located near where Kibbutz Golan was built a year later. The Syrians captured him, took him to the steps of the Cinema House in Kuneitra, which was in plain view of where the young couple lived in Kibbutz Golan a year later, and then killed him. While Omer told me this story, we could make out the red roof of the cinema and its fateful steps on which his wife's brother had been murdered, now again in Syrian territory due to negotiations after the Yom Kippur War.

To reach the ruins of Kibbutz Golan, Merom Golan's first roots on Golan soil, we turned on the bumpy road where an empty shell of a building sits that was once the former Syrian Headquarters for the Golan. There, you can stop and wander through the large rectangular building on the site. Outside is a small monument to Eli Cohen, the Israeli spy caught and hanged by the Syrians in 1965. Thanks to him, the IDF was very aware of Syria's defensive capabilities and various plans. Inside the structure you'll find ruined stairwells and graffiti. If you're brave enough to negotiate the broken stairway to the roof, you'll be rewarded with an incredible view of the surrounding countryside, now under Syrian control, which was also hotly contested during the Syrian Civil War.

Omer did not stop at the HQ. Instead, we continued to the border fence, and turned right.

"Here," he said, "We had a restaurant, here, and a gasoline station. This was the end of the kibbutz. It started here and it was inside Kuneitra too."

As he spoke, I felt a tingle of excitement. I suddenly realized that this was not my first time here. My mind flashed back to a tour bus. It was 1969. I was fourteen—with my parents in body, but not so much in spirit as is likely the case with any adolescent forced to endure a two-week trip with their parents. I remembered gazing out the window of the bus as we neared Kuneitra and seeing a gas station and restaurant arise out of seemingly nowhere. The decades that have passed since have blurred that image, but my memory was instantly clear. I had been here fifty years before.

As Omer drove past more ruins, he'd say things like, "That was the garage here," and "Here we had a little motel." Or when we saw a deep trench, he clarified, "The anti-tank ditch was dug in 74 or 75." And about the buildings they occupied, he'd said, "It was a neighborhood of Russian officers that came to help the Syrians . . . and we took all the houses . . . and made the kibbutz inside." Omer then explained the interior design of the buildings: "In every house we had three rooms, [a family in] every room, the bathroom and [kitchen was shared].

Then, Omer showed me where his home was and where Yehuda's family lived. All in all, the small community contained about twenty buildings. A few months later, when I met Omer and Yehuda at Omer's home, Omer drew a map of the community. The map made clear what our talks had not. Part of where Kibbutz Golan had been located was on land still controlled by Israel. The other part is in old Kuneitra, across the fence, on land controlled by Israel after the Six-Day War but now controlled by Syria.

Unfortunately, while the settlers of Kibbutz Golan were enthusiastic, they also had an unrelenting problem—the land was relatively flat. As a result, the Syrians could clearly see them. That meant trouble. Artillery shells fired by the Syrian army intermittently whistled through the air before exploding nearby. To protect themselves, the settlers built aboveground trenches composed of walls of sandbags with overhead metal roofs. The tunnels stretched from house to house. But as the years passed and the shelling continued, the settlers decided to move to a location less vulnerable to Syrian attacks.

The location they chose was in the shadow of the towering cone of an extinct volcano, Mount Bental. With determination, they built their new homes. But what, they wondered, should they call their new community? Should it remain Kibbutz Golan, or should it be something else? As is always the case with major decisions on a kibbutz and many minor ones, the question was put to a vote. The kibbutz charged Omer's wife with counting the ballots. Many names were proposed and received support. The name "Merom (meaning Heights) Golan" did not receive the most votes, yet it had an advantage over all others. Atalya favored that name. She told everyone "Merom Golan won."

It turned out that the new location shared the same problem as the prior site. The settlers had thought they would be safe hidden behind Mount Bental. And they were—in part. Their location protected them from artillery shells fired from their east. But it left them exposed to shells fired from the north. And the Syrians had artillery near Mount Hermon. Though intermittent, the artillery shells kept coming.

By October 1973, Merom Golan had a firm hold on the land. The community was growing, its new location, while still receiving sporadic fire from the Syrians, was no longer in the open, and it had at least the tacit support of Israel's government. Meanwhile, other communities had joined Merom Golan on the Heights. The plans of Eyton Sat, Rafel Ben-Yehuda, Dan Laner, and Yehuda, along with others, had begun to bloom.

Then, on October 6, all that was put at risk.

At 2 p.m. the Syrian army, in conjunction with the Egyptians at the Suez Canal, surprised Israel's thin, unprepared line of defenses along the Golan with an attack. The Syrians came with thousands of tanks and armored personnel carriers. Their goal was to sweep through the Golan Heights and then descend to the Hula Valley in one day. Initially, their only opposition was a couple hundred IDF tanks scattered about and a few infantrymen in prepared fortifications.

Syrian tanks flowed like waves across land south of Kuneitra. Their plan was to drive east and then wheel north, cutting behind Merom Golan. In a pincer movement, at Kuneitra, and to its north, another massive Syrian attack aimed to punch through the few IDF tanks and men in their way. The Syrians broke through in the south. In the north, the fortitude of Israel's crack seventh armored brigade, assisted by more defensible terrain, barely held them at bay.

As we drove in his vehicle in Merom Golan's fields adjacent to the Syrian border, Omer turned to me with a devilish smile before he playfully ratted out his friend. Omer said:

> *I can tell you another story [about] Yehuda Harel. He doesn't like so much this story but that's our story. At the beginning of the war we sent the children and the women down to another kibbutz. All the guys were staying in [Merom Golan] to guard the kibbutz. We didn't know exactly what's going on, what kind of war is it. So, in the middle of the night I was near the radio and I heard that they start[ed] to call all the kibbutzim from the [areas] of the Golan. 'Take all the people and get down,' I woke all the people around me, [we were at the headquarters for Merom Golan] and told them . . . they are ordering [us] to leave the kibbutz . . . . Yehuda Harel and another [said] no, we can't leave the kibbutz. You can't leave a place just because the army says.*
>
> *And I told them look, we are . . . [civilians] . . . I was an officer in the army. It's an order from the army. Now it's war. If they say we have to go we have to go.*

> *We argued about it.*
>
> *After some time, we decided to send Yehuda and the other guy to Naffekh [IDF headquarters on the Golan about five miles away] to see what's going on ... So they went.*
>
> *At 5:00 a.m. they call us. 'Do it quick!' ... What happened is they [spoke with] Raful Eitan, he was the commander .... He [said], 'I have no time for you! [Eitan knew they were both from Merom Golan]. 'Look on the map. The blue it's us. The red, the Syrians.' They saw the Syrians [were] surrounding Nafekh and ran to the radio [to call us]. 'Do it quick. Do it quick!'*

After three days of desperate fighting, the IDF evicted the Syrians from all their gains on the Golan, except at the top of Mount Hermon. The war ended a couple weeks later with the IDF holding new territory deep into Syria. Then came negotiations.

At our first meeting, I asked Yehuda about those negotiations. His answer more revealed his ideology than the events in question.

> *I can say we believed that the Golan Heights has to be part of Israel, not only because of the security reasons. Because as I said to my friends, even if Assad becomes a member of Peace Now, we don't want to leave the Golan. But I have to tell you, in my new ideology, state is not so important, reality is more important. Even my ideology before I changed it was more anarchist than communist. I don't believe in the State. I don't like big government. I don't like government. I don't like politics."*

As I listened to him then, and as I think about it now, he may not have liked politics, but he was a master politician!

Trying to refocus our conversation on the ensuing peace negotiations with Syria, I asked Yehuda if he had met Henry Kissinger, America's secretary of state who mediated the talks between Israel and Syria after the 1973 war ended. His response surprised me. He had only spoken to Kissinger once on the telephone, but he thought Kissinger was not so important.

"The problem was not Henry Kissinger," he said. "Our problem was the prime minister of Israel."

Knowing that Kissinger had written extensively about how Merom Golan's farmland stretching to the post-1967 border had created a huge problem for him in negotiations, because Syria had demanded that territory back as part of a quid-pro-quo for a ceasefire, I asked Yehuda about that. He said, "You're right," but then elaborated on the process he instigated. Yehuda said:

> *The Syrians asked for all of the Golan Heights, then part of the Golan Heights, then the hills (Mount Bental and adjacent Mount Avital among them). [To prevent their return] it was the first time we made a political movement in Israel. Because we were only about 800 people on the Golan Heights, we started a committee of the settlements on the Golan, and we made a campaign all over Israel, without the parties involved, the politicians. And we got the support of the people. I especially made a lot of conversation with [Prime Minister] Golda Meir.*

Did Meir sympathize with your views? I asked.
"Very sympathetic."
Yehuda then added:

> *[I had a] good connection with her. The government was very, very tired. I remember that she told me that the people are tired,*

and we had about . . . 200 [of our soldiers] prisoners of war in Syria. The [people] want them back. And you know, there is a war of attrition here. Till April [1974] I believe. The Syrians kept shelling and all of our children were in shelters. Not only in the night but all the days. For about six months.

Barely pausing, Yehuda continued:

She told me that the people were tired, and soldiers want to go home. The reserve soldiers. Most of the Israel[i] army are reserves. There were many months the war of attrition here . . . [The government wanted] Israel to sign very quickly the disengagement agreements because the people are tired. I told this to another friend, the commander of the Golan Heights [Yitzhak Hofi]. He said, 'the people are not tired. The government is tired!'

Yehuda said, "We begged her . . . strong[ly] not to surrender and not to give the hills. We went to all the Ministers, one by one, to convince them. It was the first time we made a political movement not to withdraw from the Golan Heights."

I couldn't help thinking that Yehuda certainly had participated in a political process that achieved the right to settle on the Heights. It therefore certainly made sense that he would have fought tooth and nail to hold on to what he and others had gained. Thus, I was not surprised that when I asked him if he had led the group that campaigned against returning the Golan to Syria, he responded modestly, "Informally."

I followed up with questions about how it came about that he met with members of *Gush Emunim*. *Gush Emunim* was a radical movement for that time. Growing in strength after the Yom Kippur War ended, it combined religious zealotry with a thirst for land that had been part of Israel in biblical times. One of its leaders was Hanan Porat. I had written about *Gush Emunim* in my book, *The Pivotal Years: Israel and the Arab World 1966—1977*. As a result, I already knew that Yehuda had met Porat. But now was my chance to hear about history from the person that actually made it.

Yehuda answered my inquiry immediately.

"You see, I was a very good friend those times with Hanan Porat. Once in this struggle against the withdrawal we made a new settlement in Kuneitra, [named] Keshet. I asked Hanan Porat to bring people because I failed to make a kibbutz there."

Yehuda's words summarized what I knew to be true. He could not convince enough people to move quickly from the Galilee to the Keshet site. Needing to make it viable while negotiations with Syria were ongoing, Yehuda called on Porat.

Yehuda's request, however, was for *Gush Emunim* to do something not totally congruent with its goals. *Gush Emunim* focused on the West Bank, known as Judea in the southern portions and Samaria in the northern areas. The Golan was not in its purview. Still, Porat answered Yehuda's call. Soon, *Gush Emunim* recruits arrived at Keshet. However, they were of a different stripe than previous Golan settlers. Religious rather than secular, they brought a new dynamic to the region. Nevertheless, they were Jews eager to hold the land. Jews working the land, marking the borders with their settlements, and not withdrawing under pressure had been instrumental for Israel's creation since the First Aliyah. Everyone on the Golan—whether secular or religious—was determined to mark the borders of the nation and preserve gains made in the Six-Day War.

Whether it was Yehuda's pressure tactics, the Israeli government's conviction, or just good fortune—with Kissinger's help Israel was able to reach a disengagement agreement with the Syrians. In return for Israel withdrawing from Kuneitra, the former Syrian capital of the Golan, and very minor withdrawals in areas contingent to Kuneitra, the Syrians agreed to stop fighting, accept zones with limited numbers of soldiers and weapons, and return their Israeli prisoners of war, who had languished in Syrian prisons for months. On a macro level that was good. On a local level, that meant returning to the Syrians some of the land where Yehuda and his fellow kibbutz members had established Kibbutz Golan. Given what he had achieved to forestall further withdrawals, Yehuda was ok with that. But he knew that a problem existed that could derail everything.

Keshet. Keshet had established itself in Kuneitra.

"The people of Keshet were very religious," Yehuda explained. "Very religious . . . . When the disengagement was signed, I knew already two days before that Israel will leave Kuneitra . . . so I was very afraid they [would not agree to] leave there." Keshet's settlers came from the Cook Yeshiva in Jerusalem. Yehuda feared they would refuse to leave "because they were very religious, and Cook said that every part of Israel you are not supposed to give [up once you gain control of it]."

With a thoughtful look, Yehuda continued. To forestall a problem, he had spoken to the two leaders of Keshet, "They were already my friends. Merom Golan helped them [get established]. We talk[ed] about it and I saw it won't be easy. But I didn't know where will be the line." By that, Yehuda meant the new border between Syria and the Israeli-held Golan.

Yehuda then said, "So after a week, there came a team to make the line. The head was a civilian, an Israeli. He said that [he had a PHD] for the Science of measuring the land, geodesy."

I had a hard time understanding Yehuda's pronunciation of the term but sure enough, when I later Googled it, I learned that geodesy is a descriptive term for the science of measuring and understanding the earth's geometric shape, orientation in space, and gravitation field. And that many organizations use its principles to mark land boundaries. Yehuda had taught me a new word.

Yehuda said the scientist came with a map that had been marked with thick pencil. Following the scientist's car was a military command car carrying barrels painted white for marking the border wherever the scientist said they should go. Two days later, a fence would be erected to replace the barrels.

Yehuda knew that the location of the new border was a serious matter. A few yards one way or another would determine whether Keshet's residents would make trouble. They had established their community in an old Syrian hospital bunker that had ten underground rooms and a hall. So, Yehuda went to the scientist and said, "It is very important that the bunker where Keshet [is] will be on the Israeli side [of the border]." He further explained, "Then I can move them to another place without breaking their religion." As Yehuda spoke to the scientist, he was also looking at the scientist's map and saw that the scientist's interpretation of the disengagement agreement would place the bunker in Syria. So, Yehuda told me, he "ask[ed] him to move it, about fifty meters, that's all, or 100 meters." Yehuda recalled the scientist saying that it was "against his honor as a Doctor of Geodesy." Yehuda added, "And I didn't convince him . . . In the morning he told his soldiers where to put the barrels."

With a gleam in his eye, Yehuda then said, "In the evening a friend, Uri Mayer, he moved the barrels."

When I asked, Yehuda said he was not there—perhaps not physically, I thought, but for sure in spirit if not as instigator. "After two days," Yehuda continued, "came the people to make the fence and that's the border now." By moving the barrels, that put the bunker "on the line, but on the good side of the line." However, given its proximity to the Syrian border and its lack of natural cover, Keshet was a particularly dangerous place. Therefore, like Kibbutz Golan before it, Keshet then voluntarily moved to a new location. But despite moving, Keshet's settlers upheld their values. They did not give up their land to the Syrians.

Yehuda also played a role in finding new land for Keshet—another task replete with difficulties. The government, which held title to the Golan, didn't recognize Keshet as a settlement. But Yehuda was consumed with placing people on the land; he didn't want the government to return more of the Golan to the Syrians in future negotiations. Yehuda had already seen how the presence of Merom Golan had had a favorable impact on the negotiations. He said:

> *We talk[ed] about it with one colonel of the army that was responsible, but we didn't have permission [from] the government to make a settlement. But I [had good relations] with people in the government, especially Yisrael Galili. He was in our movement and was in very close friendship with me and with [my father's family]. And they didn't disturb us, the government. But they said that I was responsible to move Keshet and I decided to move them to the center of the Golan because there were no settlements, no villages in the center of the Golan, and we were afraid that they would give it to the Syrians [at some point].*

The move was made in two steps. First, the Keshet residents lived near Merom Golan for about six months. Then they moved to their new home in the center of the Golan, where they still live and thrive today.

When I asked Yehuda about his goals in those days he responded that it was "to start a new wave of making many kibbutzim in Israel . . . maybe 200 or 300 kibbutzim and start again the movement of kibbutzim . . . . We didn't make the hundreds of kibbutzim, but we made thirty-three settlements in the Golan Heights. So, I don't know if I succeeded or not. I believe you have to fail because if you don't fail it means you didn't try anything."

Yehuda certainly succeeded. The Golan Heights remains under Israeli control, and thousands of Israelis now populate the Golan, which has become a tourist attraction. With the coming of a cold peace with Syria in 1974, life for residents on that high plateau became less stressful. Decades would pass without intermittent artillery rounds striking random locations, interrupting their lives, and threatening loved ones. They could now devote their efforts to deepening their hold on the land. And even though the Syrian Civil War and its aftermath, replete with Iranian and Hezbollah encroachment, has brought a few shells and rockets to the Golan's skies, on the whole the Golan remains peaceful and vibrant.

Chapter Nine

Kiryat Shmona

I had no intention of spending time in Kiryat Shmona. It seemed like one of those towns you drive though on your way to somewhere else. Highway 90 runs north through Kiryat Shmona and beyond to Metula. Highway 99's western start is at an intersection with Highway 90 near the northern outskirts of town. Heading north, shopping centers are on either side of the highway. Some are modern; others much older and looking quite worn. From the road it is hard to glean how far east or west the town goes. Other than stopping twice—once to buy a shawarma from a roadside establishment that I am charitably calling a deli, once to drop a friend off at a taxi stand—I had always kept driving toward one of the many kibbutzim in the area, Metula, or the Golan. Everything I knew of the town was confined to old news reports of deadly attacks launched by the PLO, and later Hezbollah, from just beyond the prominent mountain ridge to the west.

That all changed after I met Yamit Yanai Malul.

A friend of mine had insisted that I interview Yamit. I was leery but acquiesced. While Kiryat Shmona fit my criteria—a town very close to the Lebanese border—I had already decided to profile Metula, a few miles up the road and even more remote. What would learning about Kiryat Shmona add to my understanding of the north? It turns out quite a bit!

Yamit had asked that we meet at a *Cafe Cafe* coffee shop—yes, that is its name—located at the southernmost border of Kiryat Shmona. It took me thirty minutes to drive there from Merom Golan. Along the way, while still on the Heights, I had passed an army base and then a group of artificial-looking buildings that appeared useful for urban warfare training. Afterward, my route had taken me through rolling fields strewn with firing ranges, ruins of old Arab villages, and then the Hula valley came into view. For the first time I gained a full appreciation of Kiryat Shmona's geography as I gazed at it through my windshield while negotiating the winding roads marking my descent from the Golan. From a distance, Kiryat Shmona looked beautiful, nestled into the Lebanese hillside to its west.

I was glad we were meeting at *Cafe Cafe* because I favor the larger cups of coffee that you can purchase there, not the small espresso cups I call "thimble coffee," which many Israeli coffee shops typically serve. I had slotted two hours for our meeting. Yamit was a few minutes late. No matter. Rather than two hours, we spent four highly informative hours together and I would have been happy with more. What she had to say left me with no doubt that the story of Kiryat Shmona is very much part of the fabric of life along Israel's northern borders.

Yamit is of moderate height, pleasant appearance, and loquacious. Like many Israelis, she began by apologizing for her command of English, even though she had nothing to apologize for. Yamit expressed herself well. That led to the importance she attaches to Israelis learning English. She said that every day her two children must speak at least twenty words in English. "I am a fanatic with that," Yamit said, because it's important to start when they are little.

Yamit trained to become an attorney. In Tel Aviv she learned politics and law in school. Yamit then attended Berkley, in California, where she earned a Masters in Commercial Law but realized she was no longer eager to practice law. But law and politics go hand-in-hand in her family. Yamit's father was a former mayor of Kiryat Shmona.

Her maternal grandmother also involved herself heavily in the political arena. Yamit's grandfather immigrated to Israel in 1948 from Corfu in Greece. In Kiryat Shmona, he founded the Federated Workers Party and worked with Deputy Prime Minister Yigal Yadin. Later, Kiryat Shmona named a street after him. Thus, it was inevitable that Yamit would become an advocate for Kiryat Shmona.

Studying at Berkley challenged Yamit because of her English. Google became her Bible. And studying at Berkley was difficult for political reasons. Few there liked Israel. Many hated the country. Signs castigating Israel and supporting the BDS movement made it emotionally difficult for her to go out. So did the verbal abuse.

Yamit said, "Once I was going to buy some coffee and someone [said] where are you from?"

She answered, "From Israel and I'm studying here in Berkley."

The male inquisitor responded, "You the Jewess." "Anti-Semitism," she realized from the man's comment, "is not over."

Still, Yamit worked hard and earned good grades. To this day she questions how.

Yamit presently works as a lobbyist with Lobby99, a not-for-profit organization that advocates for the Israeli public as a counterweight to commercial interests. Twice a week, to fulfill her job duties, she leaves her home at 5 a.m. in order to spend a full day at the Knesset in Jerusalem. In addition, Yamit frequently advocates for Kiryat Shmona in public settings. And she is also now studying land politics at the University of Haifa and has performed research regarding the northern Galilee under the university's auspices as well. Previously, while working for the Israeli government, she wrote a plan for developing the Upper Galilee. In short, Yamit has focused much of her working life on defining and communicating the problems residents in the Upper Galilee face and proposing solutions for them. Thus, it was no surprise that she was eager to speak with me about the economic challenges and discrimination the residents of Kiryat

Shmona endure. But I didn't expect that her personal life would interweave with the issues we would soon talk about.

Yamit told me she married a "son" of the kibbutz and emphasized that a "son" of the kibbutz had rights she did not have. Her husband's name is Yaniv. In the 1970's, he was the second child born at Merom Golan. The distinction of being the first, of course, goes to Omer Weiner's daughter. Yaniv's father is a good friend of Yehuda Harel, whom Yamit called the "Old Lion."

When Yaniv met Yamit's father for the first time it did not go well because her father was embroiled in political battles with the area's kibbutzim. Until the late 1930s, the only Jewish communities nearby were in Metula and Kfar Giladi. Then thirteen new farming communities established themselves in the Upper Galilee within a few years, ten of which used the kibbutz model. These communities then banded together in an organization called the *Committee of the Upper Galilee Kibbutzim Bloc* (I will refer to it as the "Bloc") well before Kiryat Shmona came into being. That organization eventually morphed into the Upper Galilee Regional Council which now counts twenty-nine kibbutzim as members. Although its headquarters is located in Kiryat Shmona, Kiryat Shmona has never been a member. And there, it seems, lies part of the problem.

Yamit's father told Yaniv, "You know I don't like the kibbutzim." Her father was a member of Likud, a conservative party. Her husband had more leftist views consistent with his socialist upbringing in the kibbutz movement. "So," Yamit said with a wry smile, "I'm living the conflict."

There are also times when Yamit has Shabbat dinner with her husband's family in Merom Golan and the conversation turns into relations between the kibbutzim and Kiryat Shmona. So much so that her husband has said, "Please, please, not now!" But Yamit explains plaintively, "It is in my blood."

We then got down to business. But before I proceed, some of the history I gleaned from my research provides context.

* * *

The problem started in 1949 after the 1948 Arab-Israeli War had ended. Until then, there had been an Arab village called Al-Khalisa located just south of Kfar Giladi, at the base of the Lebanese hills. It was the center of Arab settlement in the Hula Valley. In fact, in the attack on Tel Hai almost thirty years before, Al-Khalisa residents participated. After the Israelis won the war in 1949, the 13,000 Arabs in the region fled, including the residents of Al-Khalisa. Whether they chose to leave or were forced to leave by the victorious Jewish forces, or something in between, is a subject for endless argument well beyond the scope of what I am seeking to explain.

Kibbutzim in the region and Israel's central government wanted to advance Jewish settlement of the area—but lacked volunteers. In May 1949, Bloc committee representatives met with Prime Minister David Ben Gurion to request Jewish settlement of Al-Khalisa and further development of Rosh Pina. Shortly thereafter, the central government asked for a member of Kfar Giladi to come to Tel Aviv to coordinate preparations for the arrival of some Yemenite Jews at Al-Khalisa.

On July 18, 1949, the central government literally deposited fourteen Yemenite families at Al-Khalisa. A month later another group of similar size joined them. At first the community was called Kiryat Josef, in memory of Josef Trumpledor who had died at nearby Tel Hai. Kfar Giladi voluntarily supplied the new, small community with enough foodstuffs to last them three months. In September, a member of Kfar Giladi who had served three decades before in Hashomer, went to the new community to manage it. As the numbers at Al-Khalisa continued to grow, reaching perhaps 200 people before the year ended, planning progressed for building hundreds of housing units.

At this point, it is important to recognize the backgrounds of the people involved.

Kibbutz members were for the most part Ashkenazi Zionists. As such, they were more secular than religious, motivated rather than desperate. They, for the most part, came from European countries and Russia. Most had come to Palestine to build a nation through physical labor and shared sacrifice. Although many were escaping pogroms and harsh government restrictions, they came to kibbutz life by choice. For them, their kibbutz was everything. Members shared both the backbreaking work required for their survival and the fruits of their efforts. Governance was by majority vote, and when moments of leisure presented themselves, their structure fostered social bonds within the community. This led to being somewhat insular by default. Not from bad intent but from a need and desire for mutual support and enhanced communication that would ensure communal success.

On the other hand, the Yemenites who first came to Kiryat Yosef had no say in where Israel's government placed them. All over Israel, Jewish immigrants from Arab countries throughout the Middle East and North Africa were flooding the country. Known as Mizrahi and Sephardi, their ethnic traditions were different than the Ashkenazi. Often more religious, they also lived differently, had different traditions, had different family structures, and had different attitudes in general. Physically, they bore a closer resemblance to the defeated Arabs than the victorious European Jews. And when they fled, or in many cases were evicted from their homes, they left behind all their belongings. No matter their previous economic status, they were poor refugees upon arriving in Israel. And while Israel was not ready to receive them, it welcomed them anyway. It also needed them.

Israel had just won a war. But its victory had taken a toll. Israeli forces had suffered many deaths and many more had been wounded.

The fighting had destroyed many physical structures, and for years all the resources available to Jews in Palestine had been directed toward procuring the means to fight. Now, Israel's economy and infrastructure had to recover while simultaneously finding a way to settle what became more than a million refugees arriving within a decade of the state's establishment. Israel saw its population double during the first three years after its victory, with the arrival of more than 600,000 Jews. And its population already included many refugees from the years before the war started. Of the Jews who arrived after the war, some were Holocaust survivors, but many were from the Arab lands.

Israel's government had two problems and decided to solve both in one stroke. First, it needed somewhere to put the refugees. Second, it had to figure out how to settle the areas in the north and the south, relatively far from the populous center of the country centered on Tel Aviv, Jerusalem, and Haifa. The government's solution was to create transit camps to house the immigrants. But the immigrants had no input in the matter. The government sent some to Beersheba and other places in the Negev, others closer to Gaza as in Sderot and the like. And some were sent to the new transit camp at Kiryat Yosef.

The influx of people stirred debate within the Bloc in late 1949 and into 1950. What kind of community did the kibbutzim want at Kiryat Yosef? Did they want an urban area or an agricultural community? Many of the old pioneers in the region—some of whom had risked their lives as Hashomer members guarding Jewish communities—pushed for an agricultural community. They did not want to spoil what they saw as the "special character of the area." Eventually, though, most of the Bloc's members by the end of January 1950 had agreed on an urban concept. They saw a need for laborers to help develop the area and drain the nearby Hula swamps. But events didn't wait for their decision. The national government had already decided that the transit camp at the former Arab village of Al-Khalisa would become a city.

In June, the name of Kiryat Josef was changed to Kiryat Shmona. Rather than naming the city after just Joseph Trumpledor, it would now be named after all eight who died that day at Tel Hai. But what was interesting about the name change was the letter that the Bloc sent to the government. It said, "At the same time we note that the aforementioned community is not included within our area of jurisdiction. We discussed your proposal as neighbors . . . ." Thus, making clear that Kiryat Shmona would not be part of the Bloc.

And so, what started as a transit camp grew as an independent community with its own municipal government. Between autumn 1950 and the end of 1951, the government poured thousands of immigrants into the city. They came from Romania, Iraq, India, Persia, Hungary, and at first, a few from North African countries such as Morocco. Many more Moroccans came later. From July 1950 to July 1951, the population at Kiryat Shmona swelled from 800 to 4,000. From there it continued to grow. In a few short years Kiryat Shmona became the largest community in the Upper Galilee and one of the largest transit camps in the country. Public services collapsed under the strain of such rapid growth, which Israel's government, short of resources, failed to adequately alleviate. Area kibbutzim pitched in to help. And after a stormy winter in 1950, the army provided some assistance to the growing population, but it was fleeting and not enough.

The Bloc was the only organized body that could provide consistent help. In January 1950, Prime Minister Ben Gurion delivered his "ashamed and embarrassed" address to the Knesset in an attempt to spur all kibbutzim to assist the State by devoting more of their resources towards settling the new immigrants. But the Bloc was already doing so in the north. Each kibbutz sent at least one member a day to help at Kiryat Shmona. Since the kibbutzim members were still living in somewhat Spartan conditions themselves and needed to further develop their own land, in their minds, their efforts were not insignificant.

In January 1951, the Regional Council (a governmental body that as far as I can tell replaced the Bloc), wrote to the kibbutzim that they had "not yet filled their elementary obligation to mobilize for the [transit camps] . . . . This situation cannot continue. The kibbutzim must immediately send members to the . . . Kiryat Shmona transit [camp]. The responsibility and concern for the new immigrants is too great for the matter to continue to be postponed."

Ben Gurion's and the Regional Council's requests and cajoling did not fall on deaf ears. At times there were as many as thirty volunteers from the kibbutzim working at Kiryat Shmona. They built an infant house, school, and a dining hall. Kibbutz volunteers repaired collapsed structures. The kibbutzim donated clothing, books, toys, and outdoor play equipment for the children. Volunteers developed a welfare department and rotated in medical assistance.

It was not enough to alleviate the suffering. There were just too many immigrants to help. The dining hall was built to hold 100 kids. Soon there were 350. The growing numbers overwhelmed the teachers, their supervisors, and everyone else who came to help.

One kibbutz member wrote of the coming injustice she saw, "I know that one day our demands of them, these youngsters [of Kiryat Shmona] will be the same as our demands of our own children, because we'll say, 'they grew up in Israel.' But there is a great difference, an immeasurable difference, between the developmental conditions of the two groups."

Nor could the newcomers earn enough money to improve their standard of living. Some had many children. Their salaries did not cover the costs of feeding and housing their families. As a result, living conditions were harsh, especially in the summer when crowding of up to eight beds in a room coupled with the heat and poor sanitary conditions fostered the spread of illness.

Those volunteering saw the problems. Those not volunteering did not. One volunteer wrote, "The distance in space is very small. The distance in time is whole generations." Activists at the kibbutzim recognized that, if they failed to alleviate the suffering, the gap between the kibbutzim and Kiryat Shmona would only widen with the passing of generations. They also saw a political opportunity for their socialist Zionist movement to win the hearts and minds of the immigrants. But it was not to be.

Instead, the early compassion of many kibbutz members gave way to an attitude of superiority and separatism. Meanwhile, the immigrants, mired in a hopeless situation not of their initial making, became less appreciative and increasingly angry. Many of those kibbutzniks saw the townspeople in Kiryat Shmona as lazy and backward. Many of the immigrants thought the kibbutzniks were condescending and lacked respect for their culture. The curse "Go to hell," transformed into an epithet for Kiryat Shmona residents: "Go to the kibbutz."

It seems to me both sides were wrong and right. The situation was impossible and the cultural differences vast. The new immigrants had chosen to come to Israel (many because they had no other option) because of the treatment they were subjected to in their home countries but had few choices upon arrival. In Israel, they were sent, with little support, to build new lives in ramshackle homes near the borders where their presence, like border kibbutzim before, served the nation. Having just fought a war for their survival, the kibbutzim accepted their responsibility to help yet lacked the resources to alleviate all the suffering while also maintaining and developing their own communities. Human nature being what it is, it's natural that the Kiryat Shmona residents became more frustrated, just as the kibbutzim grew more resentful. And so, troubles began in those early years, troubles that continue to this day. Kiryat Shmona, plopped in the middle of the verdant fields of all the many agricultural communities in the area, struggles with economic hardship. And while dealing with their poverty, its inhabitants see these verdant fields hemming in the boundaries of the municipality, serving as a constant reminder of what they don't have.

* * *

Yamit told me, "Kiryat Shmona is choking, she doesn't have the land. And all the kibbutzim and settlements have plenty of land, they don't use it. This is not an issue that start[ed] today. It start[ed] fifty years ago with my father."

Yamit then placed in front of me a sheaf of documents and newspapers to prove her point. Clearly, she was trying to be objective. But just as clearly, she has a perspective. One of the pieces of paper had printed on it a cartoon from 1981. It depicts an image of a human that personifies Kiryat Shmona, and a pack of six wolves, that represent the kibbutzim, tearing at the human (Kiryat Shmona). It caused a big uproar in Kiryat Shmona and the surrounding kibbutzim when it was published.

Yamit then told me about the "millionaire's speech" delivered decades ago by Menachem Begin, a former prime minister favored by Kiryat Shmona residents. It was in response to an incident that occurred nearby, at Kibbutz Manara's swimming pool. This was a period when Palestinian Katyusha rockets, fired from Lebanon, were falling frequently on Kiryat Shmona, but due to geography, not so much on the area's kibbutzim. Yamit told me the government wanted to evacuate people from the town to the kibbutzim in the region, an idea the kibbutzim resisted. Begin had heard a kibbutz member say they didn't want Kiryat Shmona people in their pool. The central idea of Begin's speech in response was "shame on you."

Yamit said this was a pivotal point. Afterward, the divisions between the area kibbutzim and Kiryat Shmona deepened. Ironically, she now lives with her husband in a kibbutz, despite her allegiance to Kiryat Shmona. She sees the divide there and also in town.

"Never going to end," she said, "until the land is justly distributed."

Yamit then told me that 23,000 people live in Kiryat Shmona on about 3,650 acres of land. The region's kibbutzim have 17,000 inhabitants and 74,000 acres of land. The Moshavim in the area have about 7,000 people and 33,500 acres of land, she said. What Yamit didn't explain—because it was tangential to her point—is that the land is not owned by the kibbutzim or moshavim. Instead, based on a system that has been in effect since the creation of Israel in 1948, the State permits those communities to use the land, but retains ownership rights.

That's when Yamit told me why she had suggested Cafe Cafe for our meeting spot. It was to make a point. The coffee shop is in a shopping center called *Big*. Located adjacent to other business on the southern part of town, seemingly, it is part of Kiryat Shmona. But it isn't. When Yamit's father was mayor, he worried that if *Big* were built it would take revenue from businesses in Kiryat Shmona. And since the shopping center would be built on land outside of Kiryat Shmona's boundaries, the city wouldn't receive any tax revenues from it. Thus, its tax base would decline causing further reductions in city services.

Yamit's father pushed Israel's government to form a land distribution committee to study the matter, along with other Kiryat Shmona land needs, and find a resolution. The town needed land to grow and thereby increase its tax base so that living conditions could be improved. However, the Upper Galilee Council wanted the *Big* shopping center on its land for similar economic reasons. Perhaps unfortunately for Kiryat Shmona, a city mayor elected after Yamit's father did not see things in the same light. In return for Kiryat Shmona receiving half of the taxes generated by the *Big* shopping center, he agreed to disband the land distribution committee and abandon the city's request for the government to re-appropriate land from the kibbutzim to the city.

To make the issue of Kiryat Shmona's lack of land clear, Yamit showed me a map of Kiryat Shmona and the surrounding area so that I would understand the stranglehold on the city. A blue line on the map marks the areas which from which taxes are paid to Kiryat Shmona. A few miles to the north sits Metula. It is a town whose economy mainly depends on agriculture. As such, it doesn't want to give up any land. Frankly, from what I have learned, farmers never do. Other areas depict agricultural fields and industrial plants. All the agriculture in the area and much of the industrial buildings are outside of the blue line—business there pay taxes to the Upper Galilee Council not Kiryat Shmona.

Yamit's father hoped to incorporate land into Kiryat Shmona as far as the turn-off to Tel Hai college, perhaps a mile up the road from the city. The next mayor's deal to accept fifty percent of the tax revenue from *Big* ended that endeavor. Yamit said that the mayor had "made the biggest mistake of his life." The government had the power to redistribute the land. The mayor gave up the town's request for that to happen. Now, kibbutzim are building houses everywhere. Non-members can buy them. Meanwhile, Kiryat Shmona has no land for new housing developments. Therefore, people with means are fleeing to homes on Upper Galilee Council land. "As a result," she said, "Kiryat Shmona is getting older and less populous." And poorer.

Nor is there room for new industrial plants. Stef Wertheimer, a visionary industrialist, built a new industrial zone on Kfar Giladi land, not Kiryat Shmona's. While it certainly provides job opportunities for members of the city, its industrial activity won't generate tax revenue for Kiryat Shmona—that money will go to the Upper Galilee Council.

And, most likely, people drawn to the area by the job opportunities created at the Industrial Park will live outside of Kiryat Shmona. A large part of the reason the industrial zone was built on Kfar Giladi land was that Kiryat Shmona did not have enough land available that would fit the needs of an industrial zone. Another reason was that the Council could afford giving more tax breaks than the city. And perhaps, it was also because during the 1948 War for Independence, Wertheimer had spent time testing his artillery designs at the rock quarry just up the road owned by Kfar Giladi.

Medical care, Yamit explained, is another issue city residents face. In fact, consistent in all the interviews I conducted throughout the north, everyone had concerns about accessibility to medical care for emergencies and for treatment of major diseases and chronic problems. Yamit told me, "One of the biggest struggles in [the last] five years, they closed the emergency center [near Tel Hai]." She explained that the only facility now operating is something akin to a walk-in clinic for common minor medical concerns. The mayor "can't convince the government to put here the emergency [center] like it was." People must go to Safed for emergencies or major problems.

Several days after our interview, the point Yamit had made to me in the coffee shop was amplified on the national stage. Prime Minister Netenyahu spoke in Kiryat Shmona to celebrate the opening of the new clinic Yamit had referred to. Normally, Kiryat Shmona is considered a bastion for Likud, Netenyahu's political party. Not this time. While the prime minister was speaking about the rights citizens have for adequate medical treatment, a political activist-heckler interrupted him, "Then why did you take away the emergency room?" she said. Netanyahu responded, "You're not interesting. You're boring us." His response created a mini-political tempest that quickly blew over. But a true emergency room in Kiryat Shmona, a city of more than 20,000, never materialized.

Our conversation then turned to economic issues in Kiryat Shmona, which mostly boil down to economic activity leaving the city for the surrounding area. Before *Big's* construction, Yamit told me, "The center of Kiryat Shmona was alive and [now] it is dying." After its construction, some city businesses left Kiryat Shmona for *Big*. Of course, that meant Kiryat Shmona would get fifty percent of their taxes rather than the 100 percent the city had previously received. Another change also took business from the city—parking! To raise revenue for Kiryat Shmona, the current mayor placed parking meters all over the commercial areas of the town. I saw those meters everywhere while driving around with Yamit, often coupled with congested parking lots. At the open-air shopping center, *Big*, parking is free and easy. Given that it's a very short drive from the city center, naturally people would go there instead of going to alternatives in town. This impacted the solvency of the businesses that remained in the city.

Yamit identified Katzrin, the growing modern town in the central Golan Heights, as a threat to Kiryat Shmona. There, she said, kibbutz enterprises coupled with private concerns are pulling new and old commercial activity from the city. Having been to Katzrin a couple times, I can attest that its wide-open shopping area and modern restaurants are attractive alternatives to Kiryat Shmona's more closed-in feeling.

And, Yamit said, the religious views of the present mayor are a problem that further detracts from the city's economic vitality. The mayor is a Rabbi. Therefore, it is not surprising that he promotes the closure of all city businesses on Shabbat, from Friday night to Saturday evening. But many residents want to shop on Shabbat, go to a restaurant, or even get a cup of coffee. So do tourists. If they can do so elsewhere, they will. Revenue from their purchases will be lost to the city and its businesses forever.

At least the new soccer stadium confers some benefits for Kiryat Shmona. Built in 1989 and remodeled in 2008, it is a source of joy and great pride for the city. Just before the turn of the century, a wealthy Tel Aviv born entrepreneur looking to help the city, Izzy Sheratsky, at the mayor's request took over the two soccer teams in Kiryat Shmona. He then merged them into one, which he named, Hapoel Ironi Kiryat Shmona. Sheratsky had been a big donor to the city, but afterward the soccer team became his biggest development project. As such, he had one ironclad rule and one mission. The mission was to develop homegrown talent. To do so, he invested in the city's youth programs. The rule was that all players had to live within city limits. At first, the team played in a fourth level, bush league in Israel. In a small country like Israel, that was the lowest of the low. But in 2012, the club won Israel's championship for all teams and qualified to join Europe's Europa league. Quite a success story amid all the decay and danger.

People now remain in Kiryat Shmona, Yamit told me, because "they don't have any alternative, [they are] stuck." The city has little money for basic public services, the schools need funding, and its public areas are not well kept. Everywhere, there are empty shells in buildings that once contained open stores and eateries but now are stark reminders of the city's economic deterioration. One visible example of the decrepit conditions devouring the city is the Kiryat Shmona Museum. Its grounds were a mess when I stopped by, its doors were locked, and the building showed no signs of regular visitation. Just a couple miles north, the Hashomer Museum at Kfar Giladi is beautiful and well kept. The contrast is stark.

And then there is the "stigma" of living in Kiryat Shmona. Yamit said when people in Israel learn that you come from Kiryat Shmona, they paint an immediate picture in their minds of who you are. That comment led us to two stories—her own and her family's.

Yamit's grandfather came to Israel with his eleven sons from Morocco. Yamit's father was a baby. Her father said that his father was always angry about coming to Kiryat Shmona because the kibbutzim treated him like a slave. Nevertheless, Yamit's grandfather's sons contributed to the State. One of Yamit's uncles was an engineer in Morocco. In Kiryat Shmona, upon arrival, he was assigned to laborious jobs—moving stones and otherwise clearing the Hula valley. Later, her uncle was among the first members of the city council. Yamit's father served with the IDF on the Golan during the Yom Kippur War. One of his brothers, one of the eleven, was killed on the Golan during that same war. They were the only family in Israel's history that had eleven boys serving and fighting for the state at the same time. Yamit's dad was a fairly high-ranking commander in the navy. He had gone to a school for military officers and received an advanced education. But while back home in Kiryat Shmona during the 1970s, the local kibbutzim, Yamit says, wouldn't allow him or any other city people in their swimming pools. These are the stories she grew up hearing. This prejudice, she says, is the root of the problem.

Born in 1979, Yamit grew up during a time when PLO and then Hezbollah Katyusha rockets and mortar shells frequently exploded in the city. While we spoke, a loud sound from outside had coincidentally punctuated our conversation. "I'm hearing now," she said, "the motorcycle, [it sounds like a shell]. When a missile [comes] it is like a whistle sound." Yamit reached a point in her youth when she could determine how close incoming fire would hit by the sound. Her home was unusual for the day: it contained a shelter. Most people had to rush from their homes to go to a public shelter but Yamit's "grandfather had money to build [one downstairs]. I'm still hearing his voice, the yelling, go down. We didn't have a siren. We had to listen and when we hear[d] the whistle then we go down."

Yamit said, "A lot of people in Kiryat Shmona [were] killed because they didn't get to the shelter, they didn't have the time. It was crazy."

When I asked if, as a child, did she think about the danger every day, Yamit's response pivoted to the present. "I tell that to the government that they are taking for granted people living here." People that have choices leave, she said, and then added, "She doesn't want [her children] to have the stamp from Kiryat Shmona." Though Yamit hadn't responded to my question, I got the point. People in the city feel stuck—they deal with the danger and economic malaise out of necessity, not choice.

Yamit then told me a personal story, which personified the problem and was a pivotal moment in her life. During her army service "everybody [told her] you don't look like [you are] from Kiryat Shmona." The comments painfully reminded Yamit of the stigma attached to her home city. So, she said, "I decided that I will tell everyone I am not from Kiryat Shmona." She would name a kibbutz or town instead. One day, while serving in the army as a draftee at age eighteen, Yamit hitchhiked home on a day off. A high-ranking officer picked her up. When he asked where she was from, Yamit answered, "Metula."

After driving for an hour, the officer asked who she knew in Metula and which family she was from. Metula is a small town. Even today, its population is less than 2,000. Even so, Yamit was determined to conceal her true home. She invented a story. "Like Mossad," she said.

After reaching Kiryat Shmona, Yamit asked the officer to pull off just north of the city, a few miles south of Metula, at the Tel Hai intersection. He responded, "Don't worry, I will take you to your home." Yamit said, "He took me to my parents' home exactly. He [looked] at me and [told] me, 'Listen, … I knew who you [were] at the minute I pulled over the car, I knew you were Sami's daughter, I don't know why you did all these tricks. But I'm going to call your father and tell him."

At the time, Yamit's father was deputy mayor of Kiryat Shmona. Her lies made him angry, as she knew he would be. Yamit had told the lies to avoid the shame of being identified with Kiryat Shmona. "And then, that minute," Yamit said, "I understood what happened." The media's focus on Kiryat Shmona after the barrage of Katyushas that hit the town in the 1980s had had an impact. The missiles destroyed property and took lives. The images also depicted the town's malaise and further created a negative perception, which, up until then, Yamit did not want to be associated with. Henceforth, Yamit had shed her youthful embarrassment and began cultivating her adult passion—the rehabilitation of Kiryat Shmona.

So, I asked her, what's the solution? The answer, Yamit emphasized, was land.

The kibbutzim, she said, don't want to relinquish any land that the government has given them for farms or to build factories on. It's also politics. Kiryat Shmona residents, by and large, support Likud. The kibbutzim support more Labor-oriented parties. At one time that political divide had everyday ramifications according to Yamit, with Kiryat Shmona residents having trouble finding work at local kibbutzim unless they carried a Mapai card (Mapai was a center-left Israeli political party that merged into the Labor Party in 1968). Even if that is no longer the case, the economic stranglehold surrounding kibbutzim have on Kiryat Shmona through circumstances of geography and history, has certainly economically and socially impacted Kiryat Shmona.

Yamit said that the city needs more land to build new neighborhoods, and to build new homes where neighborhoods already exist. Their children, as with the kibbutzim, need to have an opportunity to come home and build their own homes. If this doesn't happen, Yamit said, "Kiryat Shmona is half [its present] size in five to ten years and the population is [comprised of] people that have no alternative." And, I observed, getting older.

Yamit, however, had not yet finished her explanation. There was more—taxes. Tax revenues are needed for many things, including education. The schools, she said, are not good. "English is not well taught." One answer for the problems, Yamit thinks, is to integrate the educational programs of Kiryat Shmona and the surrounding kibbutzim. Not surprisingly, given what she had already told me, the kibbutzim refuse to do that. Instead, they work with the towns and kibbutzim on the Golan Heights to provide their children with a more comprehensive educational solution.

Yamit's answer for the tax revenue problem sounded a lot like subsidies. She said, "The government gives the same tax benefits (subsidies) to Megiddo and Kiryat Shmona. Makes no sense because of course people will [want to live] in Megiddo. I keep saying to the government the further from the center [of the country] the more the benefit taxes have to be . . . . Here we are like in the middle of nowhere. If you don't have a car you are stuck here, you can take a bus, [but it takes] four hours to Tel Aviv, it's crazy."

Yamit compared their situation in the far north, that she and all others refer to as the periphery, to Beersheba, another development town in the Negev that has grown substantially. In Beersheba there are large military bases that drive the economy as well as a train that connects Beersheba to Tel Aviv. In Kiryat Shmona there is nothing.

After a couple hours of conversation, we left *Big* for a short tour of Kiryat Shmona. First, we drove past a poultry factory. Yamit told me that her father had opposed its construction, fearing the bad smells emanating from it that might spread throughout Kiryat Shmona. After hearing her out, I found that perfectly understandable. So many of Kiryat Shmona's problems—from the perspective of its residents—come down to image. A smelly poultry plant does not help the cause.

We then drove past other built-up areas around *Big*. Located on Council land, they provide no tax revenue for the city.

Then, on a narrow road, near the main highway but not visible from it, we pulled up to Mama Hassa. It is a famous restaurant in Kiryat Shmona that has been there for quite some time. It sits in a somewhat dilapidated shopping center that was built after the restaurant opened for business. But despite attempts to change the present situation, the restaurant, now a part of the shopping center, pays its taxes to the Council—not Kiryat Shmona.

Pictures that date back to the beginning of Kiryat Shmona covered much of the wall space inside the restaurant. With music blaring in the background of the darkened room that exuded a certain ancient feel, Yamit showed me pictures on the wall of her grandfather and other family members. There was a picture of her father's brother, who had been killed during the Yom Kippur War. One other was of a beauty contest with her grandfather showing his appreciation of the view. Another was of Yamit's grandmother. There were countless pictures of other family members. And some depicted Yamit's father as deputy mayor, mayor, and even dressed up as the soccer team's mascot in 1968.

"My father loves it here . . . . All the grandchildren, they want to eat outside." But Yamit's father insists they sit among the pictures, which patriotically tell the story of their town. As we walked along the left side of the room, Yamit took me through pictures that dated back to the town's beginning in the late 1940s. A man is seen overlooking the land before it had been developed. There is even a picture of Trumpledor from decades before. She then showed me a picture of her grandfather with a socialist flag on International Day. For him, that was important. He was a socialist who fought against Franco in Spain. After he died from cancer, the city named a street after him.

Clearly, Yamit's family was rooted in the history of Kiryat Shmona, and Kiryat Shmona was rooted in Yamit.

As we drove through town, we saw pictures of the present mayor, up for re-election, hung everywhere. The mayor had held his position for a long time. But this time his chances were not good, and Yamit hoped for his defeat. The election was held a couple weeks after I interviewed Yamit. The sitting mayor lost. It remains to be seen what difference it will make.

I saw many of Kiryat Shmona's residential areas during our drive. Most had a dingy look that dated them. Yamit told me they were built in the 1950s. Among them was the street named after Yamit's grandfather. One neighborhood was filled with homes from the 1990s. I saw nothing more recent.

The commercial areas to the west of the main highway were especially depressing. It was a Sunday and businesses should have been buzzing with people. Yet it seemed that most shops at the city center and the central bus station, were closed, or the storefronts were vacant. The walkways were quiet. Very few people were around. It certainly didn't look like a profitable or vibrant environment.

I also experienced the city's parking problem firsthand. Meters were everywhere. A private concession controls them. The city only receives a percentage of the revenue they generate. Although I suspect the private company was awarded the contract because the mayor thought it could do the work more efficiently, Yamit's demeanor suggested she thought otherwise.

The only vibrancy I saw emanated from the temporary mayoral campaign offices that surrounded a small open area and some of their employees who were sitting at a table outside. We stopped to say hello.

While there, Yamit learned that Kfar Giladi's hotel had recently let go all its employees after closing for two years of remodeling and redecorating. The woman who told Yamit this had worked at the hotel for fifteen years. The hotel's closing was a huge blow for a town with few large employers. Yamit expressed empathy for her plight. But there is another side to this story. A few months later, when I met

Gideon Giladi at Kfar Giladi, we spoke about the hotel closing. The kibbutz had to do it to compete with alternative hotels in the region. Without refurbishment, the hotel would fail, and the employees would lose their jobs anyway—but without the hope of regaining them in the future. However, that business reality doesn't change the here and now. Those who lost their jobs will naturally feel despair despite receiving some unemployment compensation, which won't last forever.

And there are few alternative jobs. For example, Yamit told me, Merom Golan finds it cheaper to hire Druze from Majdal Shams than Jews from Kiryat Shmona. And getting to the Golan is not easy or dependable for city residents. She says, "If you use public transportation you have to pray to God you will arrive someday." The same is true for Metula. For some reason the busses going there do not adhere to their schedules.

My time with Yamit had a strong impact on me. Through her, I learned of Kiryat Shmona's problems and because of the interest she had kindled within me, I learned more through research. Clearly, there is a need for some form of government involvement to jump start economic development in the city. It just isn't acceptable to permit a critical northern border community to crumble. Simply put, further economic deprivation risks Hezbollah achieving a bloodless victory. Israel can't afford to pull back even an inch from any spot along its border—because an inch becomes a foot, a foot becomes a mile, and a mile becomes a region.

Before I left, Yamit told me that the government at some point had invested forty-six million shekels in Kiryat Shmona, an amount equivalent to about thirteen million dollars. But there was little to show for it.

Why, I wondered, haven't the city's residents taken matters into their own hands? Yamit seemed to suggest one reason was that religious issues might be holding them back, strict observation of

Shabbat and the like. Though not Haredi, she told me, Kiryat Shmona's residents are becoming increasingly observant and as a result business is impacted. But that is happening in many areas of Israel and on the whole Israel's economy is doing well.

Perhaps, I thought, gender equality was a problem. Yamit had told me a story about her mother that suggested traditional roles for women in Kiryat Shmona were more the rule than the exception. But that also is true in many religious areas in Israel.

And, while my research into the past had indicated that although there certainly were issues, on the whole the area kibbutzim had tried to be helpful. So it wasn't that there was no outside support for the city.

So, does the fault lay with the people of Kiryat Shmona? Some think so.

When I spoke to an Israeli friend about this, that person told me that it might have something to do with the difference between Ashkenazi and the pre-dominate Sephardi and Mizrahi ideology in Kiryat Shmona. That person felt strongly enough to consider writing about the "Crying Israeli." But I don't think so. There certainly are many instances of non-Ashkenazi Jews excelling. Avigdor Khalani, whose parents came from Yemen like many of Kiryat Shomna's initial inhabitants, was the battalion commander who saved the north in the Yom Kippur War. He alone undercuts my friend's supposition. But my friend had another, much more persuasive theory for me too. It was that people need to take responsibility for their lives rather than ask others. Left unsaid was the thought that if you create a culture of handouts, the recipients never get it for themselves. I agree with that. But Yamit's point is that it's not a level playing field. Considering the complex problems that face Kiryat Shmona, I agree with her point too.

In the end, the answer is probably both—there is a need to create better opportunities, but also to increase expectations. Nothing will change quickly, but perhaps small things will create a ripple that will eventually create a wave of change. I know that I will never drive though Kiryat Shmona again without stopping and buying something within the city limits. Perhaps readers of this book will too. Small acts matter—especially when repeated.

As for Yamit, it's funny how life gets in the way of altruistic passion. Yamit's husband refused to live in Kiryat Shmona. Yamit refused to live in Merom Golan. So, they live in a compromise location at another kibbutz—where they are buying land. But her husband "wants to go back to Merom Golan because he has the right to build there." I don't blame him. I love it there too. Their children go to a Galilee school. Yamit sees the irony and accepts that the compromises she made for her marriage conflict with her advocacy.

"I'm not the enemy," Yamit said with regard to Kiryat Shmona, "I'm sleeping with the enemy!"

Chapter Ten

Fall of the Kibbutzim

Like a receding wave, its energy spent, the kibbutz movement reached its high-water mark soon after Israel won the Six-Day War. Then its downward slide began. In 1985, that slide became precipitous due to Israel's economic crisis.

The kibbutzim that line the northern borders suffered from economic problems, as did the others. But their potential implosion had profound implications for Israel's future far out of proportion to their numbers. Historically, kibbutzim led the way for marking and holding territory. The social structure of the kibbutz lent itself to the tower and stockade concept implemented in the late 1930s. Afterward, the presence of those kibbutzim was instrumental in gaining international acceptance of Israel's borders. Without them, Israel would have been smaller and more difficult to defend. Today, if a border kibbutz along the Lebanese border were to fail, that would help Israel's enemies achieve their goals because Israel shrinks if the borders depopulate. Regarding the Golan, if nobody lives there and works the land, international political pressure to return the Golan to Syria might swamp arguments solely based on the defensive imperatives for keeping it. Merom Golan played a central role in holding Golan Heights territory after the October War. Had it not been there, the negotiated disengagement line might well have been further back, to Israel's great detriment.

Today, at least thirty kibbutzim remain within a couple miles of the confrontation line with Hezbollah and Syria. Given that there are only 270 kibbutzim throughout the country those thirty represent more than ten percent of the nation's kibbutzim, a significant number since they are concentrated on only three percent of the nation's land.

Degania is no longer near Israel's border with Syria. The Six-Day War took care of that. But the other four kibbutzim addressed in detail in this book—Dan, Hanita, Kfar Giladi, and Merom Golan—are still on Israel's northern borders. How they survived the economic and social turmoil that buffeted them—and their condition today—is both instructive and, in one case, concerning for the future. But before we look at the present-day condition of those kibbutzim through the eyes of some of their residents, it might be helpful to examine the past.

"From Each According to his Ability, to Each According to his Needs."

The concept of the kibbutz sprang from these twelve words. And it worked well for a while, especially in a time of scarcity, determination, and idealistic principle. In fact, it's hard to see how Israel would have come into being without the hard-working, young socialist pioneers who were determined to redeem the Jewish people by developing the land. Largely secular, their fervent belief in Zionism fulfilled them. Their socialistic structure built atop their democratic ideals, and their communal life that emphasized the group over the individual, gave them the strength to overcome what seems Herculean in hindsight. Those who worked harder felt sufficiently enriched by the acclaim. Those who worked less felt the shame. Both motivations pushed people to do more. Especially because they lived in a close-knit society where they took meals together, socialized together, and even in most cases raised their children in group homes rather than in parental units.

Throughout Israel, kibbutzim were once largely lionized. Rarely more than three percent of the population, their members punched far beyond their numbers in securing pre-Israel Palestine, holding elective offices in the national government, and participating in elite military units. During the 1948 Arab-Israeli War, kibbutzim played a significant role in securing the borders. In the north, that was true even more so than in Israel's center. After the war, the government leased kibbutzim large tracts of land for agricultural and industrial purposes.

Greatly revered by most, the only consistent detractors of the kibbutzim were the post-1948 immigrants, who often supplied the necessary labor for developing many of the kibbutzim and worked in their industries. As always, disparities in wealth lead to problems. Jewish immigrants from Arab and Muslim lands felt, whether true or not, "We are welcome in their factories, but our children are not welcome in their schools."

By 1950, with Israel's Independence established and its borders delineated, the kibbutzim could realistically turn to building their economic wealth, which shifted their focus from survival to something else. Soon, human nature began to override collective need. After the Six-Day War, the army became more of a role model for the nation, and as the nation's economy developed alternatives emerged. Soldiers who had lived their lives on the kibbutz did as was the habit of many who served—they took long foreign trips after completing their army service. Some did not return to Israel, attracted by the lifestyles they found in the United States and other countries. Many others returned to Israel, but not their kibbutzim. Instead, they chose city or university life over the kibbutz's pastoral environment and found the lure of entrepreneurial pursuits more appealing than being required to share resources and the fruits of their labor.

Beginning in the 1970s, the "Society of Children" led by trained supervisors came to an end. Most kibbutzim, forced by the demands of parents living there, ended the practice of group homes for their children. From then on, children slept with their parents rather than together. Parents did the parenting, not designated individuals. But now each kibbutz member's home had to be enlarged to accommodate the children. Which required money. Lots of it.

Then, in the 1990s, kibbutzim tried to evolve in response to the financial and societal challenges they faced. Many adopted "privatization of allowances." Previously, the kibbutz had provided its members with clothing, furniture, travel, and other items. After they implemented allowances which afforded some individuality; members could choose how much clothing to buy, what furniture to purchase, and when to travel. It became their decision rather than the kibbutz's. But this newfound freedom wasn't enough. People were leaving kibbutz life in increasing numbers.

All kibbutzim had communal dining halls, but as time passed other structures became commonplace. Some, perhaps, were necessary such as offices and libraries. But other improvements were luxuries, such as tennis and basketball courts, swimming pools, and even concert halls. These upgrades made life more bearable. But they also cost money.

Meanwhile, the kibbutzim continued to assume responsibility for providing its members consumables such as food and electricity as well as education, health, and support for the elderly. Without any responsibility to pay, membership abuse became routine. A constant refrain I heard from multiple kibbutz members was that the dogs and cats ate well because members fed their pets with free kibbutz meat meant for human consumption. In addition, utilities like air conditioning and heat ran in members' homes at high levels with no regard for cost. All that came to fore just as productivity at the kibbutzim began to wane. This productivity loss was much related to incentive. The compensation people received for their efforts was always the same—no matter the task being performed, the quality of their work, or the uniqueness of their talent—so people were less inclined to work hard or resist the temptation to work elsewhere, knowing they wouldn't receive a benefit any different than the next person for the quality or importance of their effort.

Simply put, the money started to run out. The principle of working to your ability and only taking what you need morphed into taking what you want and working less. But this fiscal squeeze was not reflected in kibbutzim standards of living, which across the board was too high for the money available to support it. Nowhere else could mostly working-class jobs support such luxuries. As a result, kibbutzim were being squeezed from both ends.

But instead of changing their ways, in large part kibbutzim addressed the problem by borrowing money. Even worse, the kibbutz movement had, for the most part, organized itself by 1980 into two umbrellas organizations. These organizations borrowed money collectively and then funneled these funds to individual kibbutzim. But, in keeping with their communal philosophy, each kibbutz guaranteed loans made to other kibbutzim. And then there were projects involving multiple kibbutzim that required more loans. Investment failures by the umbrella organizations further exacerbated the situation.

For a while everything held together, even when massive inflation hit Israel during the early 1980s. Fortunately for the kibbutzim, most of their loans were not indexed to the inflation rate. This meant that as inflation increased the kibbutzim received more for their products—even though each shekel could purchase less product as prices soared. For example, what once cost ten shekels a year later might cost twenty shekels. However, since the loan amount remained the same, the kibbutzim could use their inflated shekels to pay back loans that stayed the same amount. It was a great deal for the kibbutzim. Not so much for the banks.

But in 1985, the Israeli Government had had enough. Inflation had reached 400 percent. A product that cost one shekel in January, cost four shekels in December. So the government froze wages, devalued the currency by fifteen percent, increased interest rates, and broke inflation's back. However, prostrate on the altar of fiscal sanity lay countless businesses throughout Israel that went bankrupt. Also falling into the abyss were the kibbutzim. The government would no longer guarantee their debt with the banks. Meanwhile kibbutzim collective debt continued to increase. Something had to be done soon.

Stepping into the breach was a consortium composed of representatives from the lending banks, government, and the kibbutzim. At first, they tried rescheduling the kibbutz debts. That ended in failure. Due to the higher interest rates, the amount owed spiraled. Soon it was equivalent to more than five billion dollars, quite a tidy sum in those days. Finally, a deal was reached in 1989, which had to be amended in 1996 and 1999. The banks wrote off some of the debt and attempts were made to release the remaining debt from the collective kibbutzim guarantees and instead, to assign it to individual kibbutzim. However, half of the kibbutzim could not afford that. As a result, the wealthier kibbutzim assumed more of the debt and the poorer ones got a disproportionate share of the write-offs. Finally, the kibbutz financial crisis came to an end—for the time being.

And then the demographic crisis accelerated.

Not surprisingly, young people were not eager to live in failing institutions. Without structural changes, the financial crisis would return. Kibbutz members, especially the older ones, were averse to change. After all, they had poured their vitality into the collective dream. But the writing was on the wall: with the average age of kibbutz members growing higher and higher, the older members would soon have to fend for themselves. Still they feared change and fought it.

As early as 1993, Yehuda Harel offered suggestions for fixing the kibbutz crisis. As you may remember, Yehuda was instrumental in establishing Kibbutz Merom Golan in 1967, the first kibbutz on the Golan. His ideology then "was very socialist or communist." But the brutal struggle to keep the kibbutz movement alive in the 1980s had disillusioned him. Yehuda told me that, "You must make mistakes every day," otherwise you are not trying. When I asked him what his biggest mistake had been, his answer surprised me, "Socialism!" And then he explained, "Socialism failed in Russia and in Israel in the kibbutz. It made me think again and to read. And it took me five or six years and I changed all my ideology."

When I asked Yehuda for an example of what had impacted him, he said, "Bankruptcy," and that "the new generation left the kibbutz. The new generation of our children and the new generation of the youth movement that come to the kibbutz to be educated about the kibbutz . . . within a year they left."

In 1993, Yehuda published *The New Kibbutz*, in which he argued socialism had failed to maximize production while capitalism failed as a system for distribution. He suggested reversing the two—using capitalism as the framework for production and socialism for distribution. Yehuda advocated organizing factories and farming to maximize profit. Often, this would mean bringing in the best talent available to manage kibbutz operations, even if those people were not kibbutz members. This violated traditional kibbutz principles. Traditionally, each kibbutz had a governing secretary and committee that would assign members to specific kibbutz tasks. However, especially due to rotation of jobs, that did not guarantee good matches between capability and responsibility.

In addition, Yehuda argued that kibbutz members should seek work on their own that fit their talents or interests, even if that meant working outside of the community. The kibbutz committee might still have the power to hire, but not the power to require. He hoped that this would make kibbutz life more appealing—especially for young people.

However, Yehuda's newfound embrace of capitalism did not extend to the distribution of wealth. He still clung to the notion that wealth (profits and assets) should be distributed relatively evenly, while adding that a kibbutz should seek to facilitate autonomy and independence within the confines of its socialist framework. Some kibbutzniks agreed with him. Others did not—even though they saw the need for changes. Thus, the idea of the "renewed kibbutz" came into being. While its definition continues to evolve, it typically includes hiring outside managers to oversee businesses, having kibbutz members pay for their own electricity usage and food, and making salaries commensurate with the corresponding job.

But it was not easy convincing kibbutz members to change the socio-economic system they had lived in all their lives. To help them solve what often seemed to be intractable problems, many kibbutzim hired consultants. One was Israel Oz, who had been assigned by the government to work with the entity tasked in the 1990s to negotiate and administer the loan modification agreements that, for the moment, had alleviated the crisis. He was an advocate of significant structural change. I was determined to meet Oz after reading about him in David Leach's incredible book *Chasing Utopia*. On a Friday morning in Tel Aviv I got the chance to do so.

* * *

My appointment with Oz was for 9 a.m. I walked a mile or so from my hotel, adjacent to Tel Aviv's huge Azrieli Center Mall, to a sedate residential neighborhood in Tel Aviv with several multi-story buildings. Oz had been very clear. He would give me two hours. It was Friday. After that, his family was coming for a pre-Shabbat meal and I would have to leave.

Oz is a rather nondescript man of average height and weight. But he speaks with confidence.

After spending a few moments with pleasantries, I sat on Oz's sofa sipping coffee he had made me. Oz settled himself in a chair to my left. Rather than ask him first about his family, because he only could meet with me for two hours, I started the conversation by asking Oz if he is still consulting. He responded that while he still oversees the business operations of two kibbutzim, he has not actively consulted for several years. However, Oz said, "I lived for those years you are talking about, the change of the system of life for those kibbutzim, mainly in the north part of Israel, from what you would call privatization of the kibbutz. I used to manage this kind of process in around, let's say, ten kibbutzim in the Galilee and then I was a chairman of some kibbutzim."

Oz then smiled rather seriously and added that, prior to those years, he had been "for ten or twelve years . . . the chairman of the kibbutzim arrangement between the banks, the kibbutzim, the government of Israel. So, I'm familiar with the kibbutzim."

Our conversation then turned to his eighty-page bible. For each kibbutz that hired him, Oz wrote what amounted to a manual for change. When I asked to see one, he returned with several, raised one in the air and said, "This is it." When I responded that some people called it the Talmud or Bible, he laughed. One for kibbutz Sha'ar HaAmakim caught my eye. Before volunteering at Kibbutz Ma'ayan Baruch almost fifty years ago, I performed a week of volunteer work at Sha'ar HaAmakim. It was just another example of how Israel is such a small world.

But I was not there for nostalgia.

What did you learn from the consulting process? I asked.

Oz said, "You called it privatization, you called it reformation. I call it the change of the system of life, the habit of life.... And it's all the essence of it, all what it means is one sentence."

He then looked at me gravely, "Only one sentence:"

> *All the other is bullshit. The meaning of the change was and is that every member of the kibbutz will, has to be responsible for his life. And he has to be a free man. His freedom. That's it. All of it. The kibbutz is responsible for the basic income to those members who are older than 65 years old. They have to pay them. They have to be [safe] and sure enough they will [receive] a monthly income, as a pension or whatever, that's it. That's all the story!*

He paused and then continued:

> *Then it's all how to do it. How much do you want to subsidize the day care, if you want to subsidize it or not, if you want to subsidize the services [of doctors for older people].... And yes, how much and where [are] the resources for the money that you plan to [use for subsidies].... But the main idea, let them be free men! Let them be responsible. Let them take responsibility [for] their own life.*

Oz's cadence then changed. He began enunciating his words slowly but emphatically:

> *That's it! And you know what was so surprising? That those people, men and women at the age of fifty, almost twenty years ago... were so afraid that they could not manage their life. That they could not find a job, that they will not have enough income,*

that they could not handle their life. And so on and so on. All of them. But all of them, all the kibbutzim, when they realized there is no other way, you have to take responsibility of your own life, they find their way.

Despite his obvious passion for the subject, Oz ended his consulting practice. Why, I asked?

Oz responded, "It was boring. It is boring. It's the same, it is not the challenge for me . . . . Why? Because it's always the same . . . . They think they are unique. They are not unique." Wealthy kibbutzim that were fortunate enough to have a successful factory particularly frustrated him. All too often, Oz told me, people, especially young ones, did not pull their weight. As a result, the kibbutz subsidized them. That, he said, made it "a corrupt system."

Our conversation then strayed into the loan agreements he'd administered between the kibbutzim, the banks, and the government. For years the banks had willingly provided loans to the kibbutzim for industrial development, which the kibbutzim repurposed for daily living. That changed under his watch. Money lent for industrial purposes had to be used for those purposes, and the industrial assets, not the kibbutzim, secured those loans. Of course, that also meant the kibbutzim had to refrain from profligate spending aimed at increasing their members' standard of living. Easier said than done.

But why did the banks lend so much money under such risky conditions? The answer, Oz told me, was rooted in history. After 1948, Israel's government came into being. Before 1948 the leaders were the same people, then part of the Zionist organization that brought the State into being. And, he said, the kibbutzim and moshavim, "are the land occupier. They mark the border of Israel. And therefore . . . from 1920 till 1995, [the Zionist organizations] and the government of Israel after 1948, they subsidize[d] . . . the kibbutzim movement. They never ever lived on their own."

Oz continued with increasing fervor: "Always, every few years, the government, in different ways, subsidized the kibbutzim. Even when I met [with] the banks at the beginning of the nineties, I [asked], 'why you gave them so many loans?', and they said, 'We understood that always the government of Israel would take care of those loans and give us the money back.'"

Why? Because the kibbutzim had undertaken "the mission of the Israel[i] government. To hold the land. To settle all over. That's it!"

Things changed in 1988. Although the government had once again guaranteed the outstanding loans as part of the first loan restructuring, it now said that this was its last guarantee. The end of government guarantees was the final straw. Kibbutzim could not afford to go on as they were. More and more young people left the kibbutzim, seeing the writing on the wall, left for a better life elsewhere. The kibbutzim began to wither as they entered into an economic and demographic death spiral. Something had to change despite the reluctance of the older members to do so. And finally, Oz said, "Everything blew up."

Oz said there have been three major changes in kibbutz life since their inception. The first was moving the babies from "the communal hall to the home." The second were all the structural changes, the shift of responsibility from the kibbutz to the individual, that were necessary after the subsidies stopped. The third change is happening now. "And they are not dealing with it," he said. "In many kibbutzim a lot of young families are coming back . . . . It's overcrowded now. And [for] many issues they don't have the values. They don't have the understanding what is a kibbutz." Oz said they don't respect the kibbutz community and its leaders. Instead, "they are interested, let us say, [in] what is good for them. A house, education services, babysitter servicing from the grandparents, and so on."

Oz further lamented that nobody with gravitas is teaching the younger members the co-operative community values necessary for the social functioning of the kibbutz. As a result, "a lot of [the younger members] are fighting against the kibbutz," by demanding more and more. These disputes motivate "the parents and the kids [to] arrange a coalition against the kibbutz." Then, in general assembly meetings, there is chaos. In the past, peer pressure served to minimize outbursts. If peer pressure didn't work, the realization that the kibbutz secretary and the various committees could make your life miserable would serve to cool any hot tempers. Good luck getting the job you want, permission for a vacation, or a kibbutz car if you disrupted the community. But now people are free. And free people can say what they want, and they do. "So, what happened," Oz told me, "what is interesting, [is] that the big change that [took] them from dependent people to free people to independent people, is the main [problem] for the daily life of the community."

When I asked Oz what he would have done differently, he immediately zeroed in on the problem of community cohesion. Although he regarded his efforts with the kibbutzim "a big success," Oz told me, "Honestly, I didn't realize . . . what [would] happen in the kibbutz after the big change . . . . And I didn't understand then what I understand now that we have to deal with the day after. What is the meaning of being such a community?"

How should kibbutzim now address the problem he had just identified? Oz said that in order to avoid destructive internal squabbling, kibbutzim should hire outside managers to deal with the "friction points," such as health services, education, or infrastructure. Cultural issues, however, he would leave to kibbutz leaders.

My time with Oz passed quickly. Near its end, I asked about his family background. Oz told me that his mother had survived Auschwitz before coming to Israel in 1946 and that his father was a soldier in the Russian Army who participated in battles from Russia to Berlin before arriving in Israel in 1948.

I'm glad I didn't ask Oz about his parents when we first met. I wouldn't have been able to resist using my full two hours learning about them. And, of course, there was another coincidence, typical of what I had already grown accustomed to encountering. Before meeting Oz, I had spent much time interviewing residents of Merom Golan and learning its history. Decades ago, Oz had been in a youth movement. When he graduated in 1968, its leaders wanted to place him at Merom Golan. Oz refused. Imagine that. He and Yehuda and Omer could have been friends!

In 1975, Oz moved to Kiryat Shmona, spending three years as a community director. He confirmed what Yamit Yanai Malul had told me several days before. "Those who have enough money and enough opportunities just left. Those who stay over there till now, those don't have any alternative." Recently, Oz went back to Kiryat Shmona for a day to do research for his third fiction book, which is now in the works. He walked the neighborhoods and what he saw was "disgusting, unbelievable, compared to those days [when he lived there]. It's much, much worse."

Everything Oz told me corroborated what I had been told during my travels in the north. It also made me realize that I needed to ask more questions. Three months later, I returned to Israel, determined to better understand how the northern border kibbutzim had weathered the economic and social storms of the last four decades. What I learned is where I now turn.

Chapter Eleven

Kibbutz Dan Now

In February 2019, I sat down with Dorit ben Shalom Moshe, chairman of the board of Kibbutz Dan, in a sparsely furnished room that contained a conference table surrounded by sterile looking chairs. Diminutive, seven months pregnant, and nearing forty, Dorit's exuberance was noteworthy. She is filled with confidence, as is her sister Orly, who is the financial manager at Kibbutz Hanita. Orly had suggested I meet Dorit to hear a different perspective on kibbutz management. How often, I thought, do two sisters occupy similar roles for two different organizations?

Four months after Orly had suggested that I meet her sister, and several emails later, I found myself driving up Kibbutz Dan's main road, looking for its administrative offices. When I last visited the kibbutz in October 2018, I was focused on my interview with Samuel Gardi rather than the condition of the kibbutz. This time, I studied its common areas and noted the condition of its structures. After having visited many kibbutzim in the north in the span of a few months, I had a basis for comparison. What I saw concerned me. Rather than immaculate public areas I saw grounds that needed work. Many buildings were old, some plainly in need of renovation. It wasn't poverty, but in many areas it wasn't reflective of the nicer grounds I had seen in the area of the kibbutz where Samuel lived. Nor was it up to the standards of other communities I had seen. Something was amiss.

When I met Dorit, she was well into the third year of her four-year elected term. But, like much else in Israel, her role is complicated. Before the kibbutz's membership elected her, Dorit worked as a secretary for its day-to-day manager. Kibbutz Dan employs an outside manager. After her election, Dorit remained the manager's secretary while also, as chairman of the board, she was his boss. Soon, Dorit fired that manager and hired the current manager, whom she works for today. Dorit's rationale for this odd arrangement was simple. Her mother was born on the kibbutz and her grandmother and grandfather were part of the group that established the kibbutz. For her boss it's just a job. But for Dorit, "This is my home." Still, only in the kibbutz ecosystem can someone hire and fire their own boss with perhaps one exception. It is not unusual for IDF reserve officers to command reserve privates, corporals, and sergeants who, in civilian life, are their superiors. So, I guess it's better to say: Only in Israel.

We got to our topic—the present state of Kibbutz Dan—very quickly. I asked Dorit if she would run for a second term. To my surprise, she very definitively said no. "Nobody wants to" run for a second term. And then, "Especially here. Dan is very complicated."

When I gave Dorit a quizzical look, she quickly said, "Kibbutz Dan right now is of one of the most complicated situations in the kibbutz movement in Israel."

Explaining her kibbutz's situation to an Israeli from another kibbutz is difficult, Dorit said, but explaining it in English to someone from the United States was even harder. "But," she said, "I will try."

* * *

Dorit's words surprised me. My meeting with Samuel a few months earlier had left me with the impression that Kibbutz Dan was in good shape. He had told me that Dan was a "renewed kibbutz," which had evolved from its traditional format. Now there are different salaries for different jobs, and most members eat at home. Only rarely do they gather for a common meal in the dining hall. Income is no longer pooled. The percentage of members who work inside the kibbutz has practically reversed; previously ninety percent of members worked inside the kibbutz, now ninety percent work outside of it. Monthly earnings average about $3,000 to $4,000 per month and members now own their own homes. In addition, there is a social protective net. If someone has medical expenses in excess of twenty-five percent of their earnings, the kibbutz picks up the difference. As a result of these reforms, and a change in its membership structure which I will get to later in this chapter, Samuel had told me the kibbutz had reversed course, with the average age of its 300 members getting lower, mainly due to an influx of the children of members that live in most available housing on the kibbutz. The only downside of that, I thought, was that there now is little housing available to sell or rent to outsiders, as is now done to raise money and attract new members in many other kibbutzim.

Samuel said he thinks "this is much better," but misses "some parts of the old times." His wife, Haviva, felt the same. After an extended conversation about the old days, she said you "only don't change when you are dead!" But earlier on that October day, as I spoke to Samuel's older friends, I had picked up a hint of sadness when I talked with them about the old days versus the present ones. Still, Samuel and his wife embraced the need for change, or at least recognized that the kibbutz is a living organism that must adapt to survive.

Haviva and Samuel had relayed two stories to me that highlighted the community feeling that had been lost with the changes. The first involved a female friend of Haviva's that had returned to Kibbutz Dan after a twenty-year absence. She had remembered the kibbutz as a lonely yellow light in a sea of blackness when seen from a distance in the deep of night. Now, no longer a dim island in the dark, the lights of Kibbutz Dan are barely distinguishable from the glow of civilization throughout the valley. This disappointed Haviva's friend when she returned. For her, Kibbutz Dan no longer had the cache of being an isolated outpost. For me, the underlying message of the story was that isolation had bred a deep bond among members that was necessary for their survival, a deep bond that no longer was as strong.

Samuel's story spoke more to the beauty of kibbutz life that had been lost. A friend of his, now dead, who had served with him in the Yom Kippur War, had lived in Kibbutz Dan for a time. Then, a communal radio had served as a gathering point. Samuel's friend was horrified when he returned and saw that everyone now owned a radio in their own home. Similar stories are told about teakettles—they only could be found in the kibbutz dining hall for decades—but over time members acquired their own. Whether radios or teakettles, both examples and countless others illustrate the change in kibbutz culture wrought by time and the need to "renew." The kibbutz as a whole is no longer a family's focus; now the focus is on the traditional family unit of parents and children. And because of the changed security and economic conditions, kibbutz members no longer had to band together for their common good.

Still, after I left the Gardis in October 2018, I thought things were going well at Kibbutz Dan. I was wrong.

* * *

The problem is not money but status. At Dan, members have one of two statuses: one for those who became members decades ago, another for those who came to the kibbutz within the last twelve years. After the financial crisis that impacted the entire kibbutz movement, Kibbutz Dan adopted some of the principles of a "renewed kibbutz." But, Dorit told me not enough was changed to attract new members.

For ten to twenty years nobody joined. Member's children went their own way, and nobody else had an interest in replacing them. As a result, the kibbutz aged. And aged. And aged.

Finally, the kibbutz acted. It created a second type of membership for new members. They would be responsible for their own finances, like the older members, but would not be required to take on any of the kibbutz's then massive debt. Also, the new members, many of whom are children of the older members, would get the benefit of the quality of life in the north, living close to their parents, and the remaining educational and social benefits of living on a kibbutz. In return, only the older, debt ridden members, would receive any profits produced by assets of the kibbutz or proceeds from their sale. The older members would also receive a pension from the kibbutz. The younger ones would not. Nor would new members be allowed to vote on decisions regarding kibbutz assets since they had no rights to the profits and no responsibilities for the debt to date. Nor would they have any voice regarding any new moneymaking ventures on the kibbutz. However, in recognition of the differences between old and new members, the buy-in for new members, other than the cost of their homes, would be minimal.

For the older members it was a great deal. For the younger members—on the surface, in retrospect at least—perhaps not. But living in a small community isolated from the hustle and bustle of the country's urban centers comes with a certain vitality and closeness. And not being responsible for the kibbutz's debt burden was no small thing. For a while, that was enough—until it wasn't.

Eventually, the kibbutz paid off its debt and prospered. Over time, the evolving reality that the older members were "in the money," began to grate on the newer members. Acceptance of the balance previously forged in return for not taking on debt dissipated. Perhaps even more so for newer members that joined the kibbutz after it began to prosper again. Dorit is a new member. But she explained that for her, "it's okay." She knew what she was getting into. But many "people [agreed to] one deal," she said. "And now they want another."

The day before I met with Dorit, there was a membership vote regarding—of all things—marijuana! The vote illustrates the division between membership classes. The kibbutz decided to partner with a company called *Seedo* to manufacture cannabis for export. Israel's government had officially approved such activity a couple months earlier. Kibbutz Dan will become the first kibbutz to try its hand at making money from cannabis. Subsequently, others joined the cannabis bandwagon, including former Prime Minister Ehud Barak, who is involved with another company doing the same thing. But Dorit was not permitted to vote on the matter. Imagine that. She had the right to become the kibbutz's chairman of the board but could not vote on what she had been elected to manage. Nevertheless, Dorit understands. The new members did not invest their lives in the kibbutz's factories. They, she says, "[don't] get how things were here." Dorit's perspective comes from her life as a child on the kibbutz. Her mother served in the kibbutz war room while her uncle was outside fending off the Syrian army on the second day of the Six-Day War, which I described in Chapter Seven.

Still, Dorit also recognized the risks of doing nothing to alleviate the growing anger of so many members. People could leave again. The average age of the younger membership group is thirty-five or less. The average age of the older group is seventy to seventy-five. If there is no solution, the old will get older and nobody from the younger group will stay to manage the kibbutz or ease the older members during their last years.

So, Dorit has begun crafting a plan that will allow people to progress from one status to another. Currently, there is no way for members with younger status to gain the same rights the older members have. Under Dorit's plan, there would be a large buy-in. So costly that she's not sure that people will want to do it. In fact, even

Dorit's not sure that she'd be willing to do it. But, from our conversation, I gleaned that for now that is the best that can be attained in a compromise between the warring groups. And not all wars are between young and old members. Some older members are arguing with each other whether to hold the line vs. introducing a plan to moderate or eliminate the differences between membership classes.

And warring they are.

The problem with those members of the older group that are resisting change, she said, is that "they are mostly afraid. It's fear."

Kibbutz Dan's major source of revenue comes from Danpal, a kibbutz-owned company that operates on five continents. It supplies materials for walls and roofs that allow architects to infuse natural light into their designs. If sold, the proceeds could be used to guarantee payment of pensions to the older members and would eliminate some of the issues that prevent the newer members from gaining ownership rights in kibbutz assets. But Dorit accepts that the choice rests solely with the older membership.

"They have to be the ones to decide if and when they sell it," she said. "It is one of the biggest decisions they don't want us to be involved in and I think they are right."

However, many of the younger members are not as accepting as Dorit. She explained why. After army service, Dorit moved to Jerusalem with her husband, whom she fell in love with when he was a sixteen-year old boy, living like her, at Kibbutz Dan. In Jerusalem, she studied law and became pregnant with her first child. Dorit's instinct was that Jerusalem would not be a good place to raise a child. Her heart led her to return to the north to be near her mother. Dorit's husband wanted to return to Kibbutz Dan. It would seem that the stars were aligned for her return, but Dorit refused. They ended up in Kiryat Shmona for a year before he prevailed. Her fear was that no matter what her accomplishments, people at Dan "would see her as a child" and through the lens of her family. Dorit need not have worried. It did not take long for the members, new and old, to elect her to the kibbutz's top position.

It also did not take long for Dorit to realize things have changed since her childhood "in a complicated way."

"The older chaverim (friends but in this context members) didn't change enough to get along with the new ones," Dorit said, even though most new members are part of the old members' families. As a result, the social problems caused by the disparity in the status of members has seeped into families—manifesting in some children becoming angry with their parents who will not consent to their having equal membership rights. When I again asked whom do those older members that refuse change think will take care of them, Dorit responded that she thinks "their plan is to have enough money so they can hire people." But, she says, "Community is more than that, and at the end of the day it is more than who will change their diapers."

Dorit told me that the impasse is causing tremendous problems with the kibbutz's infrastructure and social cohesiveness. As I drove into the kibbutz to meet her, it was clear to me something was wrong. Landscaping has been neglected. Tennis courts are not in good shape. The older areas of the community have a well-worn look. When I asked Dorit about it, she said "[Kibbutz Dan is] a wealthy kibbutz but just for some of the chaverim. When you look at the community as a whole it is a very, very poor kibbutz . . . . There is no money for basic stuff." The new neighborhood, she told me, is nice. "But money from the factory does not get to the community." Money for the community comes from a 400-shekel (a little more than $100) fee that each adult pays. And only recently did older members begin paying that fee.

A problem Dorit recently encountered spoke volumes about the difficult environment at the kibbutz. Socializing together, of course, is one of the trademark attributes of kibbutz life. That sense of community had already diminished some time ago, with people hardly ever eating together in the dining hall or gathering on holidays. But an opportunity had arisen to potentially renew the community's spirit. Many kibbutzim commemorate the date of their establishment. For Kibbutz Dan, 2019 marked the eightieth year of its existence. Dorit and others wanted to celebrate their eightieth year with an event that would bring all kibbutz members together for food and fun. But the membership voted against it. A majority did not want to spend the money. A majority does not want to increase the monthly fees per adult. A majority thinks of themselves more than the community. "Nothing is going to happen and it's sad," Dorit said.

As we neared the end of our time together, I asked Dorit what she thought the kibbutz would be like in ten years. She responded, "It's an enigma. Ask again in a year or two. It's really about whether [everyone] will be able to become full members." As full members, the younger members would finally be able to participate in making decisions about the kibbutz's future and finances. That will be crucial, she said. "Someone has to make the decisions—not the managers you hire."

With little confidence of hearing one, I asked Dorit if there are any other proposed solutions to Dan's problems, at least on the drawing boards. Her answer was not optimistic. Other than the buy-in opportunity for younger members combined with some form of longevity requirement, nothing else is in the offing.

A couple months after our interview, I thought, most likely Dorit's time as chairman of the board of the kibbutz would come to an end. She had told me that after giving birth to her child and subsequent maternity leave, it's unlikely that she will return to work before her term is up. And that she was certain she will not run again, even though she fully intends to continue with her job as a secretary to the manager. "I need a break," Dorit said. "The last two years [were] very difficult for me and my family."

While she knew what she was getting into, the job has plainly left Dorit exhausted and frustrated. With some modest pride, Dorit told me that when she started her term, but before she fired the manager, "People didn't speak to each other." That has since somewhat improved, yet the battle between the old and new guard at the kibbutz rages on.

Dorit sympathizes with the younger generation despite many who have misgivings about her. She said, "For the young people in the kibbutz, I am only like a traitor." Conversely, she understands the fears and needs of the older members, saying, "They change like people usually change when they get older . . . . Partially they are right. [But] I don't think they are doing the right stuff to change their situation". Sadly, few at the kibbutz seem to share her perspective.

I left Kibbutz Dan saddened by what I had heard but still hopeful. Dorit had told me there were good people at Dan who could assume her position and push through the changes that were needed. And, I had learned, Dorit has no plans to leave. When I had asked her why she wouldn't leave, Dorit responded forcefully, "It's my home! My mother is getting older and my child is growing up here. This is my home. This is my family. It's very important."

I couldn't help thinking that the same is true for just about everyone else who lives there. And, I knew, the problems Kibbutz Dan faced could be solved. I knew because I had heard a similar story at Kibbutz Hanita a few months earlier. There, they had weathered the storm. Knowing that I would be returning to Hanita in a few days, my time with Dorit had made me all the more eager to do so.

* * *

Fortunately, the saga of the membership wars at Kibbutz Dan has taken a turn for the better since I interviewed Dorit. When I returned to Israel in November 2019, I heard that Dorit had resumed her duties as chairman of the board rather than leave office after her baby was born. Then, in January 2020, I learned some extremely good news. Dorit and Samuel Galdi, who had been the elected leader of the kibbutz between 2003 and 2007, have almost completed a plan to address the differences between kibbutz memberships. Samuel had pushed for creation of the two-tiered membership plan during his tenure as kibbutz leader fifteen years ago. Then, it was a necessary implementation because younger people refused to join the kibbutz, in part, because it was so laden with debt. Samuel's plan then struck a needed balance. Now, despite being part of the older group, Samuel has recognized that the differences in membership needed to be addressed now that the debt has been paid and the kibbutz has returned to profitability. Together, Samuel and Dorit have formed a productive working relationship based on mutual respect and friendship. If only politicians in Israel and the United States would do the same. Their plan will likely be presented to the kibbutz during the summer of 2020. Meanwhile, relations between kibbutz members have improved. It seems that the kibbutz is making significant headway to resolve its problems.

I was overjoyed to hear that news.

Chapter Twelve

Kibbutz Hanita Now

I met Dr. Yuval Achouch at a stone bench adjacent to a grassy public area in the center of Kibbutz Hanita. He's a man of average height, with a dark-haired but receding hairline, and the hint of a paunch typical for a sixty-year-old man. He spoke with a joyful cadence that made conversing with him an absolute joy.

Yuval promptly took me to his new home located just within the outer boundary of the kibbutz. There, I saw harsh reality intruding upon what had once been a serene view. Just beyond Yuval's backyard deck is a layer of low green trees that resemble what is in the backyard of many suburban homes in the United States. But beyond that, on the other side of a narrow gorge, stands a towering, many-story-high, dirt wall that has been scraped from the once verdant hillside. Just below the low green trees, only feet away, is a patrol road used by the IDF, a fence, and another massive dug-out vertical dirt wall. The two man-made walls circle around and meet to the east. Together they form the shape of a "U". At their base is a gorge. That gorge is in Lebanon. The hill to the west, opposite the open side of the "U," also is in Lebanon. Behind the steep walls torn into the hillside is Kibbutz Hanita.

The IDF created the dirt wall to make infiltrating the kibbutz physically taxing. The IDF removed the vegetation to ensure that its soldiers could see anyone attempting to climb the dirt wall. Soon, more security measures will be put in place. Yuval's deck provided me a bird's eye view of the security challenge that Kibbutz Hanita faces every day—and some of the countermeasures put in place.

But Yuval was somewhat wistful, saying, "Look what they did," his voice overriding the clang of construction equipment digging into the mountainside. "It was forest, everything was green. It's a pity. I'm very sad about what will be. They are supposed to build [another] wall seven meters high. That's what we'll see from our window."

Yuval, attracted by the view, had purchased his home just two years earlier. Now, he was considering putting small trees on his deck to block the ugliness. At that moment I realized it's one thing to read about Israel's plans for building a security fence along the entire Lebanese border, from the Mediterranean to Syria, and reshaping the landscape where necessary. But it's something else to see it up close and personal from a private civilian's home, knowing that as we were looking into Lebanon from Yuval's deck, eyes from Lebanon may well have been looking at us.

I became aware of Yuval after reading about him in David Leach's book *Chasing Utopia* published in 2016. After discussing the troubles kibbutzim face in general—and Hanita specifically—Leach had asked Yuval if he had ever been tempted to leave Hanita. Yuval then answered, "That is my dream now!"

Years later, I was determined to discover if that was still the case—it's not!

I thought this change of heart especially important coming from Yuval, since he has a PhD in Sociology, has written multiple articles concerning kibbutz transformation, and who for the last decade has been affiliated with Haifa University's Institute for Kibbutz Research. But even more important, Yuval is an older member of Kibbutz Hanita. Why did his dreams change for the better?

Yuval grew up in France, where he joined a Zionist youth movement in Marseilles. At the age of sixteen he visited Hanita for a week, and then performed volunteer work at a different kibbutz. On his second trip to Israel, Yuval spent six months in Jerusalem as part of a program for young Jewish leaders, another six months at Hanita, and then joined the IDF, where he became a paratrooper. In those days, French citizens could enlist in Israel's army in lieu of fulfilling their military commitment to serve in France's army. Nevertheless, after completing his IDF service, Yuval returned to further his education. But Zionism still motivated him.

Yuval made Aliyah and decided to make his home at Kibbutz Hanita. He worked as a farmer for his first decade at the kibbutz, but he yearned to teach. When Yuval saw opportunities begin to appear at local colleges for teachers with advanced degrees, he obtained his PhD in sociology. Now armed with an advanced degree, Yuval embarked on his still ongoing twenty-year career teaching sociology. His research is devoted to studying the transformation of the kibbutz in Israel. When I met him in 2018, Yuval had already lived at Hanita for thirty-four years since 1984.

Given Yuval's academic and personal background, I was eager to begin our interview. However, as is so often the case in Israel, coffee came first. Once seated and happily sipping away, I asked him whether he knew of Israel Oz. Yuval answered, "He is the father of the reformed kibbutz." But then, he said in a cautionary tone, "We are learning every day of the consequences of the change."

Yuval told me that there were three steps of privatization generally and at Hanita. The first occurred in the 1990s, when Hanita stopped providing everything for free. For the first time, members and their families had to pay for personal items like dining hall food and laundry services. But that alone was not enough to reverse Hanita's economic and social malaise. The second step was differential salaries. In 2004, Hanita began paying different amounts for different employments based on a variety of factors. But this caused problems for older members who could no longer work to the same degree as younger members, and who in some cases, no longer had the physical or mental capacity to perform any work. With the kibbutz no longer providing various services for free, how would the older members survive?

The third step was privatization of the resources [assets] of the kibbutz. Some kibbutzim gave members a percentage of the value of assets based on how long they had been members. Others divided up just the "fruits [profits] of the resources but not the resources themselves." Hanita did neither. Instead, Hanita decided to divide both the income and the assets among the older members just like at Kibbutz Dan. That, Yuval said, was a mistake.

The continued malaise, Yuval told me, caused many of his generation to leave Hanita. As a result, he said, "Our friends are not here anymore." A population that peaked at 350 members in the early 1980s was almost cut in half two decades later. When I asked why he stayed, Yuval answered, that he was "too naive. I believed in kibbutz ideology, I believed in socialism, in equality, something quite different than in France." In his first few years as a member, he thought kibbutz life at Hanita heaven. "Of course, there were problems," he said. But he had been optimistic, thinking, "We could fix it without breaking everything." So, for a while he fought against the changes, arguing for "something else, not privatization." But Yuval lost that argument.

The darkening future for kibbutzim impacted Yuval so profoundly that he wrote his PhD dissertation about the turmoil caused by kibbutz privatization. For him, it was part of his "process of mourning the kibbutz—I understood that it is finished and now you have to make something else."

He thought that for about fifteen years, including when he'd spoken to David Leach.

That's since changed. Now, he said, "I believe that there is a future for something which is not the classic kibbutz that was Hanita in the past, but that can also be something different, an alternative to a way of life outside the kibbutz. And it's very interesting that we are living that. It's kind of a laboratory we try to make ourselves at this time in this place. It is a challenge."

What changes are required now? I asked.

Yuval responded enthusiastically: "I believe that it's possible that it will not be a commune like socialism, but we can keep the idea of community and make a community with solidarity with a kind of [caring for each other], make a society where people will know each other, do things together."

But when I asked Yuval what it would take to achieve his dreams of community, Yuval responded vaguely. He said that even though they couldn't now reverse course on the principle that people must be more independent rather than dependent on the kibbutz, they needed to create an environment that fosters connectivity.

When I inquired how that might be accomplished, Yuval answered, "I don't do that. Sorel [the Kibbutz community manager] does that—and other people who are in charge—and I do it also." Although Yuval's statement might seem confusing, I understood him. He won't lead the effort, but he will support the goal. The trick, he explained further, was to create a consensus for building a form of community that emphasized social interaction. And to my surprise, he added economic interactions.

Yuval gave as an example the 2,000 dunams (500 acres) of land the government permits the kibbutz to use for economic pursuits. The land, he said, is an economic tie for all kibbutz members. Yuval told me a kibbutz member who has a PhD in biology and specializes in food for fish had brought to the general assembly a proposal to grow shrimp. The proposal needed a simple majority to carry but lost by one vote. Perhaps, he said, it had not yet been the right time to embark on such an enterprise because people had thought the kibbutz was dying and didn't want their assets invested in what they viewed a wasteful enterprise. But, had the proposal been approved, the shrimp farm would have created an economic tie among them.

Our conversation then turned to the large kibbutz factory, Hanita Coatings, founded in 1983, which makes films, including metal-coated sheeting, for industrial use. For a longtime, the kibbutz owned three quarters of the factory. In 2015, its share of the factory's profit was five million dollars. In 2017, the kibbutz sold Hanita Coatings for seventy-five million dollars and netted about thirty million dollars after the transaction closed (equivalent to approximately one hundred million shekels).

The sale of the factory has improved Hanita's environment. Before the sale, although the kibbutz was aging and losing members—the average age of its members had reached almost seventy—its older members would not permit any new members to join. As at Kibbutz Dan, older members feared diluting their interest in the Kibbutz's assets and income. Yuval, then, was also against permitting new members to join the kibbutz if that meant they would gain an interest in the factory. He explained that, although he was for socialism ten years ago when he was fifty, the kibbutz looked like it might dissolve, and he needed the factory money to support himself.

Yuval said, "I invested thirty years in this community, and it's not possible to tell me, OK, after thirty years we change the rules, somebody will come and enjoy what you invested and you get nothing for what you invested. Or they can come and decide what will be with the fruit of my investment?"

Yuval was emphatic on this point. The first few years on the kibbutz he had toiled in its banana and other agricultural fields to support the factory when it was not making money. He would never give up ownership or the right to vote to those who had not earned it. Likewise, the older members who had little or no working life left refused to allow younger members to obtain a vote because the factory was their only remaining financial support. Unlike kibbutz land, which belongs to the government, the factory belonged to the kibbutz. It was their safety net. New members would dilute ownership of the old. Other than a massive payment, like an initiation fee that few new members would be able to afford or willing to pay (like, perhaps, at Kibbutz Dan), the only solution for attracting new members was to sell the factory.

Now, Yuval said, "Selling of the factory gives [the older members] the feeling of justice." As a result, Yuval is now optimistic. There is a feeling of excitement, he said.

Yuval then explained what he believes should be done over the following two decades.

First, "Integration of new members. [We] have to renew the population," he said. For more than twenty years the kibbutz would only permit new social members that were not given the opportunity to own kibbutz assets. But Yuval said, "We understand if we have classes in the kibbutz it doesn't work." So, he advocates for one class only, full membership for all.

Second, Yuval said, the kibbutz needs to build more homes to accommodate more people.

Lastly, the kibbutz must "find a way to support the community. Community can only exist if you have good services for the population." But doing that costs money and people don't want to pay higher monthly dues. So, he said, "You have to build the business of Hanita so it will provide more resources to make the life better." That doesn't mean another big factory, but instead, many smaller concerns. And, he emphasized, "You have to renew the infrastructure of Hanita. It looks like [a] refugee camp sometimes."

Near the end of our conversation I learned that Yuval has three children— ages 30, 28, and 27. None of them live at Hanita. For them, he said, it's more interesting or exciting to live in Tel Aviv. But he told me that good people are now moving to Hanita. He's optimistic.

* * *

Sorel Hershkovitz, Kibbutz Hanita's fifty-one-year-old community manager, like Yuval, is now optimistic. Sorel is a big man with a gentle presence. Formerly a Lieutenant Colonel in the IDF who, in addition to operational commands, served a stint as liaison between its northern command and the international community, Sorel was accustomed to navigating difficult relationships to find common ground. Four years after retiring from active service, in 2016, he was elected community manager by a majority of Kibbutz Hanita members. It was a difficult time for the kibbutz: the factory had not yet been sold, its membership was aging, and pessimism ruled. Nor did Sorel's status as a social member without rights to the assets place him in a position where he could lead by giving rather than getting. But he had a vision, which he was determined to act upon. And he had the grit to see it through.

For Sorel, it is all about rebuilding the kibbutz's sense of community. For thirty years he has called Hanita home. Two of his four daughters still live at home with him and his wife while attending high school and middle school. His oldest child is in Jerusalem learning to be a nurse. The second oldest is in the army. While serving in the army with various commands, Sorel's heart remained at Hanita where, it became clear to me, it was torn by the internal strife.

Sorel, again like Yuval, met me at the stone bench. The kibbutz recently built the bench as part of its restoration of a large grassy and tree shaded playground area in the center of the community. To its west there is a dilapidated building that Sorel hopes to transform into a kibbutz library, which, in conjunction with the grassy area, would become a focal point for the community. The dining hall was to the east of the bench. Once a spot where members would gather for every meal, the hall has been reduced to a location where an outside contractor serves lunch for thirty shekels (about nine dollars and very tasty as I would later find out).

As we walked along a sidewalk cutting through the grassy area, Sorel discussed with me aspects of the playground and common areas and how they fit into his vision and the philosophy of the kibbutz. Sorel's plan for improving the common area included fixing and enlarging a concrete pad in the northeast corner. During the day, children could play on it. At night, with added electrical infrastructure, it could be used as a stage. In front of it, would be a lush field of grass. In short, he wanted to transform the common area into a cultural hub, perfect for performances, gatherings, and even weddings. All were within Sorel's vision for the future.

Previously, the grounds had fallen into disrepair while the community focused on financial issues involving the factory and attempts to create new housing. Now, he assured me, the focus had changed. Residents recognized that Hanita "must invest in our community not just in [their] personal area." While we spoke, a man I will call "Amir", who was the kibbutz groundskeeper, walked up to us. Amir rented his home on the kibbutz but was not yet a member, even though he was born here. His father had belonged to a Zionist youth group, where he met his wife. The Zionist group had sent them to live in Hanita in the early 1960s. Later, Amir tried living in Tel Aviv, and even in Paris, but then came back, he said, because "this is my home." Sorel quickly interjected, "This is home."

The idea of "home" is a common refrain I heard on every kibbutz I visited. Despite concerns for the future, many young people reared on a kibbutz felt that tug to return home. The economic uncertainties unleashed in the 1980s coupled with older members' fear for their economic survival had torn those bonds for decades. As I listened to Amir, I realized that I was seeing evidence of those bonds being re-forged. Would Sorel be able to accomplish that? Could Sorel's vision serve as a model for Kibbutz Dan and others? I wanted to learn more.

As we neared the end of the common area, I saw several rocks and dirt sections that supplemented more traditional playground equipment also present. Sorel explained that part of the philosophy underlying the playground was that the children should play with materials of the earth like sand, water, and mud. And to increase their tactile experience, parents permitted their children to play barefoot. Some in the community expressed safety concerns, asking, for example, whether the stones placed there were too high or too rough? But Sorel's response was that part of growing up is learning to handle difficult things and to become aware that "not all things [have] round edges, soft and easy to deal with. This is not life," he said, one "can't expect them to grow with a wide and open mind if not allowed even to fall."

Then he added a refrain that I heard frequently in my former life as an attorney, "We are in a country with too many lawyers, don't take it personally, they are always looking for the opportunity to sue someone. It's amazing, each letter I write I must discuss it with our legal adviser."

Perhaps his comments indicated his frustration with aspects of his present job. But I am just as certain they indicated the exasperation he felt at northern command where he served in intelligence and as a liaison with the foreign press—two jobs where he had a front row seat to legal advisers intervening regarding which targets could be struck, giving orders and advice not based on military needs but on international law and opinion.

Before nearing the administrative offices, we passed the dining hall. Sorel told me his dream was to provide meals for the community there twice a week. He explained that he wanted to reverse the pendulum that first swung from providing every meal to every resident every day for free to not providing any meals at all. Now, Sorel said, for the benefit of enhancing the community experience, the pendulum must pull "somewhere back." He explained that the total elimination of communal meals divided the members and that now they needed to find the correct balance between financial constraints and social needs.

Sorel's office was rather nondescript, but we passed it up in favor of a large conference room adorned with coffee, soda, and fruit that I couldn't stop eating. In between bites, I asked Sorel how he got to Hanita. His answer, like many, revealed a past that while unique to him was a common theme that I believe links many Israelis and must be recognized to understand Israel.

Born in Romania, Sorel arrived in Israel as a child in late 1973. Syrian and Israeli soldiers were still fighting on the Golan, even though the Yom Kippur War had ended. Sorel had no idea he was leaving Romania until the day it happened. His parents, for the family's safety, had kept it secret. In those days, Sorel said, "Jews paid Ceausescu money to release Jews." In fact, from 1967 until 1989 when Romanians, enraged by his cruel rule and failed economic policies, overthrew their dictator, Nicolae Ceausescu, and executed him, Israel paid nearly one billion dollars for permission for Jews to flee. These payments amounted to an average of $4,000 per Jew that the Romanian government allowed to escape its dictatorial rule. By 1991, the 450,000 Jews in Romania who survived Nazi concentration camps had dwindled to 18,000.

"I remember," Sorel told me, "I traveled in a train to Bucharest, it was night, we arrived at the airport, [and] in the morning Ben Gurion, Tel Aviv." All his old friends were lost to him. Immediately, without warning, he "started a new life here." Sorel grew up in Beersheba, then a development town in the Negev. There he finished high school, learned biology and chemistry, and was drafted into the air force. Six months later the IDF transferred him to the army, where he became an artillery crew member. Then he went into an officer training school and met his future wife, Dikla, who had been born at Hanita. In 1990, before he had decided to ask Dikla to marry him, Sorel visited Dikla at her parents' home in Hanita. As he spoke it was hard to tell which came first, his love for Hanita or for Dikla, but his love for both increased as he saw more of her and of Hanita.

Sorel spent most of his military life serving in the north. Initially, that happened because one of his instructors at officer training school took a position in the north and brought Sorel with him. In 1991, Sorel married Dikla, and of course as a result, Hanita. In 1992 he became a traditional full member. Both he and Dikla had to be voted in. Dikla's connection to the kibbutz didn't hurt their odds of receiving approval.

But Sorel had no idea of the severity of the impending problems. In 1992 or 1993, he said, "It was the beginning." Hanita started charging a minimal amount for groceries. "It was only a symbolic payment," Sorel said. In the past people took what they wanted, "People have cats and dogs that [ate] meat and cheese because [they] didn't pay." Sorel thought making members pay for grocery items was a good idea because it made people stop and think. But then it was the dining hall. "[You] should pay for yourself what you are taking to eat. And again from [that] place people took three or four portions . . . for the cat and dog outside."

Sorel acknowledged that because of people's selfish conduct the dining hall change was necessary. "When you start paying even symbolic pay," he said, "you are taking only your portion . . . . It was a very positive change in mind."

Then, in 1995, kibbutz members began discussing what would happen if Hanita fell apart. The impetus was both the economic crisis Israel had just overcome, partly at the expense of the kibbutzim, and growing dissatisfaction at Hanita. To permit residents in the community to build their own wealth, the membership decided to transfer homeownership from the kibbutz to the individual member that lived in the home. But of course, the devil was in the details. Homes varied by size, model, and age. As a result, some homes were worth more than others. Direct transfer of ownership would create winners and losers. Therefore, the kibbutz developed a matrix that accounted for how long the member had lived at the kibbutz and how big the home was. Those with larger homes had to pay something. Those with smaller homes might receive an additional payment. Changes like that required seventy-five percent of the membership to agree—an incredibly tough requirement, but it went through. Still, two decades later, Sorel in his present role is dealing with a few families disputing how the matrix should be applied to their situation. And, of course, given Israel's ownership of kibbutz land, there were legal problems as well.

In the late 1990s, Hanita began dabbling with differentiating salaries—but only slightly. Kibbutz leaders, working with outside consultants, evaluated each kibbutz job and assigned them specific salaries. Since most people worked within the kibbutz this made it relatively easy to achieve agreement on the salary structure. But for those members employed in private industry jobs outside the kibbutz, they were now being paid competitive rates in the commercial sector. This created a salary disparity between kibbutz members working outside of the kibbutz and those working kibbutz jobs.

In response, like other kibbutzim, Hanita instituted a progressive dues system, much like a condo fee, on its members: the more you earned, the more you paid the kibbutz. Of course, those dues were in addition to Israel's progressive tax system. The kibbutz used those dues, to fund its infrastructure projects and educational programs for children. But nobody likes it when dues go up. High-income earners did not want to pay more to the kibbutz than those who worked at the lower paying jobs on the kibbutz. In recognition of the dissension the new dues created, Hanita stopped its progressive dues program in 2012 but by then more damage was already done to at least the societal aspects of the kibbutz—whether that system also prompted more members to leave is subject to dispute. Nevertheless, the brain-drain caused by members moving away that had already started in the 1990's which had left too few qualified workers to satisfy the kibbutz's needs, was not reversed. And the 2012 replacement for the progressive dues system, a fixed amount that everyone paid regardless of income—"a very low [fee], very low [fee]," Sorel said—caused a new problem. The flat dues structure did not generate enough money to meet the kibbutz's internal needs. Maintenance decreased and buildings used for daycare and education deteriorated. As a result, Hanita's society continued to crumble.

Making matters even worse, the kibbutz simultaneously stopped accepting new members. Again, the cause was fear. As people fled, as infrastructure fell into disrepair, the fear felt by the older people nearing or already at the end of their working lives, was validated by the kibbutz's downward spiral. Their only hope was the factory, which the kibbutz started in conjunction with an outside investor, who received twenty-five percent of the equity in return for his investment. Adding new members to the kibbutz would dilute older members' shares in the factory. So the membership decided that anyone who had become a member before 2003 would share in the factory's income and in the proceeds if the factory were sold. Those who became members in 2003 or later would receive nothing, even children of the older members who saw Hanita as home, who wanted to become members, and who represented the future of the kibbutz.

The older members received a yearly dividend from the factory's profits. But they worried it wasn't enough for them to support themselves in light of the economic changes at Hanita. They felt the need for more—sooner. Sorel said with empathy and understanding: "They saw that they were older, they saw they won't live long enough to enjoy all the dividends, [they] wanted cash money now." And so, among them they reached a consensus: the kibbutz should stop investing in the factory to increase its profits. Instead, they should sell it.

Sorel's term as community manager began in February 2016. His first challenge was to convince the community "to accept new members." "This," Sorel said is "the main goal, the main effort." But he couldn't get it done "until they [sold] the factory." Older members worried that newer members would use their vote to overturn the decision that only members prior to 2003 would have ownership in the factory. Fortunately, after the factory sold, Sorel's words no longer fell on deaf ears. In July 2018, almost eighty percent of the members voted to accept new full members. It was just in time. The average age then of the remaining 166 kibbutz members was seventy. As a result of the vote, Sorel said, "I hope in 2019 we will get twenty or thirty new members. I hope." But he said it will not be easy "because we are not attractive."

Although there are 700 people, including children, living on the kibbutz, the economic issues it has experienced requires confidence in the future. There is much work to be done, which has been deferred for decades. Hanita's infrastructure, including the buildings used for day care and education, are in desperate need of renovation. I had personally walked through one of these buildings. To say it had deteriorated would be charitable. I saw ceilings stained from periodic leaks, toilets that didn't always flush properly, old paint, archaic kitchen equipment, and tile that to my untrained eye screamed of asbestos in their composition. Modernizing the facility will cost a lot. Parents already living in the kibbutz might tolerate the facility, but I doubt any parent was pleased with it. And for those thinking of joining the kibbutz, I'm sure the thought of paying to join a community that hasn't fixed the buildings used by its children would turn many off, especially because membership is not cheap.

A prospective new member must prove they have the financial resources to obtain a mortgage to purchase an existing home at Hanita, which costs on average about $300,000, or to build a new home, which costs about $500,000. That's a lot of money for a young family in their thirties or forties that, quite possibly, might include one or more partner who had just retired from the military. A prospective new member must also provide proof of their ability to obtain insurance and to secure their own pension. Two other charges are also assessed to new members: an initiation fee (since the factory was sold) of approximately $4,500, and an approximately $150 per month charge for use of community facilities and kibbutz support. Plus, new and old residents must pay an additional monthly community fee of a little more than $150.

Even if people applying for membership meet all of the kibbutz's financial requirements, they also must be approved by more than half of Hanita's existing membership. Before that vote occurs, the applicant must meet with the membership committee to ensure that their views are relatively aligned with the kibbutz's philosophy, social structures, and habits and that they fully understand the commitment they're making.

Still, Sorel is optimistic. New members will be able to build homes they desire on kibbutz land, which already contain the necessary plumbing and other infrastructure. Once members, they'll have a right to a percentage of any new income sources the kibbutz is pursuing. The educational system runs 300 days a year, rather than the 240 days schools are in session outside the kibbutz. Furthermore, the after-school programs for all children run until 5 p.m., which working parents find attractive. The kibbutz also has an appealing student-teacher ratio in grades Kindergarten through fifth grade, one educator or aide for every twelve students, that is less than half of what is normal in many non-kibbutz communities. For the older children, buses take them to school outside the community and then bring them back to the kibbutz's after school programs. And, despite the external threat posed by Hezbollah distressingly close by, the community provides children with a safe place to play. There is little or no traffic in the public area to endanger the kids, and there is a protective feel arising from the fact that most inhabitants know and trust each other. Thus, Sorel says, Hanita "is a great place to have kids," and with the changes he hopes to create an attractive place for families to move to.

"My vision," Sorel told me, "is to improve the community's facilities and services because this is what will attract the young people to be members. I told you," he reminded me, "we are not so attractive now. This is the change [I'm trying to make] . . . . With all the activities on the kibbutz, the holidays, the events we arrange, I am looking for a lively community not only a sleepy town."

But one thing confused me. During our conversation Sorel told me that he would be one of the new members. Earlier he had told me that he'd become a member in 1992. Uncertain, I asked Sorel about the discrepancy. Smiling, he responded, "Promise you won't laugh."

It turns out Sorel was a kibbutz member until he wasn't. Sorel and his wife moved away for a few years. When they returned after 2002, it was too late to become a full member again. Instead, he had to settle for the partial membership that did not allow him to vote on financial matters. Like Dorit at Kibbutz Dan, he was a manager without a vote on all things. There were about fifty people in his status. Most of the first new full members will emerge from that cadre.

Our first meeting was in October 2018. It wasn't until our discussion was nearly over that I learned how close Sorel had come to having a much darker vision for the future. The vote whether to accept new members had been in July. A few days later the kibbutz had scheduled a celebration of its eightieth anniversary. Sorel had held off preparing the remarks he would deliver to the community on that day. He said, "I didn't know what to write. If it is something that is looking forward, or if it is something . . . talking about shutting down this place . . . . It was a very difficult dilemma for me." After the community voted to allow new members he said, "I wrote down the words, and it was optimistic—looking forward." Sadly, quite the opposite was the case at Kibbutz Dan where members wouldn't even agree to celebrate its eightieth birthday!

Sorel's physical appearance belies his vitality. His cuddly smile gives no hint of the passion he has for restoring Hanita. Sorel told me, "You must first of all have the vision, to believe and push it even if you meet obstacles and people who are discouraging you, it is not easy, but you must push it. Maybe it's my education, my previous military background that you have a mission you must push it." And then he emphasized, "You must have the vision."

I left Sorel enthused by the future he sought to bring to Hanita. But I also was aware how all of that could come to an end if he weren't reelected as community manager in February 2019. Sorel told me that the kibbutz had already started building ten new homes and has room for another 150, which will take another twenty years to build. Impressively, he had found time to consider how the new residents living in the new homes would be incorporated into his vision of a cohesive community. Some of the new home sites were located on a steep downgrade from the communal areas. When Sorel spoke to the architect about that, the architect told him not to worry, people would drive. Sorel was not satisfied with that. Hanita, he said, needed to be a walking community where all would know each other. Somehow, I think Sorel will come up with a solution. And I'm certain he will win a second term despite having angered some of the older community members with his unceasing efforts.

"I am fighting for my home to make it a better place," Sorel told me. "Before me there were fifteen years [of] outside community directors which came here in the morning and went in the evening."

Sorel has the passion to transform Hanita into a community that combines the best of communal life with the opportunity to excel as an individual. It's up to the community to harness it.

* * *

Sorel is not the only key player in Hanita's resurgence. Orly Gavishi-Sotto is the kibbutz business director. She handles the money. Sorel might have the dreams, but Orly is charged with finding a way to pay for them while also generating more income for the kibbutz. Together, they make quite a team.

It wasn't until 5:30 a.m., before the sun came up on my last day at Hanita, that I really got to know Orly. The night before, at a dinner with others, she had challenged me to join her in a training run the next morning. Orly was preparing for a Christmas half marathon held each year at Me'ilia in the Western Galilee. It has become quite an event, one in which Jews, Arabs, and Christians participate. Orly had been training for some time. Several other people were joining her at 5:30 a.m. My last training run had been more than a month before. Having just turned 64 and carrying many more pounds than I should, and a few more than I admit, I was concerned. Hanita is hilly and I'm not an early morning person. I hoped adrenalin would get me through.

We met in the parking lot just south of the dining hall. It was pitch dark and the sound of something akin to crickets chirped in the background. A small group, including Orly, had already gathered. Soon, several cars pulled up. A few more runners emerged. Some came from several miles away to share in the torment. In the darkness, I couldn't tell exactly how old the people in shorts and T-shirts surrounding me were, but my best guess was that I had at least two decades on them. And, among them was Sharona—the taskmaster.

After some preliminary exercises more strenuous than I expected, we started on what amounted to a 1.5-mile run. Orly ran next to me the whole way. My strategy was to ask her a couple questions early on, that way she'd do most of the talking while I focused on breathing. I hoped the more she spoke the slower she'd run. My plan failed. But the stories she told fascinated me.

Orly, who was in her late thirties when I met her, was born at Kibbutz Dan, the oldest of several children, one of whom was Dorit, the present chairman of the board at Kibbutz Dan. Until she turned twelve, Orly had lived with eighteen other kids in a children's house supervised by a kibbutz employee. Two hours each day she'd spend time with her parents. After turning twelve, Orly moved to a different house for older children. Orly looks back at those days fondly, although she knows those days are gone. When I asked her if most people had found living in a children's house a positive experience, she told me that fifteen percent consider it a negative experience, out of which some speak loudly about their negativity. The rest feel otherwise.

Orly's worst memory of living without her parents had nothing to do with the system and everything to do with where they lived. When Orly was four years old, it was 1982. The first Lebanese War had broken out. Shells were flying and Kibbutz Dan lay directly on the border. Her adult guardian told Orly to go to the shelter. With a blanket and pillow in hand, that little girl, barely able to navigate the steps down to the cold concrete walls below, did what she was told. Orly remembers her fright to this day.

Our run took us throughout a large part of the silent kibbutz. Only the sound of many feet, my labored breathing, and hushed voices marked our way. When we returned to the parking lot, rather than relax, Sharona was waiting for us. Two sets of twenty pushdowns against the curb she barked, then two sprints, each about 200 yards, then more pushdowns, more jogging, more sprints—with Sharona yelling at me each time I returned to the parking lot, "Cliff, faster!"

When we finally finished at sunrise, I was dripping with sweat. But I felt a camaraderie with my new Israeli friends and perhaps had earned just a touch of respect. But I also felt that I had connected on a personal level, ever so slightly, with Orly, whom I hoped would cue me in further to Hanita's likely success or failure in the coming months.

Orly has three daughters, who in 2018 were ages four, nine, and twelve. Her husband was born on the kibbutz, and like Sorel, is not a full member. Nor is Orly. Later, I met Orly and Sorel at the after-school building. Arrayed in a cluster of buildings were the after-school center, the kindergarten, and the lower grade schools. Sorel proudly told me they were arranged so that no vehicles could endanger the children while they moved between buildings or the play areas. Outside many of the buildings were play areas with old appliances and toys. At first, I thought they needed updating, but Sorel explained that, like the playground, the fenced-in areas with the junky looking items were exactly what the kibbutz wanted. We want children's play to be "experiential," Sorel said. "We want them to play with stuff that is not obvious how to do it."

Many young children were inside the building we entered. Loud as it was, Orly told me it was quieter than usual because many were on a field trip. Among them were children with special needs. Orly said it is "very, very important that they are part of the group." Just outside of the door there was a basketball hoop with no net, perhaps a metaphor for the conditions I saw inside. The building for after-school activities is divided. Older children are upstairs, younger downstairs, and between them on a middle level are the bathrooms. The kids all seemed happy and boisterous. The conditions were not. The ceilings were old, stained and well worn. They leak whenever it rains. The wear and tear on the furniture made the chairs and sofas look like they had been there since the 1950s—and they have been. Also present was a kitchen area where a hot lunch is prepared for the kids. That also looks dated.

Crumbling steps led downstairs to the bathrooms. The toilets are very old and at times don't work. At times, you have to dump buckets of water in them so they operate. Below that level, is an area reserved for younger children, where it was more of the same. At least the air conditioning works well there, something that the older kids upstairs don't benefit from much. Also downstairs, I met a woman I will call "Mayel" who works with the kids. She confirmed my observations. When Mayel was a child in the 1950s, she spent time in the same rooms I had just seen. Mayel thinks the building has not been renovated since—a victim of the economic issues that had befallen the kibbutz for more than two decades.

Clearly, the condition of the building bothered Orly and Sorel. The other buildings used for the kids have similar problems. Sorel recognized that the "educational system is one of the most attractive points in our kibbutz community" and it pained him that he and Orly get many comments from parents that not enough money is put into it. Orly agreed, saying, "Education is the most important thing in this community," and feels it necessary to improve the quality of their educational infrastructure "to attract young families here."

The last room I looked at was the bomb shelter. Shelters in the buildings used for the children, Sorel told me, are connected with protected concrete entrances to the buildings and shielded by an arched roof so if something happens, "they can run directly and without exiting out and exposed to danger." The kindergartners don't even have to leave their building. There is an entrance running directly from their room into the shelter. All the teachers have keys for the shelters. The children here learn how to react to incoming rockets, shells, and terrorist attacks as soon as they join the school program. If there is an explosion before a warning siren, the kids are taught to stay close to an inside wall while crouching below a window line. As Sorel spoke, I thought of the days when I was in elementary school and was taught to crouch down in a hallway against the wall with my hands over my neck in the event of a nuclear war. That was theoretical and never made sense to me, even as a child. Here it was practical advice.

As of 2018, the last shells to land in the western Galilee were in 2014. Every day holds the possibility of them coming again.

With two days left on my visit to Hanita, I went to the train station in Nahariya to pick up my friend Mary and her daughter. We visited the Alma Research and Education Center and spoke with its founder, Sarit Zehavi, and then returned to Hanita.

Mary and her daughter stayed in a room rented from a kibbutz member. For little more than forty dollars a night, I stayed in a yurt rented by another kibbutz member. The yurt had multiple beds, heating and air conditioning, and an adjacent, small outside platform containing a room with a fully functioning shower and toilet. But the best thing was the yurt's huge covered deck from which there is an incredible view stretching past the ocean beaches of Nahariya to the faint glimmer of Acre's and perhaps Haifa's lights. To say it was magnificent would be an understatement. On the other hand, to say that the ancient refrigerator on the deck kept things a temperature other than tepid would be an overstatement. Nevertheless, the twinkling lights along the distant coastline combined with the deck's rustic and rural feel served as a great backdrop for three of us to have a heavy philosophical discussion about Zionism. As we talked, I drank the coffee Mary had brought specially for the occasion. It was a moment I didn't expect and will never forget.

On my final morning at Hanita, the three of us met Orly and Sorel for breakfast. We sat in shade cast by a tree at an outdoor table that offered a view like that at the yurt. A woman who seemed in charge took our order of omelets. Fresh bread and other Israeli breakfast staples sat at the table, tempting me. For a moment, I thought I was at a high-class resort instead of an austere kibbutz, on a mountain ridge at the fringe of Israel, with an implacable enemy a short stroll away. Only in Israel!

Orly told us that in early 2019 she would be taking a three-week class in management at Harvard as part of a one-year educational program in Israel. I was stunned but didn't show it. My shock came not from the idea, but from my surprise. My meeting with Dr. Yuval Achouch had alerted me to Hanita's problems and given me hope that solutions might be on the horizon. Sorel, during our in-depth discussion, had explained the challenges and left me convinced that he had a vision and the drive to see it through. Now I was learning that professionalism would marry practice. What I learned convinced me that Orly, Sorel, and many other kibbutz members are determined to transform Hanita to something greater than it is, and I'm certain that they'll succeed. For me, it was not what she would learn at Harvard that mattered. Rather, it was that she wanted to learn.

Our conversation then strayed to the "lone soldier" phenomena. Many boys and girls, especially from the United States, come to Israel to serve in the IDF. Emotionally, it is difficult for them. When Israeli soldiers go on leave, they have a home to return to. Lone soldiers, the term often used for foreign volunteers, do not. Their family is back in their home countries. Many kibbutzim try to fill the void. Hanita has hosted four lone soldiers. Hanita, with Israel's financial assistance, houses them, feeds them, adopts them as part of the kibbutz, and gives them a place to return to over and over again. One was from Pittsburgh. He, or as Orly put it, "my soldier," returned to the United States after his service. The second soldier came from Italy and stayed at Hanita after his service. The third, from South Africa, is still serving in the army. I learned about the fourth, now at Hanita, just before this book was published.

After breakfast we took a walk. Along our route was a music room equipped with a large piano. The room is also used for dance and yoga. We then spied the club area for kids aged twelve to eighteen. More of a hangout than anything else, Sorel said that such a place has had a positive impact by minimizing vandalism. "It's very important," he said, "It gives them someplace together to play and have activities and it prevents them from doing stupid things." I guess teenagers are the same everywhere.

A couple minutes' walk beyond we saw goats behind a fence. Orly told us goat cheese is produced from the milk the goats produce. Shortly after the goats we saw chickens and then we saw something I did not expect. An art studio. Inside, students were taking a painting class. Also, preparations were underway for an upcoming art show.

We then walked down a hill along one of the two roads that run from the gate into the kibbutz. On our left were several buildings, which I asked about. Orly said that the kibbutz rents space to several businesses. The rental income goes into the kibbutz's central fund, and some kibbutz members get jobs with the businesses. The art gallery, a glass factory, and a call center—all operate in spaces rented by the kibbutz. Some of the call center's employees pay the kibbutz to educate and provide after-school care for their kids.

Next came the most interesting business we encountered on that walk—Jullius Distillery. Inside were numerous barrels and a custom-made machine from Germany that distills fermented fruit into traditional brandy and gin. On the machine there was an inscription, "I drink, therefore I am." After a short lecture regarding making what they call "Akko gin," I sat at the small bar in the tasting area and sipped on the gin and some peach brandy, both made at the distillery. The kibbutz collects rent from that company too. In the name of "research," I stayed there for a while, "tasting" more than I should have.

I would've never guessed what Orly had up her sleeve when I first met her. She has planted the seeds for Hanita's renaissance in some of the many vacant buildings that the kibbutz no longer uses. Only time will tell if it will work, but my money is on Orly and Sorel. But it's also on Erez and the people responsible for securing the kibbutz from dangers without and emergencies within.

* * *

Erez had picked me up around 9 p.m. on my first night at the kibbutz. Born at Hanita, he studied in Haifa and served in Lebanon. In 2006, he was off duty on the day Hezbollah kidnapped the two IDF soldiers, which sparked the beginning of the 2006 war. Their loss was hard on Erez. He was their commander. It's possible that Erez would've been taken, instead of one of the two soldiers, had he not been on vacation. Erez first heard of the incident from the radio he carried with him. When Erez called in, his boss said, "It's our problem. Come here."

I had met Erez briefly a year earlier. He had accompanied me into the kibbutz's command center in an underground shelter. The next day, I encountered him again getting into a car with one of his children. But I was quite surprised when I opened the door of the jeep sitting outside the yurt and found Erez sitting inside. I had arranged a meeting with representatives of United Hatzalah, a volunteer rescue organization that provides emergency medical services. Their goal is "to fill the gap" by arriving at the scene within three minutes of an emergency call, and then stabilizing patients until the more traditional rescue services can take over and transport them to the hospital. I wanted to speak with United Hatzalah members in the north because of the paucity of emergency services in the region. Never did I imagine that Erez was a voluntary member. Along with his job as security chief of Hanita and safety officer at the recently sold factory, Erez's plate is quite full.

Erez took me down the road back to the gate and then suddenly veered left onto a dirt road cloaked by darkness and overhanging vegetation. A minute later we came upon an open area with three men around a picnic table. Erez turned on a headlamp attached to his vehicle and directed it at them. When we exited our vehicle and joined them, I saw plastic bottles of soda and a tin of pastry. Under the stars, in the middle of a forest, on a dark night, it was magical.

Surrounded by stillness, the five of us spoke for over an hour about the needs of United Hatzalah in the region. Their faces were in shadow, but their voices were clear, and every word spoken struck me. Hanita has particular needs because it is high up on a hill and can only be reached by a brutally steep, road with hairpin turns. Erez told me if he is needed on the kibbutz, he could reach a person in need within a minute. But the next closest United Hatzalah member would take five minutes or more. Traditional ambulance services could take much longer. The organization is supported by donations, but all too often the donations specify that the money must be used in Jerusalem. As a result, the north, I said, "Gets screwed." At which point one of the wits surrounding me said in reference to Hanita, "But you have a good view!" By the time we finished I committed to purchasing a defibrillator for Hanita and another for use in the region. It was the least I could do for those who were selflessly volunteering their time to save people's lives.

As Erez drove me back to the yurt, I asked him if the region was ready for the earthquake that experts predict will occur sometime in the not too distant future.

"Not enough," he answered.

Then Erez revealed his deep concern for Hanita. "I believe if something happens in this area [nobody will] come to Hanita.... My job is in Hanita, is to organize the kibbutz, [deal with] the emergency myself, my people in the kibbutz, I want everything here. What I don't have here, [in] regular times will come. But in war or big issue in the country, nobody will come. It will just be myself and my team."

Erez revealed that Hanita has an old fire truck, one he proudly showed me on our way back. In addition, the kibbutz will soon receive a newer one from the government. In recent years, his team extinguished two fires in six minutes, well before the twenty-five minutes it took for the firetruck from Nahariya to arrive!

Erez's love for Hanita struck me. I had never known anyone so passionate about where they lived. "It's the best life," he told me. "I have a daughter in the first grade, she can go to homes with friends without me. In the city, no."

Erez, then forty-two, admitted, "[My] phone never turns off. I go to the shower with my phone." He is always on alert and agrees that it is a hard life, "But," Erez said "[It] gets you so much fuel. For the soul it is amazing. When you help someone, you help him, but it gives to you so much. I believe that how much you get is the same that you give. All my life, I all the time give [without] waiting to get back."

The kibbutz, Erez told me, has changed since he was a child—if you ask him, for the good. The old kibbutz, Erez said, "[Was] not good for people that like to work. It was good for the people who don't like to work.... I like to work, I work all the time. My wife all the time says to me 'sit down, sit down, why all the time by the phone, the rescue team, go [be a] firefighter, sit down for a few minutes.'"

A remarkable man. Soon I came to realize how much more remarkable than I had thought.

That was when I spoke with Erez again two days later in the mid-afternoon, this time in the company of two other men, Dvir and Haim. We met in the same conference room I had met Sorel in, but this time without the delectable fruit that had distracted me.

Dvir, a strong looking man in his early fifties was born at Hanita, like so many others I had spoken with. He is the third generation of his family to call Hanita home. Dvir's grandfather arrived in 1939—just a year after the kibbutz was founded. Dvir now works in the factory along with Erez. In addition, he is in charge of all the emergency teams at the kibbutz. During emergencies, he is responsible for keeping community services up and running. In the army he was an officer in the combat engineers. Erez, on the other hand, is the director of security. As such, Erez is responsible for putting the resources in place and thinking strategically. Dvir is responsible for dealing with the emergency at hand—in essence, he is charged with thinking more tactically. In reality, they are close friends and work well together.

The kibbutz maintains several well-trained volunteer emergency teams under Erez's overall command, which are equipped with guns and charged with responding to all manner of emergencies. All are former soldiers. Some still perform reserve duty. They live at the kibbutz, most are available at night, fewer during the day because some hold jobs outside of the kibbutz. When I asked Erez if he knows how many are available at any one time, he answered, "Every minute. All the time."

Emergency calls of all types go to Erez for him to coordinate the response. If the army detects something of concern, they call Erez too. Then he and Dvir decide whether to investigate further and/or to mobilize the volunteers. Erez's volunteers also have a WhatsApp group to facilitate a quick reaction to any emergency. Teams are trained for a terrorist incursion and to fight fires, but not for search and rescue if there is an earthquake. This concerned all of them because, Erez said, "We know that we have to be self-sufficient."

In addition to the volunteers, a hired security guard is constantly on patrol at night. That guard, of course, is backed by the volunteers on call and supplemented by the army. A long time ago, before Dvir was born, terrorists penetrated the fence line precisely where Yuval's house, is located. The kibbutz reaction force chased them back into Lebanon before anyone was hurt.

Many people have volunteered to be on the security teams. Although all of them live at the kibbutz, not all are members. That struck me. Dvir had told me that of the 700 some people living on the kibbutz, 200 were kids and another 100 were old people. Others had special circumstances that made it difficult for them to volunteer or disqualified them. That left only 400 men and women aged appropriately to volunteer for dangerous and disruptive work. I said it was amazing that so many did (I will not provide the exact number given the dangerous people just over the border that might want to know).

Haim, an older man whom I later soon learned is sixty-nine and is Erez's father, quickly responded to my remark. He said volunteerism is higher in Israel than other countries and even higher on a kibbutz. "People are doing it," he said, "not because they have to, they are doing it because they want to be part of the community. . . . They have a commitment," whether they are members of the kibbutz or not.

There was that word again, I thought. Community.

When I asked Erez what concerned him, he immediately mentioned the Hezbollah watchtower constructed just east of the kibbutz, constructed on a high hill along the border. One morning, the kibbutz woke and saw it there. Before that morning there was nothing. Erez told me that a sniper in the watchtower could easily hit someone walking around Hanita. He knows that they are always watching. In addition, "If a lot of people come against us," he admitted that would be difficult for them.

"This is the most stressful to me," he said. "And it will be very hard and very painful for us. Because all the time when you attack [you have the advantage], you never know when and where they [will] attack you." Then he said reassuringly, "This is what I do for my living. To think all the time how to defend the kibbutz, to be organized [should] anything happen."

As our conversation wound down, I asked if all were confident in the kibbutz's future. Clearly Hanita had been buffeted by economic issues while also having to expend significant resources protecting itself from Hezbollah.

Immediately, all three responded, "Yes."

Haim explained that he came to the kibbutz in 1974. He and his wife were married at Hanita, where she was born. Now they have three children—including Erez—living at the kibbutz. The children have blessed them with ten grandchildren. They also live at the kibbutz.

Both of Haim's parents are Holocaust survivors from Poland. Both became partisans during World War II and fought the Germans from their camps in the woods. Haim's father was then married to another woman. They had two children. The Germans killed all three. Erez's grandmother was in a group shot by the Germans. She escaped and hid in the forest. Pretty and blond, she later spied on the Nazis. When Haim's grandparents married, his mother was eighteen years younger than his grandfather. Until Erez and his siblings asked, they never spoke of their experiences in the Holocaust. On holidays, Haim's grandmother would cry because she had no other family.

For me, Haim's story capped off Hanita's story. Hanita was born in fire. It lost its way for a time because its older members refused to evolve. But Hanita will endure and thrive because of the strength of its people, which has stretched from one generation to the next. The founder's children and their children have Hanita in their DNA. They—and the spouses who have joined in their mission—are on track to making Hanita better than it has ever been.

Just before we walked out, I asked if Dvir was a full member. He is. But he then turned to his friend Erez, who was not, kiddingly looked him in the eyes, and said, "Second rate!" Erez is anything but second rate, Dvir knows it, Haim knows it, and I do too. These are the kind of people that will ensure Hanita's future success. People like Erez, Sorel, and Orly along with farsighted members like Dvir, Yuval and Haim, who said we want "to have all members the same."

* * *

Four months after conducting those interviews in October 2018, I returned to Hanita and the yurt. This time I met Sorel in his office. He had won another three-year term. Seventy-eight percent of the members had voted for him. No longer burdened by concerns, he had a mandate to move forward. Almost giddy, he unveiled for me his future plans. Sorel wants to turn the rundown building adjacent to the playground into a beautiful library and children's center for the entire community. The grocery store, now in an old building along the road, he hopes to move to a more convenient location. He had also obtained approval for more homes, many of which will be multi-family units that will be more affordable for young people who want to move to the kibbutz.

In all, Sorel intends to devote more than eight million dollars to upgrading the kibbutz. Of the thirty million dollars netted when the factory was sold, seventy-four percent of it was distributed to the members at that time. The remainder went to the kibbutz. With that money, Sorel will be able to resurface roads, repair infrastructure, and modernize the community.

When I first visited Kibbutz Hanita, its need for maintenance work was clear. When I conducted interviews in October 2018, opportunity was in the air and I left optimistic. Now I was confident. Hanita has the right people, the right plan, a historic past, and a superb future to look forward to.

Chapter Thirteen

Kfar Giladi Now

One of the first things I noticed when I met with Gideon Giladi was a picture taken of Kfar Giladi Quarries (KGQ) in 2006. Owned by the kibbutz, KGQ provides material for construction purposes throughout Israel, and is a huge source of revenue for Kfar Giladi. I had come in early 2019 to speak with Gideon about Hashomer and his grandfather's role with the organization. I left after having learned much more—about the kibbutz and about Gideon.

Gideon describes himself as self-educated. His father had attended an agricultural school and subsequently revolutionized the kibbutz's approach to agricultural pursuits. He also had a talent for fixing mechanical devices and inventing new ones. As he grew up, Gideon learned from him and demonstrated his capability to resolve technical issues. When Gideon reached military age, he wanted to become a pilot. Twenty-five sons of Kfar Giladi have become pilots in Israel's air force, many others have served in special units; an extraordinary number given that never more than a few hundred people have lived at the kibbutz at any one time. Perhaps, Gideon told me, it was because of the kibbutz's proximity to the Lebanese border that made its residents live and breathe the need to defend themselves.

Gideon had a talent for sports and excelled at any he tried. As a teenager, he was on track to follow in the footsteps of the others who had become pilots. But during his physical, the IDF diagnosed him with asthma. The evaluators disregarded that Gideon had just been out harvesting in the kibbutz fields. In fact, he was not asthmatic, just sensitive to the powder in the grains being threshed. As a result, they assigned Gideon a 45 profile on a scale of 1 to 99. He could work in the air force canteen, they said. Not surprisingly, the boy who dreamed of fighting Israel's enemies in the sky rejected the suggestion he serve meals. So what could he do?

Gideon went to the person at Kfar Giladi in charge of liaising with the IDF, hoping that the kibbutz's contribution of pilots and special unit members would give him some pull. It did. Instead of the canteen, the IDF accepted Gideon into a fourteen-month engineering program offered by the air force for studying electronics. He became an expert at servicing American and French military equipment. This was a better fit for Gideon's interests and talents which had included watchmaking since he was sixteen.

After serving in the army, Gideon returned to Kfar Giladi, where he further developed his industrial and mechanical skills. Any thought of becoming a doctor was nixed by his mother, a dentist, who told him it would destroy his life, having to answer 2 a.m. calls. Instead, for the next fifty years, and still today, Gideon's life has been immersed in the mechanical challenges of KGQ. The kibbutz owned company is constantly purchasing new machines—old one's break, others are invented. He found it all fascinating. For a few minutes, Gideon took me through two rooms filled with mechanical drawings, notebooks, and the like. It was a mechanical history of KGQ and a history of his life.

"That's my baby" was written all over his face.

Twice, the kibbutz has elected Gideon general manager of KGQ. Once he was elected general secretary of the kibbutz. In his past life, he embraced leadership roles but now he seems more content, in his room, surrounded by papers and files, continuing to further KGQ's business. Ofer is now KGQ's manager. Gideon charitably says that Ofer has been the best manager ever. Ofer moved to the kibbutz in 1996 after serving in the north as an officer in the IDF and then marrying his wife, a Kfar Giladi native. Soon after Gideon mentioned his name, Ofer walked in. He looked a generation younger than Gideon, perhaps even more.

After Ofer left, and after we spoke about Hashomer, our conversation turned to the kibbutz and Kfar Giladi Quarries. KGQ, Gideon told me, represents about eighty percent of the kibbutz's effort and presumably a similar amount of its revenue. Agriculture makes up most of the rest.

The kibbutz started its first quarry in 1922, shortly after Kfar Giladi was established, but it was not profitable, so the kibbutz closed it down. In 1958, the kibbutz tried again. Now Kfar Giladi owns the local quarry and three others, plus numerous concrete asphalt plants and other construction and powder plants. KGQ is Israel's biggest producer and seller of micronized powders, made of limestone and basalt, used in plastic, paint, and other building materials. Although most is used in Israeli industries, some is exported. When Gideon saw my quizzical look, he pointed to the walls and said that ninety percent of the paint on them is composed of very fine powders like what KGQ produces.

I asked how much longer, at the present rate of production, would there be material left to mine in their various quarries.

According to Gideon, another twenty years at Giladi. Elsewhere, the kibbutz will need extensions to continue mining operations after ten years. He didn't answer how much longer after an extension mining would be economically viable at those quarries. But then he surprised me. Gideon told me that Israeli law requires that KGQ restore the land when it stops its mining activities at a site.

At Kfar Giladi, KGQ takes about a million tons of limestone and basalt out of the ground per year. In return, KGQ must pay one shekel per ton into a special fund that will be used to restore the land to something else. That equals about $300,000 per year. Over the years, with investment returns, that should total a tidy sum. Then, when there is nothing left worth mining, the fund will be used to restore the land, and since it's located in an industrial zone, another industry will likely take its place.

But as good as it is for the kibbutz, KGQ had been a source of aggravation for years. Several years ago, the kibbutz entered into a partnership arrangement with a company called "CaesarStone." Disputes arose and the two partners commenced what resulted in six years of litigation. There were claims and counterclaims in the convoluted arbitration that ensued. Finally, a year before Gideon and I met, the matter was resolved. Kfar Giladi Quarries emerged with an award roughly equivalent to sixteen and a half million dollars. CaesarStone claimed victory despite getting little in return. Gideon seemed very happy with the result. From what I read after we met, it seemed Gideon had a right to be pleased.

Our conversation was punctuated by talk of Kfar Giladi's wellbeing—both past and present— and its role in Israel's history. Kibbutz life, Gideon told me, is "not a simple way of life," and "its democratic way of life is sometimes too democratic." But he said defensively, "Our fathers and grandfathers couldn't study or learn anywhere in the world how to manage a kibbutz. They created it from ground zero. So, we have to learn it."

Like Merom Golan in some ways, Kfar Giladi was a "startup kibbutz." Alone, on the outer northern boundary of pre-1948 Israel, it was pretty much the only kibbutz in the area. Ma'ayan Baruch's founders got their start living in Kfar Giladi. Similarly, Kfar Giladi assisted the founders of Kibbutz Dan, Dafna, Manara, and others. Before those kibbutzim were founded, Kfar Giladi and Tel Hai merged after Jews returned following the death of Trumpledor at Tel

Hai. Now, Tel Hai College with its 6,000 students sits on more than sixty acres of land which Kfar Giladi had donated.

To my surprise, much of Kfar Giladi's growth stemmed from the arrival of 150 young educated Jews who made Aliyah from the Baltic states in 1932. Their numbers swamped the twenty-five Hashomer veterans, all more than forty years old, living at Kfar Giladi at the time. Very quickly, they started running the kibbutz.

"All that we have here . . . today," Gideon said, "is thanks to these people who came in 1932." I immediately thought that kind of influx is just what some of the kibbutzim I had previously met with need now.

Over the next fifteen years, Kfar Giladi played a crucial role in developing and protecting the State of Israel. Hidden within the walls and floors of its buildings were more than twenty cavities, called "sliks," in which the kibbutz hid guns from the British for the Haganah. In November 2019, I had an opportunity to see one of the sliks. It was hidden by a heavy machine with a cleverly camouflaged locking mechanism, that when unlocked, permitted it to be easily rolled away, revealing an underground room filled with a variety of weaponry. Descending into that deep secret via a metal ladder felt like descending into a forgotten history. Also, between 1922 and 1948, up to 10,000 Jews circumvented the British Mandate's ban on immigration by taking an arduous route that passed through the kibbutz after exiting Lebanon. And between 1945 and 1948, 1,300 children who had been smuggled out of Syria, spent time at Kfar Giladi. There, dressed in work clothes and hidden in chicken coups and cowsheds, they evaded capture by British authorities. Thus, Kfar Giladi is no stranger to helping others.

Still, there are residual hard feelings between some residents of Kiryat Shmona and the kibbutz. When the kibbutz shut down its hotel for needed renovations, many Kiryat Shmona residents lost their jobs. Even though they will be welcomed back when the kibbutz hotel reopens sometime in the future, the process has engendered hard feelings. Other tensions continue, with Kiryat Shmona's need for more land and more job opportunities. Sure, many Kiryat Shmona residents work at KGQ's quarry adjacent to Kfar Giladi's community and, as a result, have pensions, but that has not eliminated the lingering animosity between kibbutz and town. And even though Gideon has many friends in Kiryat Shmona and is invited to weddings and funerals of lost friends, he told me, "The roots and disputes you can still feel it."

In 2004, Kfar Giladi privatized. A movie screened in 2010 called *Keeping the Kibbutz*. It documented the change in Kfar Giladi within the context of the kibbutz movement, the changing economy, and how those changes impacted community members. Gideon confirmed that Kfar Giladi's reformation was "a major change for the community."

In the 1980s and 1990s Gideon explained, Kfar Giladi had fewer problems than other kibbutzim because of KGQ's profitability. Still, the same social issues that had already impacted others were now dragging Kfar Giladi down as well. Before privatization, everyone received the same amount of money for incidentals, with slight variations based on size of a household and the duration of someone's membership. And salaries earned from employers outside of the kibbutz went, in their entirety, to the kibbutz. After privatization, each member had to pay for what they consumed: "utilities, food, clothes and everything," according to Gideon.

Today, the kibbutz only subsidizes Friday night meals in the dining room, because "people like to see each other," said Gideon. "It's a celebration." Lunch is also served every day, but for a fee. Except on Friday, breakfast and dinner in the dining hall is a distant memory. But, Gideon said, "All production facilities remained mutual and owned by all and managed like a business . . . and salaries were differentiated."

When I asked Gideon how all the changes have impacted the feeling of community, he responded with a touch of sadness, "It is different." But then he said with more certainty than sadness that members are now more sensitive to human rights and a social democratic way of life. "What happened to our parents, they left their homes, etc. And started fresh. And now, some kids leave the kibbutz."

Gideon has three children, none of whom currently live at the kibbutz. One is an attorney, another works in a security role with the government, and the youngest lives an hour away. What he then said is true everywhere, "Nothing to do if they marry outside. You can't control it. But some do come back."

And others come.

Like Merom Golan, Kfar Giladi charges new members an initiation fee to join. At Kfar Giladi it is about $28,000 and prospective members must demonstrate they're financially able to build a home on kibbutz grounds. Furthermore, two thirds of the community must vote to accept the candidate. But now, acceptance does not require waiting. Previously, a candidate had to wait a year. Now, while there is no waiting period, a new member will not receive any distributions from the kibbutz's economic endeavors for their first five years of membership. Nor do they have the right to vote during that time period on any economic issues.

Once a member, like all other kibbutz residents, they must pay an amount equal to the taxes per member imposed by the Israeli government for each member of the kibbutz. In addition, each member must pay about $130 per month for kibbutz services and infrastructure. The total comes to a significant amount for an individual given that the typical worker in industry receives about $4,300 a month and an agricultural worker closer to $3,300 a month. Of course, managers make more.

Although most of our conversation was not about security issues, we did touch on them.

"Why do people build villages under a volcano?" Gideon asked.

Barely taking a breath, he answered his own question: "There is no explanation, you like the place, you are there, it is part of your homeland." Apparently, the 700 people living at the kibbutz, of which 292 were members in early 2019, agree with Gideon. They agree with him despite the kibbutz, encased by a fence, lying less than two miles downhill from the border with Lebanon.

"Of course," Gideon said, "A part of our life is security. It is with you all the time." In the 1970s, Gideon and other kibbutz residents armed with Kalashnikov rifles, would walk the kibbutz's boundaries. To combat terrorist activity at night, they built a fence with special electronic components, the design based in part on Gideon's experience in the air force. Gideon is no pacifist. He sees no prospect for peace soon. And he believes Israel must stay strong, must continue to innovate, and must develop the land and its industry. And they must do all this while emphasizing education. Gideon is a man who always keeps one eye on the future.

And, according to Gideon, if the Labor party ever regains power, things will improve for Kfar Giladi and all kibbutzim. Why? It comes down to land and ownership.

Gideon patiently explained to me that in Israel most of the land belongs to the State. Only two other countries, he said, have land administration like Israel—Cuba and North Korea. Like Israel, those two countries own most of the agricultural land and lease it back to users. That's good for the treasury, but not good for the kibbutzim. And it creates tortuous legal processes when kibbutzim want to repurpose the land for other uses. Previously, before the State existed, farmers received the assurance of long-term lease agreements from philanthropic institutions. Now, the State can take land from one entity and grant it to another. For Gideon, that creates unnecessary instability and cost. Of course, for Kiryat Shmona, desperate for more land to build homes and industry on, the present state of affairs offers hope.

Moving from land to internal dynamics, Gideon said the British invented Kfar Giladi's present asset sharing arrangement in the late 1930s. He describes it as a cooperative agricultural society. Under that umbrella, separate entities are created for each endeavor—Kfar Giladi Quarries, hotel, etc. "If one loses money," he said, "the other helps." The general meeting of the kibbutz runs the umbrella organization consistent with Israeli law. "Everything is democratic, sometimes too democratic," Gideon said. Most decisions only require a majority unless it involves changing certain fundamental rules, which then require a two-thirds affirmative vote. Each sub-entity, like KGQ, has its own board of governors. So do other endeavors, such as a separate organization tasked with assisting and improving the community. Profits float up to the umbrella group, which then decides how much to pay, as dividends, to members, and how much to invest in infrastructure, etc.

Despite having all this structure in place, caring for older members is as challenging here as it is at other kibbutzim. Gideon said, "They suffer a lot." The kibbutz feels obligated to care for them. In fact, the kibbutz also takes care of its younger people that are physically unable to work. They call it the "Security Net." On site is an assisted living facility with twenty-two beds; not all are filled by Kfar Giladi's elderly members because some prefer living at home where hired aides, partially paid with government assistance, help them. As a result, the kibbutz rents some of the beds to outsiders.

Overall, Gideon was quite clear. He is optimistic about Kfar Giladi's future. Never did he feel pessimism. Because the kibbutz had and has enough land, Kfar Giladi Quarries, and a knowledge base, he said, "The sky is the limit." Hopefully, his philosophy that "we are commissioners for the next generation of Kfar Giladi" guarantees that those assets address future needs rather than just being squandered on present desires.

Outside the entrance to Kfar Giladi is the kibbutz cemetery. There on a hilltop overlooking the Northern Galilee lies the body of Joseph Trumpeldor and the seven others who fell at Tel Hai a century ago. Gideon's grandfather, mother, and father are also buried there, along with his brother, who fell during the Yom Kippur War in 1973. One day, Gideon says, he will be buried here, too. It will have been a life well lived.

Chapter Fourteen

Merom Golan Now

Before October 2018, I had already spent twelve nights at Merom Golan over a four-year period. The camp-like atmosphere of its tourist cabins, the amazing breakfast buffet served in its dining hall, the evening meals in its restaurant—all of it had enchanted me. And its location in the shadow of Mount Bental—so close to the Syrian border where the civil war had then raged—only added to its mystique.

I was especially awed when, taking a friend's advice, I left my cabin before dawn and drove to Mount Bental's summit. There I saw the coffee shop, owned by Merom Golan, trenches used by the IDF that dated back to 1973 now a tourist attraction, and most spectacularly, the view stretching east over the Syrian plain almost to the outskirts of Damascus.

At sunrise, a rushing river of puffy white clouds pushed by the wind sped overhead as I watched, transfixed. The scene which included a snowcapped Mt. Hermon to the north and seemingly tranquil Arab villages in the valley to my east, seemed utterly peaceful. But, of course, that was not true. What lay below the dormant volcano I was standing on was a menagerie of terror and mayhem—ISIS and Al-Qaeda, Syrians and Iranians, Hezbollah and Sunnis and Druze, all entangled in a struggle for domination. The contrast of sky, land, and human division was striking. Such are the northern borders of Israel, whether with Lebanon or with Syria along the Golan—beauty and beast. And on the Golan, Merom Golan is at the center of it all, both geographically and historically.

* * *

I met Shefi Mor in the reception area of the kibbutz hotel. He is a man of moderate build, short cropped hair, and a kind smile. Shefi currently manages the hotel. He previously served as the kibbutz business manager. And before that, he was a cowboy. When I later told Omer, the kibbutz cowboy who had taken me to the old Merom Golan location, that Shefi had mentioned he was once a cowboy, Omer grinned and said, "I was his teacher."

Shefi came to Merom Golan while serving in the army, and then became a member in 1982. The kibbutz was very poor back then. It had no industry, and its agricultural efforts were not doing well. Things are different now. Today the kibbutz has several significant streams of income emanating from its agriculture products, industrial plants, and hospitality services. Our conversation started with the kibbutz restaurant and hotel.

The restaurant, called *Habokrim*, is a kosher steakhouse that serves meat from Merom Golan's own cattle and vegetables and fruit from its farms. I can attest, especially for Friday night dinner, its meals are memorable. Walking into the warm and charming building, you'd be surprised by its humbler origins. Steffi told me the restaurant began as a barbecue shack. Later, the kibbutz housed *Habokrim* in an old train car previously used by the IDF as a weapons warehouse.

For years, guests of the kibbutz hotel slept in the many cabins that were once the homes of kibbutz members. Shefi was one of them. The cabins though clean, are a little austere. However, my personal experience is that they are comfortable and inviting. But in 2019, the kibbutz added thirty-eight new rooms in a stand-alone building. Having stayed in one, I can say they're comparable to four-star hotels around the world.

Merom Golan was always packed with tourists whenever I visited. It was obvious that the hotel is thriving. Still, I asked Shefi whether its proximity to the Syrian border—and by extension, the fighting that had occurred there during the Civil War—affected tourism. Especially, since perhaps, once every few weeks, a Syrian shell would land on Israeli held land somewhere near the border, and because you could frequently hear the sound of fighting, particularly when standing on the top of Mt. Bental (truth be told, sometimes the explosives detonating were from IDF training ranges). In the United States, the hotel would be empty. Not so in Israel. Shefi told me, "Israelis are tough, they come." Eighty-five percent of their guests are Israelis and year around they average sixty percent occupancy annually, including weekdays and winter. When I Googled the average occupancy rate for a hotel in the United States, I learned it is about fifty-six percent. So, sixty percent is not bad for a kibbutz on the border with bombs going off and shelling nearby!

But to my surprise, hospitality is not the biggest moneymaker for the kibbutz. Nor are its industrial pursuits, even though Merom Golan factories produce motors for Israeli Merkava tank turrets and also missile parts. Instead, agriculture is the biggest moneymaker for the kibbutz. Merom Golan grows apples, grapes, kiwi, strawberries, and now truffles. Merom Golan's cattle range throughout the Golan. The kibbutz has a diversified economy, and all its parts appear to be doing well.

My main interest though, was how the kibbutz had fared since the 1980s and what the future might bring. What I learned was encouraging. Seven hundred people live at Merom Golan (a comparable number to many of the other Kibbutzim I visited); 140 of these people were members in October 2018. The non-members include children, some spouses or significant others, and renters. The average age of members was about 60 in 2018. Later in 2018, twenty-one new people became members, all of them younger, some much younger than sixty. One of them was Shefi's son. He has two other children: one living in Jerusalem, the other flying planes for the IDF.

Shefi explained to me what it's like for new members. First, they must rent or build a home at the kibbutz so existing members can get to know them and so they can get a taste of kibbutz life before deciding to join. As in other kibbutzim, a committee must also approve their membership and they must demonstrate their financial capability to build or buy a new home on the kibbutz if they don't already own one. Furthermore, they must buy stock in the kibbutz.

The buy-in is a fundamental change to the process. Shefi said, "When I came to Merom Golan, I buy nothing. My stock in Merom Golan is the years where I am here [and work]." Now, the mandatory stock purchase for children of members seeking to join is about $14,000. It's twice that if either of your parents aren't members of Merom Golan. That money gets the new member a share of the assets and the profits as well as a vote. However, the buy-in does not get you everything immediately. New members only get thirty percent of what otherwise would be their full share of the profits. They get the rest over time as they accrue more years as a member. When Shefi and I spoke, this concept had only been in effect for the last four years. Before that, I suspect, much like at Kibbutz Hanita, Merom Golan found its membership aging with no way to attract significant numbers of new, younger members to join.

Merom Golan started experiencing demographic and social challenges in the 1980s but the kibbutz reacted quickly. "The big change," Shefi said, "was in 1992. [They] started the change of the system of the kibbutz. Merom Golan was maybe the fourth or fifth to change the system in the country because Yehuda Harel is the vision guy."

Different pay for different jobs became the standard. The kibbutz no longer provided; people had to pay.

I then asked Shefi what the problem was in the 1980s that has been fixed.

Shefi answered, "The old kibbutz there was too much waste. [Now] family managing of finance became better. When I come into the kibbutz I smoke[d]. I go to the [supermarket], I take cigarettes what I want. [Now], I buy. People were taking more than what [they] need. That was a big change. Another [is the] pension." Until 1992, once you became too old to work, the kibbutz took care of you. It wasn't "personal," Shefi said. "Now everyone invests into [their] own pension plan" except for old members. "When they made the change, they protected those [who]" had no means to invest into the pension plan. It was a safety net for the elderly who had no other means to build their pension assets.

What happens, I asked, if a member wants to leave the kibbutz?

Shefi answered, "Before the change the kibbutz gave you compensation. Every year you lived on the kibbutz you got "X" amount of money." Now, I gathered, it is a much more complex calculation that considers how much one has paid in versus received.

Homes, built on land the government permits the kibbutz to use, cost on average about $400,000. A decade ago, it was a little less than half of that. Of course, mortgages are available to cover most of the cost. Despite the steep price of those homes for many Israelis, whose salaries are much less, on average, than in the United States, there seems to be a sizable demand for housing that's reflected in the rising prices.

As we spoke, I could see how much the kibbutz, and its continued success, meant to Shefi. He then told me a story that confirmed my observation.

"When I came to the kibbutz," Shefi said, "the first time in 1977. I fell in love . . . [with] the place, the openness. Every morning I come to work all my adult life I like it." The hardest thing, he told me, was "the poverty to overcome in the beginning and 1985-1992 when a lot of friends, members, left the kibbutz. Only in the last ten years members [have not left] the kibbutz. Before, when there was difficult time, very much people [left] Merom Golan."

That prompted me to ask if he now was optimistic. "Very, very," Shefi answered. "In the last twenty years you see the kibbutz growing, moving, changing." And the schools are vibrant, educating children through eighth grade, after which they go to Katzrin or Kibbutz Dafna for high school.

Next to Shefi, sat Joanna Kline. Originally from England, her parents made Aliyah in 1979. Afterward, she served in the army.

Joanna is a valued kibbutz employee in charge of reservations at the hotel. Despite living on the kibbutz in a home she and her family built, Joanna isn't a member. Nor does she want to be. Joanna enjoys the communal life and loves the natural setting, but when I had asked her if she wanted to become a member Joanna responded, "The easiest way to put it is I enjoy the kibbutz life without the headaches of the business side." She then added, "Where have I got [the money for the buy in]?"

Joanna pays the same amount for kibbutz services as members do, and the same monthly municipality fee charged by the kibbutz. If she wanted to use the kibbutz's school system for a child, like a member, she would pay extra. But Joanna doesn't receive a percentage of the kibbutz's income, nor does she want to. But that difference started a problem, one that is still causing conflict.

It was about windmills. At least that's where it started.

Not too far from the kibbutz, several large, power-generating windmills dot the landscape on a hill overlooking the Syrian border. The kibbutz thought it could benefit from building its own windmills on its own land. Some of the electricity generated would be used for Merom Golan's needs; the remainder would be sold, generating income that would be distributed among members. A deal of some sort was struck with a utility company. Members loved the idea. Non-members, including Joanna, who would not receive any of the income, hated it. Non-members weren't interested in the money. They were interested in maintaining the views that attracted them to the kibbutz. For those, like Joanna, who had built their home on kibbutz land, the kibbutz was taking something from them. But backing out of the deal with the utility company would not only mean less revenue for members, it also might create litigation risk for a damage claim against Merom Golan.

"That," Joanna said, "started something. And other things came with it." When I asked if the issue had been resolved, Shefi answered, "It's not final," whereupon both laughed.

Four months later, when I returned to the kibbutz, there had been a meeting the day before to again discuss the issue. It seems that some common ground had been reached regarding non-members serving on some kibbutz committees, but nothing had yet been finalized. Nine months later, I returned again. The issue was still ongoing!

Still, the new neighborhoods "saved the kibbutz," said Joanna during our October 2018 conversation. Shefi agreed. They brought a youthful vitality and some community-based employees, like her, to the kibbutz. And, although non-members do not know all the members, the two groups are very social with each other. And, despite their differences, Joanna told me "there is a lot of communal life.... I know in other kibbutzim it's less successful. But between the new neighborhood and the kibbutz. I can say personally it is a success."

One problem, however, still bedevils members and non-members alike—health care. The kibbutz has a medical clinic that's closed on Shabbat. But for a life-threatening emergency, Shefi told me it takes forty-five minutes to transport the victim down the Golan's windy, steep roads to the valley below and the hospital beyond. And that's only if the ambulance is nearby when called. Shefi said that when his mother broke her shoulder at ninety-six, he took her to a hospital in the center of Israel. "It was a nightmare. The traffic was impossible." And any need for specialists creates a chronic, rather than an acute problem. They are mostly in Tel Aviv, Jerusalem, or Haifa—almost two or more hours away. Only in the last couple of years has radiation therapy for cancer been available in Safed, which is about an hour's journey.

This problem, however, is not unique to Merom Golan. Every border community I visited had the same complaint. It's a big reason why they call it living on the periphery.

What I did find somewhat unique was that Merom Golan does not pay for its older members' assisted living needs. Their system has been set up in such a way that each member has been given the ability to pay for that out of their personal finances, which includes a pension that they have either paid into for quite some time, or for the very old, was subsidized.

Near the end of our time together, I asked Shefi about what the future looks like for Merom Golan. Fortunately, he said, government policy seems to be aiding the kibbutz's drive to attract new members by not permitting establishment of any new kibbutzim on the Golan. Instead, "They want to stress," according to Shefi, "the existing communities, not to establish new ones." By adopting that course, young people attracted to life on the Golan will join established kibbutzim, injecting youthfulness into their aging populace, thereby helping to ensure Merom Golan's long-term survival.

But will Merom Golan survive as a kibbutz? When I posed that question to Shefi, he answered, "I don't know. I think now the system has leveled out. All the business is together. Every family lives for itself."

* * *

From my perspective, Merom Golan has found the perfect balance between communal living and individual responsibility that Kibbutz Hanita is searching for, Kfar Giladi has created for itself, and Kibbutz Dan has not yet found. You certainly would feel that way if you spent time with Omer Weiner, the happy cowboy.

Of course, Omer is much more than the cowboy he happily portrays himself as. Not only is he a poet and photographer, he also worked on Merom Golan's business side and managed one if its factories. "The main idea when we started," he told me, "was to do everything, to finance ourselves, . . . develop things." And later he said, "We decided we don't want to suck money from the government."

While we spoke, Omer proudly showed me vast fields of apples and even kiwi. "But when we started," Omer said, "we didn't know [how]." For example, ranching. Before Merom Golan, he told me that the biggest cattle herd in Israel was less than 200 cows. "We started with 1,000 (the exact number fluctuated with each conversation). So, we had to learn it by ourselves. There was nobody to teach us."

To our right was a different field. "Here," Omer said, "we . . . are doing experiments with all kinds of agriculture that belong to the kibbutz. And we are trying new things all the time. To find new things that will feed this area. To make good agriculture that we can earn money . . . . Because the weather is not the same weather [elsewhere in Israel], here we are about [3,000 feet] above sea level, and it's cold, there is snow in the winter, we try to use all these things to come to another season in the markets."

That, he said, gives Merom Golan an advantage.

While Omer drove along the dirt roads separating those fields, I could see why Yehuda Harel had fought so hard, and so successfully, for those fields not to be returned to Syria after the October War. Lying between Kuneitra and the kibbutz, Assad had wanted them badly. And just as badly, Yehuda wanted to hold onto them. Merom Golan required them and Israel, Yehuda thought, needed them. Assad was a President, leader of a powerful army. Yehuda was a farmer, father of an idea. Henry Kissinger wrote in his memoirs about how obstinate Merom Golan was. Yehuda led Merom Golan. The farmer won.

Then, amid the Israeli minefields added after the October War, close to a mound on a hill that contained a large bunker, which is where the abandoned Keshet settlement had first took root before Yehuda convinced them to move, was a field filled with something Omer was especially proud of. "New in Israel, he said, "and we hope it will be the goldmine of the Golan Heights. It is truffles."

Extremely expensive, especially prized for their taste, and requiring specialized farming techniques, truffles are a fungus that grows on roots. While often considered a mushroom, technically they are not because mushrooms grow above ground and truffles grow below. Kibbutz members and many of their Druze employees went to Spain to learn the agricultural techniques required. Merom Golan used special oak plants to grow the roots that would bear the fungus. Good truffles could bring the kibbutz a few hundred dollars per pound, better ones, perhaps a thousand dollars.

"It will be the best agriculture in Israel," Omer said. And, "Now we have dogs for it. Special dogs from Italy to dig it. We now have about five dogs to dig it."

Talking about truffles made me forget how close we were to Syria. That momentary lapse passed when I saw a few concrete blocks, several feet high sitting along the road. When I asked why they were there, Omer told me it was so you could hide behind them from snipers across the border. "It can be snipers, it can be little rockets, like they did over there [pointing to the hill with windmills on it] . . . they killed a father and a child he brought with him."

The five dogs charged with locating and digging up the truffles are not the only dogs in Merom Golan's employ. Omer said, "I developed a system to guard the cows with dogs. They're free. They [also] guard the cows against wolves" as well as the many foxes, jackals, hyenas, and wild dogs roaming the region. The cows are scattered all over the Golan. Omer said, "Nobody is going with them and the cows you know are by themselves. These dogs [stay] with the cows and guard the herd."

The cattle herd spread out in various areas of the Golan, especially between Nafekh and Katzrin, numbers about 2,000, of which 1,200 are cows or calves. As Omer put it, the cows are for making cattle and are only slaughtered when they cannot make kids. The boys have it bad while the girls live on. They graze on far more acres of land than the average kibbutz has, an advantage stemming from being the first kibbutz on the Golan.

Omer only works about four hours a day now, troubleshooting problems with equipment and the cattle as well as coordinating with the army to ensure that the kibbutz's livestock don't interfere with IDF training exercises. But he is also a gregarious repository for an oral history of Merom Golan, always shared in a joyful manner. He has a story for everything you see, even the ditches. After the Yom Kippur War, the IDF wanted to dig anti-tank ditches all over Merom Golan's lands. The kibbutzniks, though patriotic, were also very practical. Omer told me Merom Golan said fine, but only if they were dug where they could also be used for irrigation purposes. A deal was struck.

Sadly, every beginning has an end, and I was nearing the end of my time with Omer. So, I asked him what he thought about Merom Golan now as compared to the past.

He answered, "I believed in socialism all my life. But you know, it changes. It's not the kibbutz like it was." But he was optimistic about the future. "There are very many young people that want to live in this area and want to become members in this kibbutz," he said. "Part of them come to live and be part of the kibbutz and not be members. Some of them come to be members. People that [were] born on the kibbutz [are] now coming back. Grandchildren [too]. Most of the time I am optimistic." And, he added, there is nothing that worries him about the future of the kibbutz. Even the dispute between the members and non-members over the windmills did not unduly concern him because, "The main thing that we want," he said, "is that they be here, they want to help the kibbutz. Everybody has the same target."

However, for settlements on the Golan, there is always a nagging back-of-the-mind worry about some future negotiation with Syria that will end with the Golan going back into Syria's hands, as remote as that might seem today. What Omer said next regarding that concern demonstrated the depth of his thinking. "If there will be peace, real peace," he said:

> *I told them because I was a Zionist I came to this area and if to be a Zionist I have to go down, I will go down. I will not fight for it. For peace, for my children.... For peace, real peace, open border, and then we can [drive] to Europe from here in two days .... For this, for Israel, it will be the Messiah time. You know to go from Africa to Europe in four or five days by car. And Israel will be on this highway.*

A cowboy only, Omer is not. A deep thinker, a gentle soul, a joy to be with, an Israeli Zionist—he is!

Chapter Fifteen

People of the Land

In this chapter you will meet four extraordinary entrepreneurs doing extraordinary things for northern border communities. From education to news broadcasting and philanthropy to business, their contributions, along with the contributions made by many others, have had an important impact on the region.

Sarit Zehavi

About five feet, five inches tall, with glasses and a captivating smile, Lieutenant Colonel Sarit Zehavi (ret), stood before me at a small bakery in Ma'alot-Tarshiha, a few miles from the Lebanese border. The town is a living example of what is possible within Israel when old grievances, religious extremism, and fear give way to cooperation and peace. Here, Arabs and Jews live together peacefully. Seventy years before Sarit and I met in the courtyard of the bakery the Arab town of Tarshiha saw its peaceful existence fractured by the 1948 Arab-Israeli War. Then, in 1963, rather than grow separately apart, in a courageous political-economic move, the Jewish town of Ma'alot and the Arab town of Tarshiha chose to merge and try prospering together. The experiment worked. It worked, even though in 1974, the peace of Jewish Ma'alot was fractured by Palestinian terrorists who killed Jewish children they found sleeping in a Ma'alot high school.

When I drove through the winding streets of Ma'alot-Tarshiha, I saw no hint of animus and, at least from my untrained eye, no suggestion of a divide. Sarit chose the bakery for our meeting because, in her view, it was the best in the area. I have no reason to dispute that. The smells of freshly baked bread and pastries wafted from a small, cluttered room that opened onto a small, stone patio protected from the sun on one side. The food was delicious. Our conversation, even better.

Why did I want to interview Sarit? I had already known her for two years. We first met when I had hired Sarit to guide me as well as my two brothers-in-law along the Syrian border on the Golan Heights and the Lebanese border. The Syrian civil war had been raging, and I was very interested in learning where the various terrorist groups were located, the risk they posed to Israel, and about the perspective of Israelis living along the borders.

I found Sarit, a retired intelligence officer with Israel's Northern Command, through an Internet search. Then, she ran a one-person company called "*Alma*," dedicated to researching security issues and to educating English-speaking tourists, groups organized by AIPAC and others, and American legislators and Congressional staffers from Capitol Hill. Sarit was eminently qualified due to her professional and educational background as well as her fluency in English and knowledge of Arabic in addition to Hebrew.

Today, *Alma* has blossomed into a growing group of seven full-time employees and several part-timers, located in northern Israel close to the Lebanese border. Sarit has merged their capabilities and backgrounds into the preeminent research and education facility focusing on Israel's northern border security. And Sarit has become a well-recognized expert on Capitol Hill, at AIPAC meetings, and more and more throughout the United States regarding security issues involving Israel, Lebanon, and Syria. Still in her forties, she has accomplished this while mothering five children and living so close to the Lebanese border that her family would only receive nine seconds warning of a rocket launched in their direction by Hezbollah.

But that was not the main purpose of our meeting.

I knew that Sarit was part Lebanese, Syrian, and Iranian—and all Jewish. But I was curious how those parts had come to be. After we sat down with our steaming cups of coffee and my overly large, doughy nosh, I asked her that question. With a mischievous smile she looked me in the eye and said, "There is always a story."

It turned out her story was in two parts, one for each side of her family.

Sarit's grandmother, Miriam, was born in Beirut, Lebanon in 1912, into a family that eventually included five other siblings. A few years later, Sarit's great-grandfather was called to fight in World War I. He returned with tuberculosis. In 1923, doctors recommended that he go to live in the Lebanese mountains where the air was lighter and cleaner than in the city. Following their suggestion, Sarit's great-grandfather, his wife, and two of their children—a baby girl and a four-year-old boy—moved temporarily to a mountain retreat. Their nanny accompanied them. The other four girls, including the one named Miriam, stayed home.

In the middle of the night, sometime after they had arrived at a hotel, there was a knock on their door. From outside a voice asked, "Are you Christians?".

The nanny, who was Christian, answered "Yes, we are Christians."

That was a mistake. During those times, Lebanese Muslims and Christians were engaged in bitter fighting, often with no quarter given—not too different than the brutal warfare between Christians and Muslims that intermittently engulfed Lebanon during the last three decades of the twentieth century. Upon hearing the nanny's words, the knocking stopped, replaced by a sudden shove that thrust the door open. Shots rang out, Sarit in a measured voice continued, "[The] nanny got shot, the parents got shot, the child got shot, and only the baby girl [who] was asleep, probably [because a blanket hid her] survived." The story had been known to Sarit's family for decades. But Sarit, being a researcher, looked for confirmation. An obituary she found confirmed it.

The Muslims who killed Sarit's family members almost a century past had made a mistake. Previously, a Christian family had stayed in that room. They were the targets. Sarit's great-grandfather and great-grandmother, along with their four-year-old son, were not—just collateral damage in a bitter conflict.

The remaining five girls in the family now were orphans. Their uncle took them in. But he did not want them to live with him permanently. And since they were girls, he saw a solution—marriage, as early as at twelve years of age. Miriam much later explained to Sarit that it was, "because we wanted to have joy in the family." But truly it was because her uncle wanted husbands to assume responsibility for them.

One of the girls married a man who brought her to Los Angeles. The youngest and oldest married husbands who took them to Israel. A fourth married a gynecologist who continued to practice medicine in Beirut until the 1960s. And Miriam, in an arranged marriage at the age of sixteen, married a thirty-five-year old Jewish jeweler who took her back to his home in Damascus, Syria. His name was Daniel. Daniel's grandmother had been a sister of Miriam's grandmother, which, in a way, made the new couple related.

Miriam found life hard in Damascus. In Beirut, she had grown accustomed to bathrooms and running water. Despite her husband's comparative wealth, her living conditions in Damascus were squalid by comparison.

For two decades, family life continued for Miriam, uninterrupted by outside events. In total, she had seven children, including one who died at age four when burned in an accident at home. But in 1946, riotous Arabs who wanted to drive the French out of Syria after World War II, targeted French citizens in Damascus. And, reminiscent of the pogroms in Eastern Europe, Jews became favorite targets as well. Daniel and Miriam thought about moving the family to Mexico to escape the mounting danger. But one of their children, Avraham, was sick. The closest center for treatment was in Palestine. Daniel had a French passport for travel. Miriam did not. Thus, they had no choice. Daniel had to take the sick boy to Palestine before giving further thought to taking his entire family to Mexico. And because he needed help with the boy, Sarit's Aunt Bella, Daniel's oldest child, went with him to help despite her having received a prized scholarship for study in France.

After Daniel left, when Miriam saw the Arabs attacking the Jewish community more frequently, she feared for her husband's safety if he returned and felt the need to warn him away. But given the difficulty of communications, how?

That's where the Jewish Agency in Palestine came into play. The Jewish Agency's overriding goal was to bring Jews to Palestine. Knowing that Jews in Syria were under pressure and looking to escape, representatives of the organization, who were based in Damascus, took Jewish children, with the permission of their parents, from Syria to comparative safety in Palestine. Otherwise, the Jewish Agency feared, those families succeeding in escaping Syria might scatter around the world. Then, those children would be lost to Palestine and would not play a role in creating the future State of Israel. All told, the Jewish Agency succeeded in moving roughly 1,000 Syrian kids to Palestine, usually in groups of about fifteen that would make the first step of the trip—from Damascus to the northern kibbutzim—at night by way of the Golan Heights.

Moshe was Miriam's oldest son. Many years later he would become Sarit's father. Although only eleven, he looked older. Sending him was the method Miriam chose for warning her husband. A plan made easier because even at his young age, Moshe was already connected with the Zionist movement in Damascus. So, he most likely had the desire to live in Palestine and perhaps even had the connections to get there on his own even though he was not yet an adolescent, let alone a man. But Moshe had one condition before he would agree to leave Syria. His six-year-old brother, Chaim, had to accompany him. The Jewish Agency representatives agreed, evidently realizing they would get two for the price of one! Years ago, after much research, Sarit found documents containing her father's and uncle's names. They were the youngest children to make the trip. She also verified what soon proved to be, once in Israel the agency purposively split them up!

On Moshe's neck, Miriam placed a necklace with the address of her sister in Palestine. That's where Daniel and the two children who had made the trip with him were staying. Miriam told Moshe to find his father quickly and warn him that it would be dangerous for him to return to Syria, especially because he was a Jew with a French passport. With that admonition, Moshe, bearing the weight of his heavy responsibility, left with his brother for Palestine.

From Damascus they walked part of the night and rode otherwise on "borrowed" British army trucks. When they reached Palestine, the Palestine Agency separated them. Both were sent to kibbutzim—Moshe to a kibbutz near Petah Tikva, and Chaim to a different kibbutz about three miles away. For more than a year neither brother saw each other or other family members. Moshe was told Chaim was far away but nevertheless Moshe tried to contact his younger brother. He would steal chocolate, write "Chaim" on it, and drop the candy in the mailbox, sure that it would get to him. Meanwhile, unknown by all, Daniel, Moshe's father, was living very close by in Petah Tikva.

Desperate, with her husband and two children already in Palestine at known locations and Moshe and Chaim lost, Miriam found her own way out of Syria, by way of Lebanon. With her she brought her remaining two children, both still babies. Along the way, Lebanese authorities arrested Miriam. Only because her husband had been a jeweler did she have the means to bribe her way free. One can only wonder how Miriam accomplished the journey while keeping those two young children safe and with her.

Upon arrival in Israel, Miriam searched for the missing boys. First, she found Chaim.

Miriam's first words to her son were, "I am your mother."

Chaim responded, "I don't know who you are."

Chaim's confusion was understandable, it had been two years since he last saw Miriam when he was six. So, she repeated, "I'm your mother!"

Chaim didn't respond with words, tears, or a hug. He ran away.

As he ran, Miriam had an inspiration. "Chaim, tell me where is [Moshe]."

Hearing his brother's name, Chaim stopped, turned, gazed at Miriam, and remembered.

Decades later, the family celebrated Miriam's eightieth birthday. Chaim, who evidently prides himself on his jokes, dressed as a kibbutznik, walked up to his mother, and attempted to humorously reenact the past when he asked, with a look that suggested confusion, why she had brought him here? Miriam got upset. Losing her sons for two years was no laughing matter to her—even decades later. Miriam must have been quite emotional because Sarit was eight when she witnessed it and remembers it to this day.

Miriam continued to try to find Moshe without success. Several months earlier, Moshe had come close to unraveling the mystery of his father's whereabouts on his own when Moshe met the head of security at Petah Yikvah who lived only one block away from his father, Daniel, but he was of no help. Pre-adolescent Moshe had no choice but to accept that he was stuck where he was. Then, on May 1,

1947, Moshe marched in a parade celebrating Workers' Day in Petah Tikva. By fate alone, Moshe's older sister spotted him in the throng. But like his younger brother, when Miriam rushed to the kibbutz to claim her son, Moshe ran away. Why? He feared his father's wrath because he hadn't taken care of Chaim as he had promised.

While seemingly harsh, upon investigation Sarit learned the basis for the Jewish Agency's decision to routinely separate siblings coming from Syria. The agency's paramount goal was to build the State of Israel. By separating the children, it would be more difficult for their parents, still in Syria, to find them and move elsewhere. The agency knew that just like in Eastern Europe at the turn of the century, many Syrian Jews preferred to live elsewhere than Palestine. But for Palestinian Jews to have a chance to build a nation more Jews were needed. Moshe now bears no grudge for the Jewish Agency's actions. When asked, he says that he forgives the agency. These were harsh and desperate times, he says, that cannot be judged solely by today's standards.

The lives of Miriam, Daniel, Moshe, and the other siblings in Palestine were hard. All the family wealth had been left behind in Syria. Miriam went to work as a seamstress. Moshe started working at age fourteen to provide for his parents and siblings. Daniel eventually died in poverty. But even so, Miriam and Daniel had four more children, of which only two survived childhood.

Moshe was born on November 29, 1934. On Saturday, November 29, 1947, newly reunited with his parents, Moshe was thirteen and ready to celebrate his Bar Mitzvah. His parents invited guests, made cookies, and prepared a celebration. But nobody came. Gunfire that day marked the real beginning of Israel's struggle for independence that broke out into war with its neighboring states in 1948. Shots had been fired hundreds of yards from where Moshe lived. With the survival of Jews in Palestine in question, celebrating Moshe's Bar Mitzvah was no longer in the cards.

On November 29, 2014, Sarit's family gathered to celebrate Moshe's eightieth birthday. To honor his request, they went to the Golan to the exact location where he and Chaim had walked out of Syria. A sign marks the spot. Then Sarit said to Moshe, "Daddy, give me two hours, don't ask any questions." Together, the entire extended family went by bus to Katzrin, a newly built Jewish town in central Golan. Sarit had told all of them that she had arranged a lunch at a Kosher restaurant there. It was a lie born from love. Instead of a waiter, they encountered Moshe's cousin, a Rabbi, who lived in Katzrin. And rather than first sit down to a meal, with no warning, Moshe read from the Torah. Sixty-seven years late, within miles of where he first entered Palestine, Moshe had his Bar Mitzvah.

* * *

Sarit's mother, Rika, was born in Tel Aviv. For years Sarit did not think there was anything special about her mother's background. But then she learned that her grandmother, Sarah, mother of Rika, was not born in Jerusalem as she had thought, but in Hebron in 1922. At the age of seven, during the Arab riots in the city that killed sixty-seven Jews, a Muslim family hid Sarit's grandmother, her brother, and her parents in a huge box used to hold linens. The family moved from Hebron to Jerusalem after the massacre. It's unclear whether they did so of their own volition or because of British policy that forced Jews to leave the West Bank for safety reasons. But trouble followed them. In 1936, the Arab revolt against the British made things difficult for Jews in Jerusalem. So the family fled to Beirut. But there, impoverished, they went hungry. Sarit's great-grandfather decided he would rather starve in Jerusalem than Beirut. So they headed back. Traveling south through southern Lebanon first, they had to negotiate the intervening mountains. The trip was made even more complicated by nature. Along the way, in the hills overlooking Safed, Sarit's great-grandmother gave birth to a girl.

Moshe and Rika met in the army. Moshe was her commander. Such fraternization was much more common then, than today, since it is now forbidden. They married in 1960 and lived in Petah Tikvah. Moshe served in all of Israel's wars between 1956 and 1982. In 1982, he commandeered an IDF military vehicle, and used it to enter Beirut to find the grave of his grandparents, slaughtered at that hotel after World War I. He told all whom he encountered that he was Druze. Since Moshe had green eyes, and in those days black hair, he looked the part. His personal mission failed with only one solace; he came back alive.

* * *

Sarit was born in 1976. From the age of sixteen, her passion was Middle Eastern studies. A central question drove her intellectual yearnings, why was Israel the only democracy in the region? Most of her friends affiliated themselves with the left wing of Israeli politics. Sarit leaned right. While in High School, Sarit learned Arabic. In the army after being drafted, however, she could not overcome the sexism of those times. The IDF placed her as a secretary. Frustrated, Sarit found a way out. She enrolled in an officer's course and afterward became a liaison for the reserve forces.

Although the liaison position was reserved for women, it came with more responsibility than being a secretary. As a liaison, at nineteen, Sarit was responsible for dealing with issues arising out of reserve requirements that pulled men, some in their forties, out of their daily lives and back into the army. When called to duty, they would abruptly leave their jobs, children, and educational pursuits. The disruptions in their personal lives became Sarit's responsibility to mitigate. She was the one to send them notice of their upcoming reserve requirement. She was the one to decide whether to grant requests to not report. And she was the one to find those who chose not to report without permission. "It was challenging," Sarit told me. And, she said, I "hated my commander. He was not a role model. I was disappointed there are these kind of commanders in the army."

Sarit's frustration mounted. She told her father that she will never rise beyond lieutenant in the army. Therefore, she left the IDF when her service time was up. Determined to fulfill her potential, Sarit attended Ben Gurion University where she earned a bachelor's degree and Masters in Middle Eastern Studies. Her plan was to become a professor. But that changed.

The army recruited Sarit to take a position in its research division. The job required her to work in Tel Aviv. Sarit and her new husband had just moved into a home in Beersheba days before. There, her husband was pursuing a PhD in Mechanical Engineering. Despite it requiring a 140-mile round trip commute, Sarit took the job in the research division, only moving closer after giving birth to her first son.

While still in Beersheba, the Second Intifada broke out. Without warning, bombs would go off in busses and malls. As we spoke about those days and the suffering Israelis endured, Sarit's voice deepened. Speaking quickly in precise clipped sentences, she said:

> *What you are experiencing in Israel today is totally not the experience we had in these years, in the second intifada. The experience was of constant fear. You are afraid to go to the restaurant, you are afraid to go to the mall, you are afraid to go on a bus. When you go in the bus you look everywhere to see where there is suspicious bag, who is this Arab that went on the bus, is he suspicious or not, what is he carrying, who is this guy in the mall? Your eyes were open all the time.*

> *I was on the lines to the train station. It was really busy, and I remember that every time when I was standing on the line, and you know you are standing on the line to security, and if somebody want[s] to make a suicide attack [he] can just stand on the line [without first] passing through security. And each time I was looking around. It was a totally different atmosphere than the atmosphere in Israel today.*

I then asked Sarit whether fear had always been in the back of her mind.

She responded with an answer that emphasized the psychological stress Israelis experienced during those years: "It was all the time on the front of your mind and not because I was with security, not at all. It was because it was really frightening . . . . Back then we were really afraid. And I think it is not easy to bring people to understand that."

Sarit's comments made me think about all the hoopla in the United States and elsewhere when Prime Minister Sharon decided in 2002 to complete a wall with checkpoints around the West Bank. Whatever one's views about Palestinian issues, it's impossible to discount the government's need to stop the terrorist suicide-bombers coming from the West Bank. And, perhaps in conjunction with other factors or perhaps alone, the wall worked. The incidence of suicide-bombers markedly plummeted.

On July 12, 2006, Sarit was pregnant with her second child. Earlier in the day, she had reported to work at IDF headquarters in Tel Aviv, where she served in the research and analysis division. At 9:30 a.m., the first reports of mortar shells fired by Hezbollah reached her unit. Shells were falling in Metula, in Zarit, and other border towns. "What's going on," she wondered. Even though the border in those days was not completely quiet, it was quite unusual for Hezbollah to fire so many shells at so many areas. Something, she knew, was up. Two hours later, her unit received a report that IDF soldiers had been kidnapped along the Lebanese border near Zarit.

After hearing of the kidnapping, Sarit went to her commander, asked him a question, and made a statement. The question was rather cogent considering the government's subsequent failures, "Why are we not [calling up the] reserves? What are we waiting for?" The statement was more personal. "We are going to war? I am nine months pregnant. We can't go to war!"

The 2006 war had a searing impact on Israel as a whole and, in particular, on citizens living close to the border with Lebanon. Sarit told me:

> *We understood this is war. We understood it was not going to take twenty-four hours, forty-eight hours. This is war. And I think that part of the disappointment in Israel is that the . . . Chief of Staff didn't deliver the message 'guys this is war, this is serious.' He continued to wear the official uniforms and when there is war, you don't wear these. You are going underground; you wear your working uniform. And this was part of the feeling of the disappointment of the army. He himself was not a role model.*

Despite her pregnancy, Sarit served throughout the war. Of course, I was curious what she did. When I asked, she said "professional analysis." When I inquired further, I encountered the same roadblock I have encountered with Sarit on other occasions when the answers to my questions would require divulging secret information, she said she "couldn't talk about it."

After two weeks, although the fighting continued and with Hezbollah rockets continuing to rain down on northern Israeli communities, Sarit had to reduce her involvement. The baby in her womb was making his presence known. Frustrated because she was needed, Sarit wanted to do her part. Sarit's commander said, "Don't worry, he will wait." Spontaneously, Sarit told me that it was difficult to be a mom in the army, not because of discrimination, but because duty requires long hours and "you have to choose between your job and your motherhood. It's very personal."

On August 12, Sarit's water broke. "We went to the hospital," she told me. In the car heading there, Sarit turned on the radio and heard that a truce had been negotiated to begin on Monday at dawn. "And on Monday at dawn," she said, "Mor was born."

Then, after a slight pause, Sarit told me a story that I have not since forgotten. The nurse in the delivery room asked Sarit whether the baby she was about to give birth to was a boy or a girl.

Sarit answered, "A boy."

The nurse responded, "Good, we need more soldiers."

"Why are you telling this awful thing to me."

The nurse answered, "I have one in Gaza, one in Lebanon, and one on the Golan."

Sarit left it at that but told me in reference to Mor, "I am still afraid for him. He is not afraid of anything." And then she said that a famous Israeli writer had tried to explain mothers in Israel. The writer said in an interview, "The mothers in Israel are different from any other mothers because the mothers in Israel know they raise their children to this day, when they become eighteen, and they will go to the army."

Sarit said the writer was correct. "[We] all know that, and it affects our motherhood. You hand him over."

In that moment I thought back to a ceremony, which I had witnessed near its conclusion. It was at Ammunition Hill, a hallowed spot where IDF paratroopers, at a horrible price in blood, had wrested control of a strategic location from Jordanian soldiers during the Six-Day War. There, among the Jordanian trenches stormed by young IDF soldiers, of whom many perished in the fighting, stood the families of eighteen-year-old young men and women. Mothers and fathers were literally turning their children over to the army. The scene was reminiscent of early morning gatherings in the United States where parents send their children to summer camp. But what I witnessed that day was not the joy of parental liberation. What I witnessed were children going off to war. And parents reflecting on their own personal past experiences doing the same when they were eighteen, knowing that their son or daughter might not come home alive. I will never forget that moment. And I will never forget the look in Sarit's face as she explained Israeli motherhood.

After her second son was born, Sarit returned to the army. She and her husband moved to Kfar Vradim, a community within a few miles of the Lebanese border to the north and the Mediterranean to the west. The IDF assigned her to the Northern Command and offered her a position as commander in charge of the alert desk. The offer signified how well her superiors thought of her. From that assignment, rapid promotion was likely. A future Lieutenant Colonel position, or higher, was in the offing. But at first Sarit was hesitant. When interviewing for the job, the interviewer told Sarit she would only need to work from 8 a.m. to 6 p.m. But Sarit knew better. It would require more than that. As a mother of two at that time, she was concerned. Sarit told her husband that she would not take the position.

But then the head of the intelligence unit called and asked, "Are you coming?"

The question caused her to reconsider. She decided, "Ok. I made my decision. I'll do it. I'll go for a career."

The commander of the alert desk is the person who determines, based on gathered intelligence, whether Hezbollah is going to carry out a terrorist attack. "That's it. That's my job every day," Sarit told me. I translated her duties in my own mind. Sarit had to determine every hour of every day if, when, and where shit would happen by piecing together an incomplete puzzle of observations, intelligence intercepts, and understanding of the enemy's culture and behavior. The stress must have been unbelievable. Lives of young soldiers guarding the border depended on her. The lives of residents along the borders depended on her. The lives of her family in Kfar Vradim depended on the correctness of her daily evaluation. Sarit put it succinctly; she had to constantly answer questions that included, "Where are they going to do that? How are they going to do that? When are they going to do that?" And then she added another comment that used an acronym I had previously taught her, SWAG, which means a sophisticated wild-ass guess. Sarit said, "If you don't have information . . . you have to take a SWAG. We are good in SWAG!"

After five months at the alert desk, I got "really hard pains in my stomach," Sarit said. "It lasted for a week, and I told [my husband] I can't do it anymore. . . . I took myself to the hospital." There, doctors diagnosed her with Crohn's disease. Crohn's is an inflammatory bowel disease. While there are many risk factors and potential causes, stress aggravates it. Deciding when Hezbollah would strike had taken its toll. Sarit said to me, "It was not an easy decision for me to choose career [vs] motherhood. And I knew that I was choosing. I knew that. And [at] that moment, [I knew] that my career was over."

When Sarit told her boss of the diagnosis, he looked at her and said, "You have Crohn's. You are not anymore the head of the alert desk." With that pronouncement he left the room to alert his superior of the development.

Left alone, Sarit started crying. "I felt like everything ended. What am I going to do? They will get me out of the army. . . . They dismiss people that are sick with Crohn's in the army." Up until then, Sarit had been on the fast track. Only thirty, she had felt there was no limit to how high she could rise. Sarit told me, "I dreamed to be a woman that will open the doors to other women in intelligence. And all of this was over in one moment . . . . I got Crohn's. Not only I had to deal with this crisis [of my lost aspirations], I had to deal with the Crohn's. I was really sick." And, of course, she had to figure out how she would make a living.

Fortunately, Sarit's commanders appreciated her past work. They told her that they would not dismiss her from the IDF. As long as they remained at Northern Command, she would have a job. Sarit's superiors assigned her to a specific project that she had the proper skill set to accomplish and sufficient health to perform. And she was interested in and proud of her new task. Sarit said, "I was the right person at the right time." That job opened opportunities for other projects in other places. "I am very proud," she said, "that I was the one who had done that."

However, the kindness of her superiors only provided a temporary respite. The IDF generally changes the Northern Commander every two years. When General Gadi Isenkot would be replaced by a new commander, Sarit knew that her newly acquired job position would be in jeopardy. Sarit remained in the army for a few more years. But she could only work limited hours, she knew she would not be promoted, and she fatalistically recognized that all was temporary because the army would not retain her on limited duty forever.

After three years Sarit's life took another turn that she didn't expect. Instead of losing her position with the IDF, she lost her husband.

"I didn't expect that," Sarit said in a flat voice. "It happened by surprise, he just left one day, and this was a huge crisis. I think the divorce was even worse [than the Crohn's]. I was left with two babies. I lived far away from my parents and I knew that my [ability to earn money] was in question."

And then, she said to me with emotion, "You know the new Sarit. You don't know the old Sarit."

Sarit talked with friends. She felt the need for reassurance that she was not crazy with her fears and shock. It was 2010 and she and her husband had just moved to a new home. A month later came the shock. Her husband left her, leaving Sarit with a mortgage and the two kids.

"Maybe I don't need a big home," Sarit thought. "That moment I understood I must figure out what to do if I am out of the army." She knew it was a matter of when, not if she would be dismissed from the IDF. And she knew that dismissal for Crohn's disease would mean no pension.

For four more years, Sarit remained in the army. After her boss was replaced, the project she had been working on was stopped. Work became frustrating and nobody cared what she did. In desperation for something meaningful, Sarit initiated a project of her own design. Again, nobody cared. Now, however, the fruits of her labors are still being used. Despite having reached the rank of a major, she had no future. But fortunately for her, the army had too many majors. When the IDF offered compensation as part of a program to encourage majors to leave the service, Sarit grabbed at it. Already she had beaten the odds. It was time to leave. In May 2014, she became a civilian once again.

Fortunately, while her work life was on the downturn, Sarit's personal life was on the upswing. She met her present partner, Yaron. He had two children from a prior marriage. Now living with each other, together they had another child and named her Alma. Yaron had encouraged Sarit to leave the army. But what to do now?

Sarit decided to use her expertise and passion to establish an educational and research center. Dedicated to security and geopolitical issues in northern Israel, she would focus on enhancing the English-speaking world's knowledge of the issues Israel faces along its northern borders. Sarit initiated targeted research, gave lectures, and took interested people on tours along the border. Her first lecture was in June 2014. The referral came from an old army friend in intelligence. But in Israel, events have a way of interfering with plans. War broke out in Gaza in July. Nobody was too interested in meeting with Sarit about the north during, and in the aftermath, of the seven-week war in Gaza.

Sarit used her free time wisely. While living on unemployment benefits, she built a website, studied, read, and wrote. Unlike others who left the army, Sarit was not in the reserves. At least with a reserve position, she would have earned some income when she was called to duty. But with Crohn's, a high-level person had to request her service in the reserves. Nobody did.

Then came a break.

An army contact called Sarit and asked why she was not in the reserves. Sarit responded that no one had asked for her. The contact answered, "We will get you back in the army." When her old IDF unit heard about her possible return to a different location, the commander said, "No. You are going back to your unit!" When Sarit reminded him that the unit had done nothing to request her retention in the reserves before, the commander said, "We forgot." And so, Sarit returned in a reserve capacity to her old unit. Instead of serving twelve months a year, she would serve perhaps thirty days. But she was back doing what she knew and where she was wanted.

In May 2017, on Israel's Independence Day, Sarit Zehavi received the promotion Crohn's had taken from her. She was promoted to Lieutenant Colonel. When I asked Sarit how she felt when she received the news, her response was simple and direct. "Wow. I won the Crohn's. I beat it. Because the Crohn's stopped me from having it. I beat it!"

Now, two years later, Sarit is not sure whether she can remain in the reserves and in what capacity. Her growing research center, *Alma*, named after her daughter, requires her full attention. I thought, also, that it must be difficult to compartmentalize secret information learned at IDF Northern Command from that acquired through research at *Alma*. But Sarit set me straight. Because her prior job with the IDF sometimes required her to brief journalists, she is quite adept at compartmentalizing.

Today, in a few short years, the Alma Center is well established and recognized. There, the only computer simulation of a geo-political crisis in the north involving Israel, Hezbollah, Syria, and Iran can be played by interested groups. One or more people take the role of different Israeli government Cabinet officials forced to react to a challenging and changing environment that threatens war. Based on their decisions, new hypothetical scenarios are presented for resolution that have arisen as a result of prior decisions made by the role-players.

In the field, Sarit and other *Alma* employees take individuals and groups to locations along the border where explanations accompany visual sightings. Meanwhile, in-house research is ongoing. From monitoring Arab social media, analysis of government and organizational pronouncements from all relevant countries, and conversation with experts—*Alma* now produces timely analysis consumed by individuals in Congress, think tanks, U.N. officials, and others in official positions as well as the public at large. Furthermore, Sarit's editorials are routinely published in the Jerusalem Post and other newspapers. In 2018, Sarit spoke to 18,000 at the AIPAC convention in Washington, D.C. and has since been a speaker in demand at AIPAC events, other gatherings, and even in Europe. And, in January 2020, *Alma* hosted its second well-attended day-long conference regarding security challenges in the north.

As a result of *Alma*, the north's security challenges are brought to light. The tours of the border regions given to all level of personages provide a level of understanding of the dangers unmatched by any other media. The simulation highlights the complexities that face Israeli decision makers. And Sarit's many lectures to groups small and large, editorials and articles, podcasts, social media posts, and individual meetings with those in power or with prestige inform decision makers and positively impact public opinion. Combined, all of *Alma's* activities enhance northern Israel's security by illuminating the threat.

When I asked what is most challenging for her, Sarit answered, "The challenge is to deliver a complex message in a simple way."

And when I asked if she is enthused, Sarit laughed and said, "I'm totally excited. I can't believe this is happening!"

Having seen the Alma Center, having met Sarit's employees at *Alma*, and having seen the enthusiasm they too bring, I can attest that it is happening.

But along the way Sarit received assistance from an impactful organization in Northern Israel. Called in short, the Galila Foundation, it is dedicated to improving lives and developing entrepreneurs in the North. And it is to Galila I now turn.

Yael Barlev

After my meeting with Sarit concluded, Yael Barlev joined me at the same bakery where we engaged in a wide-ranging discussion. Tall and striking, Yael is an articulate middle-aged woman who exudes competence and passion for causes important to her. Since its inception in 2005, she has been the executive director of *Galila—The Northern Galilee Development Foundation*, an organization supportive of borderline communities and other causes in the security-threatened northern Galilee.

"Galila was my destiny," Yael told me. "Because when I was a kid, I was an outsider. I grew up in a house that taught me to think different and be very self-reliant." As kids, Yael and her sibling would overhear her mother and father telling each other about their day. "There were no secrets," she says. And, Yael emphasized, they were taught to rely on their own values, not the opinions of others. Yael's mother would say to them, "If you are happy that's what is important. What other people think is irrelevant!" That upbringing fostered self-reliance and independent thinking—qualities crucial for navigating her tragic loss of one parent when she was nineteen and the other five years later.

From a young age, Yael dreamed of becoming an attorney. But after finishing her army service where she had served in a Patriot Missile Battery during the Gulf War, that dream required schooling. Not one to procrastinate, Yael moved to Tel Aviv where she planned to enroll in the requisite curriculum. There, she needed to support herself while attending school. Waitressing did not excite her, so she searched for something else.

When a friend called and asked if she would be interested in a job with a start-up company that provided software to law firms, Yael responded, "Sure!" She then didn't even know where the letters were on a keyboard, let alone feel conversant with computers. But, Yael thought, why not give it a shot?

When Yael called the firm, the firm's recruiter asked when she could come for an interview. Yael responded in her direct manner, "Now!"

The head of the company interviewed Yael. During the interview he asked whether she was comfortable with using computers. Yael answered, "No, but I am a fast learner." "Fine," he responded and hired her. Although he was the brother-in-law of the person who had told Yael of the opportunity, that connection did not get her the job. Nor, obviously, was it her experience. It was because, Yael later learned, he thought her "so motivated." And that's Yael in a nutshell. Her worldview identifies no permanent roadblocks, just obstacles to sweep away.

The job, however, derailed Yael's legal ambitions. While helping law firms incorporate her employer's software, she came to realize the legal profession was not for her. But that realization did not stop Yael from being inspired by the respectful and intelligent people she met. Yael was twenty, and "had no fear of hierarchy" and in her words, "This was the school of life. It was the best school I have had." In a small firm and left independent with only one responsibility—to perform— she thrived.

Later, after leaving the legal software firm, while eight months pregnant, Yael moved with her then-husband to Seattle, where he had received an offer to work in a high-tech firm. Not allowed to fly at such a late stage, to hide her pregnancy she covered her obvious condition. Having overcome that obstacle, Yael gave birth to her first son in the United States. Later, after moving to England, there she gave birth to a second son. From living in England and the United States, Yael learned to speak English fluently, albeit with an accent.

But living away from home did not sit well with Yael. Even though her husband was earning big money in the hi-tech bubble of the times, Yael's family and heart was in Israel. Those feelings, plus her passion for Zionism, drove her to return to the Galilee which she missed dearly. Yael insisted on coming home. "And that's the best decision I ever did in my life," Yael told me. "I [saw] my kids with their grandparents." And then she paused. Knowing Yael as I had for over a year, what I saw during that pause surprised me. Usually strong and definitive, her features softened, and a soft smile emerged. With emotion, she repeated, "Really, it's the best decision I ever made."

Upon Yael's return to Israel, the United Jewish Israel Appeal (UJIA-UK), a huge philanthropic organization based in England that is a sibling of the UJA in the United States, hired her in 2004 and her first marriage ended. Yael sighed after mentioning her hiring by the UJIA-UK and then in a confiding tone, after snapping her fingers, she told me about a defining experience she had.

The UJIA-UK, according to Yael, then thought that portraying northern Israel as needy would spur donations. Because of that policy, the UJIA-UK would not permit her to bring groups to Kvar Vradim, a northern Israel success story. Instead, the UJIA-UK wanted to highlight poverty in the region. After a while, Yael said, "My whole attitude changed. I didn't fit the organization."

Soon after, Yael lost her job at UJIA-UK. But before leaving, Yael made a connection important for her future. She met Natan Golan who, for one year, was the UJIA-UK's CEO in Israel before he, in effect, downsized himself out of a job. A former officer in the IDF and originally a British citizen who made Aliyah, philanthropy has always been at the core of Natan's professional life.

Out of work, Yael asked Natan, who she subsequently married, "What's next?"

Natan answered, "You know what, that's our chance. Instead of complaining what's wrong, what do we want?"

Yael responded:

> *I want to establish an organization [where] I will say where the money should go. They will see Israel, or the Galilee, through my eyes. They will see something different. What [is done in startups] let's do in philanthropy. I don't want people to hear about how awful the Galilee is because I don't believe [that] . . . . I want people to join our ventures because we are changing reality and [making] progress."*

To achieve her goal, Yael went online, downloaded information about how to start a philanthropic organization, rolled up her sleeves, and got started.

"At the beginning," Yael said in response to my question regarding what her biggest frustration was, "I was mostly dependent on the system. Because I didn't have personal connections with people, I was asking for money from foundations. On-line grant requests. Nightmare. And you have all those gatekeepers."

Yael also reflected on problems dealing with potential recipients. Some municipalities and organizations would overstate their needs, thinking it was a negotiation when all Yael wanted was clarity as to the amount necessary for the applicant to reach its goals so she could determine whether she could and should fulfill their requests. Drawing on what she had learned while obtaining a master's degree in conflict resolution, Yael said her educational background had provided strategies for working with those requesting funding.

"My biggest moment," Yael said, "was when I met an American donor, a leading Jewish philanthropist for whom I will use the pseudonym "Jonathan." Yael continued, "It was a life changing moment, really. Every person has [such] a moment in life." She felt that way too about Natan.

Natan, Yael said, "got me eighty percent and Jonathan did the other twenty percent and made me excellent."

When I asked Yael if she ever told Jonathan how much he meant to her, Yael answered that she thought he knew without her having to say it, and that she has communicated it in many ways. I understood her to mean that it was a bond, like family, not romantic, that was mutually nurturing. My view was confirmed when she said, "I think it is kind of a soul mate. I understand the way Jonathan thinks. And I can relate to that.... It is a specific language .... It was a major change in my life."

Galila, under Yael's direction, Jonathan's financial backing and nurturing guidance, financial assistance from others, and with oversight from her Board, has embarked on numerous projects that have benefited the northern Galilee. Several examples demonstrate the range of Galila's impact and priorities.

During the 2006 war with Hezbollah, rockets fell on communities throughout the northern Galilee. While many evacuated beyond the range of the missiles to Israel's center, others huddled in shelters within their own communities. While the rockets still were falling,

Yael and Natan learned that the shelters had no air conditioning. Those forced to endure long stretches underground sweltered in place. They had no choice but to stay put during the periodic bombardments that often lasted for hours. Determined to make a difference, Yael's Galila, through its fund-raising efforts, provided air conditioning units to a significant number of those shelters.

Another example of Galila's humanity is Yael's concern for Holocaust survivors and her determination to do what she can to ease their remaining years. Throughout the region, the last of the Holocaust survivors live out their lives. Many are impoverished or enfeebled. For them, Galila is there with many forms of assistance, including renovating more than 600 homes to accommodate nursing needs or to provide financial aid.

A quick perusal of Galila's website reveals other past and present projects. Whether it is supporting tennis academies for underprivileged youth, English studies in a high school, support for women with cancer or bringing "joy to the child" which is a program to provide support for children hospitalized for extended periods—Galila's touch is felt throughout the northern Galilee.

But from Yael's perspective, Galila's crowning achievement is its Fellows Program. It is a joint venture between Galila and Jonathan designed to "support, empower, and enhance entrepreneurs" whose activities focus on the northern Galilee. In a subsequent conversation, we discussed two of the organizations supported through Galila—Erez College and the Tennis Academy in Kiryat Shmona.

Erez College, located in Shlomi, close to the Lebanese border, is not really a college, Yael explained. Instead, it focuses on vocational and educational training for students wanting to pursue employment in industry. Rather than a four-year program, its curriculum is mainly comprised of targeted vocational courses designed to equip local residents with the skills needed by local small and medium sized industries. When in 2015, Yossi Gimon took over as Director of the college, he piqued Yael's interest. Gimon told her, "I don't want to be a grocery shop that sells each product that people want to buy." Instead he wanted to identify the needs of industry in the area and fill the gap between those needs and residents' capabilities caused by "a lack of professional training for people that want to work in the industry here." Further explaining his passion for the mission, Yael told me that Gimon told her, "Then I know the performance of the company will be better, people will have jobs, I [will] know that I [have] donated my share to this part of the world."

"I buy this idea, I like this vision," Yael said.

To fulfill his goal, Gimon has embarked, with Galila's help, on a two-pronged program to increase the college's relevance and contribution to Israel's northern communities. First, it promotes the college's vocational programs in regional high schools to offer an attractive option for students lacking interest in pursuing a traditional four-year university program. Second, Erez College representatives meet with local industries to ascertain employee skill sets needed by those companies. Then the college offers courses designed to meet those needs for the benefit of all.

When I asked Yael what type of courses are offered, she listed three examples: programs for teaching the use of cutting machines and related software, classes designed to fill the needs of the nearby offshore gas industry, and general courses regarding modern management of warehouses. At present, hundreds of students are enrolled in Erez College courses. Collectively, they will enhance the economic vitality of Israel's northern communities.

Switching gears, Yael said the Tennis Academy is a "a wonderful story." Located in Kiryat Shmona, it is run by Shaul Zohar, a Kiryat Shmona resident. His signature program teaches tennis skills to children living all over the northern Galilee "with mental and developmental challenges [to] overcome their disabilities [by] using the discipline and fun of tennis as a learning tool."

Yael first met Zohar about 2011. Then he was a tennis instructor with the ITC, Israel's Tennis Center. But *Embrace*, a different program for kids at risk, was his passion. When the ITC asked Zohar to change his role to one involving managing ITC centers throughout Israel and prospecting for funding, he was reluctant to do so. But what to do? He needed to earn a living.

When Zohar relayed his dilemma to Yael, she said, "OK Shaul, what do you want to do?"

Zohar answered, "I want to teach tennis and I want to work with kids with special needs."

"Ok, Go ahead. Establish your own business and [in addition] go and do what you dream of."

"I can't do that."

"Yes, you can," Yael insisted.

Then, Natan, Yael's husband, thrashed out a business plan with Zohar.

But still for Zohar, there was a stumbling block. "Ok, but I need to earn money."

Yael's answer came easily. "Ok. You want to work with kids with special needs. You want to do it in Kiryat Shmona and pull kids from all over the region. This is something that you give for society. It will be a Galila project. You will become an entrepreneur for tennis for kids with special needs. We will fund this initiative."

"I don't believe you," Zohar answered.

"You have to," Yael said. "Because we are going to do it. We are going to fund the program . . . . We are going to support you all the way."

At present, Zohar's program has 100 special needs kids enrolled at any one time. Affiliated with a special needs school in Kiryat Shmona, Yael told me, "He created a miracle [t]here." In January of 2020 I had the fortune of spending two hours with Zohar. He is humble, capable, and passionate. One of his students competed in China in the Special Olympics. An amazing man

However, as close to Yael's heart as Erez College and Zohar's social entrepreneur initiative is, Sarit Zehavi's *Alma* is the Fellows Program's flagship endeavor. I ascertained that from Yael's answers when I explored with her Galila's 2019 and 2020 goals. She first answered after taking a deep breath, "WOW. I can't tell you the answer to that because I know that it will be a breakthrough." And then confidently, "I don't know why. It's [a] sense. Something will happen, something big will happen."

I then asked, "Don't you think that has happened [already]?"

"I [do] with *Alma*," Yael responded. "It's huge, it's huge, it's huge! As I told you last night, *Alma* for me was the first time that I [made my mark] and said this is what I want, it will be a success, and it was!"

When I asked Yael if she saw *Alma* having a regional, national, or global impact, Yael answered:

> *It's a national and global impact. But I see it from a different perspective. It's not just the work.... It's the people that do the work. The people that are involved! This is why I told you, when we are building now Alma... we wanted to create a family. I'm using a term that is not right for [this]. This is why I said to you I am not looking for everybody to support Alma. I want only good people and it is my definition of good people.*

Wanting to learn more about Yael, I asked her for a second interview. During that conversation I learned more about Galila but also motherhood in Israel and Yael's personal beliefs. She told me that her oldest son now serves as a paramedic on the Golan Heights, which means he is in a combat unit. Her younger son is in twelfth grade, due to enter the army in another year. And, not surprisingly when I saw the gleam in her eye while speaking of her sons, Yael emphasized, "[I am] a mother before I am anything else."

In the context of her motherhood, Yael also told me, "Only by exposing yourself to certain people you have a chance to become a person that has an impact in life." And that by doing so, you "can evolve better than you can do on your own." Because of that philosophy that she attributes gaining from her parents, Yael wanted to give her children those same values and roots. "The only place that I will be able to do that will be here in the north, Yael said. "Because of the people, because of the periphery because it [helps] people to develop their relationships much deeper.... It's a more meaningful life."

By contrast, in the center, Yael told me it is you against the world. "While living in the periphery you live with the people. You don't need to prove anything. People don't look at you and measure you with the same measurement that they measure you when living in Tel Aviv, for example." In Tel Aviv, Yael said, the type of car and the clothes you wear are important, "while here they will see if you are nice and well-behaved, what you do for the community."

Then tumbled out what drives Yael, "I think that I have a role in life that it's not just for my kids and family but for the community and the country I love so much." Continuing, she said, "I believe that if you are born as a citizen of the State of Israel that you have a role with the Jewish people.... We were born here for a reason.... We have a mission in life to do good in the world. Because we know who we are.... Israelis know who they are and what they belong to." And then, "I think that it is our role to try and convey, try and give... to people who have trouble with... with identity."

When I asked Yael if as an Israeli she feels a responsibility to the world, she said, "Totally, and to the Jewish people.... First to the Jewish people around the world and then to humanity."

Our discussion of her views on life and personal responsibility brought us back to Galila. When I asked how she puts actions to words, Yael answered:

> *I believe you do that by empowering people. I can't do it on my own. The only way I can do it is with other people that see the world the same way I do. And when I find these people I actually try to empower them and give them the tools to [impact] others . . . . So I think this was the idea when we established Galila, that we will be the platform . . . to people [so that] with our support [they] can implement their dreams.*

Whether locally, or worldwide with *Alma*, Yael's passion to make a better world flows through the dozens of endeavors Galila has supported. But how does she pick from the many worthwhile projects that come before her, I asked?

> *Basically, I look for the people. Really, for the people with the stars in their eyes. . . . Each one with their different dreams. I look for these people that don't think that the system and what they have now is enough. I want the visionaries. I want the ones that say I want this place to become [better] but also have the professional background that I know they can take this dream and with the right mentoring and the right time can make it happen.*

Identifying donors with the right attributes and matching their interests with worthwhile recipients is a more than full-time task. But Yael assures me, she finds time to balance her work with family and friends, something I have witnessed firsthand with her devotion to her sons' basketball games.

But, I wondered, what about the stress of seeing your children grow into adults, knowing that the army would be beckoning? Do you endure sleepless nights worrying? I asked.

Yael answered:

> Listen, because all of us were in the army, and our parents had sleepless nights as well, we prepare ourselves. For eighteen years I [prepared] for my son to go to the army and [if] I knew that if he's going to the army . . . . and [that he will] choose to be a paramedic so he will be in the Golan heights for the next two years, with a combat unit . . . . I'm sure that [if] I could save the situation . . . I would do that. But listen this is our role . . . .

Explaining further, Yael told me that Israelis raise their children with values and love of country but when the time comes, still, "You say no, no, no." Of course, Yael said, to further explain, "We do have sleepless nights, especially when we know the tension is going up but it's ok, this is life. I'm sure that if you are a parent in New York and your kid is going out at night you have a sleepless night as well."

I first met Yael in conjunction with my own interest and support of *Alma*. Since then our friendship has blossomed and my respect and understanding for what she has already accomplished, and my admiration for her hopes for the future, has increased exponentially. While Yael rejects picturing the northern Galilee in a needy or impoverished light, she certainly would not challenge that its security challenges, coupled with its location on the periphery, leaves the region in need of assistance to maximize its potential. That is why Galila's contributions play an important role in ensuring the northern Galilee's vibrancy. And also why the northern Galilee, without Yael's passion and dedication, would experience a huge loss.

Shlomi Afrayat

Sarit and I traveled by car up a hill to a gated parking lot for my interview with Shlomi Afrayat. When I first told *Alma* about my book project, Sarit's assistant, Christina, identified Shlomi as someone I should meet. First a video journalist, Shlomi has built an impressive television news production empire in Kiryat Shmona. Together, Sarit and I entered his building, spoke to the receptionist, and soon were joined by Shlomi. On the way to a balcony where I would conduct the interview, we paused for a minute at a bar where he made us coffee. The bar seemed incongruous for the empty building that resounded with its seeming solitude.

Once equipped with refreshments, we sat outside and I attempted to begin the interview, but Shlomi stopped me cold. Fluent in English, he made clear his concern. As an investigative journalist, he had enemies. Why should he trust me? I shared with him my vision for the book I planned to write. Sarit spoke up for me as well. For a few moments it seemed touch and go. And then, suddenly, his demeanor changed. Rather than being reticent he became verbose. And as his story unfolded, I realized that I was in the presence of someone special.

"I was born in Kiryat Shmona in 1963," Shlomi began. "I lived in there," pointing to the mountains to the west that marked the border with Lebanon,

> In that neighborhood up on the hillside. And that neighborhood [was] attacked [from] Lebanon. The three terrorists came down the hill to our neighborhood in 1973 . . . . We [had] left the house three days before that. It was Pesach. They moved to a different apartment. To me, it was all our friends. The school was there. The Kindergarten. For me it was a very bad situation, we moved and two days later . . . . "

Shlomi moved to Zichron Yaakov, south of Haifa, after eighth grade. There, he attended a boarding school that "was the best four years in my life. Everything [was] there, the lovers, the friends, until now we are together. After that the army." Shlomi was in the army for five years. As part of his service, he commanded a tank company headed to Beirut along the coast road during the 1982 war in Lebanon.

After his military service, Shlomi returned to Kiryat Shmona, where he enrolled at Tel Hai College. Over the following three years, he devoted himself to learning TV and film production. To earn a living, Shlomi filmed "whatever you can film, something that someone can pay for me. And I started to film Bar Mitzvahs [and parties]. And my dream was to film news. This is what I want[ed] to [do]. But at that point just one channel here in Israel. [To] work in this channel, if you have contact with God or someone like him then you can work there."

Fortunately for Shlomi, at that time there was a company called Visnews, which then was one of only two major, independent, television news suppliers. Shlomi started working with the company as an independent journalist. He would take video footage and sell it to Visnews, who would then sell it to various television outlets. "At that time," Shlomi said, "it was a very, very bad situation here in northern Israel, 1987, 1988." Palestinians based in Lebanon launched terror attacks into Israel, some successful and some not, and shot Katyusha rockets at Israeli communities. Given the continued fighting, what was happening in northern Israel was a hot topic for newscasters. It was then he identified a business opportunity.

"At that time," Shlomi said, "Channel One filmed in film, not in video."

The significance of the filming format, Shlomi explained, was that filming in video required only two people, but film required five or six. By filming in video, he could do it more efficiently and for less. In addition, Shlomi identified an inefficiency in the film supply chain that video would eliminate. After filming in video, he could send a video cassette by taxi to Jerusalem. That would take two to three hours. There, someone would receive it and edit it. "After five hours," he said, "You can air it." Channel One's cumbersome procedure "before that," Shlomi said, was "if you film in film, it [meant] that you need a crew coming from Jerusalem, three hours, and film let's say two hours, and then they go back and develop the film. And maybe its good [for the evening news]." Maybe, because "it is old news."

Shlomi's new concept gained traction as customers realized his video would get to market before anybody else's film. Soon, everyone came to him and, "in that time [they] paid a lot if you do [it] quickly."

Not satisfied, Shlomi pushed his mastery of the process to a higher technical level. In Marjayoun, a town in Lebanon occupied by the IDF before its withdrawal in 2000, Shlomi maintained a studio from which he could send video footage by microwave transmitter to any purchaser around the world. That further enhanced his reputation as the go-to person in northern Israel for sending video footage.

Shlomi had yet another advantage over his competitors. "Coming from the army," he said, "I know everybody here." Later in our conversation, Shlomi said even Hezbollah knew of him. He would call someone he knew and ask, "Where is it, what is it?" and then go there. Soon his two brothers joined him. Shlomi worked primarily with Reuters (Reuters purchased Visnews), one of his brothers worked with AP, and the second brother with other news organizations. Shlomi's company grew. "Now," he told me, "we have forty-five here." Now, not only could Shlomi transmit anyone's video instantly, he has positioned himself to be the go-to journalist for obtaining the footage. His company, Topline Communications Ltd, has become an indispensable partner for many news organizations.

As his business grew, Shlomi did not remain satisfied with his present success. He identified another opportunity.

> *We [understood] we needed to change something. To build something here [because] when something happened all the media [comes] here. You can see someone sitting in the coffee [shop] here and the restaurant [there]. There is no place to [get together]. So, we said, do you want to build something for the media and if there is something that . . . is a problem here, . . . all the media is here. If not, we are working in the studio, even now there is Channel one, Channel two, Fox news, [there is always something happening here]. So we started building the building in 2000 . . . . . Now, we are working [with various news channels], we are working with them [all the time], every day.*

Shlomi relayed his story with a certain humbleness mixed with pride. Kiryat Shmona is an economically depressed town, far into Israel's periphery in the north. Residents often take every opportunity to flee when they can. Shlomi, rather than flee, had returned home, built a business, and provided jobs and economic benefits to the community.

But not all of his story was so cheerful.

"In 1998," Shlomi said, "I entered into Lebanon to make some story about the Security Zone." Ever since entering Lebanon in 1982, Israel had maintained a security zone to protect the northern communities. Unfortunately, that plan created new problems. Although the PLO no longer was a threat, Hezbollah had grown and actively challenged the IDF in the zone. Over two decades, hundreds of Israeli soldiers had died there.

Shlomi continued, "We are entering Bint Jbeil. Bint Jbeil is a village in Lebanon . . . . There were four roadside bombs, one of them near me, near the car, the convoy." The bomb blast hit Shlomi's left leg, severing tissue and bone. At first, he said, "I didn't feel that I was injured." But then Shlomi saw his leg bent at an unnatural angle, "So," he said, "I put the camera down and it continued to film." The film is still available online. But while the camera rolled, Shlomi's life drained away. Evacuated to Rambam hospital where he regained consciousness, Shlomi realized his situation was "very bad."

All told, Shlomi spent sixteen months in the hospital. "I was the first person in the world," he said, to have the type of surgery the doctors recommended which involved cutting bone to help it re-attach properly. The doctors encouraged him, saying "you are strong, good family, let's try to do it." But, Shlomi said, "At the same time, just to think that you are going to be more than one year in the hospital you think cut the leg [off] and let me go!"

But then a former army comrade came to visit Shlomi. He had lost a leg fighting Israel's enemies. "He told me I can be, let's say, five years in the hospital, if I know that I have leg." To emphasize his point, Shlomi's friend said, "You want your leg, even [when] you go to the bathroom."

Proudly, Shlomi used his cell phone to show me a book with pictures of orthopedic procedures performed on legs. It was titled, *Severe injuries to the Limbs*. Pictures of Shlomi, with the convoluted system of external fixation used to save his leg, was in it. Now, although he does not walk with an apparent limp, when he rolled up his pants leg to show me his injury, the deformity I saw spoke volumes about the agony he must have gone through.

Our discussion then turned to a series of events, traumatic to Israelis, in which Shlomi played an unusual journalistic role. On May 24, 2000, the IDF unilaterally, overnight, and without notice, withdrew from positions it had held since 1982 in Southern Lebanon back to Israel's recognized international border with Lebanon. The United Nations, in one of its few moments of objectivity regarding

Israel, applauded Israel's actions and certified that the IDF had withdrawn to the recognized border.

However, Hezbollah did not agree.

To foment continued conflict with Israel and, at least in part, thereby provide a basis for its continued existence, Hezbollah contended that the Shebaa Farms, a rectangular mountainous area about two by seven miles, on the southwestern shoulder of Mount Hermon in the Golan's far north, was Lebanese territory not Syria's. Thus, the organization said that because the IDF was still deployed in the Shebaa Farms, it had not fully withdrawn from Lebanese territory. Therefore, Hezbollah stated it was justified in continuing to launch attacks on Israel.

On Saturday, October 7, 2000, little more than four months after Israel withdrew from Lebanon, in a well-planned ambush, Hezbollah kidnapped three IDF soldiers on patrol in the Har Dov area of the Shebaa Farms. Israel had named that area after an IDF officer killed there by PLO forces while trying to rescue a fellow, wounded soldier in 1970. Soon after the kidnapping, Shlomi received a phone call from a person in Lebanon he chose not to name. "I didn't understand him," Shlomi said, "But it was something about the kidnap." Shlomi's suspicions were raised, but he heard no more.

"Let's say after a year," Shlomi said, "Somebody call[ed] me and said, 'look I have the footage [film] from the kidnap.' I said, Ok, what do you want? Money. How much do you want?"

The caller demanded an amount roughly equivalent to $10,000.

Shlomi answered, "I don't believe you. You need to send me some pictures of the video."

Three weeks later Shlomi received a letter addressed to him, sent to his home from the United States. He opened it and found within three pictures of the kidnapping. "Wow," Shlomi said to me. Because he is an Israeli, and a former officer in the IDF, the content "for me, it was very bad."

Immediately, Shlomi called an army contact he knew and told him he had pictures of the kidnapping. The contact said, "Don't do nothing." An hour later, a helicopter landed near Shlomi's home. The officer Shlomi contacted came into his home, reviewed the pictures, and then they discussed what to do next. The IDF wanted to obtain the video. Even more, the IDF wanted information regarding whether the soldiers were still alive. A video at least would show whether they survived the abduction. The two men decided to do nothing other than wait, knowing that the person that sent the letter would contact Shlomi soon.

Sure enough, the mystery man called. He wanted to do an exchange, money for video, in the United States. Shlomi purchased airplane tickets. By then, as he put it, "Everyone [knew] I am going to buy [the video], even Kofi Annan," the Secretary-General of the United Nations.

Two days after Shlomi arrived in Manhattan, he received a telephone call from the same person who had called him in Israel, "I have a little bit of a problem" the caller said, "I am with another guy. I'm sorry, it is not $10,000 dollars, it's $100,000." And, the caller said, the exchange must be in Las Vegas instead of New York. Shlomi agreed. It now wasn't his money at stake, and he figured correctly that the IDF would pay.

Shlomi then flew to Vegas. Although he didn't feel in danger, Shlomi checked into the designated hotel where he was to meet the caller but prudently stayed at another. However, rather than receiving the film, he received another phone call from the same caller. The caller changed the location for the exchange to Miami Beach.

Dutifully, Shlomi flew to Miami Beach. There, the caller had instructed him to be at a designated public pay phone at 2:00 p.m. "So, I [was] there, waiting, waiting." The same guy called and, to make sure that Shlomi was there, he asked Shlomi to describe something that was then going on near the public phone. After Shlomi responded acceptably, the caller said, "I need a half-million." Shlomi, with the backing of the IDF, went to a bank, presumably one specified by the IDF, and obtained the money. However, not surprisingly, the process took time and there were others with him.

Evidently, the caller spotted the people now with Shlomi. He called again and said, "I told you to be alone," but agreed to call back. Shlomi waited two days but there were no further communications. While telling me this story, Shlomi's voice markedly lowered, evidencing the disappointment he still remembered feeling, and said, "We go back to New York, after two days, said OK, done."

Three months later, somebody new called Shlomi about the video. That caller said, "Give me $25,000." They agreed to meet in Italy. Several minutes before the scheduled handover, Israeli intelligence operatives approached Shlomi and said, "You need to go back. It is not good you . . . staying here." The agents didn't like the feel of the situation and thought it too dangerous.

Shlomi refused to leave. "No, I am not going back," he said. Unless the prime minister or defense minister insisted, he said he wouldn't leave. Meanwhile, nobody showed with the video, but a written communication from someone high up in government did arrive. It said, "You are endangering yourself and your country. You need to go now." So, Shlomi left the scene, and after speaking to his lawyer, he left Italy. Shlomi's lawyer told him that if he refused, and something happened, like him being kidnapped, the government might do nothing or disavow his presence.

According to Shlomi, the Shin Bet, Israel's security agency, eventually got hold of the tape. Apparently, they obtained it without paying any money. My imagination runs as to how. Eventually, the still pictures Shlomi had in his possession were screened on public television. Subsequently, the United Nations at first denied existence of a videotape and then admitted it. Since the attack occurred near a U.N. position, there was much speculation regarding U.N. complicity in videotaping the attack and being aware of Hezbollah preparations but not doing anything about it.

The film, parts of which were eventually aired on Israeli TV, showed the three soldiers driving a vehicle along the fence line, a bomb going off blowing a hole in the fence and damaging the Israeli vehicle, and Hezbollah soldiers driving a vehicle through the hole in the fence and then pulling the three Israelis into the Hezbollah vehicle. The Hezbollah men, per multiple news accounts, wore U.N. uniforms and wore U.N. insignia. They may have driven a commandeered U.N. vehicle. The entire operation took three and a half minutes. When Hezbollah men pulled the soldiers into their vehicle, at least one soldier appeared still alive.

Three years after the kidnapping, Hezbollah exchanged the soldiers and a kidnapped Israeli businessman for more than 400 prisoners held by Israel and the bodies of dozens of Hezbollah operatives. Within Israel, based on the pictures and video, up to the moment of the exchange there was hope at least one of the soldiers was still alive.

No live soldiers returned to Israel that day. Just three bodies, one of which was a Bedouin soldier who had volunteered for service with the IDF.

After interviewing Shlomi, I researched the story further. It appears clear that Shlomi played a central role regarding the still pictures and the video. And certainly, the earnestness and compassion in which he relayed the story convinced me that for Shlomi, the existence of first the pictures and then the video profoundly impacted him to a degree far more personal than just a journalistic scoop.

Finding the story still matters for Shlomi after decades in the business. Despite his obvious pride for Topline Communications, it is abundantly clear that uncovering important stories still motivates him. During our last few minutes on his balcony, Shlomi spoke about a story he was investigating. While, per his request I cannot write of it, the animation on his face as he told me what he suspected made his excitement obvious. Shlomi is a successful businessman, but at heart he remains an investigative journalist.

As we prepared to walk inside, I asked Shlomi why he built his studio in Kiryat Shmona. He answered, "It is my home."

Downstairs, Shlomi showed me the several studios located there. Within each sectioned off space there were a maze of screens, consoles, control rooms, podiums, etc. When busy with multiple clients, it must be hectic. Topline charges 10,000 shekels, a little less than $3,000 dollars, to use the facilities for one program. From there, a news network can either broadcast a program immediately or do edits. But as impressive as the sight of all that video technology was, the roof of the building left me awestruck. From there, when shells or rockets are falling, the 360-degree view extending through much of the most northern sections of the northern Galilee, permits cameramen to locate and film the action, all from the comfort of Topline's studio building on top of a quiet hill in Kiryat Shmona. But, of course, that access comes at a cost. Shlomi charges for using it.

I left the building with one thought: I had met a fascinating person with a fascinating business, which matters much for northern Israel and its border communities.

Stef Wertheimer

Four times I have driven through Tefen Industrial Park looking for Sarit Zehavi's *Alma* offices. All four times WAZE, rather than directing me to *Alma* with its typical efficiency, sent me on circuitous routes that never quite got me where I was headed. But along the way I saw efficiently laid out streets, circles humming with traffic, sculptures, and large buildings that clearly contained manufacturing plants—all on a hill with a sweeping view of the western portions of the upper northern Galilee. Nearby is the modern town of Kfar

Vradim, with its greenery, homes, recreational and commercial areas, all seemingly laid out per a plan. It made me wonder how it all got there.

The answer is Stef Wertheimer, a multi-billionaire with a passion for industry, education, and Israel.

After Googling Wertheimer, I knew that if I could arrange an interview with him it would be fascinating. Sadly, he was not able to meet with me. The response I received from his representative was that because of the many requests to interview him, and his present age of ninety-three, I should instead read his autobiography, *The Habit of Labor, Lessons from a Life of Struggle and Success.*

Inspiration for the name of Wertheimer's book came from A.D. Gordon, who as you may recall, lived for a time at Degania in the early 1900s. Gordon wrote, "We Jews lack the habit of labor for it is labor which binds a people to its soil and its national character."

Wertheimer agreed with Gordon's thought, but took it a step further. Wertheimer sees Zionism as having had three stages: In Gordon's day it was about agriculture and developing the land, then it became about defense. But now, Wertheimer fervently believes that Israel has reached a third stage, the need to build an export industry "to fulfill our personal and national identity here in Israel." To do so, he believes it crucial to "educate both the Jews and Arabs within Israel for skills in industry so that they can be successful and, in parallel, offer technological and entrepreneurial training" to Israel's Arab neighbors. For him, that means people should be able to choose between vocational and academic tracks with equal respect allocated to both.

In 2006, Wertheimer and his son sold eighty percent of his company, ISCAR, to Warren Buffet's Berkshire Hathaway for four billion dollars with a stipulation that Israeli management remain in control of production. Seven years later, the Wertheimers sold the remaining twenty percent to Buffet for another two billion. In 2013,

Stef Wertheimer was the wealthiest man in Israel. In 2019, Forbes estimated his wealth as close to six billion dollars. Estimates of his son's wealth hover a little over one billion. Integral to amassing that wealth was Wertheimer's handiwork all over the Galilee, and especially near Israel's northern borders. Wherever I went, whomever I met, they spoke about Wertheimer with reverence. If I could not meet the man, I decided to at least read his autobiography in conjunction with reviewing other sources. I must admit, after a few pages, I was mesmerized.

Stef was born in a small town in Germany, close to the French border, in 1926 (I will call him Stef, not Wertheimer from now on, because everyone in northern Israel seems to speak of him by his first name). One out of every six residents of his town were Jews. Stef's father had lost a leg fighting for Germany during World War I. His uncle had lost his life in the same war fighting for Germany too. In his early years, Stef enjoyed a good life. His father had several small manufacturing companies. The family prospered.

But things changed with the rise of Adolf Hitler. First, in 1933, one of the streets in the town was renamed Adolf-Hitler Strasse. Then came emergency regulations permitting Germany's leader to promulgate laws without permission of the legislature. Then a German government-inspired boycott of Jewish businesses was followed by restrictions on Jewish employment. In 1935, Germany enacted racial laws that among other things stripped Jews of their German citizenship and served to separate Jews, as a class, from their fellow Germans.

Stef's father said, "The man is crazy. We need to get out of here." Preparations took more than a year. He decided to go to Palestine because he thought he could marshal his assets into enough funds to open a flour mill there, which he thought would be easier under the British governing body then ruling Palestine rather than in the United States. A few days before Christmas, in 1936, at the age of ten, Stef and his family began their journey. Six weeks later, by way of Switzerland, Milan, Venice, Trieste, and then by boat to Haifa from which they traveled to Tel Aviv, they arrived.

In Tel Aviv, Stef's father, no longer as well off as he had been in Germany, attempted to start his business. Meanwhile, Stef went to school. But Stef was a rebellious sort. He told a story in his book that demonstrated his black sheep persona and that he says was "the first of a long series of confrontations with ruling bureaucracies." Stef explained that he had a teacher in seventh grade with whom he had constant confrontations. The teacher also had a predilection for pinching Stef and others. When the teacher pinched the girl sitting next to Stef, Stef stood up and punched him. That got him thrown out of school. Afterward, Stef's angry father had had enough of trying to reign in his unruly son and therefore, rather than try to push him back into school, told Stef to get a job to help support the family.

Stef got a job as an apprentice in an optician's shop. That led to an apprenticeship in a repair shop for cameras. There, he worked with lathes, planers, and miniature grinders for precision parts. His boss at the camera shop then recommended him for a position with a renowned optician that had moved to Israel from Germany and had opened an optics laboratory. Stef worked ten hours a day in those jobs doing what he found an increasing love for. At night, he studied many additional hours to get his high school degree.

In 1943, at the age of seventeen, the British Air Force hired Stef to fix equipment on its airplanes after receiving a recommendation from the German optician Stef worked for. Then, after the war ended, Stef joined the Palmach, Israel's underground elite strike force before the 1948 Arab-Israeli War. The Palmach sent him to learn how to pilot planes, and then to learn how to work with explosives. But the British got wind of the class on explosives and arrested all the students, including Stef. For a few months, he languished in jail. After his release, Stef worked in a secret facility in Tel Aviv that produced Sten guns, a simple to produce handheld submachine gun, and bullets for the same. Doing that required him to again work with lathes and other tools for manufacturing parts. After the 1948 war started, Stef went north, where he manufactured small artillery pieces that he tested at Kfar Giladi's rock quarry.

After the war, Stef married, worked within Israel's fledgling government industries, and had two children, the second arriving in 1951. But Stef had an independent streak and was willing to take risks. Determined to establish his own business, Stef started his own company that produced tools to cut metal with. He had no financing and no capitol, but Stef had identified cutting tools made of hard metal as an item needed by many industries to fashion the metal parts they required. By then, he had moved his family to Nahariya, then a small beach town backwater a few miles south of the Lebanese border. Nearby, on a hilltop was Kibbutz Hanita. There, he used the kibbutz's machines, in return for a fee, to produce parts. In 1952, he started making cutting tools on his kitchen porch with an inexpensive machine he purchased that consisted of no more than a motor that turned a grinding wheel. With it he would shape and paint the hard metals he purchased, and then attempt to sell the cutting tool he had created.

At first, Stef wanted to name the new company after his son, but his wife, Miriam, objected. She said, "And if, heaven forbid, you go bankrupt, will Eitan always symbolize for us a reminder of this failure?" Dutifully, Stef thought of another name, ISCAR, derived from Israel and the compound carbide. Carbide, combined with tungsten, makes an especially hard and durable metal.

However, after creating fifty cutting tools, Stef realized he had a problem. There were no customers for them because they were too big. Still without money, he had no choice but to persevere. Stef took on a part-time job repairing tools owned by others, made smaller cutting-tool models, and briefcase in hand, went door-to-door to the few local companies to peddle his wares. Through determined persistence, he found a few customers willing to repeat their orders. Two years later, Israel's water company, Mekorot, gave Stef his first big sale that provided him a real income. Still, during those first five years of operation he was unable to accumulate savings, although he avoided any debt.

Throughout the early to mid-1950s, there was little enthusiasm within Israel for developing export industries. Instead, the government was devoted to settling the more than one million new Jewish immigrants flooding the country. They had come from war-torn Europe and the Muslim countries where life after the 1948 war had become impossible for Jews to maintain. Exporting required a permit not easy to obtain. Banks would not give loans for capital investment. Neither would friends or family. What industry there was focused on supporting agriculture with needed tools, sprinklers, and the like. But slowly, with time and effort, Stef's book of orders grew.

Stef attributed his early success, in part, to his "love of my product." But also, to a fundamental decision. No longer would he buy hard metal to work with; instead, he would produce it. Production required compacting powders into pill size shapes like an aspirin, then placing them in an industrial furnace that would reach temperatures from 800 to 1,500 degrees depending on the substance he was trying to create. Hard metal, he explained in his book, is a basic building block of his industry. By producing it rather than buying it he transformed his company from a workshop into a factory.

By 1958, Stef had found partner companies to work with him and found export outlets in Europe and then the United States. Nine years later, Stef began manufacturing turbine blades for jet engines. France's decision to embargo military sales to Israel caused the government to turn to Stef for an answer. Turbine blades must withstand high temperature levels and extreme wear. If even just one fails in an engine, it can cause the aircraft to crash. Stef had no experience with building that type of part. But he successfully grew that arm of his company into a huge moneymaker. In 1973, ISCAR repaired tanks and other IDF equipment damaged during the October War that raged when Israel fought off a surprise attack launched by Egypt and Syria. Stef's days of not having any money were gone for good.

As Stef's wealth grew, he turned his attention to Israel's educational system. Drawing on his experience of dropping out of school, and later that of his son, who also did not set the academic world on fire but who eventually took over running ISCAR, Stef focused on creating vocational schools. He knew that good technical schools had once existed, beginning in 1928, in Tel Aviv and Jerusalem. But over time they had waned, supplanted by universities focused on academic subjects.

Determined to fill a vocational gap he perceived, Stef's first educational venture was creation of the Zur-Nahariyah Vocational School in the mid-1960s. Located in the north, not too far from the Lebanese border, the school's three-year program focused on "practical learning"—half of the student's time would be spent in factories and the other half in the classroom. The school secured jobs for its students throughout the Galilee. Now, many of its graduates hold management positions at ISCAR, or other companies, or have started their own businesses. That school lasted twenty years until its forced shutdown after encountering bureaucratic difficulties involving recognition of the degree the students received. Later, Stef started other schools to expose young soldiers, exiting the IDF, to industrial vocational opportunities.

Then, in the 1970s, an idea that brings us to Tefen Industrial Park germinated within Stef's mind. He saw that in the northern Galilee, in the periphery near the border with Lebanon, land was plentiful but the Jewish population sparse. He also saw an opportunity to bring Arabs, Jews, Druze, and all others together. It was the beginning of what became a passion for him, "The idea of industrial parks in the

Middle East and on the borders between Israel and its neighbors is that the parks will bring industry and provide jobs, which will keep people busy working, instead of engaging in terrorism."

Stef saw the northern opportunity as a "strip of land shared by Jews and Arabs [that] seemed a place where we could start to join [hands] and work together for the welfare of both people." But before building a place to work, he believed it important to build a planned community where people would want to live. By doing that, he thought, he could transform a primarily agricultural region "into a large and joint industrial and educational center with factories, parks, and residential neighborhoods that would fill in the bare landscape of the Galilee along the border."

Stef tried the political route first for achieving his dream. He ran for mayor of Nahariya but lost. And although he served on the Nahariya City Council, he had little advancement of his dream to show for it. Stef then embraced the national political process, and for four years served in the Knesset, ending that stint in 1981. While in the Knesset, Stef soured on relying on government for fulfillment of his dream. In his book, Stef emphasized that point by writing of when a government Minister visited him at his offices at ISCAR, then located in Nahariya. The government official offered him a government loan. Stef responded, "No thank you. I don't need and don't want any government grant or loan. I'm building the factory by myself. All you can help me with is to make sure the government bureaucracy won't bother me."

While in the Knesset, Stef focused on gaining support for developing Israel's export industry. He said:

> *Give me 1,000 entrepreneurs and the Israeli economy will change completely. One thousand smart entrepreneurs will start 1,000 small enterprises in every corner of the country. And if they follow the right path, choose correct products, become familiar with the*

> *markets and their demands, export their products wisely and grow from year to year—we will reach economic independence.*

Stef received little support from his fellow legislators for building an export industry. Frustrated, he resigned two months before his term ended. Stef said, "In this State, there are too many people who look after the unfortunate and therefore the unfortunate people do not enter the circle of production, do not regain their dignity, and instead become a burden."

But before leaving the Knesset, Stef did secure one plum, the right to be a trustee for new type of industrial community he wanted to build that would be named Kfar Vradim. And he received official approval from the Ministers of Finance and of Industry to establish ten industrial parks that would house factories engaged in producing exportable goods and organizations that would personify creative entrepreneurship. The idea of industrial parks grew from a committee Stef chaired that decided the government should prioritize aggressively supporting small export-oriented manufacturers centrally placed in one location rather than rehabilitating various failing factories.

Available in the northern Galilee was a hilltop overlooking the combined town of Jewish Ma'alot and Arab Tarshiha. Adjacent was ample room to build Stef's planned community, Kfar Vradim. The location was two hours' drive from the center of the country but very close to two Druze and some Arab villages. Today, from Kfar Vradim, the green Tefen Industrial Park looms close. And from Tefen, surrounding villages accompanied by olive groves and hot, arid hills in summer that "bloom with color in the spring" compete for attention as you gaze over the surrounding countryside. But in 1981, Tefen and Kfar Vradim only existed in the dreams of one man, Stef Wertheimer.

The Tefen concept began with a bedrock founding principle, to overcome historical neglect for the Galilee. To do that the population in the region needed to increase and employment for them needed to be established. Stef's inspiration for a planned village came from Tapiola in Finland. Tapiola is a city composed of people from many income levels. Its population density is controlled, and its residences are divided by greenery into separate communities that encircle a commercial hub. As a result, residents live no more than a few miles from where most work. The idea of Tapiola was to give people there the feeling that they were living close to nature in homes that fit into the natural landscape. The private foundation that built the project called Tapiola a "garden city" in which it hoped all social classes would live in harmony. Soon, artists came to live there, and the University of Finland opened a branch in the city. Stef hoped Israel's government would embrace and support his plans but when he saw little progress on that front, he decided to move forward on his own.

At first, Stef tried to build the new town on land very close to Ma'alot-Tarshiha, but he received push back from the town's mayor and others. Some thought he was trying to take advantage of the poor local population by building a prosperous community nearby that would entice those with little economic resources to work as cheap labor. Others thought the idea racist. The mayor of Ma'alot-Tarshiha wanted the new town to be incorporated into his city. But Ariel Sharon, then minister of agriculture, stepped in to expedite the process. Some land was rezoned, other land Stef gave to the Druze community. Stef committed hundreds of millions of shekels to building needed infrastructure for the first few hundred planned homes. Meanwhile, Stef vigorously argued to those who opposed the new community that it would benefit all in the region.

Kfar Vradim, Stef insisted, would not be a traditional development town where immigrants were warehoused to hold land. Instead, a prerequisite for moving to Kfar Vradim would be that each new resident would have to bring a "dowry" consisting of "an ability to contribute to the region, whether in industry, educational services, or another field." Stef was focused on creating Jewish roots in the area, through industry and other endeavors, no less than the first settlers saw laboring to develop the land as the only way to create Jewish roots.

However, Stef had to loosen his control somewhat. Although many seemed interested in moving to the new town being built, he also realized that, unlike in Finland, he had to accommodate the individualism of many Israelis. After all, what he was trying to build was more of a "capitalist" society with kibbutz like social connections rather than a socialist community. As such, Stef wanted to create a town that had many internal connections that fostered community but also celebrated the genius of individualism. To do so, Stef reached out to James Rouse, the designer of a planned community, Columbia, built between Washington, D.C. and Baltimore, with which I am very familiar.

Stef moderated his controlling instinct by permitting different designs as long as they created a "common aesthetic." The design clustered homes together, gathered around a shared center for security since they were near the border, but in a manner that shared much open space and fostered communal connections. The cornerstone for Kfar Vradim was laid in 1981. It thrived. Now, many more homes are being built there.

And true to Stef's hopes and predictions, relations with Ma'alot-Tarshiha improved as it began to experience benefits from the new construction. Stef moved some of ISCAR's production plant there. That created good jobs within the town, although the vast majority of ISCAR moved from Nahariya to Tefen, where many town residents also eventually worked. In 2006, Stef received an award from the same Mayor of Ma'alot-Tarshiha that had opposed him more than two decades before. The award read that it was for Stef's contributions "in promoting the development of the Galilee, and the city . . . in particular." Stef received a second award in 2013. They were two of many that included the Israel prize in 1991 for his "special contribution to society and the State of Israel."

Tefen Park, on a hilltop former goat pasture, was built simultaneously with the construction of Kfar Vradim. ISCAR moved there in 1982, but the park officially opened for new tenants in 1984. Stef explained that the Tefen model "focuses on five overlapping circles: export industries, technical and entrepreneurial education, community development, cultural initiatives, and coexistence export industries."

The first circle, export industries, is designed to create jobs.

The second circle, technical and entrepreneurial education, is to unleash Israel's biggest asset— its human resources that are crucial to the nation's existence due to its lack of physical resources. As part of his vision, Stef insured that Tefen would have incubator space for emerging companies; including even patent attorneys, anything to promote export of Israeli products or intellectual prowess abroad.

The third circle includes construction of quality communities that would attract industrious employees.

The fourth circle, cultural initiatives, seems to have been derived from Stef's formative years. In Nahariya, and elsewhere, industry was viewed as low-level and dirty. By incorporating cultural pursuits, he sought to change the image of industry and those that work within in it.

The fifth circle of importance was coexistence. This, Stef in his book made clear, was of huge importance to him. He wanted to attract the best to his industrial park, without regard to religion, heritage, age, gender, etc.

Stef's plans succeeded. At Tefen, there is a sculptural garden incorporated into the grounds that promotes, "serenity, culture, beauty, and a space for work and creative activity." Also, in Tefen is an art museum and much open space. Stef writes that the park is responsible for ten percent of Israel's industrial exports, although I imagine that does not include Israel's burgeoning computer software sector.

At Tefen, in addition to the numerous huge, ISCAR buildings, are companies that range from ScanDisk which builds flash memory cards, to a Druze woman who employs dozens of females that collectively produce skin-care products for domestic consumption and export. Also, Tefen is the home of *Alma*, Sarit Zehavi's growing educational and research company that focuses on security issues along Israel's northern borders.

The Tefen model has proved itself. Stef has built five others in Israel and one in Turkey. Three more have been built by others in Israel. One of Stef's industrial parks is located on land donated by Kibbutz Kfar Giladi, where decades before Stef tested the small artillery pieces he built. Now, located next to the eastern portion of Tel Hai University, the Tel Hai Park, built in 1992, is home to ten or more companies that collectively employ hundreds of people of different faiths in the region. For its first eight years, random Katyusha rockets fired by Hezbollah sometimes interrupted work at the park. Still, the Tel Hai Industrial Park has been a success. Companies there provide internships for students at Tel Hai University. Also incorporated within its grounds is a museum of photography. The benefit to the region is beyond question.

Stef's dream for Israel's far north led him to promote his "Marshal Plan" for the region, which would provide training, jobs, and reduce poverty in the area. So far, his ideas in neighboring countries have not born much fruit. But in the far north, his fruit has made the land sweeter. And although Stef is now in his early nineties, he is still active. The man was a dreamer and still is a dreamer—a dreamer who made his dreams a reality.

Chapter Sixteen
___

Three Communities on the Border

Of the many towns or villages that dot Israel's borders with Lebanon and Syria, three stood out to me: the Jewish town of Metula for its isolation, the Druze town of Majdal Shams for its political complexities, and the Alawite village of Ghajar for the conundrum faced by its residents and their surprising solution. No discussion of Israel's northern border communities would be complete without exploring all three in detail.

Metula

Metula, Israel's northernmost town, juts into Lebanon, where it is surrounded on three sides by Hezbollah-controlled territory. There, it is a calm peninsula that is occasionally buffeted by the raging hate around it. Since 2008, its population has grown slowly, reaching about 1,600 per the last census in 2017. Agricultural pursuits make up its main industry, although a walk along the main commercial corridor, HaRishonim street, reveals sleepy looking hotels and restaurants that boom in war and mostly lie dormant or go bust when it is peaceful.

The town itself is hilly. Getting there requires negotiating a winding two-lane road that is as steep as any I have encountered in northern Israel. Most of its homes are single family, many of them quite nice looking. Outside of the residential district, fields contain rows upon rows of fruit-bearing trees. Beyond them, in most places, is a large concrete fence. And beyond that, Lebanon.

Before the concrete fence there were other fences, some of which remain. And, like many fences, the Metula fence had a gate. From 1976 to 2000, "The Good Fence," also known as "Fatima Gate," was a pathway for Lebanese citizens to enter Israel to find jobs, receive health care, attend schools, and otherwise mingle with Israelis. Additionally, after the 1982 war, it was also a pathway Israeli military convoys took to enter Lebanon until the IDF withdrew from its Southern Lebanon security zone in May 2000. Once a well-known part of Metula, Fatima Gate now is in disrepair.

I've visited Metula several times. On each occasion I was struck by how quiet it was, how beautiful the surrounding scenery was, and how ugly were the Hezbollah flags and hate-filled billboards in clear view of the town's residents—even from across the street of the grocery store.

Determined to learn what living in Metula was like—literally under the gun of Hezbollah—I returned in October 2018 to spend time with Yaniv Elhadif. Four months later I came back with a plan to walk the town and the surrounding area by myself. I find some places are best explored slowly. I understand more if I try to "feel" the environs. Metula, with its tidy, neat streets, has an ominous atmosphere that demands such introspection.

* * *

The road to Metula goes through Kiryat Shmona. Lined with palm trees and old and new shopping centers, the road comes to an intersection where a left turn will take you quickly to the western campus of the College of Tel Hai and, a little further, Kfar Giladi.

Metula lays ahead on the snaky, challenging road that cuts through agricultural fields. On the left, steep canyon walls rise to meet the Lebanese border. Over them have come Katyusha rockets and mortar shells—and sometimes terrorists. To the right, the countryside is more open and sometimes drops sharply down. At Metula, the road branches. The left branch leads to a residential area on a hill. The right branch requires a sharp right turn before splitting again. If you bear right, the road leads to a residential area. The left option continues upwards and winds around until it reaches the main road into town. There, on either side and further ahead are some older housing units, a few historical buildings, and the commercial center of town. That's where I went.

Yaniv Elhadif lives in a trailer permanently situated in his parents' backyard. The backyard is on the northwest outer fringe of Metula. From there, the beauty of the region envelops you. So does the threat.

Yaniv greeted me at his door and ushered me in. He is of average height, has a craggy face that supports a scraggly beard, and sports a long ponytail. He works mostly as a jeep tour guide—when he wants, for as much as he wants. Yaniv likes the flexibility of his job because, being self-employed, it allows him to "keep a life balance." Although not religious, he takes Fridays and Saturdays off as well many hours on other days. Yaniv could get more guide work but avoids doing so because "it's a cycle that doesn't end." Inside, I met his pregnant wife, Sivan, and his son, Adar, who was then two. Sivan, much younger than Yaniv, was sitting on a bed playing with Adar. By the looks of Sivan, I surmised that the birth of their second child would be soon.

Yaniv, now forty-five, has lived in Metula all his life except for one year spent in Los Angeles after his army commitment. Yaniv moved to L.A. to convince his brother to come home. Successful, his brother now lives in Metula as well.

Like Yaniv and his two brothers, their parents were born in Israel although his maternal grandmother came from Syria. In fact, Yaniv's parents are first cousins. "That," Yaniv said laughingly, "is why I'm a little crazy. At least I have a reason to be crazy." Crazy or not, Yaniv has roots that dig deeply into the land. On his father's side of the family, Yaniv is the twenty-second generation of Elhanifs to live in Israel.

Yaniv's parents moved to Metula in 1972. Two years later, Yaniv was born. At first, Yaniv's father worked as a glazier while his mother started the first kindergarten in town. Later, in the early 1980s, they opened Metula's first grocery store.

I asked Sivan whether she likes living in Metula.

Sivan answered that growing up in Netanya had not nurtured her, because she likes "the trees and air." People in Metula are "very different, really warm." She compared Netanya, where you "walk into [a] town [and] nobody says hello," to Metula where "you can meet people on the way, and they say hello and [you] get to know them." Yaniv agreed and said in Metula "you don't feel the city strangling you . . . you see green."

But when I asked whether a kibbutz might provide the same environment, they both said, regarding kibbutz social structure, that "a kibbutz is too much."

To me it seemed somewhat odd, the three of us talking about a languid environment, while a few hundred yards away, Hezbollah was watching, and for all I knew, waiting for the right moment to attack. That thought prompted me to ask Yaniv whether he thought about the danger.

Yaniv answered, "People live here and still maintain their normal daily life . . . [but] this is on my mind 24/7, even when [in] my home I'm thinking and making sure there is an exit." It's not so surprising that Yaniv would have that mindset. He's been living this way his entire life. "As kids," Yaniv told me, "we were shelled by thousands of missiles."

One incident stood out to Yaniv. As a child, he lived with his parents in a small house—perhaps 500 square feet—built out of cement, which, except for direct hits, made it close to bomb proof. Yaniv said:

> *One day in the summertime my mom was at the supermarket, my father is working, my brothers are not home. I'm all alone watching television, maybe ten o'clock in the morning, bare naked, having my chocolate milk. We were already trained when you hear the explosions, bombs, we knew what it is, what direction it comes from. I realized [from] the first explosions that I heard that it's a katyusha heading towards us.*
>
> *I turned around, there was a very narrow window behind me. I looked through it, over the sofa. I climbed the sofa looking through the window, the missile fell in our neighbor's backyard. . . just on the other side of the road. As kids, we were trained to react to incidents. As [soon] as I saw it I . . . jumped on the floor and covered my head."*

Yaniv was then seven years old.

> *[When] I realized it is not continuing, there is no more bombs falling, I just opened the door and I ran to my mom's work, crying my guts out, terrified, not knowing what to do, just running to my mom. I . . . feel like it was just yesterday. That's my emotions as I am talking about it. We had many, many incidents. It was one of thousands.*

Yaniv paused, sighed, and continued, "Walking down the street in Metula on a regular day it was always on our mind. We had community shelters back then . . . . So we always had to think, where is the nearest shelter? When I am going to school is a missile going to hit? If a missile is going to fall . . . is the nearest shelter in front of me? Where should I run? Is it in front of or behind me? Constantly."

Now, somewhat fatalistically, Yaniv said that he is not afraid of missiles anymore. "Every missile being launched has a target already. And it's a matter of luck. If I hear a bomb falling you hear a whistle [he then emulated the sound] and you wait for it to fall. I could run to the shelter [but] it could find me . . . . If it is supposed to hit me, it will hit me."

"Today," Yaniv continued, "my fears are that they are going to penetrate . . . . Nasrallah [Hezbollah's leader] is claiming that they are going to conquer northern villages in the next battle." In this village [Metula], he said, there is a team of soldiers serving in the reserves "and in case of emergency we are ready to respond. We are already in the village"

Yaniv is a member of that quick response team. But despite its existence, Yaniv admitted, "If you ask me, we are good only for the first second. If somebody [comes] now without any alarm . . . I could help myself, my family, my neighbors maybe. If I need to run to the other side of the street, I'll probably pass out. We are getting old, not in shape."

Stationed in town is an active army unit. Yaniv said that's not enough. "If they will start whatever they want to do, we won't be able to stop them. We are surrounded by them from three sides . . . . If our neighbors come attack Metula from five different angles, we can't respond to all!" Still, despite Yaniv's concerns, Sivan doesn't worry "because I trust him."

I was curious about Yaniv's childhood, and what Metula was like then.

His response to my question meandered from security to smuggling to the comforts of a small town. While recognizing that he saw things differently now as an adult, Yaniv added, "I feel we are more in danger than we were as a kid,"—a period when he endured regular bombings and other incidents. But the incidents, he said, were "alarms, footprints coming through the fences [that were] usually drug traffic or smuggling. Back then it was videocassettes—cheap in Lebanon, expensive in Israel. Later on, it was tobacco and cigarettes." Yaniv told me many of Metula's first residents were smugglers. They bought cheap goods in Lebanon and sold them for a profit in Israel.

The town has also grown a lot, Yaniv said. During the 1970s, Metula consisted mainly of a main street and a couple other roads. "We knew everybody and knew everybody's pet's name. All houses [were] open to us." Of the village itself, he said:

> *It was really safe. Most of our hanging places [where they would listen to music with jury rigged cassette players] were shelters . . . . Parents knew where they were and if problems they were in [a] shelter. Getting home was a little scary, because [I was] always looking sideways to make sure nobody [is] running. It's dark, you don't see anything and your imagination . . . .*

Our conversation then turned to guns and growing up. As a child, he was used to seeing weapons in the house. "My father," Yaniv said, "in the drawer next to his bed had grenades." Yaniv knew they were there but was taught not to touch them. If it were up to him, his son would learn about weapons "from the first day. It is our life!" Yaniv emphasized. But that's not the life Sivon wants for her son. She insists on protecting him from the harshness of the world they live in. That difference seemed to have been a topic of many discussions between them. Yaniv said in response to Sivon's perspective, "I think he should know the truth. I would train him how to react." Not knowing, Yaniv told me, could mean paying the "heaviest price."

But despite Sivon's desire to protect Adar, the world continues to intrude. The sound of bombing frequently reaches her son's ears as do the noises emanating from buzzing surveillance drones and passing Humvees—so much so that "Humvee" was Adar's second word!

Neither Sivon or Yaniv had said or did anything to make me feel anything less than welcome, but I felt that I had intruded long enough. I had come to see Metula from the perspective of a local resident. It was time for Yaniv and me to head out.

On the way to his jeep, Yaniv told me Metula is slowly growing, even though most people leave Metula after their army service. The growth can partly be attributed to students living in the town while studying at Tel Hai who then "fall in love with the area and stay." Like when he grew up, Yaniv said, "It's a very different vibe here, you are aware of everything, you can leave your cars open, there is no crime, it is very safe, the children can walk in the street." He could never see himself living anywhere else. Never, even though in times of war, tanks roll past Yaniv's home before moving into Lebanon, grinding the road into "powder." And even though a crack remains in the cement outside Yaniv's home where an IDF crew setup a mortar for firing at targets in Lebanon.

Parked adjacent to his parent's property was Yaniv's red jeep. He purchased it in 1996, and since has put almost 300,000 miles on it. When things go wrong, he fixes it. Two decades old and loud, it proved a perfect transport for our journey around the perimeter of Metula.

The fence on the other side of the road from where the jeep sat was not the border, yet the border was no more than a few hundred yards from Yaniv's home. Between, were orchards and family-owned fields. In some places, because of the topography, there were spots difficult for the soldiers to properly monitor from their base. "Now," Yaniv said, "[Hezbollah] can get into my doorstep, they can open my door without any notification." But the day I was there it was quiet—except for the explosions Yaniv had heard earlier in the morning.

Yaniv's comments led me to ask about the fence and the possibility of tunnels. The fence, he answered, "Was not going to stop anyone from crossing." As for tunnels, he gestured to a nearby hilltop, across the border, northeast of the town. On top of that hill is construction equipment. "If you ask the army . . . they will tell you there is nothing here—[But] one guy in . . . his kitchen felt his kitchen shaking." Others have also heard or felt something that makes them think someone is digging a tunnel.

In October 2018 when I interviewed Yaniv, the government was keeping mum about tunnels. That changed two months later, when six Hezbollah tunnels, stretching into Israel from Lebanon, were discovered by the IDF after several weeks of searching. Two of them were very close to Metula and designed to cut-off the municipality from help while a Hezbollah unit would overrun the town. Yaniv's fears were not so farfetched.

As we drove north and then east, I could see cars going back and forth on a Lebanese road distressingly close to us. Hezbollah is not supposed to be armed south of the Litani River, many miles away, but they are there, with their guns and rockets, on the border. UNIFIL, the United Nations peacekeeping force, does nothing. Very likely, some of the cars I saw contained armed Hezbollah operatives.

Earlier, Yaniv had told me, "All seems peaceful until it is not."

His words resonated as we drove on. Farther east, I saw four waterfalls across a ravine. On Israel's side of the ravine is a trail that takes forty-five minutes to negotiate at a fast walk. As a kid, Yaniv would walk to the pools below for a swim. "The bravery test we did to each other was walking alone during the night . . . down to the waterfalls." And, of course, he admitted, "We did bring girls here." Above the trail and the waterfalls is the border.

From time to time, "Hezbollah tries to provoke us [with flags]," Yaniv said. "The last one before this one had a picture with [the al Aqsa mosque in Jerusalem] with a Hezbollah soldier next to it saying in Hebrew below, 'we're coming.'"

But Hezbollah does not just direct its terror tactics to Jews. Metula, though predominately Jewish, has Christian, Druze, and Muslim residents. Some have family in Lebanon. They are afraid to talk to their loved ones in Lebanon out of fear that Hezbollah will question those family members about their connections in Metula. For example, Yaniv has a non-Jewish friend who now lives in Metula, but once lived in Lebanon and still has a home there. Yaniv showed him on the Internet where "Hezbollah [was] threatening him, showing his house, telling him they are coming, [telling him] they know where he is. I showed it to him, and he asked me not to tell his wife."

Just as Yaniv finished telling me the story about his friend, he saw another friend who had served in the SLA. Founded in 1976, the Southern Lebanese Army (SLA) was a mostly Christian Arab group of almost 3,000 militiamen that held a narrow band of territory in southern Lebanon. For the IDF, it acted as somewhat of a buffer between Israel and Hezbollah. The SLA disbanded in 2000 when the IDF withdrew from Lebanon. Most SLA members chose to accept Israel's offer to resettle in the Jewish State rather than face Hezbollah's wrath. Perhaps ten families moved to Metula. One, another friend of Yaniv's, for the longest time refused to visit Yaniv at his home because from there he could see into Kfar Kila. The friend said it was too painful for him to "see my home from here . . . my specific home."

We then turned off the residential area on the eastern side of town and onto the main commercial strip. "Not many tourists coming," Yaniv said. Many restaurants couldn't survive as a result. The hotels looked quiet. Hardly anybody was in the street. It was a far cry from the years preceding 2000. Then, because of the IDF's ongoing occupation of Southern Lebanon, the town was loaded with military personnel, tourists, and reporters.

Soon, we passed a site that Yaniv told me memorialized the "first suicide attack by Palestinians against our troops." That day, a vehicle passed a truck loaded with soldiers, on the road only yards away that is now controlled by Hezbollah. The car stopped, turned around and went by the truck again. This time, the car exploded. "All those incidents [are] like trauma for us," Yaniv said.

> *I remember exactly where I was, who was next to me, what we were doing. We were in English class in school, all the windows . . . shattered, exploding on us. Huge explosion. We ran to the shelter, fifteen minutes, twenty minutes later, they released us home. . . . From my home I saw the same spot, the [Zaka], the orthodox were cleaning . . . all the body parts, everything . . . . We saw the [Zaka] guys walking in water, knee deep . . . . They were walking with black plastic bags collecting body parts. That's our memory.*

Next was an agricultural area. A sign along the dirt road leading into the field said, "No Entry Closed — Military Area." Yaniv nonchalantly explained as we drove past it on the forbidden road, that it was "actually not a closed military area . . . [the sign] will stop the majority of people . . . [but] if you want to make it a closed military area you need to pay the farmers." I got his point—the sign stopped tourists. Not the locals.

After a few moments, we came to "The Good Fence," otherwise known as Fatima Gate. Yaniv told me the gate was named after Fatima, a woman in Lebanon living closest to the gate. We could see Yaniv's home from where he stopped the jeep. Just above us was Lebanon. No wonder he was nervous in his trailer. I was nervous where we were. Yaniv told me that a rifleman on the second floor of one of the homes in Lebanon could easily shoot us. It didn't make me feel any better when he added that, in our current position, we were out of sight of the IDF base.

"Less than a year ago," Yaniv said, "a soldier [at the base] was shot by a sniper from Lebanon . . . . This is our daily life. It is mind blowing!" But, he said, don't get me wrong, "I feel safer here than in L.A. [They know] if they hurt any citizen here, we will have to respond."

We then walked up a short hill to where "The Good Fence" once stood. The terrain was rocky and loaded with thorn bushes. Barefoot, Yaniv ignored the rocks but picked his way through the thorns. At the top were the remains of buildings. Yaniv said, "There were a few gift shops here where you could get drinks and stuff." A thirty-yard trail led to the border. In those shops an old lady, sort of a great aunt-like figure, and then her daughter, Mary, gave free coffee to the soldiers.

When we scampered down, a Humvee outfitted with a machine gun braked to a stop in front of us, interrupting our solitude. Four IDF soldiers were inside, armed to the teeth. They had come to check what we were doing there. Yaniv knew the driver. After speaking to them, Yaniv said, "They saw us walking around the border. I am happy they are coming." Happy—yes. But we had been there for a few minutes before they arrived. Anything could've happened in that amount of time. So I had just experienced an example that supported Yaniv's concerns regarding the IDF's ability to react quickly to an incursion. As we left, the soldiers were using a chain to block the entrance we had passed through.

The rest of our time together, we passed through fields filled with apple, peach, nectarine, pear, plum, kiwi, and apricot trees—as well as capers, which Yaniv explained start as a flower and then turn into a fruit. We also passed concrete border barriers that still had unfinished gaps in them. At one point, I saw a Lebanese gas station nearby. We were very close to the border, too close for Yaniv to feel comfortable stopping.

On a hill to the east in Lebanon sat a huge mansion. Yaniv theorized its owners come from Iran or the Emirates and support Iran. But more importantly, from there or other points in the Arab village, Hezbollah can see down into most of northern Israel. "They gather intelligence on us," Yaniv said. Our drive confirmed what a friend of mine had once told me while we stood at a much higher vantage point. Where the land is green is Israel. Brown is Lebanon.

On our way back we passed the site of a future Metula neighborhood. Earlier, Yaniv had told me that real estate prices were either remaining stable or heading down slightly. Even so, housing is in demand. And the town needs to get younger and wants to grow. Therefore, children of Metula will receive priority for building homes at the new site. They will have to pay construction costs but not for the land. Furthermore, Yaniv said that in Metula, "There are very few opportunities to develop. [Metula] needs high tech or more factories, more advanced occupations . . . Otherwise, . . . it will just get older and older, very few young families are coming." Not so different, I thought, than on the kibbutzim.

Soon, Yaniv said, there will be a lottery for those who wish to build in the new neighborhood. The earlier your name is called, the higher your priority for selecting a lot. Each lucky participant will get a quarter acre of land with a major stipulation: they must build on it within three years, or else lose it. They'll also be restricted from selling their new home for several years. Yaniv is interested but concerned about the cost and not eager to work harder to make it more affordable. "The problem here," Yaniv said, "Is that the last neighborhood built in Metula was twenty-two years [ago]. I applied for the opportunity but did not win." On the other hand, his mother had said to him that a huge percentage of the people living in homes in Metula are her age and they're not going to leave. I surmised from that, if he doesn't throw his hat in the ring, he might not get another opportunity.

I left Yaniv at once joyful and sad. Joyful because he had plainly decided how to live his life and felt fulfilled by the beauty and small town feel of Metula. Sad, because I saw in Yaniv's fears how fragile Metula is. But for sure, something about the town—the ominous air, the peacefulness, the solitude, the history, and the necessity of its continued existence—struck me. I was determined to return.

Four months later I did.

My plan was to meet with Yaniv again and walk every street of the town by myself to get a better sense of life there. But fate intervened. Sivan had given birth to a baby daughter they named Tehila and Israel had announced the discovery of tunnels that Hezbollah had dug from Lebanon into Israel, two of which targeted Metula. A couple weeks after their discovery, Avraham Levine of the Alma Research and Education Center had interviewed Yaniv. During the interview, Yaniv admitted he was "a little worried, obviously, because of the tunnels dug into Metula." He said, "Two weeks ago, all of a sudden, early in the morning, we are told that the operation started, detecting the tunnels, and doing whatever is needed with them. I was very shocked."

Yaniv spoke slowly and almost sadly in that interview. At one point he said, "I'm very emotional when I talk about it," not for himself but for the doomsday scenario he thinks about. Metula is at best a mile wide, he explained, and is surrounded on three sides by Lebanon. "I'm afraid," he said, "that there are still tunnels dug onto Metula from other directions." Those tunnels will allow Hezbollah fighters to avoid the high tech-fences surrounding the town. "Which means they are going to surprise us. We have a kindergarten here [and] a local elementary school. And my biggest fear is that they are going to . . . kidnap children into Lebanon. For me, that is the worst-case scenario. I can hardly imagine that. It's difficult for me to think about it."

With scarcely a pause, Yaniv continued about the war he saw coming, "If it will start, Hezbollah is planning on conquering Metula. First, controlling the only access road into Metula so nobody can come help us and then imagine what they can do in the village. Let's say . . . 200 Hezbollah terrorist soldiers will come into Metula. It will be a nightmare. Worse than a nightmare."

Yet, even with his private horror expressed for all to hear on the Internet, Yaniv's love for his home shone through. "But even here," he said, "I feel safer. I know that my brothers, not my physical brothers, all the Jewish people here, we are very united. Someone is watching my back."

Yaniv will never leave Metula. I couldn't wait to return.

* * *

In late February of 2019, I again climbed the road to Metula, but my plans for my overnight stay were in shambles. Two days earlier I had started coughing and feeling feverish. Now, I was hacking constantly and sneezing without letup. Knowing that Yaniv's wife had just had a baby, I canceled my meeting with Yaniv, not wanting to risk getting any of the family sick. And my plans for walking the town were in jeopardy as well. Rain that had been pummeling the region for two days running was getting heavier. Gusts of wind accompanied the downpour. Walking would not be a picnic. Still, Metula maintained its irresistible pull on me. Driving down HaRishonim Street, I spotted the Alaska Hotel on my right. After pulling into the parking lot, I grabbed my things and made a mad dash for the hotel. Dripping and puffing, I burst through the door and walked through the empty lobby to the front desk.

That's when I met Reuven Wineberg.

Reuven is in his mid-sixties and spoke with an accent whose joyful lilt I couldn't quite place when he greeted me. I was the only one staying at the hotel that night. Gleefully, he informed me that I was lucky; a large group was coming tomorrow, and if the Mount Hermon ski resort were open, the place would be full. But tonight, he'd upgrade me to the best room in the place. True or not about the occupancy numbers, I was glad to get the nicer room. I was even happier when a little chitchat revealed that he was the owner of the hotel and had been for a long time. When I asked if he would consent to an interview, he said he would be glad to.

I came downstairs about an hour later, refreshed from a short nap and reinforced with a wad of tissues. The hotel itself was truly unique. Its walls were solid tile and concrete. So solid they looked like they could withstand a direct katyusha hit. When I reached the lobby after walking through a darkened corridor, Reuven led me to a seat and made us coffee before we started a conversation that lasted more than two hours.

At the outset, he told me that he had been working in the hotel for fifty years. And then almost in the next breath, that his parents had survived the Holocaust. When I responded that I was a son of a survivor too, he said in his loud jovial way, "You are fucked up too!" For a few minutes we talked about how the Holocaust impacted survivors and that his mother made him miserable as a result, but then with respect he said, "The way they continue life is unbelievable."

He then told me how his parents got to Metula.

Before the war, Reuven's mother had a husband and two children. One day, the Germans came to their home, killed her husband and children, and took her away to a concentration camp to work. After the Americans had liberated her concentration camp, she was transported to a camp near Munich. That's where she met Reuven's father who had survived the war by running away from his village in Poland. Reuven's mother was sick. Even so, the couple decided to go to Israel. When they arrived in 1948, a physician told them that his mother needed to live where the air is dry, and that the best dry air is in the far north, dismissing from consideration, I suppose, the hot dry air of the Negev. So that's why, Reuven said, "She came here, at the end of the world." The government gave them one room with no lights. They married and had children. In 1953, Reuven was born.

Before Reuven's parents arrived, the multi-story Alaska Hotel had dwarfed the other structures in town. It was built in the early 1900s. The land surrounding it was used for farming and cattle. The story Reuven told me was that the man who built the hotel, a man named Brenner, went to Beirut to buy cement for its construction even though he could have gone instead to villages no more than a couple days away. In Beirut, Brenner agreed to a contract much more expensive than he could have gotten with locals for the same product. The journey on donkeys from Beirut with the supplies took three weeks rather than the few days if Brenner had used more local suppliers. But Brenner had his reasons for doing what seemed silly.

When the material arrived, it was time to pay. Brenner, according to the version Reuven told me, offered a quarter of the contract price (another version of the story I found on the web says the offer was one tenth of the price). Understandably, that reduced offer met much spirited resistance. Nonplussed, Brenner said fine, take it back. The thought of transporting the cement back to Beirut on the backs of braying donkeys with nothing in hand to show for the trouble was evidently too much for the vendor to bear. Brenner got his price.

Brenner died in the mid-1960s. By then there were several hotels in Metula. People loved to visit the town to take in the fresh air. Brenner's children, however, wanted nothing to do with the hotel business. So, they looked for a buyer. When the children asked Reuven's parents if they would be interested, they responded the building was old and they don't have the money. But the children were persistent, and likely desperate. A deal was reached. Reuven's parents would work in the hotel and open a restaurant within it. After five years, their sweat equity would constitute the required payment and then the hotel would be theirs. Reuven's first job was where I had first met him—working the front desk.

For a while business was good. People moved freely back and forth between Israel and Lebanon. There was no fence, just friendships. The official antagonistic attitude of Arab nations towards Israel took a backseat to business, trade, and leisurely pursuits. But, after King Hussein evicted Arafat's Palestinian Liberation Organization (PLO) from Jordan, the PLO took root in Lebanon and things changed. Soon, rather than Lebanese money flowing into Metula, rockets flowed through the skies before crashing into town. One day in 1970 or 1971, Reuven told me, as many as forty landed. Years later, a missile struck the hotel's garden. Shrapnel from the rocket hit Reuven's leg, requiring him to go to the hospital. Due to the danger posed by Palestinian terrorists that had taken control of southern Lebanon, Israel closed the border with a fence, and everything changed.

With his leg bleeding profusely from his wound, I'm sure Reuven experienced what he had complained about earlier—the problem of medical care. "In the periphery," Reuven told me (there goes that word again, I thought), if you need a regular doctor—no problem. But a specialist requires waiting three to four months for an appointment and there is no second opinion. One opinion he said, "And that's what you got!" It is a forty-five-minute drive to Safed. "You can die twice!" Reuven emphasized. I wondered, after the shrapnel hit his leg, if he thought he might die at least once.

Our conversation wandered though many subjects but settled for a time on business and love. Between 1982 and 2000 business was good again. The 1982 war in Lebanon had attracted journalists in droves. For many, Metula became their base. But Reuven had a problem. Across the street was a nice hotel. It was doing a good business because the IDF spokesman stayed there. Therefore, like pied pipers, so did the journalists. Reuven's hotel was empty.

One day, in 1982, a journalist crossed the street to see if there was a phone he could use in the Alaska Hotel. In those days, to make an international connection you first had to contact an operator in Tel Aviv. Before getting an operator on the line for the reporter, Reuven asked him where he was staying. Sure enough, it was across the street. As Reuven dialed for the operator, an idea popped into his head. He asked the operator to call him every five minutes to see if he needed an international line even if he hadn't first called. Reuven was then twenty-nine. The operator was a decade younger than him. They became friendly. Meanwhile, the Alaska Hotel became known in the journalist community for always having an open line. Word spread. Soon, the Alaska Hotel was full too. For a while, as Reuven put it, the IDF spokesman was the honey, "But I [found] the honey. I got the telephone!" And he found honey even sweeter than that. The telephone operator asked if he would like to meet her. Not one to miss an opportunity, Reuven invited her to Metula. That led to marriage, five kids, and after the honey ran out—a divorce. He married another.

Sadly, for Reuven, none of his children want to live in Metula. When one son said he would help out for a few days, Reuven found him exhausted in the lobby after only an hour. When he asked what's a matter, his son responded, "I ran out of energy." Being the proprietor of a small hotel is exhausting. Few kids would want to do that. But it clearly bothers Reuven that his family will one day no longer own the hotel. Two of his kids are lawyers and another married an attorney. The fourth is a television copywriter and the fifth is involved in a start-up. Some of them live in Tel Aviv. None of them are coming back to Metula.

The hardest thing about Metula, Reuven said, is business. Right now, "it is like a cemetery." You don't see cars driving or people walking. "People come here for the quiet," he said. Of course, if terrorists had come through the tunnels the IDF found, the prevailing "quiet" would have ended in a hurry. Reuven said the tunnels were found in two places. One, placed to give fighters easy access to Metula; the other was about a half mile down the hill, situated to facilitate Hezbollah's plan to block the only road heading up to town.

Metula's agricultural land encircles most of the town. Once the land was divided among many owners; now just a few large stakeholders own most of it. The fields stretch right up to the border fence. Agricultural workers farm it without being bothered by the discernible presence of Hezbollah, only feet away. Also, Metula residents own land near Ma'ayan Baruch. Months before, Phillip from Ma'ayan Baruch had pointed that out to me. I thought it odd then. But Reuven told me that Metula had received that land from the State after 1949, in return for land in Lebanon that Metula had relinquished as part of the disengagement agreement between Israel and Lebanon.

Metula also contains a surprising structure—the Canada Center. Opened for business in 1995, it was built with money donated by the Canadian Jewish Community. It's a sports complex dominated by an Olympic-sized ice-skating rink complete with stands that can accommodate more than 1,000 people. There, in 2006, the World Under Eighteen Hockey Championship was scheduled until Hezbollah's threats forced its cancellation. It's also where two Metula siblings had learned to skate so well that they competed in the 2006 Winter Olympics. But, according to Reuven, economic reality took its toll. The center lost money and the town, which eventually had to take it over, now rents it out.

The next day I walked to the Canada Center, but it was closed. Perhaps it was the leftover puddles and cloudy skies, perhaps it was the solitude of an empty complex, but I sensed that its financial issues were continuing. A sense that was compounded when several months later I returned to Metula again and this time toured the center. Reuven told me that people come from outside of Metula for the day, but don't stay. If that's the case, and I would imagine a hotel owner would know, the center has not proved to be the economic driver that I'm sure many hoped it would be.

Metula may have troubles, but Reuven's love for the place endures. "For me," he said, "Metula is something that I cannot understand, but I cannot live in other places . . . . First of all, I am connected to the hotel like I connect to air. I don't care if business is good or bad. If you take me out from here, I die. My mother was the same thing. Until she died, she was here. I cannot explain that." Even when he was in the military, because he served in the north, Reuven "ran everyday home to work with [his] mother and father [in] the hotel." When the other soldiers relaxed, he worked at the hotel.

Do the other residents, especially if there is war, share your love of Metula? I asked.

Reuven said perhaps 500 people would stay; the rest would leave. Those who would stay, he said, were primarily the farmers and business owners like him. But he is fatalistic and knows how vulnerable Metula is. "If [Hezbollah] wants to kill people here they can do it." The damage will be great. Then, with great pride, he said that if shit happens, Israelis will pull together, whatever their background.

My time with Reuven was fascinating. A few hours after interviewing him, I ate dinner in one of the three open restaurants and then walked throughout the town at night. All around, up in the air, I could see the lights of the Lebanese villages. The next morning, Reuven laid out for me a breakfast that filled an entire folding table with tempting choices. After finishing my meal, I climbed to the hotel's rooftop, where there is a catwalk. From that high spot, a 360-degree view of the surrounding countryside greeted me. Standing there, seconds turned to minutes, which could have turned to hours if I had had the time. I was by turns struck by the loneliness and vulnerability of Metula and enamored with its beauty.

Had I been born in Metula, I am not sure that I would have ever left.

Majdal Shams

High on the Golan, tucked into the southern folds of Mount Hermon, and bordering Syria, sits Majdal Shams. A Druze town of perhaps 11,000, it is the largest of the four Druze villages remaining on the Golan after the Six-Day War and counts for half of the Druze living on the Golan Heights. In Aramaic, Majdal Shams means "Tower of the Sun," perhaps referring to the town's location at a highpoint of the Golan. In today's confused reality, however, Majdal Shams is where principle battles practicality.

The town, in a beautiful setting, its streets confused, its economy flourishing, and its politics embroiled—Majdal Shams is a study in contrasts. Picturesque statues compete with new construction aimed at satisfying tourists. Together, they create a mosaic of old and new. Surrounding Majdal Shams are orchards filled with apples and cherries, but also minefields, border fences, and, until recently, the sounds and smoke of the Syrian Civil War. Its citizens are Syrian, but also eligible to become Israeli. To the west and south, roads connect the town to the rest of the Golan. To the north, up a steep, snaking, road that climbs Mount Hermon, lies Israel's only ski resort. A paradise in the making, Majdal Shams also is a conundrum.

Druze living within the borders that existed before the Six-Day War have always been automatically full citizens of Israel, have been subject to the military draft, and have served in high positions in the IDF and as members of the Knesset. Not on the Golan Heights which was taken by Israel during the Six-Day War. Here, Druze are considered Syrian citizens by the Syrian government, a political position held by most residents—at least on the surface. Bubbling below is something quite different—a realization that life is better under Israeli sovereignty than it would be under Syrian. To understand why requires a shallow dive into past injustices and present possibilities.

The label "Druze" refers to some one million people, scattered mostly in Syria, Lebanon, and Israel. They share a faith derivative of a branch of Shia Islam that manifested in the year 1016, but they are not Muslim. Believers in reincarnation, the Druze do not permit others to convert to their religion, and those that marry outside the Druze faith are ex-communicated. Although the Druze honor prophets and iconic religious figures such as Christ and Moses, Moses's father-in-law, Jethro, is their most respected prophet. Adherents are divided into two groups: Those in the know called "The Knowledgeable" and those essentially left out in the cold, "The Ignorant." The knowledgeable have the right to partake in religious meetings and view specified holy texts. The term "The Ignorant" is not meant as a pejorative comment about the four out of five Druze that fall within that category. Rather, it just describes Druze that have not undertaken the religious study and practice required to ascend to "The Knowledgeable."

The Druze have never had a nation of their own, nor do they desire one. Instead, they generally give their loyalty to the dominant power where they live. So much so that their practice is the subject of a standard joke "Why does the Druze flag have an upper end and a lower end? The upper is to wave at the conqueror when he arrives, and the lower end is to jab at his butt when he leaves!"

In the modern era, Druze fight heroically for the IDF, sometimes they have even fought against Druze in the Syrian army. In centuries past, Druze allied with Muslims against the Crusaders. Still, Druze willingness to accept political control by the majority communities they live in has not shielded them from persecution and domination, sometimes so severe that the Druze have revolted. In particular, Sunni Muslims frequently have attacked the Druze for their supposed heretic beliefs. Within pre-1967 Israel, relations between Druze and Israel have been good since the inception of the State, despite the present stress emanating from the Knesset's recent passage of its new nation-state law that declares Israel is "the nation state of the Jewish people" but is devoid of any language guaranteeing equality for non-Jewish citizens. Still, despite their anger and concern stemming from their view that the new law dishonors them, the dispute between the Druze and the government presently appears more of a seismic tremor than a fracture.

On the Golan Heights, however, things are much more complicated. Modern Syria sprang into being in 1946. As part of the new nation, the Golan Heights then came under Syrian government control. Two decades later, during the Six-Day War in 1967, Israel took control of the Golan. At that time, tens of thousands of Druze lived on the Heights. Many fled of their own accord. Many others at the behest of the Israelis. The Druze citizens of Majdal Shams, along with Druze in three other nearby towns, remained. Syria, refusing to recognize that circumstances had changed, maintained that the Druze still living on the Golan were still Syrian citizens. Most Druze agreed and there was little impetus for change because Majdal Shams remained under IDF military rule. Instead, they availed themselves of permanent resident status—called "undefined" on Israeli ID cards and accepted the benefits of living under Israeli rule while demonstrating support for Syria.

In 1981, things changed. Israel annexed the Golan. Annexation brought Majdal Shams out from under Israeli military law and created a system for local self-government similar to the Local Council system prevalent in Israel. The new law also gave Druze residents the right to become Israeli citizens. For three decades few did, but since the Syrian Civil War broke out in 2011, the numbers have increased, especially among younger residents. Now, perhaps ten percent of the town's residents are Israeli citizens.

Why the continued reluctance to become an Israeli citizen? Especially after seeing firsthand, within hearing and viewing distance of their homes, a brutal war fought in Syria by brutal people? Why would anybody want to come under control of Assad's dictatorial regime that uses torture and violence as political tools when Israel offers peace and democracy? And if not Assad, does Hezbollah or Iran, which are both now woven into the fabric of Syrian governance, offer a better alternative? Syrian towns and cities have suffered devastation on an almost unimaginable scale. A quick look at the four Druze towns on the Golan reveals opportunity. The rational answer is that Israel offers a vibrant future, Syria a dismal past likely to be repeated. But that determination does not account for one of mankind's greatest motivators—fear.

Dating back to when the Golan was taken during the last two days of the Six-Day War, Israel's government has contemplated returning it to Syria in return for peace. In the 1990s, Prime Minister Rabin secretly told President Clinton that he would do so if Syria fulfilled certain conditions. Assad refused to accept those conditions. Later, Prime Minister Barack entered into serious negotiations with Syria. Agreement on giving back the Golan foundered on a final border issue consisting of a few yards. As risky as that might have been for Israelis, for Druze residents on the Golan, even the mere possibility that Israel might one day return the Golan to Syria makes existential Majdal Shams' Druze choice whether to accept Israeli citizenship. Those that now openly support Israel will have no chance of surviving a future Syrian regime anything like that of Assad. And since they lose little other than the right to run for office and vote by not being Israeli citizens, why take the chance?

And there is more.

Many Majdal Shams residents have family in Syria, some within a couple miles of the border. Until the advent of the Internet and cell phones, they would communicate by literally shouting to each other at "Shouting Hill." Behind the border fence line and atop buildings nearby Majdal Shams Druze would gather, while the residents of their sister villages on the other side of the border would climb to the top of the adjacent hill in Syria. From there they would shout to each other. The relationships between Druze in Syrian villages and Majdal Shams are well known to Syrian intelligence. If Majdal Sham's Druze on Israel's side of the border overtly support Israel, their cousins in Syria might pay a price.

The center of activism in town is the Al-Marsad Arab Human Rights Center. Its website is replete with articles vilifying Israel's occupation and its impact. The writing is impressive, the scope of its publications wide, and its representatives' ability to advocate its position in all manner of media impressive. But try as I did to discern from the hundreds of pages I downloaded, and the quotes of its representatives that I found in numerous newspaper reports, I could not find why Majdal Shams citizens would be better off under Syrian rule than as citizens of Israel. And even in their recent publication, *More Shadows Than Lights — Local Elections in the Occupied Syrian Golan*, the author admitted that many Majdal Shams residents, especially younger ones, now believe living under Israeli "control" (I would consider changing the words "under Israeli control" to "as Israeli citizens") protects them from Syria's present government. This view has become more paramount since the Syrian Civil War started in 2011 and even more so after hundreds of Druze were killed by ISIS and Al-Queda affiliates in the nearby Syrian towns of Hadar in 2017 and Sweida in 2018.

Al-Marsad charges that Israel tried to take advantage of that change in attitude by holding local elections for all Druze villages on the Golan, including Majdal Shams. Since 1981, Majdal Shams has been administered by a mayor appointed by Israel's Minister of Interior and a Local Council. In 2017, Israel announced that rather than the Interior Ministry continuing to appoint the mayor for each town, an election would be held on October 30, 2018 for selection of a new mayor for each town. All residents of requisite age would have the right to vote, but only Israeli citizens would have the right to run for the mayoral position. Al-Marsad strongly opposed the election, believing it would legitimize what it views as Israel's continued occupation. Prior to the election, all the candidates for mayor in two Golan Druze towns withdrew, resulting in the elections being canceled there. In Majdal Shams, only two percent of the eligible residents voted. The newly elected mayor, Dolan Abu Saleh, is the same mayor that had already been appointed to office by the Minister of Interior for two prior terms, spanning a total of ten years.

I tried to obtain an interview with an Al-Marsad representative in 2018. Unfortunately, through no fault of theirs, I was unable to do so. I look forward to that in the future. However, the Al-Marsad website is loaded with information that fully explains their perspective. I salute them for their advocacy but disagree with their conclusion.

So, on the surface perhaps, the Golan Heights Druze still appear to favor Syria over Israel. But that is not the impression of Israelis I spoke with. Omer Weiner from Merom Golan told me that Merom Golan residents routinely work with Druze in the fields. When the kibbutz sent people to Spain to learn how to farm truffles, half that went were Druze. There they got along well. Despite what they say publicly, Omer told me, "If you speak with friends, all of them want to stay in Israel." The public stuff, he said, "is to be on the safe side."

Omer's comments were echoed by Samuel Gardi from Kibbutz Dan who spends much time in Majdal Shams and whose wife, Haviva taught educational practices to teachers in Majdal Shams. Samuel said the Druze are "in a very complicated situation under Israeli occupation because they are Syrians." For them, he told me, it is much less dangerous to be pro-Syrian. But both Samuel and Omer are Israelis. Were there Druze willing to openly share those feelings?

For that, I journeyed three times to Mixto, a Druze restaurant located off a desolate, bumpy, dirt road seemingly in the middle of nowhere. However, that impression might be unkind because all three times I've been there have been at night. The restaurant is replete with green vegetation artfully strung from ceiling to floor, benches covered with red cushions, and quiet, dark booths with low tables that instantly create an aura of mystery. The food, the sounds, the ambiance I would term Arabesque, but more likely are better described as authentic Druze. Jolan Abusaleh, whose family is well known in the town, owns the restaurant.

Jolan's father was one of the first to take on Israeli citizenship. After the Six-Day War, he helped some of the few remaining Jews flee Syria. I also got the feeling that he may have worked with Israeli intelligence but Jolan didn't volunteer that and I didn't pry.

While we spoke, I became concerned whether speaking to me might cause Jolan difficulties with his fellow townspeople. He assured me not. As a child, Jolan told me, he had been targeted with much abuse in school for his father's pro-Israel stance. Now, however, he said those who accept Israeli citizenship are not ostracized, and that more and more are choosing to do so even though some still choose to hide their decision. Others refuse to change their allegiance out of fear or because, he said, they don't want to lose their identity as Syrians.

Early during our third meeting, I asked Jolan for permission to record our conversation. He said no, but he did give me permission to take notes and refer to him and Mixto directly. Whether his refusal was just due to his discomfort with being recorded or, instead, his desire to maintain some opportunity to deny was difficult to discern. However, it certainly wasn't due to any difficulty with the English language. Many years ago, Jolan left his parents, seven brothers, and three sisters for a life in the United States. He spent fourteen years there before being deported over immigration issues. Now married, he has a two-year-old boy. Although his life is with his family in Majdal Shams, he clearly looks back fondly to his years in the U.S.

Jolan's family grows apples that they sell in Syria, where they get a better price than the saturated Israeli market. Beginning in 2004, despite the de-facto state of war between Israel and Syria, Druze citizens have been permitted by both governments to export apples grown on the Golan to Syria. In addition, Druze were able to traverse the border to go to school in Damascus and for other personal reasons. The crossing is at Kuneitra, near Merom Golan. Then, in 2014, the Syrian Civil War caused U.N. soldiers on the Syrian side to evacuate after some were kidnapped for a short while. The crossing closed as a result. Recently, with the end of most of the fighting, the border crossing reopened in October 2018.

The crossing into Syria is located at the end of a desultory, dirt road that curves back and forth almost a mile from Route 98, which runs on the Israeli side roughly parallel to the border. As you approach the gate, there is a large white U.N. encampment to your right, a small uneven parking lot, multiple signs warning you of your peril, and then an imposing gate complex complete with guard towers, an Israeli flag, and a tall, strongly built metal fence fully capable of stopping people and vehicles. That fence extends beyond view both north and south of the complex. Immediately adjacent to the fence, is a dirt road used by IDF patrol vehicles. On the other side is some sort of Syrian guard station, the particulars of which are out of view, the Syrian flag, trees, and the ruins of Old Kuneitra. Any attempt to closely approach the border fence brings an immediate reaction from Israeli guards posted there. To me it all seemed quite imposing, intimidating, and novel. For Druze, crossing back and forth it is reality.

Jolan told me that Majdal Sham's economy is growing. Around town there are many contractors and buildings under construction even though land availability and licensing issues create constraints. It is also a town filled with professionals: doctors, lawyers, and the like who grew up in Majdal Shams and then choose to return even though jobs for many are scarce.

Perhaps the draw for Druze to return, and tourists to visit, is the lifestyle. In Majdal Shams, there are fewer restrictions on women's dress, more money, and looser standards than elsewhere in the Arab world. Hand in hand with that is a nightlife with dancing and alcohol even though, perhaps as a byproduct, Jolan said sex crimes are on the uptick. The Arabic used by Majdal Shams inhabitants has a Lebanese Syrian accent, different than what is heard in the rest of Israel. Coupled with the climate and winter skiing, Jolan calls visiting or residing in Majdal Shams "like traveling abroad without a passport." I thought of it like a miniature Beirut in decades past, where Sheiks had gone to escape the strict laws of their home countries to play.

Speaking to Jolan, I developed a better understanding of Majdal Sham's potential. But nothing he said alleviated my concern for the emotional fault lines that lie below the surface.

The IDF, as part of its "Good Neighbor" humanitarian aid program, treated thousands of Syrians injured during their civil war from 2013 until late 2018, when the war ended. But in 2015, hundreds of Druze from Majdal Shams stopped an Israeli ambulance carrying two Syrians injured in the fighting on the other side of the border. Using sticks and stones they wounded the two IDF soldiers in the vehicle and killed one of the injured Syrians. The crowd attacked the ambulance based on their suspicion that the Syrians within had participated in attacks on Druze villages in Syria. Whether true or not, the event demonstrates how quickly serenity can turn to madness when death knocks nearby.

If Majdal Shams was a town located in some stable region of the world, it would likely be considered a hidden gem, attractive for investment. But it is not in a stable region. It is at the crossroads of one of the most dangerous places on the planet, and its loyalties lie with two countries in conflict, one of which is stable. The other is riven with uncertainty stemming from a regime with a history of terrorizing those who stand in its way and also from Iranian soldiers and Hezbollah embedded within, bent on Israel's destruction. The Syrians, the Iranians, and Hezbollah would benefit from destabilizing Majdal Shams Druze. So, while there is hope, it is hard to have confidence that Majdal Shams will weather the storm untouched.

Ghajar

Located just west of the Golan Heights, formerly within Syrian-controlled territory, and adjacent to Lebanon and Israel, Ghajar is a village of about 2,500 people with a confused identity. Despite evidence that at least part of Ghajar may be in Lebanon, its inhabitants think of themselves Syrian. Even so, they asked to become Israeli citizens after the Six-Day War. And when the United Nations insisting in 2000 and again in 2006 that Israel turn part of it over to Lebanon, Ghajar's citizens made clear their desire to remain under Israel's domain. And, despite its citizens having voluntarily become Israeli citizens in 1981, Israel's security cabinet voted to turn the northern part of the town over to Lebanon in 2010. What is it about Ghajar that created this bizarrely unique happenstance? And what is its status now?

Kurds controlled the village 300 years ago. But that historical anomaly adds nothing to our present understanding. The confusion really began in the early 1920s. Before that, the entire region was controlled by the Ottoman Empire, so Ghajar was totally controlled by the Turks. But with Turkey's defeat, Ottoman control of the region ended. Rushing into the void were the British and the French. The British accepted responsibility for governing Palestine. The French mandate covered Syria and Lebanon. Great in theory, but there was a hitch. Where were the borders? The French tried to answer at least part of that question by designating the boundary between Lebanon and Syria. Unfortunately, when it came to Ghajar, which then was a small, impoverished, out-of-the-way village, the French made a mess of things. British cartographers added to the confusion.

Now, almost 100 years later, trying to sort out the cartographic nightmare left over is impossible, although many have tried using decades old maps to support their argument. But there are so many maps, using different scales, each with their own nuances, that it is doubtful that any answer can reconcile all the arguments plus future revelations.

For example, many now believe that the line between Syria and Lebanon runs through Ghajar, with the northernmost two thirds in Lebanon and the southernmost third, bordering Israel, part of old Syria. But in 2018, an article appeared touting the procurement of an old map Syrian construction map by the College of Tel Hai. Drafted in 1965, the map places all of Ghajar in Syria. The chief of library services at Tel Hai University showed me that map while demonstrating Tel Hai's revolutionary software for organizing and displaying maps of the region. Is that map definitive? It depends what you want the answer to be. The same holds true with other maps. Perhaps then, the truth is so evasive it no longer exists. Perhaps, then, a different standard is in order—What the residents of Ghajar want. There, the answer is clear.

By the middle 1940s, if not before, Ghajar residents thought themselves Syrian, as did the various Syrian governments that successively employed coups to take power until stabilizing under Assad family rule in 1970. That mutual view is not surprising since most Ghajar's residents are Alawites, which, like the Druze, is a religious offshoot of the Shia branch of Islam. In Syria, approximately twenty percent of the population is Alawite. In Lebanon, there are comparatively few Alawites. As part of the Syrian government's responsibility to provide educational resources to its civilians, beginning in 1950, a Syrian teacher came from Damascus to teach basic reading, writing, and arithmetic. Children seeking more advanced lessons traveled to Kuneitra, a Syrian city in the Golan then hours away. Later, in the 1950s, Ghajar expanded farther north onto land also held by Syria, into an area called al-Wazzani by some but that is really part of Ghajar. Meanwhile, the Syrian army garrisoned the town and townspeople served in Syria's military. And in 1960, the Syrian census included Ghajar residents. Through all this, Lebanon never said a word.

Then came the Six-Day War. On its last day, the Israeli army rolled into Ghajar. If you think of a clock with Ghajar at its center, it is little more than a mile from Metula at nine on the clock face, Ma'ayan Baruch is at seven and Kibbutz Dan at five. Around it, was Arab owned farmland and hills that lay between it and Israeli border communities. Together, the land and the town created a U-shaped penetration that threatened all three bordering Jewish communities. Therefore, it is no surprise that the IDF expended the minimal effort required to occupy the village at the end of the war. But surprising is what happened the next day. The army withdrew because according to the IDF's maps, Ghajar was in Lebanon. Since Israel was not at war with Lebanon, the army pulled back.

But the IDF's withdrawal left an unanticipated problem.

Hundreds then left Ghajar, preferring re-settlement in Syria to what lay before them if they remained. However, the many hundreds preferring to stay in their village did not want to be a people without a country. That would turn Ghajar into a small land-locked community with few resources and no defenders in a dangerous region—a recipe for disaster.

What to do?

Syria, they recognized, was not an option. Ghajar's connection to Syria was to its east across a flat plain and over the Golan. Israel's victory and occupation of that territory severed Ghajar's connection to Syria, whose closest border was now many miles away. Lebanon did not want Ghajar then, perhaps because Lebanon's leaders did not want to be thought taking advantage of a fellow Arab nation's defeat. As a tiny, relatively powerless nation, Lebanon could not afford to fall out of the Arab world's good graces. That left Israel. Like it or not, Israel was Ghajar's only remaining choice.

Within days, the villagers petitioned the Israeli appointed governor for the occupied Syrian Golan territories for inclusion under his jurisdiction. In July, a month after the war ended, their petition bore fruit. The IDF reoccupied Ghajar, and the territory came under the governor's authority. Its citizens were happy, and their economic conditions improved. That, of course, did not please the U.N., which wanted Israel to withdraw from Ghajar without caring that withdrawal would leave Ghajar to the mercy of the Palestine Liberation Organization which, beginning in the early 1970s until 1982, used most of Southern Lebanon as a base for terror strikes against Israeli targets.

Then, in December of 1981, Ghajar residents found themselves with a choice to make. Israel's Knesset extended Israeli law to the Golan Heights, which for administrative purposes included Ghajar. For the first time, Arabs living there, who previously were citizens of Syria, could elect to become Israeli citizens. The Druze living in Majdal Shams and the other three Druze communities on the Golan overwhelmingly rejected the offer. Not so the Alawites in Ghajar. There, virtually all who were of appropriate age, although still identifying with Syria, became Israeli citizens. A Ghajar spokesman, Najib Khatib, told me in 2018 while we sat in a coffee shop in Kiryat Shmona, "We chose to accept citizenship." Israel's new citizens were then free to travel within Israel, leave the country and return on Israeli passports, and enjoy the benefits of Israel's support for basic services, governance, and protection.

Less than a year after effectively annexing Gjahar, the IDF swept into Lebanon in 1982 to push back Arafat's PLO from positions it held throughout southern Lebanon. The IDF's surge extended to Beirut and then receded to positions still many miles into Lebanon. During the eighteen years they remained in place, Ghajar grew and prospered. Unfortunately, so did Hezbollah, a Lebanese Shiite movement, supported by Iran, which hated Israel. Hezbollah's initial goal was to push Israel out of Lebanon. To do so, Hezbollah killed Israelis and those that supported them. Nevertheless, life in Ghajar was good with few worries—until it wasn't.

As part of his election campaign in 1999, soon to be Prime Minister Ehud Barak promised to withdraw the IDF from Lebanon. On May 24, 2000, two months before his self-imposed deadline, he did so precipitously after announcing his intentions, but not the date, a month before. But where to withdraw to?

In 1978, the IDF moved into southern Lebanon to clear out terrorist bases after Palestinian terrorists traveled by boat from Lebanon to Israel's coastal highway where they hijacked a bus and killed thirty-eight Israeli citizens and wounded seventy-one others. The U.N. responded by issuing Security Council Resolution 425 that called for the IDF to "withdraw forthwith its forces from all Lebanese territory," and established a "United Nations interim force [UNIFIL]" to patrol southern Lebanon. After Barak announced his intention to withdraw, the U.N. took on a new task, "Delineate a line of withdrawal so as to confirm the implementation" of Resolution 425.

What emerged from U.N. deliberations came to be known as the "Blue Line." The U.N. said it was not an international boundary. Instead, it was "a practical line for the purpose of confirming the Israeli withdrawal." Nevertheless, Israel and Lebanon treated it as a definitive border. The problem created was that the Blue Line, despite Israel's strident objection, went through Ghajar, placing its northern two thirds in Lebanon and the southern third in Israeli annexed, formerly Syrian territory. In effect, the U.N. mandated that a town be divided into unworkable pieces, each in territories at war with each other, and each unable to stand economically, politically, or socially on its own. As the only Alawite village in a region in which their Alawite identity rules their lives, division into two small pieces meant the end of their way of life. Within the town, families would be separated, mosques cut-off from their worshipers, doctors from patients, and friends from friends. With no thought of the people impacted, the U.N. made the decision based on its analysis of historical facts, not present needs.

Needless to say, Ghajar's citizens strongly objected to no avail. As a result, for the first time, the loyal Israeli citizens of Ghajar would soon be forced to live in a country they were at war with. When rumors first circulated that Barak might agree to pull out of the supposed Lebanese portion of Ghajar, Najib, the spokesman I met with, went to Jerusalem to lobby against it. He tried to see the prime minister without success and was told by another politician in a failed attempt to mollify him, "The only thing you believe in the newspaper is the date and time." Soon after, despite the admonition Najib received from the politician, the rumors came true. Seeing indications that the IDF was preparing to leave, Ghajar residents laid down in the streets in a failed attempt to prevent U.N. representatives from coming into the city. Amid the weeping, Ghajar's new U.N. regime arrived.

Fortunately, at first, despite the division appearing on maps, security for the now divided village's residents was not impacted by the IDF's withdrawal. UNIFIL soldiers, from their bases, north of Ghajar, supposedly protected the village from infiltration. Meanwhile, IDF soldiers in the southern third refrained from crossing the Blue Line. But immediately, even though Israel did not build a fence within the town dividing the two parts, village services suffered. Although electricity flowed, getting items fixed became a problem. If a washing machine broke, an Israeli repairman could not cross the line into the northern two thirds of the town. Even Israeli ambulances for the sick and injured could not negotiate the checkpoint without IDF permission.

Also, as time passed, Israel became increasingly anxious about this open wound pointed like a dagger into the northern Galilee. Because the northern Ghajar residents were Israeli citizens, they were permitted access into Israel and north, back into Ghajar. But those who wanted to could also get into northern Ghajar from Lebanon. Among the first to do so were members of Hezbollah. About a dozen operatives turned an old bomb shelter into a Hezbollah command post and erected a white tent outside. Since the only fence keeping them from entering Israel was outside of town, residents feared that Israel would construct a new fence within the town to keep infiltrators from using the part of Ghajar in Lebanon as a base of operations. As a result, the village opposed Hezbollah's presence, made obvious by the camouflage netting and their yellow flags that surrounded their base. In addition, Ghajar became a smuggler's haven—drugs and information were often exchanged for cash—all facilitated by the easy access from Lebanon into the village and for Ghajar's residents, into Israel and the rest of Lebanon.

Then, on November 21, 2005, Hezbollah attempted to kidnap IDF soldiers in Ghajar with the hopes of trading them for many more Hezbollah prisoners and sympathizers held in Israeli jails. While their mortar shells and rockets struck positions throughout the region, specially trained Hezbollah soldiers sped into the southern portion of Ghajar on all-terrain vehicles and motorcycles. Their hope was to get in and out quickly with captives while the IDF was distracted by the shelling. Fortunately, Israel had learned of the pending attack. A corporal trained as a sniper lying along the route of the attackers killed some of the Hezbollah invaders. The rest withdrew without completing their mission. Afterward, the Israelis went into northern Ghajar and blew up the Hezbollah base there.

In 2006, another war erupted between Israel and Hezbollah, started by Hezbollah's successful kidnapping of IDF soldiers along the border many miles west of Ghajar. The war had a very unsatisfactory conclusion for Israel as a whole. But for Ghajar, it brought the welcome return of IDF control. Three years later, however, the same concerns felt in 2000 about a pending IDF withdrawal arose again. In December 2009, once again, Ghajar citizens took to the streets in mass to protest. And once again, it was to no avail. A year later, Prime Minister Netanyahu told the U.N. that Israel would again withdraw from northern Ghajar and leave UNIFIL responsible for the town's security. But with the outbreak of Syria's Civil War, and the ascendancy of Hezbollah in Lebanon, the withdrawal has been deferred and at this point may never happen. Although the IDF does not routinely enter the northern parts of the village, Israel's presence remains.

Najib told me that he does not fear for Ghajar's security now. For him, the presence of the U.N., the Lebanese army, and the IDF is, for now, sufficient. However, the town, and he, remains worried that it will again be divided one day. I could see that lingering concern in his eyes. Ghajar's residents want very much to remain Israeli citizens and want nothing to do with Lebanon. But other than that existential concern, for now according to Najib, things are going relatively well. Within Ghajar there is a high level of education. His son, for example, is presently studying in the United States to become a physician. And, Najib explained, now with a twinkle in his eye, there is at least one benefit to having the high level of Israeli security that restricts outside access—when he is invited to Shabbat dinner at the homes of Jewish friends in Israel, he does not have to invite them back!

In 2018, the IDF permitted me and three others to enter Ghajar after we supplied some biographical details. When we arrived, towards evening, at the imposing gate to enter the village, an IDF soldier checked us and took our passports, leaving me feeling somewhat naked, even though we were told we'd get them back when we exited. While waiting for permission to enter, I observed other cars traveling back that were operated by residents of Ghajar. Once granted permission to proceed, we drove to a location with a set of parking spaces overlooking a shallow wadi with a U.N. checkpoint at the northern end and some houses south of us, along a ridge line that curved away to the west. Across the wadi was Lebanon, and certainly Hezbollah.

The village itself was clean and quiet. There was very little traffic and I saw little commercial activity. To say I felt a bit unsettled would be closer to fact than fiction. There was no IDF presence, no police presence, not any protective presence. Just as I realized that, my phone buzzed. When I looked to see who was texting me, I saw it was Verizon with a message, "Welcome to Lebanon."

I stayed in the town only briefly. A few months later, after learning more, I tried to go back.

I don't know why, but the IDF would not let me.

Chapter Seventeen

Terror and Katyushas

Since Israel's War of Independence ended in 1949, northern Israel has seen seven other wars—five in Lebanon and two on the Golan with Syria—that were fought by soldiers, the sons and daughters of Israelis everywhere. But also, since 1949, thousands of rockets, artillery, and mortar shells fired by the Syrian army, Palestinian terrorists, and now Hezbollah and even Iran, have spread terror, death, and destruction throughout northern Israel. Israel's civilian men, women, and children have endured them. It bears repeating what Gideon Giladi, a resident of Kfar Giladi, told me, that it was like "Living under a volcano." You don't know when it will blow, but you know it eventually will. It always does. And you know that when it does blow, it might kill you.

Terrorists

In the introduction, I described the terrorist attack on the children in the high school in Ma'alot on May 15, 1974. Forgotten in the fog of time is that it was one of three terrorist attacks that took multiple lives during a three-month period, the first happening in Kiryat Shmona on April 11 and the third, in Nahariya, on June 25, 1974.

* * *

Kiryat Shmona spreads across the base of a line of hills. From the top of those hills, where the Israeli-Lebanon border lies, it is only a mile down the eastern slopes of those hills to the town. To the north, Metula is a few minutes' drive away up a steep ravine. Unfortunately, the rough terrain in the region provides cover for anyone wishing to infiltrate into Israel. Kiryat Shmona's proximity to Lebanon and its sprawling density also makes it simple to lob rockets and shells over the crest of the rise with certainty of hitting something. In short, the town's residents provide a fat target from the air and the ground. On April 11, 1974, three Palestinian terrorists crossed the border, descended the hill, and surreptitiously entered the town.

They planned to seize a school building filled with students in order to force Israel to release 100 terrorists in its jails. But it was Passover. The school was empty. Determined to shed innocent blood, the terrorists set their sights on a nearby apartment. There, they found adults but also some of the tender young targets they had originally sought. Some they shot, their bodies later found littering staircases and halls. And some, just children, they flung out third floor windows to their deaths. One nine-year-old girl survived by hiding. Her mother, sister, and two brothers died at the hands of those murderers. When Israeli soldiers attempted a rescue, the three terrorists blew themselves up with explosive belts they were wearing. In the end, eighteen Jews died, eight of them youngsters. Fifteen more were wounded.

* * *

Nahariya is a beach town, astride the Mediterranean, a few miles south of the Lebanese border at Rosh Hanikra. There, on June 24, 1974, another three-man terrorist contingent flanked Israel's land defenses by navigating an inflatable zodiac boat to Nahariya's beach at night. Hoping to attack people sitting in a local movie house, they were spotted moving towards their target by a teenager in an apartment building alerted when they crossed a hedge. "Terrorists!" he shouted. Two Nahariya civil guard members had heard him and rushed to the scene. It was a little after 11 p.m.

The terrorists spotted the guardsmen coming for them and met them with gunfire and a grenade. The two Israeli guards fired back. Within five minutes, more security forces arrived. Also, an IDF army officer who lived nearby stationed himself at the entrance of his apartment building to prevent the terrorists from entering. The combined effect of the rapidly formed resistance was to push the attackers into an apartment building parking lot. From there, one of them broke into a nearby building. Most of the residents, realizing what was happening, locked their entrance doors and piled furniture against them before taking shelter within their rooms. One family, living on the first floor, chose an alternative option. Rather than shelter in place, Mordechai Zarnekin, fearing that the marauders would break into his unit, told his wife and two children to escape by scrambling down sheets strung together to the street. Together, after reaching the ground and then running toward the street, terrorist bullets and a hand grenade found them. Together, they died.

Within two hours, it was over. All three of the terrorists lay dead as did an Israeli soldier. Five soldiers were wounded, as was another civilian. The civilian, shot accidentally by the IDF while also climbing down the bedsheets, was the husband and father of the woman and two children now lying bloodied, still, and cold.

* * *

Tragedies, like these that occurred at Kiryat Shmona, Ma'alot, and Nahariya almost a half century ago, remain in the DNA of those who live in the north far longer than the memories. The terror of those moments, and countless others, not only impact the lives of those directly affected, they shape the prism through which many that live in the region see the world around them. All three of those incidents share the same common denominator, people at home or at schools, asleep in their beds or lolling around in their rooms, feeling safe. At their most peaceful and secure moments, fear jolted them from tranquility, hot lead and jagged shards tore their flesh. Their lives were no more. And the lives of those that live near them and the lives of generations to come were forced to come to terms with the fact that people live nearby, just over a border subject to penetration, that hate and kill for political purpose or no purpose at all.

The terrorist attack on Nahariya in 1974 was not the last in that town. Five years later, on April 22, 1979, what came was worse. Four Palestinian militants, led by Samir Kuntar, like the terrorists in 1974, and like terrorists in 1978 who landed on a beach south of Haifa before killing thirty-eight Israelis on a bus, employed a boat leaving from Lebanon to evade border patrols before arriving at an Israeli beach. This time, again in Nahariya. After killing a policeman, they entered an apartment building. There, they planned to kidnap two people and take them back to Lebanon. When they tried breaking into one of the units, a resident shot at them, killing one of the terrorists. But the remaining three, after encountering another Israeli who escaped them, broke into another apartment and took Danny Haran and his daughter, Einat, hostage. Einat's mother, Smadar, escaped by hiding with her two-year-old daughter, Yael, in a crawl space.

Quickly exiting the apartment, the three Palestinians made their way to the beach where their boat lay waiting. Also waiting were Israeli police and special forces. Gunfire erupted. Bullets disabled the boat. Rather than surrender, Kuntar shot Danny in the back, in full view of his daughter, and pushed his head under the waves to ensure he was dead. His blood lust not satisfied; Kuntar then used the butt of his rifle to crush Einat's head against the rocks dotting the shore. During the ensuing firefight, one of the other terrorists died. Kuntar and his remaining accomplice eventually were captured.

Meanwhile, during the moments of madness in the apartment building another tragedy unfolded. Fearful for their lives, Smadar covered Yael's mouth to stop her from whimpering. Smadar feared that the noise would lead Kuntar and his killers to her and Yael. Remembering her "mother telling [her] how she had hidden from the Nazis during the Holocaust," Smadar thought, "This is just like what happened to my mother." But not quite. By putting a hand over Yael's mouth, Smadar accidentally smothered her.

The events of that night horrified all of Israel. Nevertheless, in 2008, Israel released Kuntar as part of a one-sided prisoner swap with Hezbollah during which Hezbollah returned the bodies of the two IDF soldiers it kidnapped in 2006 in return for Kuntar, five other prisoners, and the remains of 200 others. Sarit Zehavi remembers working at the alert desk on the day of the exchange. Regarding the two IDF soldiers, "Until the door opened," she said. "Maybe, until the last moment [there was hope] they were alive."

But that November was not the first time that a terrorist organization had worked to gain Kuntar's release. In 1985, after terrorists hijacked the Italian cruise ship Achille Lauro and threw wheelchair bound Leon Klinghoffer overboard to his death, release of Kuntar led the list of their demands.

Upon Kuntar's arrival in Lebanon, the Lebanese president along with Hezbollah leader, Hassan Nasrallah, greeted him with a hero's welcome. Bashar Assad gave Kuntar Syria's highest medal. Mahmoud Ahmadinejad, Iran's former president, honored him in 2009. Reportedly, soon thereafter Kuntar began climbing the ranks of Hezbollah's leadership until 2015, when an Israeli air strike ended his days on earth. In the process of setting up a Hezbollah cell among the Syrian Druze near Israel's border with Syria, forty years after shattering Einat's skull, the aberration of Kuntar being set free had finally been put right.

Israeli authorities have never addressed whether Kuntar was their target.

* * *

March 12, 2002 saw a different type of attack. Rather than attacking people fast asleep in their apartments, this time, two terrorists crossed the border near Kibbutz Hanita. There, the fence laden with technological wizardry designed to detect intrusions failed because the terrorists had used a "trapeze ladder" to "sail" over the fence without touching it. Safely across, wearing IDF uniforms to cloak their true purpose, they made their way to a hillside overlooking the road from the border town of Shlomi to Kibbutz Matzuva. From there, after killing a shepherd tending his flock, they fired weapons and threw hand grenades at civilian vehicles on the road.

Before being killed by IDF security forces, the two terrorists killed an IDF officer and four citizens. Two of the citizens were a mother and her fifteen-year-old daughter that lived in Kibbutz Hanita. Innocently, they had descended the winding road in the family car. Their ride back up that road was to their funeral, attended by hundreds. In a *New York Times* article written two days later, a young immigrant from Russia said, "We were used to Katyusha rockets, but terrorists in Shlomi? This is something completely different. Then you knew it was coming from the other side. Now, it's like you've been stabbed in the back."

Another middle-aged woman, Nurit Naaman, said that the aftershock reminded her of her childhood years living on the border, "There was fear then," she said. "Personal security was close to zero. We felt unprotected. Now there's exactly the same atmosphere, but today it's more personal—the danger is more tangible."

Katyushas

In October 2016 I found myself in a jeep heading up another steep, winding road—this time to Kibbutz Kfar Giladi. It was my first time there. Earlier that day, I had met a former IDF officer who I will call "Boaz" in Merom Golan's dining hall. He had agreed to show me around some northern Israel historical sites with military significance. Our day started with walking battlefields from the 1967 and 1973 wars, after which we headed down the Golan, across the narrow valley composing the northernmost part of the finger of Israel, and then to the turn-off for Kfar Giladi.

After turning right from the road heading arrow-like for the border, we quickly veered slightly right again before easing into a rectangular parking lot. Ahead of us, to the north, stood the entrance to the kibbutz. A grove of trees shaded the eastern side of the lot. Between the trees and the parking lot a chiseled stone wall several feet high graced the outskirts of Kfar Giladi's cemetery beyond. Within, the "raging lion" statute stood silent guard over Joseph Trumpledor's grave and a century of Kfar Giladi's departed. But we were not there for them or Trumpledor.

Near the center of the wall, the entrance beckoned. But after exiting the jeep I didn't heed the silent invitation. I couldn't. Instead, my head swiveled, my eyes riveting first on one jarring vision and then another. And another. There was no sound except a whisper of wind. To the right of the entrance were a few flags bunched together. Below them were pictures of twelve men, some young some middle aged. Accompanying the pictures were flowers. In the parking lot, was a depression, roughly a couple feet in diameter, where something had clearly torn the surface.

To the left of the opening to the graveyard stood three large stone monuments with words etched on their faces. On top of them were small rocks and pebbles placed in the same manner as on grave markers at a Jewish cemetery. Lying at their feet, the twisted remnants of a Katyusha. Also standing starkly alone, a black pole, with irregular holes punched through it, highlighted by a brownish discoloring.

Some of the simple words on the stone wall bear repeating, "In the Second Lebanon War, on August 6, 2006, here fell twelve paratroopers . . . ."

Behind me, Boaz explained. The soldiers were members of a reserve paratrooper brigade. A brigade he commanded. Some of the unit's members were already in Lebanon. The ones in the parking lot before us, were preparing to go. Standing against the wall and leaning on vehicles lining the lot, they, in the time-honored tradition of soldiers at war, were passing the time. An alarm went off. It meant Hezbollah had fired more Katyushas. Where they would land nobody knew. Hezbollah had already fired thousands towards Israel since the war began on July 12, and many more would be fired before it would end. Hezbollah rockets struck Merom Golan, Kibbutz Dan, Ma'ayan Baruch, Metula, Rosh Pina, Kibbutz Hanita, and most other communities in the north. Alarms were a constant. Explosions commonplace. But familiarity breeds complacency. Those soldiers didn't flinch. Even after only four days under fire, the risk seemed small.

The Russians first developed the Katyusha rocket system during World War II. The Soviets used heavy trucks as a platform to launch volleys of as many as forty-eight up to four miles. German soldiers learned to dread their distinctive scream as they descended from the sky to wreak havoc. The Germans called them "Stalin's organs," but their name actually came from a Russian song about a girl pining away for her lover who is away on military service. In 2006, Hezbollah possessed 15,000 of them. Easy to set-up and fire, the missiles lacked accuracy but not lethality. Packed with explosives and layers of serrated steel or small metal spheres—designed to tear into human flesh with devastating impact—anyone standing unprotected near where a Katyusha lands is unlikely to survive.

The depression in the concrete near the curb did not come from wear and tear. It was the epicenter of death. There, a Katyusha had fallen. One moment twenty-seven men were standing. The next moment, in a growing pool of blood, a dozen were on the ground, their lives seeping away. The other fifteen were wounded. Today, the black metal pole across from where many of them fell stands today as a monument to their torn flesh. If shrapnel can so easily slam through metal, flesh does not stand a chance.

Boaz did not leave his vehicle while I sought to absorb what I saw. In a measured, sad voice—quite different than the confident tone I had grown accustomed to all day, he explained what happened to his men—and the aftermath. Boaz went to every funeral, visited every family, and to this day keeps in touch with many. But at the ceremony commemorating the creation of the memorial site in 2007, he said that presently in Israel, people are "too busy dealing with their own weaknesses. I've met the family members of the fallen soldiers, and I noticed only strengths—not weaknesses—which can help the people live their lives in a territory surrounded by enemies." I couldn't agree more about the people I have met.

One of them is Bethe Shoenfeld.

* * *

I met Bethe at the Western Galilee College located in Akko (Acre), about ten miles south of the Lebanese border. The college itself looks like any small college in America, complete with dormitories, several multiple-story classroom buildings, open areas and, of course, plentiful food. There, 2,500 students of obvious multiple ethnicities and ages further their education. There, in a small, almost claustrophobic room, is where I sat down to interview Bethe.

Bethe had first come to my attention only a couple weeks before when I had searched on Amazon for books on Northern Israel and found her book, *The Routine of War: How One Northern Community Coped During the Second Lebanon War.* Composed of Bethe's daily diary supplemented by multiple interviews, I found it an interesting study of the struggle for normalcy in an abnormal world. After reading it, I reached out to her. Fortunately, Bethe agreed to meet with me.

Bethe, now in her sixties, grew up in Pikesville, Maryland, a town I know well because my college girlfriend lived nearby. It has a strong Jewish community, many of which are Orthodox, and many of its residents are affluent. But not Bethe. She attended a conservative synagogue, her family was not wealthy, and her parents divorced. There, she did not feel community. After attending the University of Maryland and working in a restaurant in Baltimore to raise money, she traveled to Europe.

Immediately, I felt an affinity. I too attended the University of Maryland. I too had worked a job to fund a backpack trip to Europe. But I went in the summer, Bethe went in the winter when "it was too fucking cold."

The cold led her to fly to Israel for some relief. An older woman that she had met before leaving for Europe had suggested she visit Kibbutz Gesher Haziv if she ever went to Israel. Bethe decided to do so. Located two and a half miles from the Lebanese border, it is within walking distance from one of Israel's most beautiful beaches along the Mediterranean, Achziv. In her book, Bethe said "On a normal day you would think you had found the Garden of Eden." Having been to the beach and the outskirts of the kibbutz, I almost agree. Perhaps not heaven, but certainly idyllic.

The year was 1980. There Bethe experienced the feeling of community that she felt lacking while growing up. There she became a volunteer, and there she met Asher, whom she would eventually marry.

Bethe made Aliyah in 1981, arriving again at Gesher Haziv on July 13, 1981. Not yet married, but ready to begin a monogamous relationship, Asher greeted her. As did katyushas from Lebanon. For Bethe, it was the beginning of a long-standing relationship with both.

For ten days, Katyushas fired from Lebanon rained down on northern Israel.

> *It was a Saturday night at 9:13 p.m. There was a barrage of Katyushas. I was sitting in our one-room little apartment at the time. We were watching the news. We had a black and white television. [The] lights went out. Asher was already on the ground pulling me under the bed while I was trying to figure out what was going on, and I think the thing that really weirded me was all the lights went [out]. What had happened? A Katyusha had fallen across the street. It had hit the electrical lines and it just knocked everything out.*

Asher's job was to tend the kibbutz's turkey flock. After the barrage ended, he decided to check on their wellbeing. Bethe screamed out, "You can't leave me here!" But he did. Katyushas were part of the way of life. So were the turkeys' well-being.

Although the attack impacted Bethe greatly, she decided to stay. For the next two years, until the first Lebanese war, no more rockets came. When the war started in 1982, so again did the Katyushas. After the war ended, periodically, the Katyushas would still come. Periodically until July 12, 2006. Then came the deluge.

Until 2006, for Bethe, the occasional Katyusha became part of the fabric of their lives—almost routine. "Yea it's scary," she told me. "It sounds like this, phfff!-yeaaaah-phff," followed by an explosion. Especially at night, she would hear when they were launched on the other side of the high hills marking the border. In her book, Bethe said, "The noise is probably the worst. If it falls near you there is a loud crack and then deafening silence. If it flies over you, you hear a whoosh as it wizzes by." During the two and a half decades between wars, when she heard anything it was mostly whooshes. Until 2006.

When the Second Lebanon War started on July 12, 2006 with Hezbollah's cross-border kidnapping of two Israeli soldiers and killing of eight others, Bethe, her husband, and their youngest child were in the United States. Her son was serving in the IDF on the border with Lebanon, and her sixteen-year-old daughter, Shanie, was home on the kibbutz. As part of a diversion for the kidnapping and then as part of the ensuing thirty-four-day war, Hezbollah launched 4,000 missiles at Israel. Many flew near Bethe's kibbutz, Gesher Haziv. Twenty-four struck the kibbutz. Twenty-four!

On that first day, Shanie was scheduled to take a math exam necessary for her to graduate from high school. Soon after the first rockets hit Israel, the head of the math department told Shanie and the other students that nearby Kibbutz Hanita and Matzuba were under attack by Hezbollah but that they should not panic, and the exam would go forward as scheduled in the afternoon. From their school they could see the hilltop border a couple miles away and the military post there. Shanie said "there was a lot of smoke coming out of that base." In response, the IDF was shooting towards Lebanon, and in return the Katyushas kept coming into Israel. Still, the math exam went forward. During it, Shanie said, "I kept hearing the loud noises of rockets landing nearby."

After the exam, adults told Shanie to go to the community shelter or her security room, called a *"mamm'ad,"* built to provide some protections against rocket attacks in her home. But there was something else she needed to do first—walk her dog. Shanie's path took her closer to the hills and there she saw "it was burning up and full of smoke. All the smoke was very close to Kibbutz Hanita . . . ."

The next day, fear in the kibbutz increased. A Katyusha fell twenty yards from where Shanie had stood the day before. During my conversation with Bethe, she told me that if you are in the open and standing, a Katyusha striking the ground twenty yards away will likely injure or kill you. That hit brought home the reality to many kibbutz members of their frailty even though it was not the first time the kibbutz had been hit by a rocket—that distinction dates to a PLO launched missile in 1970. But it also created a new routine. Bethe quoted then seventy-eight-year-old Eugene as saying, "You have to use common sense with everything, especially in a war. When it was intense, and it was intense at times, I would go into the security room. So that became a routine as well." In her *mamm'ad*, the explosion awakened Shanie.

But the *mamm'ads* were not a complete antidote to death from the sky. *Mamm'ads* usually were a small room, required by law in any new construction, that had reinforced concrete walls, floor, and ceiling coupled with metal window shutters. Supposedly, they would protect the inhabitants from the Katyushas. But, as relayed to Bethe by Hannah Troy, "There is a story that [when someone drove a nail] into one of the walls . . . in order to hang a picture . . . it pushed the nail straight through to the other side!" Imagine what shrapnel propelled by an explosion would do.

Nor were the more deeply dug community shelters ready to receive people. Many were in poor condition with water pooled on their floors. Most lacked air conditioning. This was the situation that Yael and Natan Golan's philanthropic organization, Galila, strove mightily to correct after becoming aware of the deficiency.

Two days into the war, three quarter of the kibbutz's population had evacuated to places south. But Shanie remained and Bethe was still in the United States. Bethe only learned of the war during a stopover in Dallas on her way from Los Angeles to BWI airport in Baltimore. Bethe and Asher gave little thought to bringing Shanie to the United States. Israel was Shanie's home. Nor did they leave for the United States right away but stayed glued to the TV and the Internet. Nine days into the war, they arrived at Ben Gurion Airport where Shanie met them. From there they took a taxi the 100 miles back to Gesher Haziv because trains had stopped running north of Haifa due to the Katyushas.

Back home, Bethe and Asher struggled to adjust to the new normal of deadly fire arching over them and sometimes dropping near. In the same day, Asher mowed his lawn and fought a brush fire started by a Katyusha. Bethe once drove to the border to pick up her son who had a weekend pass. Along the way, she saw several Israeli tanks shooting into Lebanon from the roadside.

Those kibbutzniks that remained with Bethe adjusted too. Some tried to predict when Hezbollah would most likely send more rockets based on past conduct. Common wisdom was that Hezbollah would mostly launch Katyushas during the day out of fear that the dark sky would make it easier for the IDF to determine their launching point. Some argued that particular times in the morning and afternoon were more likely to see the rockets fly. And for some, there was a certain joy in their newfound freedom to drive as fast as they wanted on the roads because there was nobody on them, including the police.

Bethe wrote of her husband saying with regard to driving, "The routine was that if there was a rocket attack, or if you heard a siren, you stop the car and find a place to lie down on the side of the road for two to three minutes."

Others employed different strategies. One said, "When I'm in the car and there have already been rockets that have fallen—I won't stop the car and lie on the ground because you don't know where the next Katyusha will fall, on this side of the car or on the other. So, I believe that you need to continue driving, fast, in order to get where you need to go."

And another, "It was unpleasant on the roads. We know the Hezbollah are there and that at any second they can shoot a rocket at you and you don't know where it's going to land. It's a more intense feeling than if you're home or in your kibbutz."

Two weeks after Bethe returned to Israel, she drove to the local hospital to check on her father-in-law, David, hospitalized there. Because of the missiles, the hospital moved many of its patients into the basement for their protection. But not the children and those on the maternity ward. They stayed in their first-floor rooms, dependent on the three floors above for protection. The administration did not want to risk them being infected by the sick patients sequestered below.

While walking towards her car in the hospital parking lot after her visit, Bethe heard a rocket blast. Looking urgently for nearby cover, she only saw a grove of avocado trees. Quickly, she sought shelter amid the wood trunks and crouched down. It would have been safer to lie down, but vanity and practicality prevented her—she was wearing white pants. Later in the day, Shanie asked Bethe to drive her to see David too. After dropping Shanie off, Bethe once again headed home. And once again the Katyushas came.

Upon hearing a sudden loud crack that she knew was the sound of a Katyusha strike, Bethe pulled off the road, hopped out, and crouched in a ditch by the side of the road. After a minute or so, she saw that the ditch, as part of a water drainage system, tunneled under the road a short distance way. Thinking that safer than an open ditch, and no longer so concerned about keeping her clothing clean, she wedged herself in there. Later, when Bethe felt safe enough to leave her unsavory sanctuary, she returned to the kibbutz. There, Bethe looked back south. A plume of smoke rose from where she had come. Later, when Asher returned from picking up their daughter, a mission Bethe insisted he do rather than her after her two close calls that day, he reported that the rocket had fallen fifty yards from her car.

Meanwhile, in Kibbutz Hanita during the war, work went on in the two factories. For a while, fortune seemed to smile on the kibbutz that lay a stone's throw from the border. Most of the Katyushas arched overhead along a path destined for Gesher Haziv and elsewhere. Most, but not all. Two landed in the factory parking lot where two men had just exited their car. One required minor treatment, the other surgeries to repair his leg, riven by shrapnel.

In Kiryat Shmona, Katyushas fell as if in a long, drawn-out hailstorm. People died, buildings crumbled, and all-around town massive forest fires threatened all that remained. For thirty-four days it was a living hell. Then quiet.

One kibbutz member told Bethe regarding returning to normalcy after the war, "The days after—for about two weeks you are still jumpy—every time a window shook you were kind of feeling a little bit [then a pause before continuing], your nerves were a little on edge. It took a while before you realized that things were quiet." Bethe agreed with that assessment, writing that after the war ended it took a couple weeks to feel normal again. "And even now," she wrote, "I have this feeling that it's not finished—that there is unfinished business here somehow." She wrote those words in 2007. Now, in 2020, those words still ring true. Now, more than ever.

Bethe Schoenfeld's book, part memoir part compendium of the experiences of others, offers a revealing look into a small community struggling with a world in which, without warning, absurdity interrupted normality, and death threatened the living. Many headed south, beyond range of the missiles. Many others chose to remain, particularly those with membership ties to the kibbutz. Those who stayed gained strength from the ordeal, but some also carry emotional scars.

In Gesher Haziv the Katyushas did not kill anybody even though one struck the elementary school there, others started fires and caused other damage, and fear of them interfered with the kibbutz's economic livelihood—especially management of the agricultural fields because hired help refused to work with the crops during the war. But outside of the kibbutz, Hezbollah missiles killed forty-three civilians, including four in nearby Nahariya where fate caught up to one person sitting on her porch and a second while bringing clothes from a shelter to his little daughter. And, although spared death, the Katyushas injured well more than a thousand.

When I asked Bethe why she wrote her book, she answered because "we never thought it was going to be as long as it was," and to explain what "became the new normal." However, in the book, Bethe said, "Maybe writing this book is my way of coping with the war." All along Israel's northern borders, Israelis have had to learn to cope with Katyushas. I don't think, as Bethe suggested, it is a "new normal." It just is "the normal." A world where pockmarked streets mark where rockets have fallen and discolorations encircling jagged holes are the enduring monuments to whizzing shrapnel. In the north, which many still love, bombs and blood mix all too frequently for some and shape everyday life for all.

The incidence of Katyushas falling on northern Israel has slowed, in recent years. But that has not ended the concern. In 2017, Sarit Zehavi spoke movingly to 18,000 people at the annual AIPAC conference in Washington, D.C. The fifteen-minute YouTube video of her talk is online. "We are seven miles from the Lebanese border," Sarit said, "and thirty-four miles from Syria. That's like from here to Baltimore." Sarit speaking of the last few years continued, "It has been relatively quiet on this border. You know there have been some twenty instances here where a rocket or mortar landed in a village . . . in addition, three soldiers were also killed during this time . . . but there was no escalation, no prolonged conflict. And for us believe it or not, twenty rockets in twelve years, it's pretty quiet! But I am not sure this will last." Then, quietly and with concern, "And my kids and I, well, we have only nine seconds to get to the shelter."

The cavernous room hushed as the import of Sarit Zehavi's words sunk in. Hers is a normal family in an abnormal world where there are nine seconds to run to the safe room in her house. Nine seconds that separate life from death. I have been in her safe room. It is narrow, congested, and in the center of the first floor of her home, adjacent to the kitchen and the family area. Upstairs are the bedrooms and outside a fenced in yard out back, and a play area alongside the entrance. There, five children, two of hers, two of her partner's, and one of both, come and go, eat and sleep, play and study. Nine seconds for seven souls to get to the room lined with concrete walls, squeeze in next to the desk and bookshelf, close the door, and huddle together—it simply won't happen.

During the evening of December 21, 2015, Sarit's family came close to finding out whether nine seconds would be enough to find safety. Hezbollah fired three rockets at the Western Galilee. Although they landed fifteen minutes away from her home, the sirens warned the entire region of their approach. A Palestinian entity claimed responsibility for the missiles but as Sarit puts it, "For those that speak the Middle Eastern language, it is clear they were only a proxy." Hezbollah or its proxy fired the rockets, likely in response to the death of Samir Kuntar the night before.

Terrorists and Katyushas are simply a fact of life along Israel's northern borders. A sublimated dread for the living, never dissipating but not debilitating—unless they happen to fall nearby.

Chapter Eighteen

Yesterday, Today, and Tomorrow

The Lebanese Border

After spending several hours with Samuel Gardi and his wife, Haviva, at Kibbutz Dan in 2018, I drove west on busy, two-lane Route 99, which in the United States would be characterized as a country road but in northern Israel serves as a main east-west artery. However, I did not journey far. About a mile down the road, it intersects with Route 918, an even more rural road. There I made a left, and then another immediate left onto a dirt road, more bumpy than flat, and laced with potholes filled with water from the thunderstorm that had just passed through. That track, which ran parallel to Route 99, led me back the way I had come for several hundred yards before I encountered a paved road on which I turned right. A couple minutes later I reached the end of my journey. Alone, with a bright sun shining, a blue sky above, and a stillness in the air, I contemplated what had happened here twenty years before and had brought me there that day.

Just after 7 p.m., on February 4, 1997, two helicopters cut through the dark, foggy night. Both headed towards Israel's security zone in Lebanon bringing troops, one for its Beaufort Castle position, an old crusader fort on a hilltop several miles into Lebanon, and the other to the "Pumpkin" military post written so eloquently about by

Matti Friedman, in his haunting book, *Pumpkin Flowers: A Soldier's Story*.

Israel's security zone in South Lebanon, no more than a few miles wide, came about to protect Israel's northern border communities from terrorist penetrations and rockets after the IDF withdrew from the positions it held deeper in Lebanon at the end of the First Lebanon War in 1982. In it, twenty to twenty-five IDF soldiers lost their lives every year due to conflict with Hezbollah and others. To avoid casualties, the IDF began relying on helicopters for transport rather than road convoys that were susceptible to ambush. And, although there were no human terrorist penetrations into Israel during that time, the security zone did not entirely prevent Katyusha rockets from intermittently targeting Israel's border communities. In short, the South Lebanon security zone was an oozing sore.

In midair, over Moshav She'ar Yashuv, the two helicopters collided. Spiraling downward, one crashed into the Moshav; the other, hit the ground several hundred yards away, in Kibbutz Dafna's fields, where it lay for several hours while exploding ammunition kept rescuers at bay. There, just down the road from Kibbutz Dan, all seventy-three soldiers and airmen aboard the two craft perished.

The impact of the disaster was felt throughout Israel. Ezer Weizman, Israel's then president, paid condolence calls on each of the families that had lost a loved one. Children wrote poems and the "Four Mothers Movement" was spawned. Started by the mothers of four of the downed soldiers, the movement challenged the need to remain in Lebanon, their passion driven by the loss of their children. The Four Mothers movement was at first marginalized and ridiculed but gained steam as the human and economic cost of the IDF remaining in Lebanon mounted.

The memorial I walked to after exiting my car has two parts. The most prominent contains seventy-three large, jagged, brownish-tan stones arranged in sections of green grass divided by white walkways, surrounding a central, circular pool fed by a narrow channel. Within the pool, written on seventy-three black rocks, are the names of the seventy-three that died. But the most moving for me, hidden in a wooded area with a rushing stream and the sound of birds chirping, is a seemingly haphazard memorial. There, hanging on eucalyptus trees are remains from one of the fallen helicopters and pictures of some of the fallen souls along with their names etched in stone. Wooden benches permit silent contemplation in relative comfort.

The helicopter tragedy occurred little more than halfway from when terror began to emanate in earnest from Lebanon in the 1970s, and when I visited the site in 2018. As such, the helicopter tragedy offers a perfect vantage point, anchored in time, from which the evolution of terrorism faced by Israel's communities bordering Lebanon, both before and after the crash, can be explained.

At first, the Palestinian Liberation Organization (PLO) and its offshoots, with Yasser Arafat at the helm, led the terror campaign against the northern border communities. The PLO was dedicated to the destruction of Israel and creation of a Palestinian state on its ruins. Before 1970, southern Lebanon was mainly at peace with Israel. As a result, the then porous border facilitated trade and interaction between Israelis living in the northern border communities and Lebanese living in southern Lebanon. But after King Hussein evicted the PLO in Jordan during the early 1970s, many Palestinian terrorists found a new home in Lebanon and established a base in southern Lebanon, adjacent to Israel. Their presence upset a tenuous political balance between Christians, Sunni and Shia Muslims, and the Druze. That would eventually lead to a civil war in Lebanon in 1975. It also led to increased terrorism and increasing numbers of PLO launched Katyushas directed at Jews in northern Israel.

The ongoing PLO's terrorist attacks emanating from Lebanon, culminating in one in 1978 that killed thirty-five Israeli citizens and wounded seventy-one others along a coastal road south of Haifa, spurred Israel to launch Operation Litani into Lebanon on March 14, 1978. Its goal was the destruction of PLO bases south of the Litani River, which flows several miles from the border, in order to secure northern Israel. The operation lasted a week, after which, under pressure from the United Nations, Israel agreed to withdraw in return for the U.N. creating a new force, UNIFIL (United Nations Interim Force in Lebanon), charged with maintaining order in Southern Lebanon.

On paper, perhaps, UNIFIL was a good idea worth a try. In practice, it was a failure. When the IDF withdrew from its positions south of the Litani, the PLO moved back in, and terrorism and Katyushas again became the order of the day.

Cloaked by darkness on April 7, 1980, five PLO terrorists cut through the fence dividing Lebanon from Israel. From there, they sneaked into Kibbutz Misgav Am, a smallish, hilltop border kibbutz just south and west of Metula. Their target? The sleeping quarters for kibbutz children. At the entrance stood Sammy Shani, there to repair broken light fixtures. Armed with only a screwdriver, he tried to stop them from entering the building but failed, losing his life in return. Kibbutz residents quickly stormed the building, succeeding in freeing several children and three women sleeping on the ground floor, but failing to stop the terrorists from moving to the second floor. There, before the terrorist incursion started, slept seven toddlers and one male adult.

The terrorists' goal was to negotiate release of many prisoners held in Israeli jails. After negotiations broke down, IDF soldiers swiftly attacked. In the end, one toddler died, four others were wounded, the terrorists shot the adult that had been with the children, and the IDF killed the terrorists after losing one of their own to terrorist fire. Whether two-year old Eyal died from terrorist bullets, or in the initial attempt to rescue her by kibbutz residents is not clear. What is clear is that terrorists had targeted Eyal and the other children. After the attack a kibbutz member told a *New York Times* reporter, "For a long time, we didn't use this nursery. It would have been too shocking for the children. We waited until a new generation of children was born, and they are the ones who use it now." But for Misgav Am residents, the memory is eternal.

In 1982, for a variety of reasons, Israel's army returned to Lebanon, this time moving as far as Beirut. Once again, as with Operation Litani, the PLO precipitated the IDF's entrance into Lebanon by employing terror as a political weapon. Before Israel's incursion into southern Lebanon, thousands of Palestinian terrorists posed a constant threat to the livelihood and security of Israelis living along the border. In 1981, for ten days, Palestinian Katyushas ended any semblance of normal life in Kiryat Shmona and threatened the lives of Israelis from Nahariya to Metula. The specific triggering excuse used by the Israeli government for entering Lebanon in 1982 was the attempted assassination of an Israeli diplomat in England by a Palestinian terrorist group not affiliated with the PLO. However, the memory of hundreds, if not thousands, of Katyushas launched by the PLO at targets in northern Israel along with the death of two-year-old Eyal in Misgav Am and so many others—coupled with the likelihood of more of the same—was the real reason. If citizens in Israel's northern border communities, as well as in communities farther south were to live a normal life, Israel had to act.

Unfortunately, the First Lebanon War in 1982 did not achieve its underlying purpose—peace in the northern Galilee. While the IDF did successfully evict the PLO forever, the IDF's presence in Lebanon did much to spawn an even more virulent force.

At first welcomed by Shia Muslims in southern Lebanon who had been treated poorly by their PLO occupiers, the Shia increasingly saw the IDF as enemies rather than rescuers. Soon, a new movement rose, part indigenous but also as a result of Iranian machinations. Its name—Hezbollah.

Initially, Hezbollah had another rival for Shia power, the more moderate but still virulent Amal movement. However, over time, Hezbollah proved itself the most lethal and effective group. In 1983, Hezbollah killed 241 American peacekeeping soldiers and fifty-eight French soldiers in Beirut on the same day by employing truck bombs. Two other vehicle-borne Hezbollah bombs a year apart killed another 100 IDF soldiers in Beirut and Tyre.

Supported by Iran, after Israel withdrew from Beirut in 1985 to the security zone in southern Lebanon nowhere more than a few miles wide, Hezbollah mounted increasingly murderous attacks on the IDF and its Christian allies within that zone. Over the years, more than 200 IDF soldiers lost their lives as a result and many more suffered wounds. However, during those fifteen years, Israel's northern border communities lived in relative peace. Still, as the years passed, and the human and economic cost of the continued occupation mounted, internal domestic pressure to leave Lebanon increased.

The horrific number of deaths caused by the two helicopters colliding, the Four Mothers movement that emerged, continued Hezbollah attacks that bled Israel's youth, and Israel's electoral process in 1999 all combined to move public opinion. In 1999, Ehud Barak beat the incumbent, Bibi Netanyahu, for the prime minister position. One of newly elected Barak's promises during the election in 1999 was that he would get the IDF out of Lebanon within a year. In an abrupt attempt to end Israel's Vietnam, during the night of May 24, 2000 Barak did so without first notifying anybody outside the IDF. When the sun rose on May 25, the IDF was done with Lebanon, but Hezbollah was not done with the IDF. Israel's northern border communities were once again exposed to terror and Katyushas.

Since 2000, Israel has fought another war in Lebanon, this time with Hezbollah, during which more than 4,000 Hezbollah Katyushas hit Israel's northern border communities. Those rockets killed innocent citizens, caused significant damage, and started numerous forest fires. They also served as a reminder, as did the attack on Matsuva junction in 2002, that Hezbollah was back to business as usual—threatening citizens living along the northern border with Lebanon with being hit by a rocket with seconds warning or being killed by a bullet without notice.

Simply put, Hezbollah's goal is the destruction of Israel. It first disguised that objective by calling for Israel's eviction from Lebanese territory. But its leader, Sheikh Hassan Nasrallah has left no ambiguity regarding Hezbollah's strategic objective, stating that Israel is a "cancerous growth" and that "the only solution is to destroy it without giving it the opportunity to surrender."

Designated a terrorist organization by many nations of the world, including the United States, Hezbollah presents an existential risk to Israelis living along the northern borders. With thousands of battle-trained soldiers, and up to 150,000 rockets in its possession compared to the 15,000 on hand in 2006, Hezbollah has the largest non-state military capability in the world and dwarfs the capabilities of many nations as well. During the 2006 war, Hezbollah fired an average of 120 rockets per day. Today it is estimated that Hezbollah has the capability to fire thousands per day, many of which able to carry a larger payload and travel a longer distance with more accuracy than in 2006. And along the Syrian and Lebanese borders with Israel, Hezbollah operatives are ever present and occasionally have sneaked into Israel from Lebanon during the last two decades for surveillance and mayhem. Cumulatively, all these Hezbollah capabilities present a constant risk to the safety and security of Israel's northern border communities.

One new method Israel has employed to stop Hezbollah from infiltrating the border or firing through, or over, the chain-link fence that marks much of Israel's border with Lebanon now is a huge concrete wall. Presently under construction, when finished, the almost thirty feet high wall will stretch more than eighty miles from the sea to Metula.

Another method involves changing topography. Just outside Kibbutz Hanita's fence, a massive earth-moving project has removed vegetation and cut into the hillside that rises up from a ravine to the hilltop where Hanita sits. Before, terrorists could use the rough terrain as cover while creeping up the slope, as did the terrorists that killed Israelis at Matzuva junction. Now, terrorists will have to negotiate hundreds of feet of open terrain and sharp, angular slopes. The scar in the earth, painful as it is to view, is far less painful than the risk to Hanita's inhabitants should Hezbollah choose to attack.

However, neither higher walls nor changed topography are effective defenses for all threats. And in December 2018, northern border communities received another reminder of the determination and caginess of their enemy. On December 4, the IDF initiated operation Northern Shield. For the next forty days, the IDF hunted Hezbollah tunnels that it had reason to believe crossed under the border fence and into Israel. Using seismic tools and radar, eventually, the IDF found six, three near Metula and three near Zar'it, like Metula, located on the Israeli side of the border with Lebanon. In addition, many more tunnel starts were identified in Lebanon that had not yet crossed under the border fence into Israel.

The first tunnel discovered, just south of Metula, 220 yards in length, extended forty yards into Israel. It was large enough to permit tens if not hundreds of Hezbollah operatives to move quickly into Israel where they could block IDF soldiers trying to relieve Metula from a simultaneous attack. In conjunction with two more tunnels with exits close to Metula, the tunnels gave Hezbollah a strategic option; take an Israeli town, kidnap and/or kill its inhabitants, and then hold it for a considerable period of time. The same was true for Zar'it, where the other three tunnels gave Hezbollah the same opportunity. The sixth tunnel, found on January 13, 2019 near Zar'it, was the largest and most sophisticated of them all. Cutting dozens of yards into Israel, it had electrical lighting, rails for moving heavy loads and people, garbage disposal, and even stairs cut into the ground.

More recently, Hezbollah appears to be investigating using swarms of explosive laden drones to overcome Israeli defenses. At least one Israeli company has heralded a solution to that problem that it reportedly has provided to the IDF—the ability to take over simultaneously up to 200 enemy drones.

Then, in late summer 2019, Hezbollah threatened to attack Israel in retribution for two drones that exploded under mysterious circumstances in Beirut. Reports are confusing as to the origin of those drones and their target. But it appears that the explosions destroyed a Hezbollah facility used to increase the accuracy of its missile hoard. In response, the IDF ordered its soldiers not to use open border roads and ordered the same for civilian traffic. After a Hezbollah missile destroyed an empty military ambulance and narrowly missed an occupied military vehicle, the IDF responded by firing 100 shells at Hezbollah targets. And, it ordered the border communities to open and make ready their shelters for the first time in many years. Having seen a couple of those shelters, that will take much work by the residents.

And so, Hezbollah's plans for Israel's communities strung out along the Lebanese border have become clear. In the event of war, or in some scenarios short of war, special units trained to breach Israel's borders will attempt to move through, over, or under the fences and walls arrayed to stop them. Supported by thousands of Hezbollah soldiers, some hardened by having fought in Syria, and under cover of salvos of rockets numbering daily in the thousands that will target civilian centers, military bases, industrial plants, and fall randomly as well, the invading units plan to enter border towns, kibbutzim, and villages for propaganda purposes and terrorist designs. Knowing that they would not hold their conquests for long against Israel's much stronger military force, the only conceivable purpose of their mission is to kill and kidnap, terrorize, and destroy. The hours, or even minutes, that Hezbollah would be in control would measure, for them, the extent of their victory. And for the residents of those communities, the terror and injury they would endure would be devastating.

The Syrian Border

After the 1974 negotiations that produced a cessation of hostilities, but not peace, between Syria and Israel, border communities along the Golan experienced quiet for forty years. Terrorists did not cross the border, bullets didn't fly, and shells did not land where people lived. However, fear that Israel might return the Golan to Syria in exchange for peace continued to haunt those that had built their homes on the Golan, started factories in their communities, and nurtured crops and cattle on the Golan's soil.

In 1999, that fear almost became a reality. While Prime Minister Rabin had hinted at the prospect of giving up the Golan in return for peace, Prime Minister Barak initiated direct negotiations with the Syrians to make it a reality. At first, Yehuda Harel, from Merom Golan told me, "We were afraid of a temporary agreement with Syria to give [the Syrians] half of the Golan. Now we know it wasn't possible because the Syrians want[ed] one hundred percent or nothing."

But, I persisted, weren't you concerned that Barak would give it all back?

Yehuda responded first with his view on democracy. "I believe in democracy and Israel is a democratic republic," he said. "And I told you, I don't like governments, and . . . what is the main wish of every Prime Minister?" he asked. Then, with little pause, he answered his question with a slight smile: "The main vision of [a] Prime Minister is to be a Prime Minister! And therefore, it meant people. Because democracy, one philosopher I believe in said 'what is the advantage of democracy? Not good decisions, not good leaders. It is the only system you can change the government without bloodshed.' That's it." And since Barak wanted to remain in his elected position, Yehuda thought then that if he could convince enough people to support holding onto the Golan, he would succeed in convincing Barak to step back from the brink.

"Therefore," Yehuda told me, "We never tried to fight the government by being extremist. We had [an] opposite strategy. We were very moderate, and we [spoke] soft words." Their slogan was "The people with the Golan—Ami Golan." Yehuda's rational was that "to win in a democracy you have to have the center . . . . The extremists against us, we cannot change them. The extremists with us it does not pay to [put effort into] because they are with us, but the center is about sixty to seventy percent, and you can make it with love not [craziness]."

"With Barak," Yehuda said, "It was the same. He knew that he had to go to elections." Yehuda contended that the polls showed "sixty percent were against withdrawal from the Golan but half of them were ready to give half of the Golan Heights for a peace agreement." Half would have meant that Merom Golan would have gone to the Syrians. Half would have also meant that the rest of the Golan would have been indefensible because it is a flat plain. Because democracy demands that those who wish to achieve a result must advocate their cause, Yehuda leapt into action.

But advocating for a cause to the public at large is, at best, an indirect path to a decision maker in a democracy. Personal diplomacy matters too.

In early January 2000, Prime Minister Barak was an hour from boarding his plane. In Shepherdstown, West Virginia, he planned to meet President Clinton and Syria's foreign minister with hopes of reaching a peace deal with Syria that would also encompass issues with

Hezbollah in Lebanon. Only one stumbling block stood in his way before leaving—Yehuda Harel.

"We were four people from the Golan Heights," Yehuda told me. "And he came with about four or five assistants. We made it a very difficult hour for him. I told him that our children, they were small children, they cry when they see him on television because they were afraid of him, he's the bad man for them . . . . Some of his assistants cried. After an hour," Yehuda continued, "somebody said he had to go to the plane. And [Barak] said, 'tell them I will go there in an hour.' So we sat there about two and a half hours . . . It was very sentimental. We tried to make it very difficult for him."

One tactic Yehuda used was to remind Barak of a mutual friend, Micha Frichman. Frichman had served with Barak in the same unit in the army and was a kibbutz leader on the Golan. A Syrian shell that had hit his kibbutz cut Frichman's life short. Yehuda told Barak that if he would give back the Golan to the Syrians that "everyone will remember Micha Frichman as one who [made] a kibbutz in Eretz Israel and you will be remembered as one who destroyed twenty-five kibbutzim." Yehuda said, "It made a [big] impression on him. I believe he was not certain what to do . . . . I know when he [left] Shepherdstown he didn't walk out with [an agreement]."

In Shepherdstown, the Syrians refused any deal that did not return every inch of what Israel had taken. "That helped us," Yehuda said. And:

> *We made the biggest demonstration till then in Israel, more than 200,000 people in Tel Aviv. And [Barak] said to journalists, 'Did you hear about . . . the demonstration?' And he said it was a very important demonstration. So, he decided not to sign. I don't know if it was because of Assad, because of us or because of himself. But I am sure [our] conversation helped very much, the demonstration helped, and Assad helped.*

When I asked Yehuda if he thought there was any future risk that Israel would return the Golan to Syria he answered:

> *I believe you can't know the future . . . . But I believe that every year it becomes more difficult to move off the Golan Heights because the people of Israel see the Golan Heights as part of Israel, because of how it looks, when they eat the food, they drink the wine, they have friends there, and every year about two million visit the Golan Heights . . . . It's part of Israel.*

The Syrian Civil War that began in 2011 and has only recently wound down in 2019 proved the folly of ever giving back the Golan. Only miles, and sometimes yards from the border fence, fighting raged between Syria's army and its proxies versus the rebel forces from various factions. In one spot along the border, an ISIS-affiliated group controlled a small swath of land and in other areas groups affiliated with Al-Qaeda controlled territory—neither a force that one would want to have in control of high ground overlooking the Hula Valley and the rest of northeastern Israel. But perhaps because the rebels and the Syrians had their hands full with each other, despite the infrequent mortar shell and missile that would stray over the border into Israeli controlled Golan, the Golan's border communities remained untouched. No civilians died. No terrorists brought terror. For Israelis, peace ruled the day.

That has now changed.

Syria, with help from Iran, Russia and Hezbollah has won. But although Bashar Assad remains the titular head of Syria, Russian bases remain on Syrian soil. And the Iranians maintain a military presence in Syria that is accompanied by grassroot Iranian efforts highlighting Iranian culture and that provides economic support to Syrian citizens.

In addition, an Iranian inspired plan is in the process of altering the demographic landscape by impeding the return of Sunni Muslims to strategically important areas.

But as bad as Iran's targeting of Syria's civilians may be, what is worse is that with Iran's help, Hezbollah is slowly building a foothold along the Syrian Golan border with Israel. Now, Hezbollah's efforts seem confined to building rapport with the Syrian citizenry, recruiting cells within the population to augment the small number of Hezbollah forces already there, and collecting intelligence. But like a malignant cancer, Hezbollah's presence is sure to grow unless cut out, and cutting it out may well prove impossible. Therefore, soon, border communities such as Merom Golan, may well face what Kibbutz Hanita, Metula, and other border communities face along the Lebanese border—terror and Katyushas. Nevertheless, people on the Golan have reason to be more optimistic about their future than ever before. For them, President Trump's statement that the United States recognizes Israel's sovereignty over the Golan Heights was extremely important because it removed much of what little doubt remained that Israel might one day leave the Golan.

Despite the current relative calm on the Golan, the IDF recognizes what it is facing and has responded to the threat in a number of ways. Israel replaced the old, dilapidated fence, in place since 1974, with a much stronger one, taller and with many technological enhancements. And in January 2020, I observed another, newly built earthen wall, augmenting the already present fence separating Syria from the Golan in some locations. In addition, regular army forces that include elite units have replaced reserve forces assigned to the Golan. These new forces more aggressively patrol the border areas. And, in further recognition of the growing threat, the IDF has increased its numbers in the area by creating a new regional division for defending the Golan. Also, Israel's air force has launched numerous strikes against observed weaponry that could jeopardize civilians in the north.

Recently, that included wiping out a small group of Iranian proxies actively preparing an explosive laden drone for launching at an unknown northern Israel target.

In the days immediately preceding the final edits of this book, an event occurred with potentially cataclysmic impact on Israel's borders with Syria and Lebanon. For years the Kurds in Syria's north-eastern region, in conjunction with American forces, battled ISIS. More than 10,000 Kurds died before achieving victory. As a byproduct of those battles, the Kurds prevented the Iranians from using a northern land route to supply Syria and Hezbollah with weapons for use against Israel. Similarly, in the south, American forces blocked another route. Only a more difficult and perilous middle route was open to Iranian exploitation. That all changed on October 6, 2019, when President Trump announced American forces would immediately withdraw from Syria.

Days later the Turkish army, seeking to create a buffer zone, attacked the Kurds in Syria. For years, Turkey had been thirsting to do so—only held back by the American presence along the Syrian border with Turkey—driven by its hatred of Kurdish terrorists living within Turkey that are aligned with a different Kurdish group than the Syrian Kurds. Due to America's precipitous abandonment, the Kurds in Syria had no choice. They have now aligned themselves with Syria and Russia and probably will not take steps to interfere with Iran's designs. This means the northern land route through Kurdish territory will most likely become open to Iranian exploitation. And if the United States completes its withdrawal, very likely the southern route will as well if U.S. forces do not block it from inside Iraq.

All this does not bode well for Israel. Even before the American withdrawal, Israel had been required to launch far ranging attacks of various kinds. Now, with more land routes to interdict, that will become more complicated and likely less successful. As a result, Israel will face a much more lethal foe, and Israel's border communities will face even more challenges.

But in February 2019, when I rode along the border in a jeep driven by Omer Weiner, the events of October 2019 were still seven months away. That day it was raining, the air misty, and visibility poor. What I did see did not elicit any tension in me. Nor did I feel tense several months earlier when I rode with Omer then on the same roads. On both occasions, through the fence, I saw in Syria empty fields and barren ruins. Yet I knew both times that it was possible, perhaps even likely, we were being watched by people I couldn't see and who may well have had guns pointed in our direction. When I asked Omer if he felt any concern driving near the border, he said, "I'm aware but it's not in my mind." When I asked him whether he ever worried someone might shoot at him he answered, "I don't think about it."

Medical Care

For many, northern Israel is in "the periphery." Only a couple hours' drive from Tel Aviv, it is truly a world apart. The center of Israel teems with universities, industrial pursuits, software and Internet firms that rival Silicon Valley, medical centers, and a variety of cultural pursuits equal to anywhere in the world. In the north, there are colleges, some culture, a growing industrial plant, but a profound lack of medical services. Of course, there is a hospital in Safed and another in Nahariya, but they don't have sufficient specialists for the very sick. And both, for those in need of emergency care, are very far from the farthest reaches of Israel's northern borders. Nor does the medical facility in Tiberias fill the gap for significant illnesses or injuries.

Sorel, from Hanita, told me how difficult it was to obtain treatment for his knee when he needed surgery for a garden-variety knee ailment. One that practically anywhere in the United States would be scheduled within a week or two. In the north, for him to get a surgery date, he was told it would take four months. An MRI? Up to three months wait. In Tel Aviv, two hours away, the next week. Fortunately, he was able to find a better solution in Haifa, perhaps forty-five minutes' drive when conditions are good. Two weeks later he had his surgery.

The same is true for cancer treatment. Until 2017, those in need of radiation treatment needed to go to Haifa. Now, there is a radiation treatment center in Safed, but that still requires a long drive from home and back for those living on the border.

Shefi Mor, from Merom Golan told me much of the same. In good weather it would take up to forty-five minutes to get someone who had just had a heart attack on the Golan to the hospital. And that would require negotiating roads difficult to drive in good conditions let alone bad weather or at night. Shefi had a problem of a different nature. "My mother is ninety-six," Shefi said. "Last week I [took] her to the hospital. Because she broke her shoulder [I took her] to a big hospital in the center of Israel. It was a nightmare. The traffic was impossible."

Part of the problem is the lack of emergency care facilities. A true emergency facility once existed in Kiryat Shmona, but fiscal issues forced its closure several years ago. In October 2018, a new facility opened, but this one is only capable of treating common ailments, not life-threatening emergencies on a twenty-four-hour basis.

Earthquakes

Although Hezbollah and Iran are fully capable of fomenting a disaster along Israel's northern borders, so is nature. In 1837, a destructive quake, estimated in excess of 6.2 on the Richter scale, caused a landslide that devastated Safed, located close to the Lebanese border. In 1927, near Jericho on the now Israeli held West Bank, another major earthquake struck. The fault line that produced those earthquakes extends from Mozambique in Africa into southern Israel, through the Jordan rift valley, and into northern Israel, and then Syria. Experts expect it to produce a major earthquake about every 100 years.

On July 7, 2018, fear mounted that nature was on schedule. A minor quake, 3.4 on the Richter scale with an epicenter a few miles northwest of the Sea of Galilee, in the valley separating the Golan from the mountains bordering Lebanon and not too far south of Kibbutz Dan and Metula, shook the ground. Three days before, a 4.3 Richter scale earthquake hit other parts of the northern Galilee. Several aftershocks followed. And then everything quieted, probably only for a while.

Experts say that northern Israel is at high risk for an earthquake ranging from five to 5.9 on the Richter scale and that one of the city's most at risk is Kiryat Shmona, but that all communities in northern Israel are endangered. Given that a 5.0 earthquake is thirty times stronger than a 4.0 quake, that is concerning.

The most likely area in the north to be hit by a large earthquake stretches from approximately Zar'it up to Metula, coincidently where Hezbollah's tunnels were found. To address the problem, Israel promulgated requirements in 1980 that new construction be designed to withstand earthquakes. But that left older buildings still at risk. Recognizing the problem, Israel's government issued National Master Plan 38 in 2005. Plan 38 was designed to provide incentives for builders to strengthen pre-1980 buildings against earthquakes. In return for fixing designated existing structures for free, contractors received the right to build one or more stories filled with apartments on the roofs of buildings they have hardened and keep the proceeds from their sale. This promising idea, however, has been snagged in litigation over who has the right to do what when existing tenants disagree with the plan.

When the 2018 earthquake swarm hit, public attention was again drawn to the earthquake problem. The government promised to address the issue further but to date nothing significant has emerged.

On the ground in the north, the problem seems particularly acute. Much of Kiryat Shmona sits on a hillside that seems prone to landslides like the one that devastated Safed in 1837. Nearby Kfar Giladi seems equally susceptible to the same fate. Metula and Kibbutz Hanita are connected to Israel by difficult narrow roads cut into the mountains. Even if an earthquake doesn't destroy those communities, landslides and rock falls will likely cut them off from help. Help for building collapse rescues. Help for the wounded. And, perhaps, help from an opportunistic Hezbollah that could easily choose that moment to embark on the same mission that the recently discovered tunnels were designed to facilitate.

Putting it all Together

Given the problems faced by those living in Israel's northern periphery, I thought it wise to see if political leaders were doing anything about it. My experience with politicians has been mostly negative. With few exceptions, I have found those that I have met short on leadership courage but long on personal desire, short on vision but long on platitudes. So, I had little optimism when I walked into Sivan Yechieli's office, the mayor of Kfar Vradim.

I left hoping I had met a man who will one day be Israel's prime minister.

Sivan's second mayoral term was just ending. When first elected, he committed to only running for two terms. Sivan stuck to his promise. The popular mayor's name was not on the ballot for the election coming in the next couple weeks.

Sitting at his desk when I walked in, Sivan quickly left his chair to greet me before ushering me to a small table at the foot of his unassuming office. He was fifty-four years old when we met, of average height but seemingly in excellent health. Born in Zar'it, about twenty-five miles from Kfar Vradim, after serving in the army Sivan rose to become vice president of a tech company before becoming mayor. There his efforts to promote public welfare began.

In addition to his mayoral duties, Sivan headed a committee composed of representatives of all the municipalities in the region, charged with planning how to keep basic services running during a war with Hezbollah and recovering afterward. Sivan explained that the committee's responsibility extends along a large swath of territory from the Lebanese border to almost six miles inland and west to east from the sea to Kiryat Shmona, Ghajar, and beyond. His voice, calm and quiet, had a confidence and command that drew my attention to him.

While sipping the tea Sivan had offered me, I thought it appropriate, given his regional responsibilities, to ask him why people choose to live in the north with its dangers and challenges.

Sivan answered, "Complicated question . . . . The ideal of Israel, those who came to Israel, was to settle the State. One of the ideas we had . . . [to] hold territory, [was] not by means of military force, by means of settlement." Kibbutz Hanita embodied that ideal. To "hold the ground where Jews **would** be," he emphasized. "That," Sivan said, "was the idea of the Zionist movement . . . led by the kibbutzim . . . . [S]ettlement in the rural area was based on that ideal." And the essence of Zionism, he explained to me, "was to live close to the borders, the periphery. We wanted to go to the periphery." And so, he said regarding settlement in the northern Galilee, "It is the essence of Zionism, coming here, holding the ground, fighting for it, fighting physically and fighting every day to make [a] living to sustain life." Then, Sivan said:

> *Come the fifties and immigration from Morocco and other places. And [the government] want[s] to put the Zionist idea on them as well and they send them to Kiryat Shmona, and Shlomi and Ma'alot and different places in the periphery believing that by doing so they are doing them a big favor . . . helping them fulfill the Zionist dream. The only problem was it wasn't their dream. So, the immigrants that came here felt they were shoved to the periphery. You hear them say to the 'asshole' of Israel.*

All along, Sivan continued, you "find two different types of communities in the north. Communities that saw themselves as pioneers, the forefront of Zionism and communities that felt they were second . . ., that weren't given a fair chance . . . . That conflict and tension between the two types of communities is almost until today. Today," he said, "the tension is much more relieved for two reasons." The first is that the government is doing more. The second, because those neglected feel they have a better chance. That, he said, is "creating a little more balance."

Sivan is a capitalist at heart and believes strongly in freedom of choice. Government, he says, regulates too much and has too much control over how people spend their money. Thus, it was no surprise, when he spoke so highly of Stef Wertheimer, who developed Tefen and Kfar Vradim.

Sivan told me with approval that Stef had said, "The main values I am going to promote is creativity and creation, making industry and art, working on the human spirit." That fit well with Sivan's view of Zionism that he told me had three phases. Phase one . . . bringing Jews to Israel. Phase two . . . building an army for defense and phase three . . . economic independence. "Stop the shnoring with world Jewry," Sivan said. Create export industries instead and become self-dependent.

Our digression into economic issues over, we returned to discussing the border regions. After a short conversation about the transition from PLO control of southern Lebanon to Hezbollah, Sivan and I spoke about his relevant military experience. During his service, Sivan became an officer in an IDF reconnaissance unit. What he didn't say, but I knew, was that soldiers in IDF reconnaissance units are the cream of the crop, trained in commando and special forces roles, often gathering intelligence behind enemy lines. It is dangerous work performed by the best of the best.

"When I first was in Lebanon," Sivan told me, "Hezbollah was a small extreme organization, it wasn't a strong organization. Amal was [the] strong Shiite organization." He continued, "I remember when I . . . was commanding a post in Lebanon, the Division commanding officer came in." Rather than indicating concern regarding Hezbollah's capabilities, his superior officer mocked the organization while Sivan briefed him, transforming its name to one with more Yiddish roots, "Hizboli."

But Hezbollah was not something to be mocked. Part of Sivan's responsibilities was to bring convoys in and out of Lebanon. That experience has contributed to his overall view. Especially, the beginning of the suicide attacks. "I lived it, and therefore I have a vivid memory. I understand the process that led the Arabs from where they were to where they are. It has a lot to do with us. People don't understand it."

"And why is this?" Sivan asked.

With little pause, he answered his own question, "When we were strong doing something," they did something else. And then:

> Eventually, what's a suicide attack? Suicide attack is eventually an understanding that I have no other means but to go all the way. Because I am not going to win any other form of fight . . . It's an act of desperation. It's a result of [our] success. It's not a

result of something else. If you don't have to kill yourself, you don't want to kill [yourself]. You want to kill them.

Sivan served more recently as a reconnaissance officer in Gaza. There, he had another experience that is directly relevant to living on the northern borders. A fence equipped with technological innovations that sense when the fence is touched, and then notifies trained personnel to react to those informational inputs, surrounds Gaza. Alongside the fence is a dirt road. Sivan told me that the IDF calls that road "Hoovers."

The concept behind the fence and the path was that whenever someone touched the fence while trying to sneak into Israel, soldiers would go to where the fence had been touched. But the Gazans, realizing that soldiers would come, started purposely touching the fence and then ambushing the soldiers when they would arrive. The IDF reacted by creating a new path, Hoovers B, about 100 yards from the border in order to avoid ambushes. "I couldn't stand it," Sivan said. "We are losing our sovereignty!", he told officers there.

With the construction of Hoovers B, soldiers could not go to Hoovers A without higher level approval. But, Sivan told me, resorting to using Hoovers B would mean thousands of soldiers would be required to deal with the growing number of incursions of increasing depth that would result from pulling back from the fence line. Instead, he suggested, "If you put observation points in several places . . . you can take care of it. The Chief of Staff approved the plan. I wrote the plan and they executed it," he said. But the Gazans adapted. Rather than go through the fence, "The result was they go underground." When that was blocked by IDF innovations, they used rockets, and then kites. In effect, Iron Dome led to kites. His points were two: Never give up sovereignty over the ground and the enemy always reacts.

Regarding the north, Sivan thinks the Golan, and perhaps Kiryat Shmona, have received far more government assistance than the rest of northern Galilee. "The result is that this area [was] quite neglected."

Then, the 2006 war made things worse. "It was a major event." Hezbollah's capabilities came as a surprise. "The Israeli public," Sivan said, "did not internalize the fact that we are going to suffer in the war." Even though objectively Israel won a great victory, "the internal discussion was that it was a loss." That sounded eerily like North Vietnam's Tet offensive in which it suffered a huge military defeat but gained a strategic political win for its struggle to shift public opinion in the United States.

"Over 100,000 houses were demolished in Lebanon," Sivan said.

> *The devastation in Lebanon was as if it was nuked.... But still the Israeli public [was dissatisfied]. What I concluded from that is this. Most of the war was in the home front. It wasn't [at the front lines]. It was civilians. Civilians don't [attack], it's not an attack battle, it's a defense battle. In a defense battle it's very difficult to define victory. No one made an attempt to define victory.*

Sivan, having diagnosed the problem in 2006, then suggested the solution.

> *Now I have done that. I've decided I'm going to define for the northern and home front command [victory]. They accepted my definition.... I said the following: 'An external shock may happen, always an external shock may happen. You suffer a loss. OK. You have an earthquake. People will die. There is nothing you can do about that. You can do a lot of things but once it*

happens, . . . those who are unfortunate die . . . . The question is, how to make that still a victory?

Sivan again answered his question, as was often his habit with me, by saying that first, it is important to:

look at the community and say . . . this is the place where we begin before the event. Now, a crisis is where you have an external shock that things before the crisis are not the same after the crisis. If we are able to create the plans [ahead of time] to take the casualties, to take the blow, but to cope with it in such a way from a social point of view we are better at the end of it than before it then we have won.

Sivan's focus was on the community. He realizes that if Hezbollah launches 1,000 or more rockets a day during a war, or an earthquake knocks buildings to the ground—people will die despite his best efforts. But if the community is stronger at the end, that's the essence of victory. "So," he said, "You can define your goal for victory in a defense battle as well."

Coincidently, I had then just finished reading Sebastian Junger's book, *Tribe*, which had a great impact on me. In it, Junger writes about how in bad times, such as hurricanes, all elements of society come together to overcome the devastation. When I asked Sivan about whether that was his philosophy, he said, "It is exactly the same!"

Sivan got his inspiration for defining victory after reading *The Black Swan: The Impact of the Highly Improbable,* in which the author argues that most impactful events are unpredictable and not discernible from a progression of past events. "History does not crawl, it jumps," the author writes. For Sivan, the book was a jumping off point for grappling with his core problem: ensuring a community's survival after an unpredictable event.

Sivan explained, "Most systems are fragile. You can make systems that will be more resilient. OK. You can make it out of metal, but even metal [has weaknesses]. But what about systems that will benefit from disaster?" fully recognizing that there will be losses. "In a stock exchange," he continued, "that would be certain options that would go up and down. The stocks fall and you make a fortune. So, can you make a benefit from a disaster? But what happens about a society? How do you build that?" Saying "benefit" is difficult to say and hear, Sivan admitted, because it means benefiting from loss of life and that is not remotely equivalent to loss of stock value and the like. "But as a society you can benefit and that is something . . . that has to be said. You can improve."

Sivan's thesis is really no different from that of religion, parenting, and many other forms of self-help. He says, "You [can] grow from crisis." But he says, "If you look at the media, if you look at the internal talk, [that] is not their agenda. But we can make [it] our agenda."

But talk is cheap. What, I asked Sivan, has been done in furtherance of the northern Galilee achieving a defensive victory. He responded, "First of all, I'm the main pusher for the government's plan for [preparing] for our region to be in battle, so they approved the program of 5 billion shekels (about 1.4 billion dollars), . . . extending it over a period too long [in] my opinion."

When I asked what must be done as part of the plan, Sivan responded, "Three things, it is easy to say. One, warning. The warning systems should be perfect. The warning systems in the north have to be the best. Today, they are not . . . . If I don't know that the rocket is going to fall on my head, I cannot even lie down. If I lie down, I improve my chances of surviving by eighty percent. Ok, it's not a small issue."

"Does that mean a general warning or one specific to location like Iron Dome?" I asked.

He answered, "It's very specific. The system is very specific. But I'm not worried about specific. I'm worried that from 0 to 4 kilometers, we don't have a warning for mortars. And we are going to do that. We are going to cover that. It is about 100 million shekels (twenty-eight million dollars). That was approved. It's going to happen."

"The second thing," Sivan continued,

> is continued functioning of the local authorities. That means we have to have certain stores of food, medicine, and stuff like that, water of course, that we are able to supply. And, we must have the method . . . to supply it in times of crisis. So therefore, a person would feel, that you know, shit happens, but I'm at home and I have something to eat and drink. And someone is looking at me and I've got medical staff here, volunteers and everything, that can give . . . first aid . . . . All these things have to be in place.

"The third thing," Sivan said,

> is just shelters. Increasing substantially, the amount of shelters both in private homes and in public facilities. So, we will be able to [meet the need]. If we have these three things, we will be far more prepared for any[thing]. There are other things. We want to evacuate people, so we have to protect the road, but take the things I am talking about—that is the major need.

My hour with Sivan seemed like only a few minutes. When an aide came in the room to tell him he had to leave for another appointment I was surprised at how quickly the time had passed. But as he got up to go, Sivan emphasized "These are the issues that are in my blood."

Sivan left a lasting impression on me. He is a practical capitalist and during his two terms a practical politician who believed in people exercising freedom of choice with as little as possible government interference. After two terms in office, he kept his promise to return to the private sector rather than coast to future electoral victories. That, in itself, is unusual for a popular politician. But his background in the army and his vision for the future set him apart as well.

Sivan thinks strategically. He would mourn every life lost in a crisis and had been working hard to provide the warning necessary, along with the resources required, to minimize those losses. But his focus is also on ensuring that the lives of the living improve after a crisis by pulling together as a community. That requires practical steps but also psychological preparation.

Sivan's genius was in providing a definition of defensive victory that would pull the community to a better place and that did not require divining in advance all aspects of the crisis that will come. And, just like during his experience with the "Hoover" route in Gaza, Kibbutz Hanita and other border communities hold strategic terrain. While it might be easier to defend Hanita, and the other communities, if they moved to a different location, that would result in Israel losing sovereignty over its land under pressure, and as a result, pressure would increase everywhere. If only some of the residents move because of the dangers and hardships, it would decrease the economic viability of those communities for those who remained. Inevitably, that would lead to the demise of the community, and a loss of sovereignty. Then, the same process would start over again for the next line of communities, and then the next. So, just like Sivan's adamant opposition to creating "Hoover B," the courage and determination of the border communities should be admired and must be supported.

Sivan's linkage of the Zionist movement to the need to hold land so that Jews could fill in behind particularly moved me. But that same love of the land is infused within almost all whom I interviewed, along with the idea of service to a community. Erez, the security chief at Kibbutz Hanita, said it best:

> *I have a weapon in the home," he said nonchalantly regarding his security responsibilities. "We understand if we don't do it, nobody do[es] it. This is what happens in a small community. In Tel Aviv, you [ask] someone to volunteer, [they] answer why? How much money you pay? Here, I don't think how much, I don't think about what I get. I think if I make this kibbutz, this area, a better [place]. This is my fuel."*

Even though he agrees it is a hard life, Erez says, "For the soul, it is amazing."

Throughout the north I met amazing people. People devoted to the Zionist dream. People devoted to their country and devoted to holding the land for those who will come after them. People who "want to do something for the community . . . save a life."

"Why do people build villages under a volcano?" Gideon Giladi from Kfar Giladi said to me, "There is no explanation. You like the place, you are there, it is part of your homeland."

Pictures

Yeduda Harel with Cliff Sobin

Omer Weiner with Cliff Sobin

Sarit Zehavi

Yamit Yanai Malul

Cartoon Depicting Kiryat Shmona and the Kibbutzim

Gamla

2006 Hezbollah Kidnap Site of Two IDF Soldiers

418 *Living in Heaven, Coping with Hell*

Changing the Topography -- Lebanese Border
Outside Kibbutz Hanita

Tel Hai Courtyard Where Trumpledor was Shot

Acknowledgements

First, and Foremost, this book would not have been possible without my wife, Julie's, patience, support, and thoughtful suggestions. Not only did she accept my absences during three trips to Israel in 2018, 2019, and 2020 to conduct interviews, she also graciously read early versions of *Living in Heaven, Coping with Hell* multiple times to help stamp out typos and to offer suggestions for improvement.

Craig Dowd provided me with crucial support, from copy editing to structure. Without Craig, I would have violated nearly every grammatical construct in the English language.

I also benefited greatly from insightful comments and corrections given me by beta readers Christina Hen, Dr. Yuval Achouch, Sorel Hershkovitz, Phillip Pasmanick, Yamit Yanai Malul, Samuel Gardi, and Mary Grossman. Also, I am grateful to Yael Barlev, whose direct questions helped keep me on the path that I chose for the book

I also would be remiss if I did not thank all those that allowed me to interview them for this project, of which many have appeared in these pages. Without fail, everyone I spoke to enthusiastically shared their time, thoughts, and experiences with me. I am awed by all of them.

And a special thanks goes to Sarit Zehavi and Christina Hen. Without Sarit and Christina this project would not have been possible. Both suggested potential interview targets, Christina scheduled many of my interviews, and Sarit accompanied me on a few of them during which she translated when necessary.

Sources and Background

Overview

I first became acquainted with Israel's northern borders in 1969, when as a fourteen-year-old, I briefly visited the region while on a bus tour with my parents. However, other than a brief foray onto the Golan Heights, I have no memory of the days we spent in the region. The same cannot be said about my return as a volunteer at Kibbutz Ma'ayan Baruch two years later. Those three weeks have never left me. Although my world was then only the kibbutz, its fields, and the work, from then on, my heart and soul intertwined with the land of Israel. Nevertheless, I did not return until two decades later and then again not for another sixteen years.

But in 2014 things changed. My oldest daughter, Jessica, was living in India at the time with her husband. My wife and I decided to visit them for the second time in less than a year. However, rather than travel directly to Bangalore where Jess was living, I decided to stop in Israel for four days first, leaving my wife to journey alone before meeting up with my family in Mumbai.

After studying my options, I decided to spend three nights at Kibbutz Merom Golan. Israel's heroic defense of the Golan during the 1973 Yom Kippur War had been a subject of study by me for me for forty years. That, along with my general interest in the Six-Day War and the Yom Kippur War, coupled with my dissatisfaction with most books on the subject that viewed those events individually rather than collectively, had led me to initiate research for a two-volume book I published in 2017, *The Pivotal Years, Israel and the Arab World 1966*

– *1977*. So, it should come as no surprise that I had wanted to walk the battlefields and soak up the feel of the Golan. Since Merom Golan seemed centrally placed for what I wanted to do, I stayed there.

What came as a surprise to me was the connection I felt with the land at Merom Golan, and elsewhere throughout the region.

Three years later I returned, this time with my two brothers-in-laws. Again, I spent three days at Merom Golan. But this time I hired two guides, both reserve officers in the IDF. One was Sarit Zehavi. The other was Boaz. For me, both were fateful choices. Both have become good friends. And both were instrumental in providing me with background for writing this book.

The following year, I returned again. Again, I stayed at Merom Golan for three days. Again, I spent time with Sarit and Boaz. This time I visited Kibbutz Hanita for the first time where I met Orly.

That trip was followed by another, this time with my wife and another couple. Of course, we stayed at Merom Golan for three days. And it was during that trip that I read David Leach's *Chasing Utopia: The Future of the Kibbutz in a Divided Israel* (ECW Press, 2016). Like me, Leach worked as a volunteer on a kibbutz in northern Israel, albeit for much longer. His book, which focused on the kibbutz movement in Israel, motivated me to translate my love for the northern border region and respect for its people into this book.

Invaluable for overall direction and understanding, in conjunction with Leach's book, was Martin Gilbert's *Israel: A History* (Key Porter, 2008), Bernard Reich's *A Brief History of Israel* (Checkmark Books, 2018), and Augustus Richard Norton's *Hezbollah: A Short History* (Princeton University Press, 2018). Collectively, those works kept me on course and gave me insight as to which events and communities I should focus on. Read in conjunction with numerous articles from three Israeli English language newspapers—*The Jerusalem Post*, *Haaretz*, and the *Times of Israel*—and after reviewing multiple websites, I became well-positioned to better target my research.

However, it goes without saying, that despite the best efforts of those I interviewed to educate me, and the efforts of the authors of the numerous well-written works I consulted, all errors in this book are mine alone.

Prologue

Although there are many newspaper articles, websites, and book excerpts that describe the events and provide background regarding the murder of the children at Ma'alot, none triggered my emotions like the film *Their Eyes Were Dry* (2007) by Brandon Assanti and the letter written by Ilana Ne'eman. My thoughts regarding how much importance to place on that event for understanding the psyche of Israelis in the region were affirmed after reading a seventy-page report written by Liav Nakar for his High School class in Israel, some fifty years later. In painstaking detail, that report took me through the tragedy and left me no doubt that to properly tell the story of the northern borders and the people who live there, I had to lead with Ma'alot.

However, since I wanted this book to mix elements of history, current affairs, and personal investigative-travel, I felt the need to explain the roots of my passion for the region. That required re-visiting Kibbutz Ma'ayan Baruch. There, I interviewed Philip Pasmanick in 2018. I also found invaluable for re-kindling my memories and providing further background, Hugh Nissenson's *Notes From the Frontier: An American's Experiences on a Border Kibbutz Summer 1965/June 1967* (The Dial Press, Inc., 1968) in which he told of his experiences volunteering at Kibbutz Ma'ayan Baruch.

Chapter One: Gamla

The seminal source for that time period is Flavius Josephus's book written two thousand years ago, *The Wars of the Jews*. The version I read was translated by William Whiston and published as an Ebook (Wilder Publications, LLC, 2014). Also, extremely informative was information I gleaned from [*A History of Gamla*, Accessed 2019. https://www.academia.edu/29097513/A_History_of_Gamla], [*Gamla*, Accessed 2019. http://www.jewishmag.com/40mag/gamla/gamla.htm], [*Gamla*, Accessed 2019. https://biblewalks.com/sites/Gamla.html], [*The Camel Backed Mountain*, Accessed 2019. https://www.timesofisrael.com/gamla-the-camel-backed-mountain/], and [*Ein Keshatot the Golan Heights Hidden Gem Opens to the Public*, Accessed 2019. https://www.jpost.com/Israel-News/Culture/Ein-Keshatot-the-Golan-Heights-hidden-gem-opens-to-the-public-569111].

However, no source amply described the solemnity and solitude of Gamla in a way that satisfied me. To do that, I walked the grounds of Gamla Nature Reserve, hiked to Gamla, read the informational signs, saw the relics and ruins, and felt the wind. I did that twice. The second time with plenty of water!

Chapter Two: Rosh Pina, Pogroms, and the First Aliyah
Several sources combined to cue me into the history of Rosh Pina, the pogroms, and the First Aliya. They included, Arieh Avneri's *The Claim of Disposession: Jewish Land-Settlement and the Arabs 1878-1948* (Transaction Books, 1984), Eric Gartman's *Return to Zion* (University of Nebraska Press as a Jewish Publication Society, 2015), Yosef Gorny, *From Rosh Pina and Degania to Demona: A History of Constructive Zionism* (MOD Books, 1989), Aharon Kellerman's *Society and Settlement: Jewish Land of Israel in the Twentieth Century* (State University of New York Press, 1993), Benny Morris's *Righteous Victims: A History of the Zionist - Arab Conflict, 1881-1999* (Alfred A.

Knopf, 1999), Simon Schama's *Two Rothschilds and the Land of Israel* (Collins, 1978), and Leslie Stein's *The Hope Fulfilled: The Rise of Modern Israel* (Praeger Publishers-paperback, 2003). In addition, I learned much of the David Shorb family story after Accessing, in 2019, https://www.dnathan.com/bucshester/familystory/.

I also spent time walking the streets of old Rosh Pina on two separate visits in 2019 and, while seated on a bench overlooking the Huleh valley, listened to the poignant, melancholy story recorded by the father of Nimrod, an IDF soldier who died in his tank while fighting Hezbollah during the 2006 Lebanon War. Later, I hiked the several mile journey on the old road used by Rosh Pina's early settlers, now a rough path, cutting through the mountains from Rosh Pina to Safed.

Chapter Three: Degania and the Second Aliyah
No study of Degania is complete without reading Joseph Baratz's *A Village by the Jordan* (The Amalgamated Printing Company in Israel, LTD., 1958). As one of Degania's initial settlers, his memoir offers a fascinating look at life in Degania and the mindset of its early inhabitants. Regarding Moshe Barsky, Chazan Meir's article *The Murder of Moshe Barsky: Transformations in Ethos, Pathos and Myth* (Israel Studies, Spring 2006) provides both detail and balance.

Also informative were Yosef Gorny's *From Rosh Pina and Degania to Demona: A History of Constructive Zionism* (MOD Books, 1989), Israel Defense Forces's *Ha'hagana* (Ministry of Defense Publishing House, 1985), Aharon Kellerman's *Society and Settlement: Jewish Land of Israel in the Twentieth Century* (State University of New York Press, Albany, 1993), Henry Near's *The Kibbutz Movement: A History* (Oxford University Press, 1992), Terence Prittie's *Eshkol: The Man and the Nation* (Pittman Publishing Corporation, 1969), Robert Slater's *Warrior Statesman: The Life of Moshe Dayan* (St. Martin's Press, 1991), and Leslie Stein's *The Hope Fulfilled: The Rise of Modern*

Israel. (Praeger Publishers-paperback, 2003). Similarly, Yitzhak Rubin's movie Degania*: The First kibbutz Fights Its last Battle* (Teknews Media Ltd, 2010) provided interesting glimpses into the community and its transformation.

Also, in 2019 I spent several hours interviewing a kibbutz resident while walking the grounds of Degania, traversing its agricultural fields, viewing the Jordan river from where the Kvutsa first started, and listening to the long recording from a kiosk-like structure there. Also helpful were the pictures, film, and historian at the kibbutz's museum.

Chapter Four: Hashomer, Tel Hai, Kfar Giladi and the Third Aliyah

The time I spent interviewing Gideon Giladi in 2019 could not have been more valuable. Through his eyes, words, and emotion, I felt rather than just heard the history described in this chapter. Later in 2019, I gained a further feel for Kfar Giladi's past when I met with Amnon Nir and walked with him through a portion of the kibbutz and then clambered down the steps to the kibbutz's main "Slik" used before 1949. Also, my visit to Tel Hai, the Hashomer Museum at Kfar Giladi, and the cemetery outside of Kfar Giladi prepared me to better assimilate the information I gleaned from the many written sources I reviewed.

Among the sources most helpful to me were Arieh Avneri's *The Claim of Disposession: Jewish Land-Settlement and the Arabs 1878-1948* (Transaction Books, 1984), Eric Gartman's *Return to Zion* (University of Nebraska Press as a Jewish Publication Society, 2015), Yosef Gorny's *From Rosh Pina and Degania to Demona: A History of Constructive Zionism* (MOD Books, 1989), Israel Defense Forces' *Ha'hagana* (Ministry of Defense Publishing House, 1985), Aharon Kellerman's *Society and Settlement: Jewish Land of Israel in the Twentieth Century* (State University of New York Press, Albany, 1993), Benny Morris's *Righteous Victims: A History of the Zionist -*

Arab Conflict, 1881-1999 (Alfred A. Knopf, 1999), Leslie Stein's *The Hope Fulfilled: The Rise of Modern Israel* (Praeger Publishers-paperback, 2003), and the website, Accessed 2019. http://www.zionistarchives.org.il/en/datelist/Pages/KfarGiladi.aspx

Chapter Five: Kibbutz Hanita
Hanita's origin as a Tower and Stockade kibbutz is the subject of the film "*On To Hanita*" which is in The Spielberg Jewish Film Archive and can be viewed at the Hanita Museum located on the kibbutz's grounds. In addition to information at the museum, Wikipedia's website for Kibbutz Hanita, Accessed 2019. https://en.wikipedia.org/wiki/Hanita provides a helpful summary of events surrounding the origin of Hanita. Also informative are Arieh Avneri's *The Claim of Disposession: Jewish Land-Settlement and the Arabs 1878-1948* (Transaction Books, 1984), Yosef Gorny's *From Rosh Pina and Degania to Demona: A History of Constructive Zionism* (MOD Books, 1989), Aharon Kellerman's *Society and Settlement: Jewish Land of Israel in the Twentieth Century* (State University of New York Press, Albany, 1993), Robert Slater's *Warrior Statesman: The Life of Moshe Dayan* (St. Martin's Press, 1991), and Leslie Stein's *The Hope Fulfilled: The Rise of Modern Israel* (Praeger Publishers-paperback).

And worthy of particular mention is Christopher Sykes's *Orde Wingate: A Biography* (The World Publishing Company, 1958). Wingate was a peculiar, driven man possessed with immense leadership skill and military talent. Although only part of the book is about his time at Hanita, I found myself captivated by the story of his life.

Chapter Six: Degania, May 1948
Dan Kurzman's *Genesis 1948: The First Arab-Israeli War* (Da Capo Press, 1992) was invaluable for learning details of the battle at Degania and placing it in context with the events in the region as a whole. Also

helpful were Joseph Baratz's *A Village by the Jordan* (The Amalgamated Printing Company in Israel, LTD., 1958), Leslie Stein's *The Making of Modern Israel: 1948-1967* (Polity Press, 2009), Robert Slater's *Warrior Statesman: The Life of Moshe Dayan* (St. Martin's Press, 1991), and Daniel Gavron's *The Kibbutz*: Awakening from Utopia (Rowman & Littlefield Publishers, Inc., 2000).

Chapter Seven: Kibbutz Dan
Leaving a lasting impression on me were my interviews in 2018 with Samuel and Haviva Gardi, Yossi Lev Ari, and Amiram Efrati. Also, very helpful were Yigal Kipnis's *The Golan Heights: Political History, Settlement and Geography Since 1949* (Routledge, 2013) and Benny Morris's *Righteous Victims: A History of the Zionist - Arab Conflict, 1881-1999* (Alfred A. Knopf, 1999).

Chapter Eight: Merom Golan
I first learned the significance of Merom Golan when I read Gershom Gorenberg's *The Accidental Empire: Israel and the Birth of the Settlements, 1967 – 1977* (Time Books, 2006). Without Gorenberg's book I doubt I would have been equipped with the knowledge to conduct the interviews of the Merom Golan's members that I obtained in 2018 and 2019. Two other books also deserve mention as having been a significant resource for this chapter. They were Henry Kissinger's *Years of Upheaval* (Little, Brown & Co., 1982) and Yigal Kipnis's *The Golan Heights: Political History, Settlement and Geography Since 1949* (Routledge, 2013). In addition, Janes Bennett's January 17, 2004 article in the New York Times, *Hoofbeats and Tank Tracks Share Golan Range* and the Eretz Staff article, *A Tale of Five Decades* (Eretz Magazine, Feb 15, 2018) provided necessary background information.

But memorable and most informative was the time I spent with Yehuda Harel and Omer Weiner. They both selflessly spent time with me in 2018 and 2019. Yehuda graciously gave me an English-language version of a book he wrote about Yitzhak Tobenkin and Omer twice drove me to the remains of Kibbutz Golan, the forerunner of Merom Golan. Both times along the way, between stories of his past and that of Merom Golan, Omer pointed out the various agricultural pursuits of the kibbutz and explained their background. To say my time with both men was a delight would be an understatement.

Chapter Nine: Kiryat Shmona
This chapter would not have been possible without the more than three-hour interview Yamit Yanai Malul permitted me in 2018, our drive together throughout Kiryat Shmona, and the dinner we had at *Mama Hassa* in 2019. In addition, Israel Oz shared his views with me regarding Kiryat Shmona. Also helpful was Raymond Russell's, Robert Hanneman's, and Shlomo Getz's *The Renewal of the Kibbutz: From Reform to Transformation* (Rutgers University Press, 2013). However, the most valuable written source I read for learning the Kiryat Shmona story was Amir Goldstein's *The kibbutz and the Ma'abara (transit camp): The case of the Upper Galilee Kibbutzim and Kiryat Shmona, 1949–1953* (Journal of Israeli History, March 2016).

Chapter Ten: Fall of the Kibbutzim
Anyone hoping to understand the Kibbutz in the modern era must read David Leach's *Chasing Utopia: The Future of the Kibbutz in a Divided Israel* (ECW Press, 2016). In addition, most helpful for me was Daniel Gavron's *The Kibbutz: Awakening from Utopia* (Rowman & Littlefield Publishers, Inc., 2000) and Raymond Russell's, Robert Hanneman's, and Shlomo Getz's *The Renewal of the Kibbutz: From Reform to Transformation* (Rutgers University Press, 2013). But more important than all was my interview of Israel Oz.

Chapter Eleven: Kibbutz Dan Today

My Interviews with Dorit ben Shalom Moshe in 2018, Samuel Gardi in 2018 and 2019, Haviva Gardi in 2018, and my conversation with Gardi in January 2020 provided the information necessary for this chapter. In addition, I reviewed several press releases regarding Kibbutz Dan, including the Seedo Corporation Press Release, *Seedo Partners with Kibbutz Dan for First-of-its-Kind Fully Automated Indoor and Containerized Commercial-Scale Cannabis Farm* (March 19, 2019).

Chapter Twelve: Kibbutz Hanita Today
For me, my first visit to Kibbutz Hanita in 2017 was a game changer. Since then, I have returned four times and my family has worked with the kibbutz on a small-scale to enhance its infrastructure. Walking its outer perimeter while gazing into Lebanon and seeing the Hezbollah controlled tower on top of a hill within sniper shot of the kibbutz had an impact on me. So did the drive up the mountain to the top where the kibbutz is now located and the film and displays in the Kibbutz Hanita Museum. Combined, physically spending several days at Hanita significantly contributed to my understanding of the kibbutz's history.

Most important, however, were the interviews I conducted, supplemented by the chapter on Hanita in David Leach's *Chasing Utopia: The Future of the Kibbutz in a Divided Israel* (ECW Press, 2016). In 2018, I interviewed Dr. Yuval Achouch, Sorel Hershkovitz, Orly Gavishi-Sotto, Erez, Dvir, and Haim. In 2019, Sorel Hershkovitz allowed me to interview him again.

Chapter Thirteen: Kfar Giladi Now
Three sources provided me most of the information I needed for this chapter. First, and foremost, was Gideon Giladi who generously spent considerable time with me in 2019 and recommended that I meet with Amnon Nir who provided me with interesting tidbits about the

kibbutz. I am also grateful to Tessa Moran who arranged for me to have access to view *Keeping the Kibbutz*, a movie directed and produced by Tessa Moran and Ben Crosbie (2010) which covers the reformation of Kfar Giladi.

Chapter Fourteen: Merom Golan Now
This chapter is primarily based on my interview of Joanna Kline and Shefi Mor in 2018 and that of Yehuda Harel and Omer Weiner in 2018 and 2019.

Chapter Fifteen: People of the Land
This chapter is primarily based on two extensive interviews of Sarit Zehavi in 2018 and the many hours we have spent together over the last three years, interviews of Yael Barlev in 2018 and in 2019, my interview of Shlomi Afrayat in 2018, and Stef Wertheimer's *The Habit of Labor: Lessons from a Life of Struggle and Success* (Overlook Press, 2015).

Chapter Sixteen: Three Communities on the Border
The Metula portion of the chapter is based on my interview of Yaniv and Sivan Elhadif in 2018 and Reuven Wineberg in 2019. Also immensely helpful, was the almost two hours Yaniv spent driving me in his jeep around Metula, its agricultural fields, and along the border. In print, I found John F. Burns's *Metula Journal, It's Raining Not Rockets but Rocks: This is Peace?* (New York Times Sep 18, 2000) very helpful. I also spent quite a bit of time wandering Metula's streets during the day and at night and viewing the region from the top of the Alaska Hotel.

The Majdal Shams portion was greatly benefited by information gleaned from Jolan Abusaleh in 2017 and 2018 as well as from Omer Weiner and Samuel Gardi in 2019. In addition, Al-Marsad's website, https://golan-marsad.org, has a treasure-trove of documents, all of which I downloaded and read. And, as always, David Leach's *Chasing Utopia: The Future of the Kibbutz in a Divided Israel* (ECW Press, 2016) provided insight as well.

The Ghajar section was helped immensely by Najib Khatib, who spent an hour with me in a coffee shop in Kiryat Shmona. I also spent much time carefully reviewing Asher Kaufman's *Contested Frontiers in the Syria-Lebanon-Israel Region: Cartography, Sovereignty, and Conflict* (Johns Hopkins University Press, 2014) and Yigal Kipnis's *The Golan Heights: Political History, Settlement and Geography Since 1949* (Routledge, 2013). Also useful was Nicholas Blandford's *Warriors of God: Inside Hezbollah's Thirty-Year Struggle Against Israel* (Random House, 2011).

Chapter Seventeen: Terror and Katyushas
I reviewed perhaps 100 articles, websites, and books for this chapter. The most helpful were Nicholas Blandford's *Warriors of God: Inside Hezbollah's Thirty-Year Struggle Against Israel.* (Random House, 2011), Richard Gabriel's *Operation Peace for Galilee: The Israeli-PLO War In Lebanon* (Collins Publishers, 1984), Yigal Kipnis's *The Golan Heights: Political History, Settlement and Geography Since 1949* (Routledge, 2013), Norton, Richard Augustus' *Hezbollah: A short History* (Princeton University Press, 2018), Bethe Schoenfeld's *The Routine of War: How One Northern Community Coped During the Second Lebanon War* (Artzy Books, 2007), and Leslie Stein's *Israel Since the Six-Day War* (Polity Press. 2014). Two newspaper articles and a letter to the United Nations also deserve mention: Richard Bernstein's *Scarred kibbutz is Ambivalent About Invasion* (New York Times, July 20, 1983), William Claiborne's *Israeli Troops Quash Palestinian Raid* (Washington Post, April 8, 1980), and a letter dated March 15, 1982 from the Permanent Representative of Israel to the Secretary-General of the United Nations.

For personal views of how terror and Katyushas affect people, my interviews with Sarit Zehavi in 2018, Bethe Shoenfeld in 2019, and my time with "Boaz" at Kfar Giladi's cemetery cued me into the emotional impact of what the people along the northern borders endure. It wasn't just what they said, but the tone of their voices and the look in their eyes. And that leads me to the four times I have visited the site just outside the cemetery at Kfar Giladi, where a katyusha took the lives of twelve IDF soldiers and have read the inscriptions in stone. Every time I go there, I feel the same chills, the same horror, and the same reminder of how tenuous life is.

Chapter Eighteen Yesterday, Today, and Tomorrow
Books I relied on include Nicholas Blandford's *Warriors of God: Inside Hezbollah's Thirty-Year Struggle Against Israel* (Random House, 2011), Matti Friedman's powerful *Pumpkin Flowers: A Soldier's Story* (Algonquin Books, 2016), Yigal Kipnis' *The Golan Heights: Political History, Settlement and Geography Since 1949* (Routledge, 2013), and Augustus Richard Norton's *Hezbollah: A Short History* (Princeton University Press, 2018).

Multiple articles also deserve note. They include Ibrahim Abu Ahmad's *Iran's Grassroot Actions in Syria* (Alma Research and Education Center, July 28, 2019), Patrick Cockburn's *Israel Buries Helicopter Crash Dead* (The Independent, February 6, 1997), Tal Beeri's *The Tunnel Theory—The Iranian Interest Above All* (Alma Research and Education Center, October 10, 2019), Diane Bletter's *The Dire Lack of Bomb Shelters in the North* (Jerusalem Post Magazine, November 22, 2019), Amos Harel's *20 Years After: The helicopter Crash That Changed Israel's Fight with Hezbollah* (Haaretz, February 4, 2017), Adam Harvey's *Israel-Lebanon Blue Line Wall to Offer War-Hit Locals Peace of Mind, but Some Fears Persist* (ABC News, November 23, 2018), Yoav Limor's *Avoiding South Lebanon 2.0* (Israel Hayom, April 25, 2019), Gal Luft's *Israel's Security Zone in*

Lebanon - A Tragedy? (Middle East Quarterly, September 2000), Toi Staff's *20 Years on, Israel Marks Helicopter Disaster that Claimed 73 Soldiers* (Times of Israel, February 15, 2017), Toi Staff's *Galilee Struck by New Earthquakes, Rattling Northern Israel* (Times of Israel, July 8, 2018), Michael Bachner's and Toi Staff's *New Earthquake Hits Northern Israel, as Cracks in Readiness Exposed* (Times of Israel, July 9, 2018), Toi Staff's *State Comptroller: Israel Unprepared for major Quake, Ignoring Warnings* (Times of Israel, July 18, 2018), Toi Staff's *IDF Chief: Hezbollah had Grandiose Attack Plan to 'Shake Israel'* (Times of Israel, January 10, 2019), D Wachs's and D.Levitte's *Damage Caused by Landslides During the Earthquake of 1837 and 1927 in the Galilee Region* (Ministry of Energy and Infrastructure, June 1978), Sarit Zehavi's *Who is the boss in Syria and how does in affect Israel's Security?* (Alma Research and Education Center, October 29, 2019).

Several websites served as a jumping off point as well. They included, 1997 Israeli Helicopter Disaster, Accessed 2019. https://en.wikipedia.org/wiki/1997_Israeli_helicopter_disaster, Four Mothers (anti-war protest movement), Accessed 2019. https://en.wikipedia.org/wiki/Four_Mothers_(anti-war_protest_movement), Israel Lebanon Blue Line Wall War Hit Locals Peace of Mind, Accessed 2019. https://www.abc.net.au/news/2018-11-24/israel-lebanon-blue-line-wall-war-hit-locals-peace-of-mind/10550690, and Galilee Earthquake of1837, Accessed 2019. https://en.wikipedia.org/wiki/Galilee_earthquake_of_1837.

My interview with Mayor Sivan Yechieli in 2018 was extremely valuable. I also learned much useful information for this chapter from my interviews with Yehuda Harel in 2018 and 2019, Omer Weiner in 2018 and 2019, Sorel Hershkovitz in 2018 and 2019 and when Sorel took me into Kibbutz Hanita's main shelter and command center, Shefi Mor in 2018, and the two interviews and time I spent with Erez in 2018.

In addition, my three visits to the Helicopter Memorial Crash Site, one each during the day in 2018 and 2019 and once more at night in 2019, reminded me that losses in Israel are felt by all Israelis. There, inscribed in stone, are the names of seventy-three souls lost in that horrific accident more than twenty years ago. There, I saw a large Israeli family gathering to grieve over a loved one who was one of those who fell from the sky decades ago. And there, during the stillness of the night, I contemplated what those living in the north endure and the dangers all Israelis still share.

A Request

If you enjoyed this book, please consider taking the time to write a short review on whichever platform you purchased it. I would greatly appreciate it.

And, I invite you to check out my new projects, thoughts, and ideas at www.CliffordSobin.com.

About the Author

Cliff Sobin is a writer with a special interest in Israeli/Jewish history. He also was the managing partner of his law firm from its inception in 1991 until he retired. Cliff has spoken to numerous groups regarding his mother's Holocaust experience, his books regarding Israel, and workers' compensation. His written work includes books, articles, and blogs concerning Israel, Maryland Workers' Compensation, Jackson Hole, and database application design. He now serves on the international advisory board for Alma.

www.ingramcontent.com/pod-product-compliance
Lightning Source LLC
Chambersburg PA
CBHW070522010526
44118CB00012B/1047